Contemplating Violence
Critical Studies in Modern German Culture

AMSTERDAMER BEITRÄGE
ZUR NEUEREN GERMANISTIK

79 2011

Herausgegeben von
William Collins Donahue
Norbert Otto Eke
Martha B. Helfer
Gerd Labroisse

Contemplating Violence
Critical Studies in Modern German Culture

Edited by
Stefani Engelstein and Carl Niekerk

Amsterdam - New York, NY 2011

Die 1972 gegründete Reihe erscheint seit 1977 in zwangloser Folge in der
Form von Thema-Bänden mit jeweils verantwortlichem Herausgeber.

Reihen-Herausgeber:

Prof. William Collins Donahue
Chair & Director of Graduate Studies
Department of Germanic Languages & Literature
Duke University - 116D Old Chemistry - Box 90256
Durham, NC 27708, USA, E-Mail: wcd2@duke.edu

Prof. Dr. Norbert Otto Eke
Universität Paderborn
Fakultät für Kulturwissenschaften, Warburger Str. 100, D - 33098 Paderborn,
Deutschland, E-Mail: norbert.eke@upb.de

Prof. Dr. Martha B. Helfer
Rutgers University
172 College Avenue, New Brunswick, NJ 08901
Tel.: (732) 932-7201, Fax: (732) 932-1111, E-Mail: mhelfer@rci.rutgers.edu

Prof. Dr. Gerd Labroisse
Sylter Str. 13A, 14199 Berlin, Deutschland
Tel./Fax: (49)30 89724235 E-Mail: labroisse@t-online.de

Cover Image: Abstract in rood 1
© Jelly Timmer 2009, www.jellytimmer.com

All titles in the Amsterdamer Beiträge zur neueren Germanistik
(from 1999 onwards) are available online: See www.rodopi.nl
Electronic access is included in print subscriptions.

The paper on which this book is printed meets the requirements of "ISO
9706:1994, Information and documentation - Paper for documents -
Requirements for permanence".

ISBN: 978-90-420-3294-1
E-Book ISBN: 978-90-420-3295-8
©Editions Rodopi B.V., Amsterdam – New York, NY 2011
Printed in The Netherlands

Table of Contents

Acknowledgements	7
Contributors	9
Stefani Engelstein and Carl Niekerk: Introduction. Violence, Culture, Aesthetics: Germany 1789–1938	13

I. The Other Side of Modernity: War and the French Revolution

Stephanie M. Hilger: Sara's Pain: The French Revolution in Therese Huber's *Die Familie Seldorf* (1795–1796)	35
Stefani Engelstein: The Father in Fatherland: Violent Ideology and Corporeal Paternity in Kleist	49
Jeffrey Grossman: Fractured Histories: Heine's Responses to Violence and Revolution	67

II. Imagining the Primitive; the Return of the Repressed

Laurie Johnson: The Curse of Enthusiasm: *William Lovell* and Modern Violence	91
Lynne Tatlock: Communion at the Sign of the Wild Man	115
Carl Niekerk: Constructing the Fascist Subject: Violence, Gender, and Sexuality in Ödön von Horváth's *Jugend ohne Gott*	139

III. Violence in the Age of Globalization; German Culture and Its Others

Barbara Fischer: From the Emancipation of the Jews to the Emancipation from the Jews: On the Rhetoric, Power and Violence of German-Jewish "Dialogue"	165
Mark Christian Thompson: The Negro Who Disappeared: Race in Kafka's *Amerika*	183
Claudia Breger: Performing Violence: Joe May's *Indian Tomb* (1921)	199

IV. Modernism, Modernization, and Representation

Lutz Koepnick: The Violence of the Aesthetic — 227

Patrizia McBride: Montage and Violence in Weimar Culture: Kurt Schwitters' Reassembled Individuals — 245

Peter M. McIsaac: Preserving the Bloody Remains: Legacies of Violence in Austria's Heeresgeschichtliches Museum — 267

Index — 289

Acknowledgements

The present volume is based on the conference "Violence in German Literature, Culture, and Intellectual History, 1789–1938" which took place October 14–16, 2005, at the University of Illinois (Urbana-Champaign), organized by Carl Niekerk. This book, *Contemplating Violence: Critical Studies in Modern German Culture*, is the result of joint editing by Carl Niekerk and Stefani Engelstein.

The conference was made possible by the generous financial support of a number of institutions and organizations: the College of LAS (Liberal Arts and Sciences) at the University of Illinois (state-of-the-art-conference program), the Mellon Foundation, the Department of Germanic Languages and Literatures, the Unit for Criticism and Interpretive Theory, the German Academic Exchange Service (DAAD), the Foreign Language Building Fund, the Program in Comparative and World Literature, and the Illinois Program for Research in the Humanities. In the early stages of the planning process discussions with Karin Crawford, Anthony Everett (both now Bristol, England), and Stephen Jaeger (now Los Angeles) were extremely helpful in developing the intellectual potential of this conference. Mara Wade, Head of the Department of Germanic Languages and Literatures, and Lawrence (Larry) Schehr, at the time Associate Dean of LAS, provided encouragement for this project, as well as their time and many practical suggestions.

We are grateful to our colleagues Cori Crane, Stephanie Hilger, Michael Rothberg, and Yasemin Yildiz at the University of Illinois, and Roger Cook, Brad Prager, Carsten Strathausen, Sean Ireton, Kristin Kopp, and Sean Franzel at the University of Missouri for their ongoing help. Special thanks also to Laurie Johnson, Richard Foley, and Lutz Koepnick who were immensely supportive, both through their versatile intellectual input and their willingness to step in and assist with many practical matters. Thanks in addition to two graduate assistants at Illinois, Mary DeGuire and Carsten Wilmes, and to an undergraduate assistant at Missouri, Lindsay Lutz, for the many different ways in which their contributions made the conference and the book possible.

On May 24, 2010, during preparations for this volume, one of the contributors, Barbara Fischer, died in a car accident close to her home in Tuscaloosa, Alabama, a great loss to the field of German Studies. Our thoughts are with her family. In memory of Barbara, the University of Alabama has established the Barbara Fischer Memorial Fund (Box 870101; Tuscaloosa, AL 35487) to support student scholarships.

Contributors

Claudia Breger is Associate Professor of Germanic Studies and Adjunct Associate Professor of Communication and Culture and Gender Studies at Indiana University (Bloomington). Her research and teaching focus on 20th- and 21st-century literature, film, and culture, with a particular emphasis on the interrelations of gender, sexuality, and race, as well as literary, media, and cultural theory. Her book publications include: *Szenarien kopfloser Herrschaft – Performanzen gespenstischer Macht. Königsfiguren in der deutschsprachigen Literatur und Kultur des 20. Jahrhunderts* (Freiburg im Breisgau: Rombach 2004); *Ortlosigkeit des Fremden. "Zigeunerinnen" und "Zigeuner" in der deutschsprachigen Literatur um 1800* (Cologne: Böhlau 1998).

Stefani Engelstein is an Associate Professor of German and Director of the Life Sciences & Society Program at the University of Missouri (Columbia). Her areas of expertise include German and British literature and the life sciences of the eighteenth and nineteenth centuries. Her 2008 book, *Anxious Anatomy: The Conception of the Human Form in Literary and Naturalist Discourse* (Albany: State University of New York Press) analyzes literature, natural history, medicine, and aesthetics to explore the importance of shifting representations of the body for theories of human subjectivity, gender, volition, ethical behavior, and political organization. Engelstein is currently researching the eighteenth- and nineteenth-century fascination with sibling incest, which she sees as a mechanism for establishing and working through new understandings of individual and collective identities in an era of global exploration. She has published articles on such topics as *Antigone*, fraternity, Kleist and amputation, Kafka and aesthetics, sibling incest in Karoline von Günderode and Thomas Mann, and reproductive strategies in E.T.A. Hoffmann.

Barbara Fischer was Professor of German Studies at the University of Alabama (Tuscaloosa). Her research interests included eighteenth- and twentieth-century German literature, German-Jewish studies, Holocaust studies, and migrant literature. She published on Lessing, Mendelssohn, the contemporary playwright George Tabori, art in Nazi-Germany, and cultural hybridity. She is the author of *Nathans Ende? Von Lessing bis Tabori* (Göttingen: Wallstein 2000) and the co-editor with Thomas C. Fox of *A Companion to the Works of Gotthold Ephraim Lessing* (Rochester, New York: Camden House 2005). Barbara Fischer died in a car accident close to her home in Tuscaloosa on May 24, 2010.

Jeffrey Grossman is Associate Professor in the Department of Germanic Languages and Literatures at the University of Virginia. He is especially interested in problems of literary theory and cultural change and transmission. His book *The Discourse on Yiddish in Germany from the Enlightenment to the Second Empire* (Rochester, New York: Camden House 2000), reflects these interests. He has also written articles on the reception of Walter Benjamin in English, Wilhelm von Humboldt, Heinrich Heine, the Yiddish writers I.L. Peretz and Sholem Aleichem, as well as problems of translating such writers. He is currently working on a book tentatively titled *Heinrich Heine's Contested Afterlives: Between Jewish Writing and German Literature.*

Stephanie M. Hilger is Associate Professor of Comparative Literature and German at the University of Illinois (Urbana-Champaign). Her research focuses on class and gender in British, French, and German eighteenth-century literature. Her articles on these topics have appeared in *College Literature*, *Colloquia Germanica*, *Eighteenth-Century Studies*, *The French Review*, *Lessing Yearbook*, *Neophilologus*, and *Seminar*. Her book *Women Write Back: Strategies of Response and the Dynamics of European Literary Culture, 1790–1805* was published by Rodopi in 2009. The present article is part of her current project on German-language representations of the French Revolution in the late eighteenth and the early nineteenth centuries.

Laurie Johnson is Associate Professor of German, Comparative and World Literature, and Criticism and Interpretive Theory at the University of Illinois (Urbana-Champaign). Her books are *The Art of Recollection in Jena Romanticism: Memory, History, Fiction, and Fragmentation in Texts by Friedrich Schlegel and Novalis* (Tübingen: Niemeyer, 2002) and *Aesthetic Anxiety: Uncanny Symptoms in German Literature and Culture* (Amsterdam: Rodopi, 2010). Johnson has published articles on Friedrich Schlegel and the practice of animal magnetism, psychosomata in Romantic psychology and literature, and Early Romantic philosophy and aesthetics. She is working on projects on Romanticism and the films of Werner Herzog, and on a volume of new psychoanalytic interpretations of fairy tales.

Lutz Koepnick is Professor of German, Film and Media Studies at Washington University (St. Louis). Koepnick has published widely on German literature, film, media, visual culture, new media aesthetic, and intellectual history from the nineteenth to the twenty-first century. He is the author of *Framing Attention: Windows on Modern German Culture* (Baltimore: Johns Hopkins University Press 2007); *The Dark Mirror: German Cinema between Hitler and Hollywood* (Berkeley and Los Angeles: University of California Press 2002); *Walter Benjamin and the Aesthetics of Power* (Lincoln: University of Nebraska Press 1999); and of *Nothungs Modernität: Wagners Ring und die Poesie der Politik* *im neunzehnten Jahrhundert* (Munich: Wilhelm Fink Verlag 1994). Koepnick is the co-author of *[Grid < > Matrix] / Screen Arts and New Media Aesthetics 1* (2006), and the co-editor of three anthologies: on sound in modern German culture, on the exile of German visual artists and filmmakers in the United States, and on the global connections of postwar German cinema. His current book project is entitled, *On Slowness: Toward an Aesthetic of Delay and Deceleration*, a project exploring different strategies of deceleration in various media of twentieth and twenty-first century artistic practice, in particular in photography, film, opera, music, installation and new media art, and prose fiction.

Patrizia C. McBride is Associate Professor of German at Cornell University. She is the author of *The Void of Ethics: Robert Musil and the Experience of Modernity* (Evanston: Northwestern University Press 2006) and articles on J.M.R. Lenz, Adolf Loos, Jörg Haider, Hermann Broch, Kurt Schwitters, and Bertolt Brecht. She co-edited *Legacies of Modernism: Art and Politics in Northern Europe, 1890–1950* (New York: Palgrave Macmillan 2007) with Richard McCormick and Monika Zagar. Her teaching and research interests include eighteenth- to twentieth-century literature and culture; modernism and theories of modernity; the intersection of literary theory, philosophy, and political theory; and visual studies. She is currently working on a book project on the theory and practice of montage in Weimar culture.

Peter M. McIsaac will be Associate Professor of German and Museum Studies at the University of Michigan in Ann Arbor starting in September 2011. Before this, he taught at York and Duke Universities. His publications include *Museums of the Mind: German Modernity and the Dynamics of Collecting* (College Park, Pennsylvania: Penn State University Press 2007), and, as co-editor, a special issue of *New German Critique* on contemporary German literature (2003). His articles have appeared in *The German Quarterly, Monatshefte, Literatur für Leser*, and *German Life and Letters*. He is currently writing a book that situates Gunther von Hagens' Body Worlds with respect to German traditions of German anatomical display and the dynamics of globalization.

Carl Niekerk is Associate Professor of German, Comparative and World Literature, and Jewish Studies at the University of Illinois (Urbana-Champaign). His teaching and research interests include modern German literature and culture, early anthropological theory, psychoanalysis, literature and sexuality, and the history of nature. He is the author of *Bildungskrisen. Die Frage nach dem Subjekt in Goethes 'Unterhaltungen deutscher Ausgewanderten'* (Tübingen: Stauffenburg 1995); *Zwischen Naturgeschichte und Anthropologie. Lichtenberg im Kontext der Spätaufklärung* (Tübingen: Niemeyer 2005); and *Reading Mahler: German Culture and Jewish Identity in Fin-de-siècle*

Vienna (Rochester, New York: Camden House 2010). Together with Michael C. Finke he edited *One Hundred Years of Masochism: Literary Texts, Social and Cultural Contexts* (Amsterdam and Atlanta: Rodopi 2000).

Lynne Tatlock is Hortense and Tobias Lewin Distinguished Professor in the Humanities at Washington University (St. Louis). She has published widely on German literature and culture from 1650 to the 1990s, particularly in the late seventeenth and the nineteenth centuries. Her interests include the novel and its origins, the construction and representation of gender, reading communities and reading habits, nineteenth-century regionalism and nationalism, the intersection between fiction and other social and cultural discourses. Her most recent publications include articles on the construction of gender in Grimmelshausen's pseudo-autobiographical novels, Gustav Freytag's alternative address to national community, concepts of work and profession in early modern novels by musicians, disease and community in Raabe's *Unruhige Gäste*, and a co-authored investigation of displacement in Kleist's "Bettelweib von Locarno." She has undertaken two literary translations of novels by women, Marie von Ebner-Eschenbach's *Their Pavel* (*Das Gemeindekind*) and Gabriele Reuter's *From a Good Family*, and has published a scholarly edition and translation of Justine Siegemund's *The Court Midwife* and of selected meditations from Catharina Regina von Greiffenberg's *Leiden und Sterben Jesu Christi*, and *Der Allerheiligsten Menschwerdung, Geburt und Jugend Jesu Christi* for The Other Voice (University of Chicago Press). Her activity as literary translator has kindled her interest in translation and cultural mediation and has led her to undertake an extended project on women as translators, the publishing industry, and transatlantic culture.

Mark Christian Thompson is Associate Professor of English at Johns Hopkins University. His areas of interest include nineteenth- and twentieth-century American, British, and German literature; Modernism; African-American literature and culture; psychoanalysis; cultural studies; literary theory; philosophy; and aesthetics. His work explores the interrelatedness of African-American expressive culture and European thought, often finding problematic, at times undesirable yet nevertheless existent, confluences between the two. He is the author of *Black Fascisms: African American Literature and Culture Between the Wars* (Charlottesville: University of Virginia Press 2007). He is currently working on a book about the complex interplay between fascism and Jazz in twentieth-century German literature and critical theory.

Stefani Engelstein and Carl Niekerk

Introduction. Violence, Culture, Aesthetics: Germany 1789–1938

Violence has become a ubiquitous topic of public concern in today's world: from debates over the consequences of its representation in entertainment, to the grim reality of wars and of genocide from Iraq and Afghanistan to the Sudan. In the form of terrorism both as a real strategy and as a rhetorical tool employed by politicians, or of torture carried out by governmental and semi-governmental agencies across the globe, violence dominates contemporary political, ethical, and social debates across the world today. With such a range of manifestations, locations, and agents, discussing violence as a single topic involves serious complications. It is therefore all the more urgent that violence be studied in its historical, local, and global contexts.

To approach violence as a topic productively, it becomes necessary to explore simultaneously how individuals construct (or remember) the communal histories and cultural identities that frame instances of violence; it is also important to ask how acts of violence are linked to such processes of identity formation themselves and how individuals conform to or resist pressures to participate in violence. The essays in this present volume take this challenge seriously, interrogating notions of culture, community, and agency as constitutive for theories of violence. Our contributions focus on the vexed treatment of violence in the German cultural tradition between two crucial, and radically different, violent outbreaks: the French Revolution, and the Holocaust and Second World War. In focusing on this period, this volume has two goals: to elucidate trends in theories of violence leading up to one of the most horrifying genocidal outbreaks in history, and also to provide a glimpse of the stakes involved in ongoing discussions of the legitimate uses of violence, and of state, individual, and collective agency in its perpetration. The chapters will examine attempts to come to terms with the structure, ramifications, legitimacy, or illegitimacy of violence as explored through a variety of cultural forms from literature to museum planning to film to critical theory. By analyzing violence in these textual realms, the volume also interrogates the extent to which violence resists theoretical description or normative legislation. In particular, recent history has shown that textual violence is so intertwined with practice that it, in a sense, leads us to the limits of theory. "Violence" is situated on the boundaries where the discursive and the non-discursive engage each other.

Looking at the history of theorizing violence in the modern period, it is possible to distinguish a number of different but intersecting nodes of debate, including the role of the state, the status of violence as a means or as an end, the agency behind the use of force, and the role of collective identity in perpetrating violence. Early modernity conceptualized violence primarily as "instrumental", that is: as a means to achieve a certain goal.[1] Individual agency was most frequently envisioned as violence against other individuals or as part of a communal assent to subjugation to the state. At the edge of communal assent, however, lurked the possibility of group dissent, and the contours of a shadowy second form of communal bond, potentially but not necessarily coextensive with the state: that of group identity. These fracture lines in the simple structure of power and agency have emerged explicitly into theory since the mid-nineteenth century. While these concerns occupied thinkers across Europe, a disproportionate number of writers on the topic were German: Kant, Clausewitz, Marx, Freud, Weber, Benjamin, Schmitt, to name just a few, all reflected in detail on the problem of violence.

From the early modern period, theories of violence have notably revolved around conceptualizations of the origin, structure, and role of the state and the legitimacy of its exercise of force. In the last decades, however, and at an accelerating rate in the new century, theories of violence have begun to manifest a seismic shift in the understanding of collective action. This theoretical shift reflects real changes in the global political and social landscape: while theories of state power and use of violence accompanied the rise of the modern nation-state, we are now witnessing the weakening of state authority and the rise of new cultural affiliations whose structures bear no relation to traditional state agencies. Today, Samuel Huntington's "clash of civilizations" theory,[2] which claims that violence is determined by one's identity within existing cultural networks, has achieved paradigmatic status, although it has also been challenged vigorously. Meanwhile, considerations of the nature of non-state collective actors and actions have been taken up by writers such as John Arquilla, David Ronfeldt, Veena Das, Arthur Kleinman, and Amartya Sen.[3] Upon closer inspection,

---

[1] Beatrice Hanssen: *Critique of Violence: Between Poststructuralism and Critical Theory*. London-New York: Routledge 2000. P. 18.

[2] The term "clash of civilizations" was introduced into public debate by the neoconservative political scientist Samuel P. Huntington in an article: Samuel P. Huntington: The Clash of Civilizations? In: *Foreign Affairs* 72.3 (1993). Pp. 22–49. He revisited the idea later in Samuel P. Huntington: *The Clash of Civilizations and the Remaking of the World Order*. New York: Simon & Schuster 1996.

[3] John Arquilla and David Ronfeldt: *Networks and Netwars: The Future of Terror, Crime, and Militancy*. Santa Monica, California: RAND 2001. Veena Das and Arthur Kleinman: Introduction. In: *Violence and Subjectivity*. Ed. by Veena Das, Arthur Kleinman, Momphela Ramphele, and Pamela Reynolds. Berkeley: University of California Press 2000. Pp. 1–18. Amartya Sen: *Identity and Violence: the Illusion of Destiny*. New York-London: Norton 2006. (Issues of Our Time)

however, the dichotomy between old and new theories of violence reveals permeable boundaries. New theories linking violence to identity in fact illuminate important questions of individual and group agency that were always already lurking beneath the surface of the discourse on violence and the state.

Thomas Hobbes, the first modern theorist of the nature of violence, erected the state as the only barrier to perpetual warfare between individuals. This condition arose from an intrinsic desire for freedom combined with the perception of power in the hands of any other individual as a threat to that freedom. Ceding power to an authority that protected citizens against each other could be said to serve merely as a displacement of violence onto the state whose control was also a form of violent imposition. Hobbes gives a definition of war and peace that undermines such a reading, however: "So the nature of War, consisteth not in actual fighting; but in the known disposition thereto, during all the time there is no assurance to the contrary. All other time is PEACE".[4] It is the assurance of a bulwark against violence, rather than an alteration in the conditions of desiring violence, that allows the state to usher in peace through force. Over time, the valence of the state's relationship to violence has fluctuated in accordance with the emphasis laid on its various roles as peacekeeper or as sole executor of violence. Far from being mutually exclusive, these roles are in fact codeterminate.

Within the modern German intellectual tradition Immanuel Kant embraced Hobbes's view of interpersonal strife inhibited by state control, but downplayed the violence implicit in such state power. For Kant, violence is inherently instrumental; it can never be a goal in itself, but only a means through which individuals, or groups of individuals, seek to achieve something. Inherent to "Gewalt" as a form of power ("Macht"), is an element of force, a certain physicality, even though this element does not necessarily manifest itself in the form of violent behavior.[5] In the first addendum to his essay *Zum ewigen Frieden* (*Toward Perpetual Peace*) from 1795, his most important text on the problem of violence, for instance, Kant states that public law finds its origin in the force ("Zwang") that accompanies "Gewalt".[6] Of course in Kant's view such a use of force is only legitimate if it serves the law, that is, if it is in accord with a moral imperative. By adopting a modified form of the social contract espoused in different forms by Hobbes and Rousseau, Kant

---

[4] Thomas Hobbes: *Leviathan*. London: Penguin Books 1988. P. 186.
[5] Immanuel Kant: *Kritik der Urteilskraft*. In: *Werkausgabe*. Ed. by Wilhelm Weischedel. Frankfurt am Main: Suhrkamp 1993. Vol. 10. P. 184.
[6] Immanuel Kant: Zum ewigen Frieden. Ein philosophischer Entwurf, in: *Studienausgabe*. Vol. 11. Pp. 191–251. Here: P. 231. Toward Perpetual Peace. In: *Practical Philosophy*. Trans. and ed. by Mary J. Gregor. Cambridge: Cambridge University Press 1996. Pp. 311–352. Here: P. 371. See also Hanssen: *Critique of Violence*. P. 20.

legitimates the authority of a republican state as a projection of the will of the people. The state thus actually becomes for Kant a synonym for peace: "Daß ein Volk sagt: 'Es soll unter uns kein Krieg sein; denn wir wollen uns in einen Staat formieren [. . .]' – das läßt sich verstehen" ["It is understandable for a people to say, 'There shall be no war among us, for we want to form ourselves into a state [. . .]"].[7] In this odd formulation the state is not merely a means to quell violence, but takes up the position of an end. To insure perpetual peace, this same procedure must be repeated on the international level, where the state, now granted the agency and authority of personhood, joins together with other states in a league of nations that can enforce public law internationally.

Gewalt in itself is thus neither good nor bad for Kant. *Gewalt* without freedom or law equals Barbarism; but if it serves freedom and the law, *Gewalt* is the foundation for Republicanism, as Kant states in his *Anthropologie* of 1798.[8] It is a paradox that in Kant's thinking only through "an evolutionary republicanization of forms of domination that have arisen through violence" is a society possible "in which all willfulness and violence has been banished from human social relations".[9] The categorical imperative demands banishing caprice or desire, and hence also individual predeliction, from the use of violence, which is only permissible if backed up by a universalizable rational deliberation. The question of violence is directly tied to modernity's ambition to legislate itself. Modernity's success, one could conclude, depends on the ability to contain the problem of violence: to suppress undesirable forms of violence and to foster desirable, or at least necessary, forms of violence. As in Hobbes, then, individuality aligns itself with unjustified violence while collectivity represses it through justified force. There is one important borderline case for Kant, and that is revolution.

Most of the texts in which Kant reflects explicitly on the issue of violence were published after the French Revolution of 1789. Kant's intense interest in the French Revolution is linked to its status as a radical break in the standing of a constitution and hence of law and rights, which nonetheless grounds those rights. In *Der Streit der Fakultäten* (*The Contest of Faculties*), Kant therefore reveals an extreme ambivalence about revolution. While he rules out revolution as unjust,[10] he nonetheless comes to the conclusion that a civil society

---

[7] Kant: Zum ewigen Frieden. P. 212. Kant: Toward Perpetual Peace. P. 327.
[8] Kant: *Anthropologie in pragmatischer Hinsicht*. In: *Werkausgabe*. Vol. 12. Pp. 395–690. Here: P. 686.
[9] Wolfgang Kersting: Politics, Freedom, and Order: Kant's Political Philosophy. In: *The Cambridge Companion to Kant*. Ed. by Paul Guyer. Cambridge UK-New York: Cambridge University Press 1992. Pp. 342–366. Here: Pp. 361, 362.
[10] Immanuel Kant: Der Streit der Fakultäten. In: *Werkausgabe*. Vol. 11. Pp. 261–393. Here: P. 360n. Immanuel Kant: The Contest of Faculties. In: *Political Writings*. Ed. by Hans Reiss. Cambridge: Cambridge University Press 1991. P. 184n.

governed by "Freiheitsgesetze" ["laws of freedom"] can only be achieved after a long process, "nach mannigfaltigen Befehdungen und Kriegen [. . .]; ihre Verfassung aber, wenn sie im großen einmal errungen worden, qualifiziert sich zum besten unter allen, um den Krieg, den Zerstörer alles Guten, entfernt zu halten" (364) ["after innumerable wars and conflicts. But its constitution, once it has been attained as a whole, is the best qualified of all to keep out war, the destroyer of everything good" (187)]. Revolution is thus unjust and yet, as Kant lost faith in reform it came to seem necessary to achieve a just civil government. Kant thus saw the widespread sympathy towards the French Revolution as a sign of the universality of a moral disposition which inclines humans toward a republican government that safeguards their rights.[11] Revolution thus teeters on the boundary of universalizability.[12]

It is productive to read Kant's deliberations on violence in tandem with a piece of popular culture like Beethoven's *Fidelio*, an opera whose roots can also be traced back to the French Revolution.[13] The opera shows how violence is embedded in a variety of complex power structures, an insight that problematizes the idea of a purely instrumental use of violence by gesturing to a disturbing attractiveness and persuasiveness Kant was blind to, which seem to raise violence to the status of an end in itself. For Beethoven not only individuals but the state apparatus is implicated in violence, while individuals possess the ability to accede to or to resist its pull. *Fidelio* stages the story of Florestan, a political prisoner of some kind, wrongfully imprisoned somewhere not far from the Spanish town Sevilla, and of his wife Leonore, who attempts to liberate her husband disguised as a man (Fidelio). The jail's supervisor, Rocco, is nominally in charge of Florestan, but in reality is a reluctant jailer who only acts on the orders of others. Florestan's fate is decided by the governor, Don Pizarro, who acts solely on his own behalf and authority,[14] and at one point (in act 1, scene 5)[15] seeks to tempt Rocco into murdering Florestan for money. This act is (narrowly) avoided by the chance arrival of the minister, Don Fernando, who gives the prisoners back their freedom. It is clear that the use of violence, namely Florestan's incarceration, is in conflict with the law. One could argue, however, that violent acts like these create a network of practices that, if persistent, can start to

---

[11] Kant: Der Streit der Fakultäten. P. 358. Kant: The Contest of Faculties. P. 182.
[12] See also Kouvelakis's discussion in Stathis Kouvelakis: *Philosophy and Revolution from Kant to Marx*. Trans G. M. Goshgarian. London: Verso 2003. Pp. 23–43.
[13] Bouilly, the author of the original French version of the libretto, witnessed a story similar to that of Florestan and Leonore during his tenure as an administrator and public attorney in the French town Tours in 1793–1794. See the editorial commentary in Ludwig van Beethoven: *Fidelio. Textbuch, Einführung und Kommentar*. Ed. by Kurt Pfahlen. Mainz: Atlantis-Schott 1997. P. 125.
[14] Ibid. P. 103.
[15] Ibid. P. 45.

function as a kind of unofficial, alternative form of the law. *Fidelio* also illustrates the way that potentates can set up boundaries to shield themselves from the physicality of the violence they command. Interestingly, the opera offers a model of resistance against violence through the example of Leonore. Physical violence is countered by Leonore's intelligence and cunning, in particular her willingness to adopt a new identity that includes a different gender. The opera not only advocates political freedom; at a time when gender roles became more prescriptive, *Fidelio* openly advocates gender-role-switching. It thus recognizes and valorizes the ability of an individual to step outside cultural codes.

Fidelio articulates the failure of Kant's project by emphasizing the allure of using force to increase power, i.e. using force to increase the opportunity to use force again. Faced with the tendency of violence to escalate, counter-violence proves less effective than nonviolent modes of resistance. Part of the opera's critical impulse is also that it thematizes the difference between the theory and the practice of violence. And yet, the rupture between theory and reality is not wholly inaccessible to theorization. In an exemplary way, *Fidelio* anticipates some of Walter Benjamin's ideas about violence in his essay *On the Critique of Violence* (1921). The starting point of this essay is the observation that nobody asks any longer under what conditions and for which goals the use of violence is legitimate. Instead violence is seen as "Naturprodukt" ["natural product"] or "Rohstoff" ["raw material" / "commodity"].[16] It is tempting to read this as a direct comment on Kant's first addendum to *Toward Perpetual Peace* in which he warns, in the context of his discussion of the legitimacy of violence, against interpreting what happens as "bloßer Mechanismus der Natur" ["mere mechanism of nature"], but instead advocates seeking rules to master the use of violence.[17] Benjamin does not dismiss the relationship between violence and nature the way Kant did; after Darwin, who is mentioned explicitly (180), and after Freud's positing of an innate aggressive drive, Benjamin can no longer deny violence as a basic component of human action (a point that is illustrated by Don Pizzaro in *Fidelio*).

Benjamin also brings to the fore the contradictions inherent in Kant's model. Like Kant, Benjamin sees violence as creating law, something that is particularly clear in times of war (183). No conflict can be resolved into a juridical treaty without at least some element of violence (190). Judicial institutions can only maintain themselves by keeping the population conscious

---

[16] Walter Benjamin: Zur Kritik der Gewalt. In: *Gesammelte Werke. Aufsätze. Essays. Vorträge*. Ed. by Rolf Tiedemann and Hermann Schweppenhäuser. Frankfurt am Main: Suhrkamp 1991. Pp. 179–203. Here: P. 180.

[17] Kant: Zum ewigen Frieden. P. 232. Kant: Toward Perpetual Peace. P. 372. It is not unthinkable that in this passage Benjamin is taking issue with Kant's essay directly; Benjamin mentions Kant's essay explicitly later on (Zur Kritik der Gewalt 185–186).

of the latent presence of violence in them (190). In order to achieve a societal order without violence, therefore, first the use of violence is necessary. Benjamin radicalizes this paradox: violence is by necessity part of the functioning of the institutions of the law, even if it appears to be absent. Toward the end of his essay, Benjamin adopts the concept of myth to illustrate the functioning of violence in the legal sense (197–203). To understand legal violence as mythical is helpful because myth, in Benjamin's work, functions beyond truth or falsehood.[18] Myth is characterized by its own autonomous dynamic. It is therefore no surprise that one particular issue in Benjamin's essay that gradually gains in urgency is the question of the conditions under which individuals can use violence legitimately – something that in general is seen as undermining the legal system (183). Benjamin's sympathy is clearly with nonviolent forms of resistance; the issue of the legitimacy of strikes as a means to protest social injustice plays a major role throughout the essay.

While Kant's deliberations on violence, in particular in the first addendum of his essay *Toward Perpetual Peace*, can be understood as motivated by a profoundly modern desire to resolve the issue of violence rationally – ultimately on the basis of a consensus-model – Benjamin's essay, in contrast, is an expression of modernity's frustration with its inability to regulate violence. As such, it is not only representative for the early twentieth century, but also illuminating for what has come since. And yet, one could say that modernity's disillusionment with its powers to regulate violence is already visible in an opera like *Fidelio*. Particularly troubling is the break between the actions of Don Pizarro, who is supposedly executing the law, and those of the minister, formal representative of the law. We see here the tendency of violence to exceed its instrumentality, to live by its own dynamics, and to create new law. While Don Pizzaro's violent behavior exemplifies the latent mythical aspect of the law, Leonore personifies a form of nonviolent resistance that is pacifist and yet outsmarts the authorities in charge – a mode of countering violence Benjamin would certainly have respected.

In one important particular, however, Benjamin's strike differs from Leonore's actions as a model for countering violence – the strike is collective rather than individual. This distinction points towards a shift in thinking about violence over the course of the nineteenth century. Kant's version of state-formation, like that of Hobbes, essentially allows for only two actors: individuals *and* (or perhaps more accurately, *or*) the state. While the consensus

---

[18] See Winfried Menninghaus: Walter Benjamin's Theory of Myth. In: *On Walter Benjamin: Critical Essays and Recollections*. Ed. by Gary Smith. Cambridge, Massachusetts-London: Massachusetts Institute of Technology Press, 1991. Pp. 292–325. Here: Pp. 298–299. See in this context also Lutz Koepnick's deliberations on mythic residues in pre-fascist modernity in *Walter Benjamin and the Aesthetics of Power*. Lincoln-London: Nebraska University Press 1999. Pp. 160, 161.

necessary to form the state might seem to require group negotiation, it is more properly an acquiescence on the part of each individual to the state apparatus in tandem with the same decision by other individuals, rather than a mutual agreement within a community. By the time Benjamin enters these debates, collective action by various kinds of groups is a live question. Between Kant and Benjamin, the dynamics of social struggle had been redefined by Marx, who, through the concept of class warfare, introduced a new understanding of group identity and collective action.

By the late nineteenth century, moreover, the second half of Hobbes's equation, the violent force required by the state to impose upon its subjects a stable condition, was much less likely to be theorized as *peace* than as, at best, détente, and at worst, undeclared war. As Max Weber put it succinctly,

> Heute dagegen werden wir sagen müssen: Staat ist diejenige menschliche Gemeinschaft, welche innerhalb eines bestimmten Gebietes – dies: das 'Gebiet' gehört zum Merkmal – das Monopol legitimer physischer Gewaltsamkeit für sich (mit Erfolg) beansprucht.
> [Today, however, we have to say that a state is that human community that (successfully) claims the *monopoly of the legitimate use of physical force* within a given territory – the 'territory' belongs to the definition.][19]

Weber's emphasis on the state as a community is striking. Still more importantly though, Weber's definition of the state is firmly historicized, just as it is firmly politicized. The state's claims to a monopoly on violence are without external foundation, its territorial boundaries are open to challenge from neighbors, and its range of political actors is the product of ongoing struggle. The violence that it exercises, by definition legitimate, is bidirectional: outward and inward.

Although Weber appropriates part of Hobbes's argument here, there is a definitive historical break that separates Weber's argument from the earlier views of Hobbes and Kant. Hobbes situates state power in opposition to the tendency of people to fight among themselves, and emphasizes obedience as the duty of the citizen in return for its protection.[20] Kant posits a state that successfully quells internal violence through republicanism and is in turn open to incorporation in a peaceful world community. For both Hobbes and Kant, therefore, the tendency towards violence can be brought into equilibrium in different ways. For Weber, as for Benjamin, and for Marx and Engels before them, what looks like equilibrium is only the successful and likely temporary

---

[19] Max Weber: Politik als Beruf. In: *Gesammelte politische Schriften*. München: Drei Masken Verlag, 1921. Pp. 396–450. Here: P. 397. Max Weber: Politics as a Vocation. In: *From Max Weber: Essays in Sociology*. Trans & ed. by H. H. Gerth and C. Wright Mills. New York: Oxford University Press 1958. Pp. 77–128. Here: P. 78. Italics in the original, but translation modified.
[20] Hobbes. P. 272.

deployment of force. Where Marx and Engels saw class as the underlying category that divided society into group actors, Weber identified a more complex and varied set of potential power-wielders: ethnic groups, political parties, and individual actors, all of whom might seek "die Macht lediglich um ihrer selbst willen" ["power for power's sake"].[21] To use Hobbes's definition, the "known disposition [to fighting]" (186) is thus a permanent condition of modern states.

In light of this widening of the debate over the legitimacy of the use of violence to non-state actors, the development of a right-wing discourse that reaffirmed the priority of the state in matters of force is unsurprising. What is perhaps surprising is the continued relevance of, and recent surge of interest in, one proponent of a theory along these lines, Carl Schmitt.[22] A member of the Nazi party and a committed totalitarian, Schmitt seems an odd choice for contemporary theory to return to. But Schmitt's 1930s theory of decisionism, combined with his work on partisan warfare and on the twentieth-century demise of a European *jus publicum*, has been called upon to analyze current conflicts between states, and between states and nongovernmental organizations, broadly understood.[23] For Schmitt, the defining political act is

---

[21] Weber: Politik als Beruf. P. 437. Weber: Politics as a Vocation. P. 109.

[22] As an example of this renewed interest in Carl Schmitt, see for instance the 2009 thematic issue of *Telos* on Carl Schmitt and the Event, and the *South Atlantic Quarterly* issue 104:2 (2005) on World Orders: Confronting Smith's *The* Nomos *of the Earth*. Recent book length studies of Schmitt include: George Schwab: *The Challenge of the Exception: An Introduction to the Political Ideas of Carl Schmitt between 1921 and 1936*. New York: Greenwood Press 1989. John P. McCormick: *Carl Schmitt's Critique of Liberalism: Against Politics as Technology*. Cambridge-New York: Cambridge University Press 1997. Jeffrey Seitzer: C*omparative History and Legal Theory: Carl Schmitt in the First German Democracy*. Westport, Connecticut: Greenwood Press 2001. Raphael Gross: *Carl Schmitt and the Jews: The "Jewish Question," the Holocaust, and German Legal Theory*. Trans. by Joel Golb. Madison: University of Wisconsin Press 2007. The MLA International Bibliography records 167 articles on Schmitt from 2000–2009 compared with 32 from 1956–1999.

[23] Carl Schmitt: *Der Begriff des Politischen*. Berlin: Duncker & Humblot 1991. Carl Schmitt: *The Concept of the Political*. Trans. by George Schwab. New Brunswick: Rutgers University Press 1976. Carl Schmitt: *Theorie des Partisanen*. Berlin: Duncker & Humblot 1963. Carl Schmitt: *Theory of the Partisan*. Trans. by G.L. Ulmen. New York: Telos Press 2007. Carl Schmitt: *Der Nomos der Erde im Völkerrecht des Jus Publicum Europaeum*. Carl Schmitt: *The* Nomos *of the Earth in the International Law of the* Jus Publicum Europaeum. New York: Telos Press 2003. Berlin: Duncker & Humblot 1974. President Bush's declaration "I'm the decider" (4/18/2006, qtd. in "President Bush Nominates Rob Portman as OMB Director and Susan Schwab for USTR". http://www.whitehouse.gov/news/releases/2006/04/20060418-1.html. Downloaded 6/4/2008), to end debate over a ill-advised, poorly-managed, and unpopular war, seems an uncanny parody of Schmitt's emphasis on the act of deciding who is a friend and who an enemy as the defining action of politics.

the creation of friends and, even more importantly, of enemies. This theory, first published in *Der Begriff des Politischen* [*The Concept of the Political*] in 1932, declares that this political opposition must be understood as distinct from moral judgments of good and evil or aesthetic judgments of beauty and ugliness. The enemy thus should not be hated and reviled, but simply understood as existentially opposed to one's own political unit.[24] Such a unit is paradigmatically a state, but political friend/enemy constellations can also crystallize around a "religiösen, moralischen, ökonomischen, ethnischen oder anderen Gegensatz" ["religious, moral, economic, ethical, or other antithesis"], which will become political "wenn er stark genug ist, die Menschen nach Freund und Feind effektiv zu gruppieren" (37) ["if it is sufficiently strong to group human beings effectively according to friend and enemy" (37)]. The theory posits such units as politically equally sovereign, with conflict between them amounting in the final extreme to a civil war. This bilateralism serves as a justificatory cover for the unmistakable anti-Semitic subtext when Schmitt defines the enemy as "der andere, der Fremde, und es genügt zu seinem Wesen, daß er in einem besonders intensiven Sinne existenziell etwas anderes und Fremdes ist, so daß im extremen Fall Konflikte mit ihm möglich sind" (27) ["the other, the stranger; and it is sufficient for his nature that he is, in a specially intense way, existentially something different and alien, so that in the extreme case conflicts with him are possible" (27)].[25] Schmitt's formulation thus legitimates lethal hostility towards an "other", under the guise of an operation conducted with duel-like fair-play.[26] Schmitt declares Clausewitz's famous quote that war is "eine bloße Fortsetzung der Politik mit anderen Mitteln"[27] ["a mere continuation of politics by other means"], faulty, because war operates according to different strategies than politics once begun.[28] He nonetheless intensifies Clausewitz's intertwining of the political and the military by formulating a state that is always already

---

[24] Schmitt: *Begriff*. See in particular Pp. 26–30. Schmitt: *Concept*. Pp. 25–29.
[25] See Raphael Gross: *Carl Schmitt and the Jews*. Pp. 177–184.
[26] Schmitt uses the duel analogy explicitly is his 1950 *Der Nomos der Erde*. P. 115 (*The Nomos of the Earth*. P. 143). By stating specifically that in the European *jus publicum*, whose demise he mourns, the enemy is not something "'das vernichtet werden muß'" (114), Schmitt distances his theory from responsibility for the Holocaust, which he studiously avoids mentioning throughout this work. Indeed, the word "Vernichtung" is applied to war tactics he specifically identifies with the air bombing of civilians, thus displacing the German genocide of the Jews with an image of German victims. There is nonetheless no doubt that his earlier work lends itself to an understanding of the Jew as a religious and cultural enemy of the German *Volk*.
[27] Carl von Clausewitz: *Vom Krieg*. Bonn, F. Dummler 1952. P. 108.
[28] Schmitt: *Begriff*. P. 33. Schmitt: *Concept*. Pp. 33–34.

war-oriented, a state whose primary political action is positioning itself in hostile opposition.

Schmitt categorically rejects Kant's utopian view of a political organization which is potentially all inclusive, and hence without enemies.[29] Partisan warfare, of course, presents a challenge to the model of the state as the only institution with political agency, which is why Schmitt eventually turned his attention to explaining it. Writing on partisans in 1963, Schmitt is clearly still rankled by the partisan fighters in France and Poland during the Second World War, who took political decisions into their own hands and continued to identify Germany as an enemy even after the surrender of their governments. Schmitt perceptively notes an increase in such partisan tactics as guerrilla warfare worldwide since the Second World War, a tendency that has only intensified since the 1960s. To be legitimately political, however, he assumes that partisans must associate themselves with a small core of regular army troops and a line of command suited to take up the position of statehood if their war should succeed.[30]

While Schmitt failed to predict the ultimate disappearance of statehood as the goal of combatants unaffiliated with states, he did identify a crucial trend in warfare towards increasingly non-hierarchical organization outside the bounds of state authority. John Arquilla and David Ronfeldt, writing just before the attacks on the US on September 11, 2001, refer to this new type of conflict as a *netwar*. The primary feature of netwar combatants, according to Arquilla and Ronfeldt, is their networked organization, which has replaced traditional hierarchies. Communication is enabled by new cell phone and internet technology, and their small, dispersed, and semi-autonomous units make them hard for state armies to engage effectively.[31] The most remarkable thing about Arquilla and Ronfeldt's analysis, however, is not their description of non-state warfare, but their adaptation of the word *war* itself. While Clausewitz claimed that "War is a continuation of politics by other means", Foucault reversed this statement and declared that "Power is war, the continuation of war by other means", and hence "politics is the continuation of war by other means".[32] The goal of politics, in other words, is not to suspend the application of force, but to maintain it. Arquilla and Ronfeldt enact Foucault's

---

[29] Schmitt: *Begriff*. P. 54. Schmitt: *Concept*. P. 53–54.
[30] Schmitt: *Theorie des Partisanen*. See in particular Pp. 92–93. Schmitt: *Partisan*. Pp. 90–92.
[31] John Arquilla and David Ronfeldt: *Networks and Netwars*. P. v.
[32] Michel Foucault: *'Society Must be Defended': Lectures at the College de France, 1975–1976*. Ed. by Mauro Bertani and Elessandro Fontana. Trans. by David Macey. New York: Picador 2003. P. 15.

declaration; for them *any* campaign run in a networked fashion is a net*war*, leading them to such paradoxical statements as

> For a seminal case of a worldwide netwar, one need look no further than the ICBL [International Campaign to Ban Landmines]. This unusually successful movement consists of a loosely internetted array of NGOs and governments, which rely heavily on the Internet for communications. Through the personage of one of its many leaders, Jody Williams, this netwar won a well-deserved Nobel peace prize. (5)

Distinctions between war and peace have entirely collapsed here. By calling all organized, goal-directed action *war*, Arquilla and Ronfeldt displace questions of violence, while pushing the complicity of power and violence that had been increasingly acknowledged from Kant to Benjamin to its logical extreme. Significantly, the research of Arquilla and Ronfeldt was funded and published by the U.S. Department of Defense. While their theory would seem to point to the demise of the state, not only as Kant, but also as Weber and Schmitt understood it, their priorities still lie primarily with protecting the sovereignty of states, above all that of their own patron-government, even as they encourage a strategic reorganization that mimics that of netwarriors.[33]

Arquilla and Ronfeldt are not alone in analyzing the traits of a new type of military activity that explodes assumptions about combatants and geography. Paul Virilio in *Ground Zero* notes the "disappearance of a real battlefield".[34] The extent of this kind of amorphous warfare is new, but tactically it is also the descendent of Schmitt's partisan-warfare, whose own debt to the soldiers of the French Revolution Schmitt notes in turn. Arquilla and Ronfeldt name the unique strategic pattern of their netwarriors "swarming": the "seemingly amorphous, but deliberately structured, coordinated, strategic way to strike from all directions at a particular point or points, by means of a sustainable pulsing of force and/or fire, close-in as well as from stand-off positions".[35] This pattern builds on the behavior of Schmitt's partisans, who attack and vanish into the landscape, but whom Schmitt theorizes as autochthonous and thus firmly anchored to their land, unable to go global like today's non-state actors.

While some violent organizations recruit and operate internationally, Veena Das and Arthur Kleinman have pointed out that the great majority of violence today involves individuals, acting voluntarily or under coercion, committing violence in their own living space, as in civil war, ethnic conflict, and local terrorism. The question of violence no longer focuses either on the individual's exercise of freedom at the expense of others or on the state's ability to restrict such overreaching, but instead on group affiliation. It is precisely this shift

---

[33] Arquilla and Ronfeldt. Esp. Pp. 15–16.
[34] Paul Virilio: *Ground Zero*. Trans. by Chris Turner. London: Verso 2002. P. 43
[35] Arquilla and Ronfeldt. P. 12.

that opens up a space for looking at violence in a cultural context: violence as somehow related to the values and investments that tie the individual to what is conceptualized as a homogenous and highly coercive "culture".

Precisely German cultural history offers us tools to describe and understand how cultural identity and violence are mutually dependent. In Germany, where questions about violence since 1945 always appropriately begin and end with reference to the Holocaust, the issue of agency has long occupied public attention, but never more than since the publication of Daniel Goldhagen's *Hitler's Willing Executioners*.[36] Goldhagen's research revealed the widespread participation of ordinary citizens in the murder of Jews during the Holocaust. While his stated aim was to uphold the notion of the uniqueness of the Holocaust in the sad history of genocide, his work, by focusing on ordinary individuals, actually illuminates strong links to more recent ethnic cleansing and genocide in the former Yugoslavia and Rwanda, where large numbers of ordinary individuals attacked neighbors in their own communities. Goldhagen's work could be seen as an early indicator of new tendencies in the study of violence, which has begun to focus on the forging of group affiliations strong enough to justify murder, while calling into question the central role of state authority.

This explains, at least in part, why violence should become a topic of interest in cultural studies. "Culture" has been embraced by public discourse as one tool to describe the origins and contexts of violence today, at the latest since Samuel Huntington's coining of the term "clash of civilizations". In part this can be explained through the observation that culture – in its many different manifestations: as a shared religion, as a shared literary or artistic tradition (popular or elite), or simply as a set of shared values (explicitly or implicitly) – functions by simultaneously bonding and excluding. On the one hand, the evocation of culture is particularly well-suited to creating group identity or social cohesion where these were lacking. On the other hand, culture also defines itself through boundaries that de-legitimate, and in the worst cases dehumanize, a set of individuals whom it (sometimes but not always mutually) defines as outsiders. A number of contributions to the current volume study these mechanisms for creating national or ethnic cohesion, an operation often accompanied by a combination of fascination and abhorrence for the "other".

Looking at German cultural history can also help us recognize the complex interactions of culture and identity, far beyond the mechanistic schematisms and epistemological simplifications of neo-conservative critics like Huntington. For Huntington, the group we belong to determines our actions, and there is no space left even for multiple group affiliations, far less for individual choices.

---

[36] Daniel Jonah Goldhagen: *Hitler's Willing Executioners: Ordinary Germans and the Holocaust*. New York: Alfred A. Knopf, 1996.

Civilizations are, in other words, bound to clash. But does our identity, whether envisioned as religious, ethnic, cultural, or all three, indeed become our destiny?

Disputing this idea forms the core of Amartya Sen's recent book *Identity and Violence: The Illusion of Destiny*.[37] Sen offers a highly critical analysis of identity politics and violence: violence, in his view, is "promoted by the cultivation of a sense of inevitability about some allegedly unique – often belligerent – identity that we are supposed to have and which apparently makes extensive demands on us" (xiii). The reality, according to Sen, is that we do have a choice about our identities, which we choose out of multiple potential ones available to us.[38] Chronologically speaking, the last text discussed in this volume is *Jugend ohne Gott*, published in exile by Ödön von Horváth in 1937. But we could have ended with Kurban Said's German-language novel *Ali und Nino*, also published in 1937 at the brink of World War II. *Ali und Nino* is one of the rare examples of germanophone literature in German literary history. While the exact authorship of the novel long remained uncertain, it has now become clear that Kurban Said is one of the pen names of Lev Nussimbaum (1905–1942), who during the Weimar Republic also published books under the name Essad Bey.[39] Lev Nussimbaum was born in Baku, Azerbaijan. His father was an oil millionaire; his mother a political activist who sympathized with the Soviets and was apparently friends with Stalin. Nussimbaum was the son of Jewish parents, but later in life converted to Islam. In the late 1920s and early 1930s he was located in Berlin where he worked as a journalist specializing in the "East".

---

[37] Amartya Sen: *Identity and Violence*. Esp. Pp. 10, 40–46.

[38] Sen's text seems a bit naive in the extent to which he underplays constraints upon such choice, not only in the possible form of force from an authoritarian regime, but also in more complicated ways such as expectations that permeate both the individual and society. Identities cannot be assumed and set aside entirely at will. Lenore in *Fidelio* gives indications of the way that the role can come to inhabit the person as much as the person inhabits the role.

[39] The following biographical information is taken from Tom Reiss: *The Orientalist: Solving the Mystery of a Strange and Dangerous Life*. New York: Random House 2005. To anyone even remotely familiar with Nussimbaum's work, it should have been obvious that he is the author of *Ali und Nino*, even before Reiss's research incontrovertibly confirmed this. We now know that Nussimbaum had the name Kurban Said registered as a pen name of Elfriede von Ehrenfels, the wife of a friend, in order to be able to publish in the Third Reich, while his other books had been banned because of his Jewish background. And yet, the 2003 German edition of the text and the American 1999 edition of the text still claim the work is written by von Ehrenfels and "vermutlich" ["presumably"] by the "Kaffeehausliterat" ["coffee house author"] Lev Nussimbaum. Kurban Said: *Ali und Nino. Roman*. München-Berlin: List 2003. P. 2.

Ali und Nino is situated in Baku around the time of the Russian revolution and narrates the story of the romantic relationship between two high school sweethearts: Ali Khan Schirwanschir, Muslim and native of Baku, and Nino Kipiani, Christian of Georgian descent. In an unusually lucid manner Kurban Said explores the cultural conflicts that the relationship between Ali and Nino brings to light. It is very much a conflict between East and West that Said describes. The book documents (and criticizes) in an exemplary way the orientalist and occidentalist clichés that shape the interactions of the different ethnicities in Baku.[40] The East is seen as steeped in tradition, full of autocratic regimes and potentates, and backward in its treatment of women. The West is portrayed as materialistic (obsessed with money; prone to alcohol), opportunistic, and in general out of touch with history, tradition, and the values associated with them. The book shows how such stereotypes are ubiquitous, and are in great need of critical interrogation.

Read in the context of its author's ideological investments – Nussimbaum was a conservative nationalist and rumored to be an admirer of Mussolini – *Ali und Nino* would seem to be a straightforward defense of a "heroic feudal life"[41] in multi-ethnic Baku, both irrevocably lost by 1937. But it is precisely the issue of violence that makes a more differentiated reading possible. At the center of the novel is the kidnapping of Nino by Ali's (Christian) friend Nachararjan. That Nachararjan is a Christian, like Nino, is important. In general, the kidnappings of brides are associated with the East, and not with the (modern) West.[42] Yet Nachararjan feels his kidnapping of Nino is legitimate in the interest of protecting her from the "savage" East (144). In this, the book offers a clear example of how the images cultures manufacture of each other can serve to legitimate precisely those practices a culture claims to reject. Ali kills Nachararjan, but he saves Nino – against the advise of his friends and, eventually also, his father, all representative of the culture in which he lives.[43]

As questionable as we may find the use of violence in *Ali und Nino*, the text shows that violence is also the product of a choice made by an individual at a certain point in time; it may be linked to beliefs, to a cultural code, but the person who makes that decision certainly also has the option of acting against such beliefs (codes). In the case of Ali's actions, the choice between violence and non-violence is not in any way the result of a negotiation of different

---

[40] For basic definitions of these concepts and a genealogy of their history, see: Edward Said and Ian Buruma and Avisha Margalit. Edward Said: *Orientalism*. New York: Vintage 1994. Ian Buruma and Avisha Margalit: *Occidentalism: The West in the Eyes of Its Enemies*. New York: Penguin 2004.
[41] See Reiss: *The Orientalist*. P. 100.
[42] Kurban Said: *Ali und Nino*. Pp. 106, 109.
[43] Ibid. Pp. 150, 156.

identities. Instead, his action can be understood as a critical response to what *his* culture prescribes him to do; it is the issue of a *cultural* identity in general that is at stake here. This is also clear from Ali's subsequent actions. To avoid becoming the victim of a blood feud, Ali flees to a mountain village in Dagestan, represented as lying beyond all ideological or cultural divides. Soon Nino joins him, and the two marry and live a simple and conflict-free life – a utopia that can only be maintained for the short term, until political reality catches up with the couple. Ali decides to join the fight for an independent Azerbaijan, and eventually dies in a hopeless battle rather than following Nino and their child into exile. Again, this choice has much to do with violence, but little with cultural codes.

In the cosmos of *Ali und Nino*, violence is never just a means for a purpose; violence cannot be contained and leads a life of its own; and while violence is bound to people making choices, it also often affects a great number of people who have no choice or have themselves made a choice against violence. At the brink of World War Two, Lev Nussimbaum, as Kurban Said, wrote a novel revealing a utopian longing for a world where identities did not matter. There is a lot one can criticize about the ideology of *Ali und Nino* or its author. But the book raises critical questions, and for that reason it is perhaps the kind of text that would be of benefit to German scholars, in- and outside the class room.

Raising such questions about violence and society now and in the past is precisely what *Contemplating Violence: Critical Studies in Modern German Culture* intends to do. Our hope is that the essays in this volume, by studying German literary, cultural, and intellectual history from 1789 to 1938, will contribute their share to a contextualization of the history of violence, as incomplete as any attempt to understand violence will necessarily be.

Although many of the articles in this collection return to similar or intersecting issues, the contributions can be divided roughly into four groups following a trajectory that begins and ends with investigations into the strategies for manipulating and deploying violence, in particular through representation. While the first set of essays orbits the French Revolution, the last set focuses on the aesthetic strategies of Modernism, but the overlap in their concerns reveals the subterranean link between aesthetic theories conceived in the Romantic period and violent disjuncture. In between these bookends, the essays primarily scrutinize three sources of violence: violence as an irruption of the primitive or repressed, violence as an outgrowth or feeder of identity politics, and violence as a structural component of institutions, of authority, or of representation itself. These roots of violence are not mutually exclusive, but build on each other. The volume as a whole thus considers approaches to violence that attempt to theorize actual violent outbreaks through rhetorical strategies and vice versa.

The first three essays in this volume focus on the aftermath of the French Revolution of 1789 (well into the nineteenth century), and in particular interrogate the extent to which "violence" forces us to rethink that revolution's objectives and effects. Stephanie Hilger discusses Therese Huber's novel *Die Familie Seldorf* (1795 / 1796) not just as a response to the French Revolution itself or its increasing levels of violence, but also as a response to the violence inherent in revolutionary gender rhetoric that posited the wholesome mother as the foundation of the healthy republic. The female protagonist's irreparably injured body thus allegorizes the failure of the search for a "new, viable body politic". While Huber "weighs positive and negative outcomes" of the French Revolution specifically, Heinrich von Kleist in contrast sees the violent underpinnings of (any) political ideology as unavoidable, as Stefani Engelstein argues in her reading of a number of texts by Kleist. Kleist's potentially critical insight that ideologies are artificial constructions does not keep him from investing in violent ideals that usurp bodily functions such as maternity and paternity in the interest of political machinations. Kleist demonstrates that one can deploy aesthetic strategies as an ideologue without therefore being a partisan. Jeffrey Grossman explores the subtle theorizing on violence that emerges from Heinrich Heine's encounter with what Bourdieu calls symbolic violence, namely the institutional constraint within the habitus of an individual. To the extent that this very constraint operates on his public poetry, its form comments on the functioning of violence itself, but only at the risk of obscurity and misreading. More open discussions of social uses of power, such as exist in his journalism, are clearer at the cost of being less revealing. Uncovering his views on violence thus becomes a work of archeology analogous to the attempt to unearth "the violence embedded in the institutions themselves".

These first three essays are united by their focus on the discrepancies between the theory and practice of the French Revolution of 1789. One can conceptualize this break between violence as theory and violence as practice as a return of the repressed; violence is but one symptom that modernity has not convincingly been able to master the forces it unleashes.

The second set of essays in this volume shifts to consider explicitly the involuntary recurrence of phenomena that at first sight would seem to have no place within modern society, delving into realms of primitive, unconscious, or compulsive drives. Laurie Johnson's contribution on Ludwig Tieck's novel *William Lovell*, written like Huber's novel in 1795 / 1796, seeks to understand violence as an involuntary side product to its protagonist's overabundant emotional life, the "enthusiasm" that forces him compulsively to repeat self-defeating or masochistic experiences that evade rational control. Paradoxically, on some level Lovell seems to desire these uncanny repetitions of violent experiences; they are the result of, or at the very least associated with, an impetus for rebellion in the interactions with his immediate environment. The violent and uncanny other becomes personified in the novel Lynne Tatlock discusses, Raabe's *Zum wilden Mann* (1874). The primitive image of the "wild man" in Raabe symbolizes an alternate, destabilizing way of reading German political history, in particular the German unification of 1871. The prosperous lifestyle of the novel's protagonist is only possible because of the cruel and evil life of his antagonist (one example of the figure of the wild man to which the title refers) to whom he owes his material belongings; one is unthinkable without the other, and moral intentions emerge as entirely irrelevant in the novel. Just as the apothecary and the executioner are revealed to be intricately intertwined, so narration itself has the potential to both poison and heal. Carl Niekerk's essay on Ödön von Horváth's 1937 bestselling novel *Jugend ohne Gott* illuminates how fascism attempted to exploit this subterranean source of violence by colonizing humans' sexual and violent drives in the interest of its totalitarian, hyper-masculine, and racist agenda. Horváth's unconventional and highly critical reading of fascism, however, shows that such a return to "nature" may, in the end, very well work against such an agenda.

While the contributions by Hilger, Engelstein, Johnson, and Niekerk explicitly reflect on the gendered agenda underlying the modern discourse on violence and its critique, the collection's third set of contributions discusses the increasingly prominent ethnic and racialist dimensions shaping modern violence. Entering the vigorous debate over the nature of German-Jewish interchange, Barbara Fischer focuses on the fraught power dynamics inherent in the dialogic form. She exposes the German-Jewish dialogue as a tug of war over the signification of such iconic figures as Lessing and Goethe within a framework of conceptualizing Jewishness, Germanness, and nationhood. Jewish and non-Jewish attempts to build a narrative of inclusive Germanness through shared culture in the interest of Jewish participation were dangerously turned back upon their authors to represent Jews as a threat to the integrity of Germanness. These reformulations sharpened into escalating efforts to silence the Jewish voice. Mark Christian Thompson's contribution on Kafka's novel *Der Verschollene*, earlier known as *Amerika*, investigates the exact nature of the novel's protagonist's self-identification as "Negro", which Thompson traces to a photograph of a lynched African-American male in a picture book of America that Kafka owned. Taking issue with a critical history that reads the protagonist's self-identification as purely abnegatory or negative, Thompson instead explores the way that becoming Negro "serves as an allegory of the process of becoming artist", by enabling a transformational subject-formation. Also exploring the violence of a cultural encounter, Claudia Breger uses Joe May's popular film *Das Indische Grabmal* [*The Indian Tomb*] from 1921 as a test case to develop a theory of narrative performativity that challenges the opposition generally drawn between narrative and performance. Exploring the cultural work of performance *within* a narrative context, Breger recasts performativity as "a process of de- and re-contextualization, which re-assembles significations". May's film demonstrates, however, that in the absence of a Butlerian concept of negotiation within representation, a deconstruction of authority "unfold[s] only through a proliferation of violence". The film exploits an orientalizing aesthetic, without, however exculpating European authority or desire. Through her engagement with performative and film theory, Breger also bridges the gap to the volume's final set of essays.

The volume's final three essays undertake an intense engagement with representation, and in particular ask how the emergence of new ways of conceptualizing the visual intersects with the history of violence. Lutz Koepnick seeks to write the early-twentieth-century history of the visual as the product of a dialectical tension between attempts to contain the overabundance of images, a "violence of visual overflow", on the one hand, and the celebration of such an assault on the viewing eye as a way to "produce new forms of knowledge" on the other. Proponents of both theories, however, unexpectedly shared the conviction that aesthetic value lay in "rigorous adherence to the logic of [the] medium", which would in turn re-educate human perception and hence society. While contemporary cinema has continued to work with both focus and shock, it has, however, detached the violence of perception from any pretensions to social remolding. Patrizia McBride's contribution to this volume shows how two texts by Kurt Schwitters from 1919 and 1922 utilize the aesthetics of montage as an aesthetic procedure to conceive of human agency in new ways. In the midst of celebrations of the New Man and in the aftermath of the First World War, Schwitters's reflections on disemboweled and fragmented bodies call attention to the violence legitimized by a rhetoric of heroic sacrifice, while eschewing the substitution of the artist as a transfiguring hero. Montage provides a cognitive medium for reconceptualizing subjectivity that acknowledges the lack of ontological integrity both of experience and of bodies. The grotesque mixture of humor and dread that pervades Schwitters' tales "thematize[s] the absence of an adequate ethical frame of reference which [however] it presents as a challenge rather than a condition to be mourned". Finally, Peter McIsaac's contribution on Vienna's *Heeresgeschichtliches Museum* [Museum for Army History] brings questions of aesthetics and violence to bear on institutional memory, critically interrogating that museum's visual strategies for dealing with Austria's violent past. McIsaac offers a case study of how narrative strategies of embellishment and exclusion in the museum functioned and continue to function in the interest of creating a coherent and "desirable" genealogy for the Austrian nation. He argues for adopting an approach to curating exhibits that incorporates the museum's own history – its past use of artifacts in the interest of ideology – into its displays in order to prompt reflection that would "bring the violent past into productive relationship with the present".

The contributions to *Contemplating Violence: Critical Studies in Modern German Culture* undermine the notion of violence as an intermittent or random visitor in the imagination and critical theory of modern German culture. Instead, they make a case for violence in its many manifestations as constitutive for modern theories of art, politics, identity, and agency. To prevent the transition of violence from latency to outbreak, it is important to recognize and reflect on this pervasive role. The following essays serve to contribute to that debate.

I. The Other Side of Modernity: War and the French Revolution

Stephanie M. Hilger

Sara's Pain: The French Revolution in Therese Huber's *Die Familie Seldorf* (1795–1796)

This article discusses Therese Huber's Die Familie Seldorf *(1795/6) as a novel in which the embattled female protagonist's body incorporates the search for a new, viable body politic initiated by the French Revolution. Huber tests various late eighteenth-century discourses on femininity in the figure of Sara Seldorf: the ideal of the virtuous bourgeois daughter, allegorical representations of virginal Liberty and the image of healthy Republican motherhood. Each discursive representation fails to accommodate the violence experienced by Sara when she becomes an active agent in the political events of her time. The novel's portrayal of the violence inflicted upon Sara's body and of her precarious position in the new body politic expresses the late eighteenth-century uneasiness of those who, like Huber, were swept away with initial Revolutionary enthusiasm and then began to suspect that the Revolution might not have resulted in radical social change but in a different sort of revolution, a return to old patterns of violence and corruption.*

The French Revolution was an event that crossed linguistic and national boundaries and was thematized in a variety of genres, as the example of the German author Therese Huber (1764–1829) demonstrates. In one of her letters, Huber expresses her enthusiasm for the ideals of the French Revolution:

> Wie ich 18–19 Jahre alt war, jauchzte ich der Todesstunde entgegen. Später wünschte ich lange Jahre beim Gesang des Marseillermarsches zu sterben – das machte mir wohl noch Freude, denn was diese Verse ausdrücken, war doch das lebendigste Gefühl meines Lebens.
> [When I was 18–19 years old, I looked forward with exultation to the hour of my death. Later, I wished for years that I would die to the sound of the march of Marseille – this still brought me joy, because what these lyrics express was the most lively sentiment of my life.][1]

Huber's reaction to the events happening across the border is full of pathos, enthusiasm and a sense of personal renewal. Her description parallels the initially positive reaction of many contemporaries who praised the fight for liberty, equality and fraternity. Yet, in contrast to those who only talked or wrote about the French Revolution, Huber became a political agent. She and her first husband Georg Forster – also known for his participation in Captain

---

[1] Magdalene Heuser: Nachwort. In: *Die Familie Seldorf*. Hildesheim: Georg Olms Verlag 1989. Pp. 347–382. Here: P. 362. All translations are mine, unless otherwise noted.

James Cook's second circumnavigation – were active proponents of the *Mainzer Jakobinismus*, the attempt to establish a republic in German-speaking lands that was based on Revolutionary principles. Yet, their active role forced them to eventually leave occupied Mainz. Forster went to Paris and Huber left for Switzerland in December 1792, where she started writing as a way of contributing to the dwindling family income. *Die Familie Seldorf* was Huber's first novel and was published under her second husband's name, Ludwig Ferdinand Huber in 1795 (Part I) and 1796 (Part II).[2]

Using her husband's name – L.F. Huber – was one of Huber's strategies to construct her authorial identity in late eighteenth-century German-speaking literary circles. This gesture enabled her to work within eighteenth-century publishing conventions and the underlying perception of writing as an unfeminine activity.[3] So did the choice of a title for her first novel. An appropriate heading was important since, most of the time, the author's identity was eventually revealed, either by herself, her publisher or her acquaintances. By calling her novel *Die Familie Seldorf*, Huber foregrounds the domestic plot and thereby obscures not only the novel's setting during the French Revolution but also its explicit thematization of Revolutionary politics. Huber's anonymity and her apparent subscription to the equation of femininity with domestic family life were preemptive moves against accusations of being immoral, on the one hand, and unpatriotic, on the other. These defensive gestures were all the more important since she had already been criticized for her relationship with Ludwig Huber during her marriage to Georg Forster. She legitimized her affair with Huber by marrying him after Forster's death, yet her contemporaries' image of her remained tainted by her second marriage's extramarital origins. At the same time that the title echoed the association of femininity with domesticity through its focus on the Seldorf family, it also strategically concealed Huber's discussion of the Revolution at a time when anti-French sentiment developed as a result of the Revolutionary wars between France and other European powers. The French Revolutionary wars provided fertile

---

[2] Part of the novel had already appeared in the journal *Flora*, edited by Ludwig Ferdinand Huber, in 1794.

[3] The following works provide important insight with regard to women writers' negotiation of discourses of modesty and propriety. Ros Ballaster: Women and the Rise of the Novel: Sexual Prescripts. In: *Women and Literature in Britain 1700–1800*. Ed. by Vivien Jones. Cambridge: Cambridge University Press 2000. Pp. 197–216. Cheryl Turner: *Living by the Pen – Women Writers in the Eighteenth Century*. London-New York: Routledge 1992. For a specific discussion of this issue in German-speaking lands, see Susanne Kord: *Sich einen Namen machen: Anonymität und weibliche Autorschaft, 1700–1900*. Stuttgart: Metzler 1996; and Barbara Becker-Cantarino: *Schriftstellerinnen der Romantik: Epoche-Werke-Wirkung*. München: C.H. Beck 2000.

breeding ground for a sense of common linguistic, national and political identity in the fragmented German territories. Veiling the novel's political reference was all the more important since *Die Familie Seldorf* does not condemn the French Revolution outright but carefully weighs its positive and negative outcomes.

Therese Huber's strategic negotiation of discursive prescriptions regarding gender and writing permeates the entire novel. She thematizes Revolutionary politics but only in the context of the titular family. This characteristic has been noted by the earliest critics of *Die Familie Seldorf*. In his 1984 article, Helmut Peitsch explores the "aktuell[e] politisch[e] Thema und konventionelle Romanstruktur" ["contemporary political topic and conventional narrative structure"][4] and asks the following question: "Verhindert [. . .] eine konventionelle Romanstruktur von vornherein eine Parteinahme für die Revolution?" ["Does a conventional narrative structure necessarily preclude support for the Revolution?"] (249). Identifying Huber's political stance was at the forefront of early critical interest in the novel. With the dissemination of feminist analyses, this question soon gave way to an inquiry into the author's position on gender. The research question was often posed as such: Was Therese Huber a feminist author and should she, therefore, be included in a growing eighteenth-century (counter)canon of women writers? Critics disagree with respect to the degree of Huber's feminism. While most observe her challenge to society's patriarchal structures[5], some argue that "die gängigen Weiblichkeitsmuster im Roman weitgehend erhalten [bleiben]" ["current models of femininity largely persist in the novel"],[6] while yet others strive to demonstrate "to what extent her agenda can be understood as a 'progressive' one in gender terms".[7]

---

[4] Helmut Peitsch: Die Revolution im Familienroman: Aktuelles politisches Thema und konventionelle Romanstruktur in Therese Hubers *Die Familie Seldorf*. In: *Jahrbuch der deutschen Schillergesellschaft* 28 (1984). Pp. 248–269. Here: P. 248.
[5] Barbara Becker-Cantarino: Revolution im Patriarchat: Therese Forster-Huber (1764–1829). In: *Out of Line-Ausgefallen: The Paradox of Marginality in the Writings of Nineteenth-Century German Women*. Ed. by Ruth-Ellen Boetcher Joeres and Marianne Burkhard. Amsterdam-Atlanta: Rodopi 1989. Pp. 235–253. Todd Kontje: Under the Father's Spell: Patriarchy Versus Patriotism in Therese Huber's *Die Familie Seldorf*. In: *Seminar* 28.1 (1992). Pp. 17–32. Also see Todd Kontje: *Women, the Novel, and the German Nation, 1771–1871: Domestic Fiction in the Fatherland*. Cambridge: Cambridge University Press 1998. Pp. 60–73.
[6] Inge Stephan: Revolution und Konterrevolution: Therese Hubers Roman *Die Familie Seldorf* (1795/96). In: *Der deutsche Roman der Spätaufklärung: Fiktion und Wirklichkeit*. Ed. by Harro Zimmermann. Heidelberg: Carl Winter 1990. Pp. 171–194. Here: P. 194.
[7] Anna Richards: 'Double-Voiced Discourse' and Psychological Insight in the Work of Therese Huber. In: *Modern Language Review* 99.2 (2004). Pp. 416–429. Here: P. 419.

While the above cited arguments are all valid and have prompted meaningful readings of *Die Familie Seldorf*, the broader question remains why critics implicitly – and perhaps unconsciously – desire to find a progressive, unruly and feminist voice in a late eighteenth-century text by a female author. Does all literature by women have to be feminist or politically progressive in order to be worth scholarly attention? The unquestioned assumption of a necessarily seamless overlap between literature by women and feminist literature significantly limits the study of eighteenth-century literary voices as it rejects writers who are less explicitly feminist and who consequently become categorized as conservative and therefore not worth reading. Therefore, avoiding this uncritical equation is crucial for understanding all eighteenth-century literary production but especially that of the post-Revolutionary years. Many women authors of the 1790s and the early 1800s escape classificatory attempts into "progressive" and "conservative" groups since they consciously and carefully negotiate discourses regarding writing, gender and politics. Reading their literary production outside of the value judgment implied by this classificatory binary allows for a more nuanced understanding of the negotiatory processes at work in the heavily politicized post-Revolutionary years. Consequently, rather than arguing for or against Therese Huber's feminism or circumscribing her political position, this article will explore Huber's use of the protagonist's female body as an allegory for the search of a new, viable body politic. Sara's mutilated corporeality demonstrates not only the bankruptcy of the aristocratic *ancien régime*, but also bourgeois Revolutionary discourse's problematic construction of healthy womanhood as the basis for a robust national body politic.

The story of Sara Seldorf resembles that of the German *bürgerliche Trauerspiel*, in which the female protagonist, usually from the upper middle class, is first seduced, then betrayed, and eventually abandoned. In this respect Sara Seldorf's itinerary resembles that of Lessing's Sara Sampson. Yet, whereas typical bourgeois tragedies focus on the seduction narrative and are situated in vaguely historicized eighteenth-century bourgeois interior spaces, *Die Familie Seldorf* is set explicitly during the French Revolution and its exterior spaces of conflict. Huber thereby consciously yet carefully widens her narrative's political implications. The characters are all actively involved in political activities, and Sara not least. Sara and Theodor are the children of officer Seldorf. Theodor's friend Roger – grandson of Seldorf's neighbor Berthier – loves Sara, who does not reciprocate his feelings and is, instead, seduced, betrayed and abandoned by Graf L. While the narrative of seduction echoes the plot of bourgeois tragedies, the novel's beginning also immediately establishes the political context and thereby diverges in its implications from the dramatic genre. Father Seldorf, a French officer of German origin, fought in the American War of Independence. While Seldorf initially vacillates in his political sympathies, he eventually succumbs to the wiles of the Royalist Graf L and therefore opposes his Revolutionary neighbor Berthier. The patriarchs' growing ideological differences are continued by their offspring's political leanings. Theodor – first sympathizing with the Revolutionary cause – joins the Royalist side, while Roger remains loyal to the Revolution. Sara, like her father, succumbs to Graf L's promises. Eventually, however, she learns that he is already married. Moreover, Graf L unknowingly wounds and ultimately kills his and Sara's common child in the post-Revolutionary chaos. Driven by her desire to murder Graf L, Sara cross-dresses, joins the Revolutionary forces and participates in the execution of the King. Thus she gradually abandons the role of the bourgeois tragedy's dutiful daughter, who mourns the loss of her virginity to an aristocratic rogue, and instead increasingly implicates herself in events happening outside the realm of her father's domain.

Unlike Sara Sampson, who dies in her room as a result of her lover's betrayal and the consequences of his intrigues, Sara Seldorf leaves her father's house in search of Graf L and becomes an active political agent when she joins the Revolutionaries. Her private desire to avenge her daughter's death is mixed up with political justifications for her actions. Her body, already affected by the aristocrat's betrayal, further comes under attack by the surrounding violence:

> Um [Sara] her jauchzte der blutdürstige Haufen, jauchzte convulsivisch aus ihm selbst die sich sträubende Menschheit, und wollte das Aechzen der Erschlagenen, durch die er seinen Weg bahnte, überjauchzen [. . .] Flüche, wildes Geschrei, schallendes Gelächter tobten um Sara, die schweigend mit gezüktem Dolch, im Ausdruk des bittersten Grimms vor ihnen hergieng [. . .] Vor ihr stürzten die Unglüklichen, Erbarmen flehend, nieder; hoch stand sie mit erhabnem Angesicht unter dem wälzenden wogenden Gewühl der Mordenden und der Sterbenden, ließ ihr Auge kalt über die Erschlagnen hingleiten, und spähte nur nach ihrem Opfer. [. . .] Sara, mit fliegendem Haar, das weiße Gewand vom Blut der Erschlagnen, über welche sie schritt, befleckt, hebt den Arm, hebt das Eisen, das sie für diesen Augenblick rein bewahrt hatte.
>
> [The bloodthirsty mass jubilated around Sara; out of it, struggling humanity jubilated convulsively, and attempted to drown out the groans of the slain, through which it made its path [. . .]; curses, wild screams, peals of laughter raged around Sara, who, silently and with drawn dagger, walked in front of them with an expression of most bitter wrath. [. . .] The unlucky ones threw themselves before her, asking for compassion; she stood there with lofty countenance among the rolling and billowing turmoil of the murdering and the dying, and she let her gaze glide over the slain ones and only peered for her victim. [. . .] Sara, with fluttering hair, her white gown stained by the blood of the slain ones, over whom she marched, raises her arm, raises the iron tool that she had kept pure for this moment.][8]

---

[8] Therese Huber: *Die Familie Seldorf*. Ed. by Magdalene Heuser. Hildesheim: Georg Olms Verlag, 1989. Vol II. Pp. 167–168.

On the one hand, the bloodstains on Sara's white gown represent the loss of her role as the virginal bourgeois daughter and her move beyond father Seldorf's realm. On the other, the bloody smudges also indicate her absorption of the surrounding violence as a fuel to avenge her child's death. Her personal suffering and the painful groans around her have hardened Sara; her white dress is that of an angel of death. The virginal gown transforms itself into a shroud and her fluttering hair becomes the extension of Sara's murderous thoughts. Huber's vivid description creates an image of Sara as a corrupted version of the figure of Liberty. Joan Landes describes this allegorical representation of the Revolution's ideals in contemporary paintings, which were crucial to the imagination of a new body politic based on an uncorrupted female body:

> Attached to her tricolor sash, she wears a lion-headed sword, attesting symbolically to her triumph over superstition, despotism, and the monarchy. Syncretically combining Christian and republican symbols, this virginal figure wears the phrygian cap, yet is surrounded by an aureole. She is figured as young, innocent, and pure; precisely the kind of transparent, natural representation that a reading of Rousseau inclined the revolutionaries to adopt.[9]

Joan Landes's analysis of *La Liberté Patronne des Français* (1795)[10] highlights Liberty's youth, her innocence and her purity. She is a Rousseauian ideal of femininity. Her sword is an extension of social and political justice. By contrast, Sara holds a dagger, a weapon devoid of associations of honor, nobility and chivalry. Revolutionary ideals have been transformed into personal vendettas with this instrument for cruel stabbing. While Sara is young, she is no longer pure. Her dress has been soiled by her implication in the *Terreur*. The virgin's aureole has been replaced by the betrayed mother's wild hair. Sara is an image of Liberty gone awry, an anti-Rousseauian representation of amazon-like femininity based on vengeful motherhood.

Sara's main motive is not the fight for Liberty per se, but her desire to kill Graf L, who is the novel's representative of the old, corrupt social order. Hers is a personal and a political vendetta. *Die Familie Seldorf* therefore represents what Lynn Hunt has termed the family romance of the French Revolution. The story of the nation is told as a narrative of family relations, which was "a kind

---

[9] Joan Landes: Representing the Body Politic: The Paradox of Gender in the Graphic Politics of the French Revolution. In: *Rebel Daughters: Women and the French Revolution*. Ed. by Sara Melzer and Leslie W. Rabine. New York-Oxford: Oxford University Press 1992. Pp. 15–37. Here: P. 28.

[10] The painting that Joan Landes analyzes is *La Liberté Patronne des Français* (c. 1795) by Louis Charles Ruotte, after Louis-Marie Sicardi, finished by Jacques-Louis Copis, after Boizot (Source: S.P. Avery Collection, Miriam & Ira D. Wallach Division of Art, Prints, and Photographs, The New York Public Library, Astor, Lenox and Tilden Foundations).

of prepolitical category for organizing political experience".[11] The father/king is killed, usually by his sons and replaced with new models of authority. In *Die Familie Seldorf*, the generational conflict is displaced by the female protagonist's desire for her aristocratic lover's death. Sara neither behaves like the innocent domestic daughter of the family romance, protected from the dirty realm of politics, nor like the allegorized Revolutionary figure of Liberty. Sara does not fit into her contemporaries' images of femininity during times of war but instead questions their implications. In Huber's novel, the female body becomes a space for enacting the violence of the changing body politic and for exploring new social and political possibilities beyond conventional national imagery. Sara's body – caught in-between the old and the new – embodies the search for post-Revolutionary signification theorized by Peter Brooks:

> The loss of a system of assigned meanings is followed by one where meanings must be achieved, must be the product of an active semiotic process in which the body is newly emblematized with meaning.[12]

The novel's detailed description of Sara's suffering illustrates Brooks' general observation that, in "the popular genre of melodrama (during the Revolution), we have a kind of literalistic realization of this new importance of the body as the site of signification" (Brooks 44–45). At the center of Huber's melodrama stands Sara, bruised and battered, a signifier of the post-Revolutionary search for meaning, open to signification yet also closed to simplifying signifieds such as the idea of the innocent bourgeois daughter, the allegorical figure of Liberty and also the image of the Republican mother.

Sara literally embodies the search for meaning following the destruction of the king's body and the national body politic. The king's body had occupied a special place in the legal and popular imaginary of the Old Régime. Its meaning transcended its physicality since it was both private and public, material and spiritual. Contemporary discourse tied the king's body to the nation's body politic:

> The material body of the king, which hungered, lusted, and suffered, was connected with the figurative body of the kingdom through ritual, representation, and rhetoric [. . .]. The French monarch [. . .] inherited his crown from his predecessor and derived his authority from the Deity, not from the people [. . .]. Differentiated, like the organs and limbs that composed the human body, by the distinctive but complementary functions assigned to them by the Creator, subjects were

---

[11] Lynn Hunt: *The Family Romance of the French Revolution*. Berkeley: University of California Press 1992. P. 196.

[12] Peter Brooks: The Revolutionary Body. In: *Fictions of the French Revolution*. Ed. by Bernadette Fort. Evanston: Northwestern University Press 1991. Pp. 35–53. Here: P. 44.

subordinated [. . .] to their divinely ordained ruler [. . .]. He maintained public order by adjudicating conflicts and restoring harmony among the various parts of the body politic, which could not collaborate or survive without a head to direct them or, for that matter, with more than one head in charge.[13]

In the same way that this *ancien régime* rhetoric justified absolutism, the discursive convergence of the king's body and his body politic was also instrumentalized by the Revolutionary imaginary. The king's body was presented as corrupted by a life of luxury and leisure. The dis-ease of the body politic was attributed to the disease of the king, who was portrayed as effeminate and weakened.[14] Since the king's body had become a site of corruption, Revolutionary rhetoric constructed a counterpoint, the image of the clean, healthy, robust and virtuous Republican woman/mother based on a reading of Rousseau. Corrupt effeminate manners were replaced with healthy Republican motherhood, itself based on the image of the clean bourgeois daughter and the virginal image of Liberty.

Huber's novel tests the applicability of Republican images of femininity on her protagonist. Sara's body challenges the discursive ideal of healthy Republican motherhood in the same way that it rejected the image of the bourgeois virgin and allegorized Liberty. Her body eludes Republican rhetoric when she becomes physically unable to care for her dying daughter, wounded by Graf L:

> Ihr [Saras] zwischen Todesschwäche und Fieberfantasie abwechselnder Zustand war mehrere Tage verzweifelt [. . .]. Die arme Kleine hätte vielleicht die Gefahr ihrer Wunde überstanden, wenn nicht die Veränderung ihrer Nahrung, da Angst und Krankheit Sara's mütterliche Brust schnell ausgetroknet hatten, und selbst die Milch, die sie noch in der schreklichen Nacht des zehnten Augusts die Unvorsichtigkeit gehabt hatte, ihr zu reichen, ihre Säfte verderbt hätten. Der Zustand ihres Kindes, und das fürchterliche Räthsel ihrer eignen Lage gaben Sara's Nerven bald eine solche Spannung, daß ihre Kräfte wie durch ein Wunder aufzuleben schienen. (Vol. II, 140–141)
>
> [Her [Sara's] condition, alternating between the weakness of death and feverish fantasies, had been desperate for several days [. . .]. The poor little one might have survived the danger of her wound, had there not been the change in diet since fear and disease had quickly dried out Sara's maternal breast. She might have survived

---

[13] Jeffrey Merrick: The Body Politics of French Absolutism. In: *From the Royal to the Republican Body: Incorporating the Political in Seventeenth- and Eighteenth-Century France*. Ed. by Sara E. Melzer and Kathryn Norberg. Berkeley: University of California Press 1998. Pp. 11–31. Here: Pp. 12–13.

[14] See Roy Porter's article on the effects of consumption – in its double sense – on the king's body and his body politic. Roy Porter: Consumption: Disease of a Consumer Society? In: *Consumption and the World of Goods*. Ed. by John Brewer and Roy Porter. London-New York: Routledge 1993. Pp. 58–81. Also see the articles in the collection edited by Sara E. Melzer and Kathryn Norberg: *From the Royal to the Republican Body*. For complete bibliographical reference, see note 13.

had not the milk, that she been imprudent enough to give her in the terrible night of August tenth, spoilt her juices. Her child's condition and the terrible mystery of her own situation soon put Sara's nerves in such tension that her strength seemed to revive miraculously.]

Sara attempts to conform to the ideal of Republican motherhood by breastfeeding her daughter. This causes her to poison her child, who becomes a literal and figurative victim of the wound inflicted by its father and its mother's desire for avenging this act. Sara is consumed by the intensity of her revenge wish, which strips her maternal breast of its function.[15] Her body is not only unable to perform its Republican mission, but its disease also positively counteracts the establishment of a solid republic through healthy children. The ideal of healthy Republican motherhood, itself constructed as a counterweight to the diseased aristocratic body politic of the *ancien régime*, is now replaced by the bruised and battered body of post-Revolutionary Sara Seldorf.

In addition to questioning the woman's role as bourgeois daughter, virginal Liberty and Republican mother, *Die Familie Seldorf* also displays ambivalence toward the related concept of hygiene put forward by the medical discourse of the post-Revolutionary years. Health was erected as an ideal for the middle classes, which could be attained through the cultivation of hygiene. Dorinda Outram observes that the medical profession focused on the individual's control and management of the "non-naturals", which "were factors external to man which inevitably and continuously influenced his physical well-being: air, food and drink, motion, rest, sleep and waking, evacuation and retention".[16] The idea of the individual's control of his/her own body was a manifestation of the "tendency to desacralize the body, to remove it from any theological frame of reference" (Outram 49). Unlike the King's body, that of the bourgeois citizen was not orchestrated by God but by the individual's management of the external "non-naturals". Sara's example displays the contemporary awareness of these factors' effects on a mother's health and that of her offspring. In addition to being consumed by her desire for revenge, Sara is tired, feverish and unable to supply her body with enough nutrients for her daughter. Yet she is unable to control these elements because the circumstances of her personal involvement in the political conflict force her to live in hiding. Sara masquerades as a male Revolutionary fighter because this presents her with an opportunity to follow the Royalist Graf L and avenge his

---

[15] In this context, Simon Richter argues that Sara's "breast becomes overdetermined both as the site of persistent maternal feelings and as the site of ruin". Simon Richter: *Missing the Breast: Gender, Fantasy, and the Body in the German Enlightenment*. Seattle-London: University of Washington Press 2006. P. 208.

[16] Dorinda Outram: *The Body and the French Revolution: Sex, Class and Political Culture*. New Haven-London: Yale University Press 1989. P. 47.

betrayal. On the one hand, this cross-dressing allows Sara to assert her agency, yet, on the other, the mental and physical strain associated with it robs her of the life juices central to her own and her daughter's health. Sara's body illustrates contemporary perceptions regarding health and hygiene, yet the novel also points at the limited usefulness of medical discourse in times of war and conflict, especially for women.

The detailed descriptions of Sara's physical suffering demonstrate the limitations of contemporary medical discourse, which does not offer solutions to those whose body is no longer under their control. Sara's body is repeatedly projected into a liminal space between existence and annihilation. After a particularly fierce battle, Sara is carried to a hospital, where she is in constant fear of being unmasked as a woman:

> Sie hatte den Muth, über vierzehn Tage lang eine Quetschung, die ihren linken Arm lähmte, und die Schulter bis zur Brust hinab mit gestoktem Blut schwärzte, für sich im Stillen zu ertragen. Das einzige Mittel, das Zufall und List ihr zu erhalten möglich machten, Salz und kaltes Wasser, durfte sie sogar nur verstohlen anwenden, und sie mußte sich das frische Wasser, wonach ihr Fieberdurst so heiß verlangte, entziehen, um ihr darein getauchtes Schnupftuch, mit etwas Salz, das sie unter allerlei Vorwänden sich verschafte, des Nachts auf ihre Quetschung zu legen, die durch den heftigsten Schmerz in Eiterung überzugehen drohte. (Vol. II, 253)
>
> [She had the courage, for fourteen days, to silently suffer a contusion that paralyzed her left arm and shoulder down to her chest with stagnated blood. She could only furtively apply the sole remedies that she had procured by coincidence and ruse, salt and cold water. And she had to renounce the fresh water that her feverish thirst demanded heatedly in order to immerse her handkerchief in it and place it during the night, with some salt, that she procured by all sorts of pretexts, on her contusion that threatened to turn into an abscess, accompanied by the fiercest pain.]

Sara has been wounded so severely that her body is on the brink of disintegration. Her flesh is putrefying and her blood infected. Rather than risking the discovery of her true identity by a doctor, she furtively treats her festering bruise with the only external remedies available to her. Sara displays an awareness of hygiene as a remedy to her situation; she cleans and disinfects and thereby sacrifices her desire to drink. Her suffering demonstrates how difficult the control of the "non-naturals" is for those who live on the margins of society and in its liminal spaces, especially those created by a society in turmoil and upheaval.

This lack of control illustrates the dark side of the discourse of hygiene, its masochistic aspect. Sara's attempts at hygiene are intimately entwined with the pleasure she experiences through her pain. This pleasurable pain allows her to regain a sense of control over her body while foreshadowing her total annihilation:

> Jedes neue Leiden schien ihr ein Schritt zu dem Ziel ihrer Laufbahn. Still und lauschend auf die Annäherung des freundlichen Genius, der endlich die Fakel ihres Lebens umstürzen würde, lag sie da in unsäglichen Schmerzen, und studierte die

mannigfaltigen Wendungen des Todes in ihren Unglüksgefährten um sie her. (Vol. II, 253–254)

[Every new suffering appeared to bring her one step closer to the goal of her career. She was lying there quietly, in immense pain, and listened for the approach of the friendly angel who would finally overturn the torch of her life. And she studied the manifold turns of death in the fellow sufferers around her.]

Surrounded by the dying, Sara patiently awaits her own disintegration, all the while attempting to prevent it through hygienic measures and thereby prolonging her suffering. Sara's view of her body is characteristic of Gilles Deleuze's concept of masochism, which "in its material aspects is a phenomenon of the senses (i.e., a certain combination of pain and pleasure); [and] in its moral aspects [. . .] is a function of feeling or sentiment".[17] Sara's pleasure at the disintegration of her body is entwined with her feeling of moral duty to restore its functioning through hygiene. Pain becomes an integral part of Sara's body and the post-Revolutionary body politic. These painful sensations are the last reminders of a sense of control lost in Sara's post-Revolutionary world. Her physicality forces a rethinking of contemporary political rhetoric that widened the implications of the medical discourse on health and hygiene from the individual body to the body politic by showing what lies beyond simple slogans and images.

In *Die Familie Seldorf*, the emerging body politic following the French Revolution is a necessarily diseased one, incomplete and always on the brink of destroying itself. Sara survives, yet hers is a body in danger of annihilation and mutilation. The body politic following the French Revolution is a fragile construction. Outram argues that "the Revolution failed to construct a 'modern state' [. . .]. Rather, what occurred was a series of transformation scenes, in which forms of government and ruling factions succeeded one another with bewildering rapidity and in which public space itself became increasingly crucial and increasingly ambiguous, as the introduction of mass political participation put new stresses on the ability to retain power" (3). Sara embodies these violent transformations; her body changes rapidly and becomes an ambivalent signifier representing post-Revolutionary questioning and experimentation. *Die Familie Seldorf* demonstrates the absence of an easy conclusion to the family romance. One body politic cannot simply be replaced with another one; the effects of violence and suffering deny easy substitutions. Not even the destruction of the representative of the *ancien régime* brings about a sense of closure. Sara does not become whole again, even though she witnesses the annihilation of the old body politic in the burning of Graf L's corpse:

[Sara] stürzte fort, den Leichnam des Geliebten zu erobern [. . .]. Den folgenden Tag wurde der Sarg, mit vielen erbeuteten Fahnen, Reliquien, Heiligenbildern, auf

---

[17] Gilles Deleuze: *Masochism: Coldness and Cruelty*. New York: Zone Books 1989. P. 101.

dem behaupteten Schlachtfeld verbrannt [. . .] und Sara's zitternde Stimme erstarb in dem rauschenden Hymnus der Menge, da sie die lezten Ueberreste dessen der ihr alles gewesen war, der sie dem Glük und der Menschheit entrissen hatte, in röthlichen Flammen emporlodern sah. (Vol. II, 263–264)

[Sara hurried away to conquer to corpse of her beloved [. . .]. The following day the coffin was burned with many captured flags, relics and saints' images on their victorious battlefield [. . .] and Sara's trembling voice died in the swelling hymn of the mass, when she saw the last remains of the one who was her everything, who had robbed her of happiness and humanity, consumed by red flames.]

When Sara finally witnesses what has motivated her all along, she does not feel satisfied. She cannot begin anew; her past has left its mark on her. Her physical and emotional wounds have become an integral part of her identity. The pain inflicted on her body is extended to the post-Revolutionary body politic. The Revolutionary discourse of a healthy body politic based on the ideal of healthy motherhood is an illusion. Wholeness has become impossible in the violent reality that surrounds Sara. The search for it leads to contradictions and dark spaces. The family romance has, from the beginning, been a melodrama and turns into a gothic narrative at the end.

There is no closure to the stories of Sara, the family Seldorf and the national family during the immediate post-Revolutionary years marked by the *Terreur* and its aftermath. Huber's novel is characterized by what Elizabeth MacArthur has called a "devious" ending.[18] The female protagonist does not get married. She instead achieves a degree of independence that sets *Die Familie Seldorf* apart from other novels' socially conformist happy endings. At the end of the novel, Sara and Robert, the neighbor who has loved her since childhood, meet again. While he nurtures hope for a romantic reunion and eventual marriage, Sara makes it clear that she cannot imagine a new beginning that denies the violence that she has experienced:

[W]as auch Dein sterbender Vater wünschte – es kann noch geschehen! [. . .] Sara, wir wollen seine Hütte wieder aufbauen! Wir wollen seine Bäume wieder pflanzen – um seine Ruhestätte ein Paradies schaffen! – Sie riß ihre Hände aus den seinigen, und bedekte ihr Angesicht: O nie, nie! rief sie schaudernd – Dein reines Kinderherz neben mir, der von Geistern umringten? (Vol. II, 345)

[[W]hat your dying father also wished for – it can still happen! [. . .] Sara, let us rebuild his hut! Let us replant his trees and create a paradise around his resting place! – She tore her hands from his and covered her face: O never, never! she cried with horror – Your pure child's heart next to me, the one who is surrounded by ghosts?]

Sara cannot return to what Roger presents as the idealized, apolitical and uncontroversial space of her father's past. His reference to Seldorf's hut

---

[18] Elizabeth J. MacArthur: Devious Narratives: Refusal of Closure in Two Eighteenth-Century Epistolary Novels. In: *Eighteenth-Century Studies* 21.1 (1987). Pp. 1–20.

reminds her instead of all those who have died. Roger's hopeful statement becomes Sara's litany:

> So mußten die redlichen Männer dahin – Thirion, der seine Freude an meiner Raserei hatte – und Raimond, mein lezter guter Engel [. . .] und der fürchterliche Joseph [. . .]. Die arme Nanni, die treue redliche Martha! [. . .] Meine theilnehmende Babet, ihr Gatte – und dann der Mann, dem die Erde nicht einmal ein Grab gegönnt hat. (Vol. II, 343–344)
>
> [So the upright men had to die – Thirion, who took pleasure in my frenzy – and Raimond, my last good angel [. . .] and the terrible Joseph [. . .]. Poor Nanni, faithful and honest Martha! [. . .] My compassionate Babet, her husband – and then the man to whom the earth did not even grant a grave.]

The death of these characters, who have all accompanied Sara part of her way, becomes part of her mutilated identity: "O wie sinnreich hat doch das Schiksal mir jede Art von Wunden versezt!" ["Oh how ingeniously fate has inflicted all sorts of wounds on me!"] (Vol. II, 344).

Sara's acknowledgment of her mutilated identity triggers her rejection of an institutionalized attachment to Roger. In Sara's eyes, marrying him would deny her past. Instead, she creates a patchwork of relations that questions traditional social roles and acknowledges the fragmentation of her individual body and the collective body politic. She establishes an alternative community outside of social prescriptions. While her vision is not a utopia, it is a social experiment.[19] She envisions the bond of friendship between herself and Roger to be strong enough to care for Hyppolit, the orphaned son of Graf L and his wife, whom her brother Theodor had put in her care. Sara, who has lost her own daughter with the count, becomes his *Ersatzmutter*. The reunion scene with Roger seems to promise the family idyll of a reconstituted nuclear family: "der Kleine sah sie an, kam herbei, lehnte sich klagend an Sara's Schooß, und Roger, der Sara nicht berührt hatte, zog ihn an sich, und schloß jezt sie und ihn zugleich in seinen Arm" ["the little one looked at her, came toward her, leaned plaintively against Sara's lap and Roger, who had not touched Sara, pulled him close to him, and now simultaneously embraced both him and her"] (Vol. II, 335). Yet the novel does not end with these words; it deviates from the happy ending that it seemingly outlines.

Instead, *Die Familie Seldorf* closes with a melodramatic scene in a gothic setting. Sara, Roger and Hyppolit seek refuge from an approaching thunderstorm in the burial vault of Graf L's wife. The alternative social community that Sara has established is a patchwork assembled from the fragments of the French Revolution and now symbolically comes under attack. At the same

---

[19] For an analysis of women authors' construction of alternative social communities, see Alessa Johns: *Women's Utopias of the Eighteenth Century*. Urbana-Chicago: University of Illinois Press 2003.

time that it bears hope for the future, it is also a precarious construction at whose center stands Sara's body and the possibility of its annihilation. Hyppolit expresses this possibility when he speaks the last words of the novel:

> Dort, dort wo meine Mutter schläft, sagte er [Hyppolit] schmeichelnd – Was dort? fragte Roger erschroken, und blikte hin – Dort mache ich Sara ihr leztes Bett – Roger schauderte; der Sturm heulte in den Mauern, ein heller Bliz erleuchtete das Gewölbe, und laut schluchzend sank Roger zu Sara's Füssen. (Vol II, 345–346)
> [There, where my mother sleeps, he [Hyppolit] said cajolingly – What is there? Roger asked with fear and looked in this direction – This is where I will make Sara's last bed. Roger shuddered; the storm howled in the walls, bright lightning illuminated the vault and Roger sank to Sara's feet, sobbing loudly.]

Thunder rolls, lightning strikes, Roger shudders, and so do we. While Sara has survived the violence of the Revolutionary years and the novel outlines an alternative model of existence, the fear of the unknown projects her once more into the liminal space that she just seems to have escaped. The seams in the social patchwork might come loose. The body politic of her alternative community is in danger of being destroyed by external forces as random and yet as cyclical as lightning and Sara's body could be buried in the same vault that holds the aristocrats' corpses.

While Therese Huber's *Die Familie Seldorf* outlines alternative social possibilities, it also casts doubt on their viability during a time marked by violence and destruction. The search for a new body politic through the figure of Sara Seldorf remains inconclusive. The model of the corrupt aristocratic body politic is rejected, but so are Republican images of femininity. Sara cannot be a virginal daughter, idealized Liberty or a healthy Republican mother. The nation's innocence has been lost; its virginity cannot be recovered. Huber's graphic depiction of the female protagonist's physical pain highlights the intensity of suffering on the level of the individual body and the body politic. *Die Familie Seldorf* demonstrates the bankruptcy of the post-Revolutionary national discourse of hygiene, eager to recreate a sense of integrity and wholeness. In this sense, Huber's novel reflects the typical late eighteenth-century uneasiness of those who were swept away with initial Revolutionary enthusiasm and thereby transcends any classificatory attempts into pro- and counter-Revolutionary literature. *Die Familie Seldorf* expresses the suspicion that the Revolution might not have resulted in a radical social change but in a different sort of *revolution* – a return to old patterns of corruption and violence, as cyclical as weather patterns and thunderstorms and yet seemingly as random as the target of a lightning strike.

Stefani Engelstein

The Father in Fatherland: Violent Ideology and Corporeal Paternity in Kleist

This article analyzes the interdependence of paternity, nationality, and aesthetics in the work of Heinrich von Kleist to explore his paradoxical underlying relationship to the issue of ideology. Kleist maintains that paternity and nationality are mutually constituted through language and then anchored to bodies through acts of violence. Male bodies are conscripted for war, simultaneously validating both fatherhood and fatherland. The domestic sphere to which female bodies are restricted is no-less-risky; there they serve as a medium for propaganda that establishes bonds between men. Because this process of exploitation is rendered visible on the surface of Kleist's texts, his work escapes common assumptions about ideological writing. By denying his warriors and soldiers the autochthonous character Schmitt claimed as the hallmark of a partisan, Kleist also evades labels of partisanship assigned to him by Schmitt and, more recently, Wolf Kittler. Kleist's alertness to the artificiality of ideology does not, however, amount to the critique desired of him by so many critics. Instead, he desperately embraces the violent consequences of ideology as the only foundation for identity.

In the late eighteenth and early nineteenth centuries, the human body entered politics. Indeed, a transformation of the understanding of the body coincided with the creation of the human as a political subject in ways that have been much discussed since Foucault's excavation of the interlocking medical, sociological, and biological discourses that have come to define both body and subject. At the turn of the nineteenth century the view of the body as a machine that had dominated the seventeenth and early eighteenth centuries did not disappear. Rather, it was sublimated into an organic model that continued to understand the body and its organs in terms of purposes. The question of the body's teleology not only affected methodological debates about the natural sciences, but defined the significance of the body, i.e. defined the body both as a signifier, and as a determinant, of the meaning of being human. The material of the body was scrutinized, anatomized, interrogated for clues to a final purpose according to which society could be organized. As Emma Spary points out, "increasingly, toward the end of the [eighteenth] century, justifications for social, racial and gender hierarchies were located within the fabric of the body itself" (195).[1] Even Kant occasionally succumbed to the temptation

---

[1] Emma Spary: Political, Natural, and Bodily Economies. In: *Cultures of Natural History*. Ed. by Nicholas Jardin, James Secord, and Emma Spary. Cambridge: Cambridge University Press 1996. Pp. 178–196.

of imagining a final purpose for humans which could be derived, albeit negatively, from the body; namely the body's failure to provide evidence of a final purpose for humans inside the realm of the natural and physical, constituted one part of his argument in favor of intellectual and communal activity as the ultimate purpose of human endeavor.[2]

The disciplines that turned toward the materiality of the body around 1800 in search of such purposes varied widely. Aesthetics, natural history, and surgery, but also the political rhetoric of revolution and of empire converged upon the human body as their source of authority and authenticity. Because it does not generate meaning, however, the body cannot sustain this role. Its failure to signify independently provides ideal conditions for the rise of ideologies. These ideologies share a strategy of naturalization by which they legitimate themselves through a claim to read the truth from the organization of the body, combined with an assumption that nature is normative. Against the background of this ferment over the body, the work of Heinrich von Kleist becomes particularly revealing. Again and again, Kleist exposes the mechanism by which ideology is constructed, undermining its claims to natural authority at every turn. This exposure is not, however, a critical endeavor; in spite of his recognition of the manipulation required to construct ideology, Kleist's ideological commitments are very real. Kleist's work therefore implies another path to ideology, one that acknowledges and accepts its constructed nature. Significantly, however, Kleist's refusal to locate the source of authority in the body does not represent a turn away from the body. Instead, Kleist documents the way in which ideology functions through the regulation of the body itself.

---

[2] Kant argues against the natural end of happiness in favor of a cultural final purpose in §82–84 of the *Critique of Judgment*. While he allowed for the purposiveness of organs, Kant rejected the conclusion that their purposes could determine the final purpose of the individual. The definition of the organism was important not only for Kant's understanding of teleological judgment. Jonathan Hess has demonstrated the political implications of the organism for Kant, who deployed the organic body as a metaphor for a republic in which individuals are simultaneously ends and means. In this way the republic contrasts with an absolutist state in which individuals are merely means, and which Kant figured as a machine. While Kant thus reconstitutes the body as a political relationship, as Hess argues, we should not lose sight of the fact that the political body was intended to supersede the physical body as the locus of autonomous activity. Immanuel Kant: *Kritik der Urteilskraft*. In: *Kants gesammelte Schriften*. Ed. by die königlich preußische Akademie der Wissenschaften. Berlin: G. Reimer 1908. Vol. V. Jonathan Hess: *Reconstituting the Body Politic: Enlightenment, Public Culture and the Invention of Aesthetic Autonomy*. Detroit: Wayne State University Press 1999.

There has been a subtle shift in the aspects of Kleist's work which have received attention in the last several decades. Although the emphasis on his aesthetics typical of the eighties has persisted, it now exists alongside both a newer critical interest in the structure of the family, particularly the role of paternity, and an engagement with the violently nationalistic tendencies of his late works. What has been overlooked is the interdependence of these concerns. An examination of how these issues intertwine will offer some illumination on the long-debated question of ideology, in Kleist's work and beyond it. Kleist's nationalistic writings arose in the period of 1808–1809 after the Prussian invasion and defeat by Napoleon, but before Friedrich Wilhelm III repudiated the treaty he had signed allying Prussia with France in the wake of this defeat. These works of Kleist's invoke a metaphorical family whose structure replicates that established for individual families in his work, enacting their inherent violence on a larger stage. Like paternity, nationality consists of a symbolic investiture combined with the rhetoric of a blood tie which, at Kleist's historical moment, was equally unavailable to empirical investigation in both cases. Indeed, the role of the father in conception was hotly contested until the 1840s.[3] The absence of a direct physical tie between father and child, and between individuals and a nation, does not exclude the body from the construction of paternity or of nationality, but it does render the corporeal component retroactive. At stake in these constructions, Kleist insists, is ultimately the viability of subjectivity itself, and the demands placed on the body to subordinate itself to an identity that either subsumes or annihilates it are commensurate with these stakes.

The 1809 poem *Germania an ihre Kinder* is a call to arms from mother Germania to her children, a trope that raises expectations of an autochthonous

---

[3] There was a debate over the purpose of sperm cells from the time of their seventeenth-century discovery. Although some "spermaticists" argued that the sperm contained a miniscule encapsulated form of the fetus, most naturalists believed that female eggs played this role in reproduction. Competing theories which emphasized both a male and female contribution to conception did not uniformly identify sperm cells as the crucial male component. Spermatozoa were widely assumed to be parasites through the 1830s when they were given their name (*sperm animals*) by Karl Ernst von Baer, the biologist who first observed the mammalian egg in 1828. Rudolf Albert von Kölliker established in 1841 that sperm were cells originating in the testes and in 1843 Martin Berry proved that conception occurs when the sperm enters the egg. For a history of embryology, see Jane Oppenheimer: *Essays in the History of Embryology and Biology*. Cambridge, Massachussetts: M.I.T. Press 1967; Scott Gilbert: *A Conceptual History of Modern Embryology*. New York: Plenum Publishing Co 1991; and Clara Pinto-Correia: *The Ovary of Eve. Egg and Sperm and Preformation*. Chicago: University of Chicago Press 1997.

Volk defending the body of the motherland out of which they were born.[4] *Germania* flouts these expectations, however, instituting an image of the nation that resolutely denies any attempts at naturalization, while nonetheless erecting the same edifice of obligation that normally accompanies them. In this and other works of these years, like the infamous *Katechismus der Deutschen*, Kleist cements the link between the concept of the fatherland and that of fatherhood, between patriotism and filial duty. All the while he insists that paternity is not derived from an originary physical act, but rather constituted through language and then projected onto the body of the child through acts of violence. Rather than reinforcing the primary status of motherhood as an authentic relationship emerging from a direct physical bond, this paradigm instead turns the woman's body into an intermediary that can serve its purpose only through self-annihilation. National identity intervenes in this internal family paradigm by appropriating and redirecting violence in two directions: externally to construct the enemies of the nation, and internally in a demand for self-sacrifice that incorporates the nation. The body of the nation is thus for Kleist neither the land nor a populace, but is composed of mutilated and dead fighters who not only legitimate, but create the fatherland in a macabre aesthetic act, the art of war.

Kleist's delineation of paternity defers the physical mechanics of insemination from an originary moment of conception to an action by the father upon the children. The dynamics of this displacement can be clearly observed in *Die Marquise von O. . .*, a text dedicated to interrogating the means of establishing paternity when it cannot be confirmed by the mother. The rape of the Marquise is invisible to her, because she was unconscious when it took place, and is equally invisible to the reader, for whom it is marked only by the infamous punctuation mark – the dash. The disturbingly sexual reconciliation scene that later occurs between father and daughter in this novella has often been read as rendering visible what is hidden by this dash. But what purpose does this repetition and substitution serve? The father's action reinstitutes his

---

[4] Patricia Herminghouse and Magda Mueller trace the outlines of a history of the figure of Germania in their introduction to *Gender and Germanness*. They document Germania's roles as mother, virgin, and the embodiment of the nation. In this nationalist symbolic, Germania is the female counterpart of Arminius / Hermann, the leader of the Germanic tribes in their successful fight against the Romans in the 1st century CE. Like Arminius, Germania is generally depicted armed. My argument in this article is that Hermann and Germania also serve Kleist as idealized gender models in his nationalistic works, but that the specific valences of these figures shift in a way that reveals the inward as well as outwardly directed violence at the heart of any construction of nationality. The protective function of these armed figures becomes merely a cover for the threat they pose to their own populace. See Patricia Herminghouse and Magda Mueller: Looking for Germania. In: *Gender and Germanness: Cultural Productions of Nation*. Ed. by Patricia Herminghouse and Magda Mueller. Providence: Berghahn Books 1997. Pp. 1–20.

paternal claim to his daughter, which he had severed upon discovering her pregnancy. While the blatant sexual content of the scene has led some critics to list the Marquise's father as a suspect in her earlier impregnation, I would argue that such a suspicion is beside the point.[5] In a narrative obsessed with identifying "the Father", the Kommandant consolidates the role of fatherhood, collapsing generational difference by reenacting the physical component of paternity directly upon his child. His traumatized response to his daughter's rape signals the crisis it precipitates in his own identity. The rape has provided overwhelming evidence that the sexual act alone does not and cannot bind a father to a biological child without the mediation not only of the mother's body, but also of her knowledge and the institutions of a community. It is the undermining of the Kommandant's own position that provokes his declaration that he no longer has a daughter. To reestablish his identity as father, he must take a more certain route by dismissing the intermediary mother. The mother literally stands between father and daughter in the reconciliation scene until, stepping aside, she permits direct contact between the two. The Kommandant remains standing, while his daughter the Marquise "ihn aufrecht hielt" ["held him upright"] until a series of convulsive spasms allows him to relax. This orgasmic exchange takes place just before the more frequently cited moment when the Marquise lies on her father's lap while he kisses her "gerade wie ein Verliebter!" ["exactly like a lover!"] (II:138), but I believe that these kisses are already symbolically post-coital.[6] The crisis between fathers and children in Kleist's writing is often precipitated by the child's sexual activity, whether willing as in *Das Erdbeben in Chili* and *Der Findling*, or coerced, as in *Die Marquise von O. . .* and *Die Hermannsschlacht*.[7] Only in *Die Marquise von*

---

[5] Irmela Marei Krüger-Fürhoff suggests this reading as a possibility in the course of her persuasive argument about the construction of female passivity, both in relation to epistemological and sexual desire, as the ideal quality for both daughters and brides. Irmela Marei Krüger-Fürhoff: Father-Daughter Incest in Heinrich von Kleist's The Marquise of O. . .. In: *Women in German Yearbook* 12 (1996). Pp. 71–86.

[6] All citations from Kleist will be taken from Heinrich von Kleist: *Sämtliche Werke und Briefe*. Ed. by Helmut Sembdner. München: Deutscher Taschenbuch Verlag 1987. All translations are mine.

[7] This model generally holds true for both daughters and sons. In *Der Findling* the son's attempted rape of his step-mother is the final provocation for the filicide – the sexual activity is thus willing on the son's part, though not on the step-mother's. In *Das Erdbeben in Chili* after Josephe and Jeronimo have a child out of wedlock, Jeronimo's father murders him, but interestingly Josephe's father tries to save her from execution. Both *Prinz Friedrich von Hamburg* and *Die Familie Schroffenstein* share some common features with this model as the threat of execution in the one, and the double filicide in the other, follows the courtship of children or foster-children. The conceit is distinct in *Die Familie Schroffenstein*, however, since the children are in disguise and the filicide (although not the murder) is hence unintentional

O. . ., however, does the father reenact the sexual event. In the absence of this substitution, fathers consolidate their power over daughters, as they do uniformly over sons in Kleist, by intruding on their bodies with outright and sometimes murderous violence.

It is not precisely the conflict between *nomos* and *bios*, legal paternity and biological paternity, that permeates Kleist's work. Instead the symbolic entitlement codified by legal documentation that enables paternity must be validated by a biological act that follows rather than precedes it.[8] Foster and natural children are equally at risk throughout Kleist's work because their status is not reliably distinguishable.[9] David Wellbery and Silke-Maria Weineck have offered two related models for understanding Kleist's portrayal of fatherhood.[10] Wellbery has identified two opposing instantiations of fatherhood in Kleist, on the one hand the wild, murderous power associated with nature, and on the other the upholder of law associated with culture, and correlated these to natural and legal paternity. He sees the oscillation between these poles in Kleist's work as mutually enabling, but I would go farther and argue with Weineck that for Kleist a filicidal potential does not merely arise out of extreme catastrophes that eliminate legal authority, but in fact underlies all order:

> Fatherhood is the master metaphor for order – the harmony of nature under the aegis of culture – and hence evokes that which threatens it, namely socio-political, intellectual, and natural revolution, which all equate to patricide in the semiotic system of oppositions that organizes patriarchy in general [. . .]. In the Kleistian context, Fatherhood is always already Laiusian rather than Oedipal, and hence proceeds under the sign of filicide – attempted or real, fantasized or enacted. (79)

The uncertainty and still more the indirectness of fatherhood amplify the violence required to inscribe paternity onto the body of the child, providing

---

[8] As Silke-Maria Weineck notes in her excellent discussion of shifting conceptions of paternity in the eighteenth century in relation to Kleist, "the hierarchy of *bios* and *nomos* – the hidden procreative act and the public documents that declare a man a father – is not as stable as it may look". My argument here is significantly indebted to Weineck's reading. Silke-Maria Weineck: Kleist and the Resurrection of the Father. In: *Eighteenth-Century Studies* 37.1 (2003). Pp. 69–89. Here: P. 70.

[9] The debates over adoption in Kleist's work are not therefore moot. On the contrary and as Helmut Schneider has perceptively argued, by undermining the status of the adopted child as a sign of ethical choice and emancipation, a trope most evident in Lessing's *Nathan der Weise*, Kleist exposes "reason's delusion about its power to generate itself". Helmut Schneider: The Facts of Life: Kleist's Challenge to Enlightenment Humanism (Lessing). In: *A Companion to the Works of Heinrich von Kleist*. Ed. by Bernd Fischer. Rochester, NY: Camden House 2003. Pp. 141–163. Here: P. 145.

[10] David Wellbery: Semiotische Anmerkungen zu Kleists *Das Erdbeben in Chili*. In: *Positionen der Literaturwissenschaft: Acht Modellanalysen am Beispiel von Kleists Das Erdbeben in Chili*. Ed. by David Wellbery. Pp. 69–87.

identity often at the literal cost of life. The father not only has a prerogative over the life of the child, but constructs the signifying capacity of the child's body, which then in turn constitutes the child's identity as a constant and pervasive presence. The idea of nation, of Fatherland, imitates and intervenes in this dynamic, creating a mechanism that displaces but does not eliminate the violence involved in fashioning paternity, by dedicating the body of both father and child to the fatherland.

Kleist's *Katechismus der Deutschen*, rightfully notorious for advocating absolute war with France and written in the same year as the poem *Germania*, is subtitled *Zum Gebrauch für Kinder und Alte* [*For the Use of Young and Old*]. The relationship between the interlocutors in this text, in other words, begins as merely generational, and not familial. The dialogue itself soon creates the identities of questioner and questioned, not only constructing a paternal/filial relationship between them, but crystallizing paternity in collusion with nationality. The dialog thus answers ontologically rather than epistemologically the primary and primal question: "Sprich, Kind, wer bist du?" ["Speak, child, who are you?"] (II:350). The child's answer "Ich bin ein Deutscher" ["I am a German"] is soon refined to "Ich bin in Meißen geboren, und das Land, dem Meißen angehört, heißt Sachsen; aber mein Vaterland, das Land dem Sachsen angehört, ist Deutschland, und dein Sohn, mein Vater, ist ein Deutscher" ["I was born in Meissen, and the land to which Meissen belongs is called Saxony; but my fatherland, the land to which Saxony belongs, is Germany, and your son, my father, is a German"] (II:350). While the land to which Meissen belongs is *called* Sachsen, the fatherland *is* Deutschland, and in the symbolic investiture of naming the nation, the child creates himself as son, his interrogator as father, and both as German, or more precisely as a single German composed of the dyad father/son: "dein Sohn, mein Vater ist ein Deutscher" ["your son, my father, is a German"]. This relationship is thereafter performed in the constant repetition of the expressions "mein Vater" and "mein Sohn", creating a paternity entirely divested of any biological underpinnings. Indeed, the structure of the text in the form of a catechism also allows a religious rather than familial understanding of the terms which would then imply the celibacy of the father. The materiality of the fatherland is similarly discredited, as Germany's continued existence is reaffirmed in spite of its absence on a map.

What is this nation if not a geographical area? In *Germania an ihre Kinder*, Kleist constructs a vision of the nation entirely dissociated from the materiality of the land or the life of the *Volk*. While mother Germania does first invoke her seemingly autochthonous sons as her protectors, she quickly effaces herself as the foundation of the nation, as the grounds for war, and as a biological progenitor for these sons. Whereas in the *Katechismus* father and son mutually constitute each other, the sons in *Germania* are their own fathers, climbing into and then out of Germania's "Schoß" ["lap" or "womb"] (I:26). Kleist rules out the fields or their destruction, the women or their rape and murder, the cityscapes or their abandonment as sufficient grounds for conducting war against the French. In the process, he validates a traditional mythic affinity between women's bodies and the fertile land, only to reject this particular myth as the foundation of national identity.

Instead, he explicitly replaces mother with father and concrete with abstract as the foundation of nationhood. Kleist initiates not only a sliding series of substitutable ideas, but the very idea of substitution itself, as the ruling trope of nationhood and adequate grounds for war:

> Gott und seine Stellvertreter,
> Und dein Nam, o Vaterland,
> Freiheit, Stolz der bessern Väter,
> Sprache, du, dein Zauberband,
> Wissenschaft, du himmelferne
> Die dem deutschen Genius winkt (I:27)
> [God and his representatives,
> And your name, o fatherland,
> Freedom, the pride of the better fathers,
> You, language, your magic bonds,
> Science, you, distant as the heavens
> Who beckons to German genius]

While God would seem to anchor this chain, the plurality and nonspecificity of his surrogates create an unease which is intensified by the elision of the Fatherland in favor of its name. What is described here is the mechanism by which language, substitution, the name of the fatherland, and the pride of the better fathers mark the entry into a symbolic relationship that creates the Fatherland and the identity of its members. Precisely this mechanism is enacted in the *Katechismus*.

The interdependence of public institutions and private family dynamics has always been a necessary element of paternity. The idea of consolidated state power as a natural extension of a God-given paternal authority had already endured some revolutionary reversals by the early nineteenth century, and the search for a natural foundation for paternal authority within the family was on-going. In Kleist, however, we encounter the family as truly internally dysfunctional, and the state as a questionable ally. Institutional intervention contributes to the murder of sons by fathers in works from *Der Findling* to *Das Erdbeben in Chili*. However, the nation conjured up in the political writings of 1809 is not identical with patriarchal state institutions or with a paternal King. With the Prussian king idling in East Prussia, Kleist's catechism advocates joining the Austrian army to fight Napoleon. His version of nationalism does not involve surrender of individual will to a particular individual or to his representatives, but rather to an ideal construct in which fatherhood and fatherland become mutually constitutive of each other and of the individual, because all are equally untethered. This is truly magic, the *Zauberband* described in the citation above.

With a string of substitutions invoked as a justification for war, the fathers and sons who are mustered to defend them are all the more vulnerable in their very concrete, but utterly replaceable, bodies. A Germany whose borders cannot be found on a map must create those borders in the material substance of the wounded and dead:

> Dämmt den Rhein mit ihren Leichen;
> Laßt, gestäuft von ihrem Bein,
> Schäumend um die Pfalz ihn weichen,
> Und ihn dann die Grenze sein! (I:26–27)
> [Dam the Rhine with their corpses;
> Heaped with their bones, let it
> Bow foaming around the Palatinate,
> And then be the border!]

This verse sounds at first like foreshadowing for the nationalistic Rhine poetry of the nineteenth century. While the poems of the 1840s *Rheinkrise* by Nikolaus Becker and Max Schneckenburger used natural markers to delineate borders as natural or claimed certain features of the landscape as innately and immutably German, Kleist here deploys nature in an entirely different way.[11] Far from being immutable, the Rhine itself must first be diverted from its course by violence before it is worthy of becoming a political marker. The landscape must first be manipulated and only then becomes meaningful. Kleist has not chosen the setting of the verse arbitrarily. The region of Rhineland-Palatinate was precisely where he fought as a young officer against the French Revolutionary army from spring 1793 to summer 1794. Kleist participated in the siege of Mainz after it proclaimed itself a republic and voluntarily allied itself with France, and fought full-scale battles with heavy casualties at Pirmasens, Kaiserslautern, and Trippstadt.[12] As part of the siege of Mainz, the Third Battalion of the King's Guard Regiment in which Kleist served blockaded bridges across the Rhine under fire. Kleist's unit experienced the

---

[11] See Nikolaus Becker's *Sie sollen ihn nicht haben, den freien deutschen Rhein* and Max Schneckenburger's *Die Wacht am Rhein*. Hoffmann von Fallersleben's famous and eventually infamous *Lied der Deutschen* can be read in this same tradition, although, significantly, it refers to rivers other than the Rhine to delineate boarders.

[12] For more on Kleist's military service and its relationship to his perception of the body and of signification as fragile, see Stefani Engelstein: Out on a Limb: Military Medicine, Heinrich von Kleist, and the Disarticulated Body. In: *German Studies Review* 23.2 (2000). Pp. 225–244.

heaviest fighting during the two-day battle of Trippstadt in July 1794, when several units, including Kleist's, were offered a special commendation by the newspaper:

> Sämmtlich Truppen haben nicht nur alle in ihre Schuldigkeit gethan, sondern auch neue Beweise ihren Standhaftigkeit, Unerschrockenheit und ihres Eifers gegeben, und dadurch ihren alten Ruhm behauptet; besonders aber haben das 1ste und 3te Bataillon Kön. Garden Gelegenheit gehabt, ausgezeichnete Beweise von Muth und Standhaftigkeit an den Tag zu legen. (*Berlinische Zeitung*, 26.7.1794)
> [The assembled troops not only did everything required of them, but also added new evidence of their steadfastness, composure, and zeal, thereby reaffirming their established reputation; particularly, however, the 1st and 3rd Battalion of the King's Guard had the opportunity to bring to light exceptional evidence of courage and steadfastness.]

The battle at Trippstadt was not victorious, however, as the destruction of communication lines forced a retreat.[13]

The campaign ended with the 1795 Treaty of Basel when, in return for territories east of the river, Prussia relinquished to France the west bank of the Rhine. Prussia thus lost the entire area where Kleist had fought and which his poem advocates reincorporating through the accumulation of corpses and the reinscription of the nation on the landscape. France held the Rhineland until the 1815 Congress of Vienna, four years after Kleist's death. The contested nationality of this area was further complicated by the voluntary allegiance of Mainz with France, an allegiance based on political affinity rather than national identity, which resulted in the deployment of Kleist's regiment against a "German" city. The insecure identity of the Rhineland is therefore something Kleist had experienced on his own body. The violence of the poem is thus not only outwardly directed at the French. A nation that is not a sum of its members, but constitutive of them, demands the sacrifice of its own people as eagerly as those of its enemies. In the catechism, the son assures the father that even the death of every German man, woman, and child would not indicate that the struggle had been a mistake. The nation supercedes its people, precluding their political choice, and enlisting them in the service of a fatherland without which they are nothing.

The position of women in this constellation is no less dangerous than that of men. Germania's self-exclusion as a motivation to defend national identity does not serve to protect women by placing them outside the conflict. Kleist had written to his fiancée Wilhelmine von Zenge, "daß der Mann nicht bloß

---

[13] Carl von Reinhard: *Geschichte des Königlich Preußischen Ersten Garde-Regiments zu Fuß zurückgeführt auf die historische Abstammung des Regiments vom 1. Bataillon Leibgarde, dem Regiment Garde und dem Grenadier-Garde-Bataillon. 1740–1857.* Potsdam: Verlag von Aug. Stein 1858. P. 215.

Verpflichtungen gegen seine Frau [hat], sondern auch Verpflichtungen gegen sein Vaterland, die Frau hingegen keine andern Verpflichtungen hat, als Verpflichtungen gegen ihren Mann" ["that the man does not only have obligations to his wife, but also has obligations to his fatherland, the woman on the other hand has no other obligations except obligations to her husband"] (II:506). While men are expected to sacrifice themselves for the nation directly, women perform the same sacrifice within a domestic sphere. Their bodies serve as catalysts for the construction of the aggregate of men. Both forms of sacrifice entail equal risk, but the exploitation of women's bodies reveals more clearly the source of the threat as internal to the dynamic of nationhood rather than external to the nation itself.

The way such internal family relationships serve the nation is most clearly evident in the 1808 drama *Die Hermannsschlacht*. With this play, Kleist engages a long tradition of depicting Hermann or Arminius as a Germanic hero in his successful struggle to expel the Romans from German lands.[14] In the oeuvre of an author obsessed with carnage, *Die Hermannsschlacht* distinguishes itself for gruesome acts of violence. In one scene a father murders his young daughter after she has been gang-raped. Hally, so draped and veiled that her father recognizes her identity only from her feet, is permitted not a single line of dialog. Her father solicits her voice only after her death, when he cries rhetorically "Hally! Mein Einziges! Hab ichs recht gemacht?" [Hally! My one and only! Did I do right?"] (I:389). Like Hally, the Marquise was also raped by invading troops. The Marquise's father, however, threatens to kill her only when he believes she has been involved in an affair, but considers proof that she was raped also proof of her innocence and justification for her readmission into the family. Hally's father, on the other hand, knows when he kills her that his daughter has been brutally attacked. He offers the audience no justification for his action. But there is another crucial difference between the

---

[14] Carl Niekerk and Hans Peter Hermann have explored the intersection of nationalism and gender in Kleist. Hermann documents the increasing misogyny of nationalist discourse through the investigation of eighteenth-century depictions of Hermann by Johann Elias Schlegel, Klopstock, and Kleist. Niekerk, however, demonstrates that Kleist in *Die Hermannsschlacht* allows Hermann to manipulate the symbolism of sexuality rather than merely conforming to it. In so doing, Hermann deviates from traditional heroic depictions of the sexuality of the soldier who defends and monopolizes the honor of women under his protection. Hans Peter Hermann: Arminius und die Erfindung der Männlichkeit im 18. Jahrhundert. In: *Machtphantasie Deutschland: Nationalismus, Männlichkeit und Fremdenhaß im Vaterlandsdiskurs deutscher Schriftsteller des 18. Jahrhunderts*. Ed. by Hans Peter Hermann, Hans-Martin Blitz, and Susanna Moßmann. Frankfurt am Main: Suhrkamp 1996. Pp. 161–191. Carl Niekerk: Kleists Männer, ihre Sexualität und die Nation. In: *Weimarer Beiträge* 45.4 (1999). Pp. 569–583.

two fathers. The Kommandant has surrendered to his daughter's rapist militarily (although he is not aware at the time that the opposing military commander is also the rapist), while Hally's father pledges revenge. By escalating the violence already directed at Hally's body from rape to murder, the father reclaims his paternal right, and through this act recommits himself to the fatherland. Hally thus serves a purpose dead that she could not have served alive. Hermann orders her body to be dismembered and the pieces sent to the heads of the German tribes to incite them to revenge against the Romans. Her body becomes a physical medium of propaganda that cements their allegiance to each other. Unsurprisingly for a play in which rhetoric is never grounded, however, the Romans are the least likely suspects for the rape, which was almost certainly carried out by marauding Germans strategically ordered by Hermann to pillage and rampage while dressed as Romans in order to cement public opinion against them.

The exploitation of Hally to encourage armed resistance is particularly spectacular because she falls into the category of things explicitly named as not worth fighting for. What is worth fighting for, Hermann narrows to a single word that we need to consider more closely here, the word *Freiheit*.[15] Hermann is an adherent of a scorched-earth strategy, advising the gathered chiefs,

> Kurz, wollt ihr, wie ich schon einmal euch sagte,
> Zusammenrafen Weib und Kind,
> Und auf der Weser rechtes Ufer bringen,
> Geschirre, goldn' und silberne, die ihr
> Besitzet, schmelzen, Perlen und Juwelen
> Verkaufen oder sie verpfänden,
> Verheeren eure Fluren, eure Herden
> Erschlagen, eure Plätze niederbrennen,
> So bin ich euer Mann – : (I:546)
> [In brief, as I said before, if you'll,

---

[15] Bernhard Greiner also situates the question of freedom in the center of the drama, but for him the question is "wie man aus einem in der Idee der Freiheit perspektivierten teleologischen Denken herauskomme und auch nicht, wie man – abstrakt – in solch ein Denken hinein gelange" ["how one can move outward from teleological thinking based in the perspective of the idea of freedom, and not how one can arrive abstractly at such thinking"] (106). Greiner therefore focuses on the necessity of transforming the abstract and ideal into a physical motivational sign, in this case Hally's body, which then takes on its own overdetermined valences and demonstrates the warped relation of sign to world. Greiner does not ask, however, what is meant by the idea of freedom to begin with, taking for granted that "Die Idee der Freiheit ist ein absoluter Wert, wer Mensch sein will, muß sie bejahen" ["The idea of freedom is an absolute value; whoever wants to identify himself as human must affirm it"] (106–107). Bernhard Greiner: *Kleists Dramen und Erzählungen*. Tübingen: Francke Verlag 2000.

Round up wife and child,
And bring them to the other bank of the Weser,
Melt the gold and silver plate,
That you own; pearls and jewels –
Sell or pawn;
Lay waste to your halls, your herds
Destroy, your plazas raze,
Then I'm your man – :]

Appalled, one chief contends, "Das eben, Rasender, das ist es ja, / Was wir in diesem Krieg verteidigen wollen!" ["You maniac, that's exactly / What we want to defend in this war!"]; to which Hermann replies in a supreme rhetorical move, "Nun denn, ich glaubte, eure Freiheit wärs" ["Well now, I thought it was your freedom"] (I:547). The disconcerted chief finds it hard to argue against this word, which is here startlingly empty of content, invented as the ultimate value in the moment of being named. The word *Freiheit* is mentioned in lists of justifications Kleist gives for the war against Napoleon in the *Katechismus* and in *Germania*, but in *Die Hermannsschlacht*, it stands alone. What can freedom mean in this context? Not independence (*Unabhängigkeit*) which Kleist contrasts with freedom and explicitly rejects in *Über die Rettung von Österreich*. When Hermann threatens to abandon the leaders should they not capitulate to his radical strategy, and therefore also to him, he detaches the word freedom from any conventional political or personal referent, and attaches it to his concept of a victory for its own sake. As Raimar Zons remarks, "Allerdings. Die Freiheit, die Freiheit aber auch von alledem, was den Fürsten beschützens- und bewahrenswert scheint" ["Absolutely. Freedom, but also freedom from everything that the princes find worthy of protecting and preserving"].[16] Freedom becomes the marker of the nation's lack of foundation and simultaneously a slight of hand that obscures this lack, a magic trick, in short, to come back to the *Germania* citation above. It represents freedom from the materiality of the land, its products, and its residents, but freedom also from the need for justification and accountability.

Carl Schmitt called *Die Hermannsschlacht* "die größte Partisanendichtung aller Zeiten" ["the greatest partisan poem of all times"], a judgment clearly echoed by Wolf Kittler in his work on Kleist.[17] Both writers seem to mean by this that the play legitimates and advocates "total war" as a means to free

---

[16] Raimar Zons: Von der 'Not der Welt' zur absoluten Feindschaft", Zeitschrift für deutsche Philologie 109:2 (1990). Pp. 175–199. Here: P. 187.
[17] Carl Schmitt: *Theorie des Partisanen*. Berlin: Duncker & Humblot 1963. P. 15. Carl Schmitt: Theory of the Partisan. Trans. by G.L. Ulmen. New York: Telos Press 2007. P. 7. Wolf Kittler: *Die Geburt des Partisanen aus dem Geist der Poesie*. Freiburg: Verlag Rombach 1987. P. 15.

the homeland from foreign occupation.[18] Both writers also place Kleist in the company of Gneisenau, Scharnhorst, and Clausewitz as theoreticians of the partisan war. One can, however, be a theoretician without being an advocate, as Schmitt himself demonstrates, and even being an advocate of partisan fighting does not make one a partisan. Kittler compares Kleist's play to the handbook for Brazilian revolutionaries by Carlos Marighella, *The Manual of the Urban Guerilla* (Kittler 235). *Die Hermannsschlacht* can certainly be read as a manual, a how-to guide, but there is a vast gulf between the intended audience of Kleist's work and that of Marighella's. Marighella provides instructions for effective action on the part of those who are already committed to a cause; Kleist provides instructions about motivating, or more accurately, manipulating a populace to take up a cause. The difference lies in the attribution of agency, and on this issue hang the linked questions of ideology and of partisanship. The partisan, after all, is motivated by an ideology, whether that of revolution, of religion, or of the inviolability of the homeland. But the person who mobilizes an ideology is a partisan of a different order: in Kleist's case the cause to which he is committed is a *need* for an all-consuming cause. He is a partisan of nationalism, rather than a partisan of the nation. When Schmitt describes the partisan fighters in terms of their autochthonous or telluric character which binds them to the earth and motivates them to rise up and fight for it, he is succumbing to a myth that Kleist had long since dismantled. While Schmitt grants these autochthonous warriors spontaneity, he denies them the ability to make decisions, and thus excludes them from the realm of the political. Kleist, on the other hand, revokes even their claim to spontaneity. The real and fabricated cruelty of the invaders that Hermann uses to motivate the masses is explicitly differentiated from Hermann's own motives for the war. The *Volk* in *Die Hermannsschlacht* are crucial for victory, but the people must be provoked, manipulated, and led.[19] They therefore also fail to

---

[18] Kittler claims that *Die Hermannsschlacht* promotes "de[n] totale[n] Krieg, der nicht einmal haltmacht vor der Zerstörung der Ordnung im eigenen Land. Es ist der Partisanenkrieg, wie ihn Carl Schmitt beschrieben hat" ["The total war that does not stop even at the destruction of order in one's own land. It is the partisan war, as Carl Schmitt described it"] (230). It was Kittler in this book who first focused on Kleist's military concerns as crucial to his texts, initiating the avenue of inquiry that this article follows.

[19] I concur here with Lothar Bornscheuer's claim that Kleist did not see the *Volk* as a self-sufficient political power (221) and that the play is therefore not a partisan work in the sense meant by Schmitt and Kittler. I strongly disagree, however, with Bornscheuer's conclusion that Kleist was merely trying to find an audience in a time of nationalist fervor and was not himself nationalistic. Leaving aside the question of whether making Kleist a hypocrite provides an acceptable ethical excuse for a work of blood-thirsty hatred, I am not sure what we gain, critically, by inventing

fulfill Kittler's more positive theory of the partisan fighter, for whom love of fatherland allows the upholding of a paradox in which discipline and freedom, although mutually exclusive, nonetheless coexist. Instead, Kleist documents the reinscribing of discipline, or rather abandonment to an assigned cause, *as* freedom, which is then constituted as *Vaterlandsliebe* in an act of rationalization. It is not the partisan who is created in the process, but the fatherland, its subjects, and the concept of nationality itself.

This notion of freedom sheds new light on the controversy surrounding *Die Hermannsschlacht* as political propaganda, as well as the parallel controversy surrounding Kleist's attitude towards paternal violence within the family. In the realm of the family, the question could be configured: Is Kleist reinscribing the power of patriarchy, is he critiquing it, or is he merely documenting its resilience?[20] In the realm of nationhood, we could pose the analogous question: Is *Die Hermannsschlacht* a piece of propaganda, as suggested by Kleist's own repeated association of its potential success with the prevailing political

---

an exculpatory persona for Kleist external to his work. We are obligated to take seriously the work itself, and in this and much of his other writing Kleist is a rabid supporter of the cause of nationalism, which is not quite the same as being a partisan of the nation. Lothar Bornscheuer: Heinrich von Kleists 'vaterländische Dichtung,' mit der kein 'Staat' zu machen ist. In: *Dichter und ihre Nation*. Ed. by Helmut Scheuer. Frankfurt am Main: Suhrkamp 1993. Pp. 216–236.

[20] Silke-Maria Wineck and Anthony Stephens, for example, argue that Kleist performs a radical critique of patriarchy. Marjorie Gelus reads Kleist's work more ambiguously as the "battlefield for [. . .] the split within himself between the steadfast upholder of patriarchal values and the androgynously subversive dismantler of stable meaning" (60). My claim is that the inherent instability of meaning that Kleist illuminates is precisely what drives him to resurrect the power of patriarchy at any cost. While Kleist does reveal the lack of natural justification for paternal dominance, as Stephens claims, I argue here that its tenaciousness is not ironic ("schwer geprüfte oder ironisierte väterliche Gewalt" [Stephens 227]), but foundational. As such, Kleist does give an undeniable, if pained, endorsement to patriarchy as the only prospect for grounding subjectivity. Joachim Pfeiffer provides evidence that the father's dominance is undermined in works such as *Der Findling* and *Die Marquise von O...*. It is true that the Marquise's father cedes power within his family as within his city to the Graf, but the Graf gains this power only by displacing the Kommandant as "the Father", and Piachi's failure to impose an identity on his foster son Nicolo in *Der Findling* elicits the escalation of power from force to violence that culminates in Piachi's murder of Nicolo. See Anthony Stephens: Kleists Familienmodelle. In: *Kleist Jahrbuch* (1988–1989). Pp. 222–237. Marjorie Gelus: Patriarchy's Fragile Boundaries under Siege: Three Stories of Heinrich von Kleist. In: *Women in German Yearbook* 10 (1994). Pp. 59–82. Joachim Pfeiffer: *Die zerbrochenen Bilder. Gestörte Ordnungen im Werk Heinrich von Kleists*. Würzburg: Königshausen & Neumann 1989.

atmosphere of resistance against the French occupation?[21] Or, in its brilliant clear-sightedness about its hero's diabolical strategies, is it a critique of the illusory nature of national identity, created through propaganda that instrumentalizes its audience?[22] Or is it, as some have argued, "merely" an aesthetic experiment?[23] Kleist displays explicitly the steps involved in conjuring up the nation, thereby exposing the artificiality of the naturalizing effect. The element of Kleist's work that has frequently been read as ambiguity in his nationalism, and that presumably led the Prussian government at the time to reject and censor his work, is this repudiation of the naturalistic argument. Can then a work that documents the construction of an ideology be read as ideological? Terry Eagleton makes the common-sense assertion in *Ideology* that, "It is part of what we mean by claiming that human beings are somewhat rational that we would be puzzled to encounter someone who held a conviction which they

---

[21] Bernd Fischer, for example, in "Fremdbestimmung und Identitätspolitik in *Die Hermannsschlacht*", labels *Die Hermannsschlacht* propaganda. Although Fischer does not cite Schmitt, Fischer's reading has much in common with Schmitt's definition of the political as distinguishing between friends and enemies. Here and in *Das Eigene und das Eigentliche*, Fischer points to the ambivalence of the work, which "hinterfragt implizit die Idee, die es in voller Konsequenz vorführt" ["implicitly questions the idea that it exhibits with all its consequences"] (*Das Eigene* 319). In "Fremdbestimmung" he situates the fervor of the *Befreiungskrieg* in an anticolonial context, leading him to question the prudence of founding national identity on an anticolonial hatred ("Fremdbestimmung" 178). Lawrence Ryan reads the failure of *Die Hermannsschlacht* as evidence of Kleist's unsuitability for writing propaganda. The political elements of the play are for Ryan only a superficial veneer over the deeper conflict between heart and reason, between spontaneity and law that pervade Kleist's work. Bernd Fischer*:* Fremdbestimmung und Identitätspolitik in *Die Hermannsschlacht*. In: *Kleists Erzählungen und Dramen. Neue Studien*. Ed. by Paul Michael Lützler and David Pan. Würzburg: Königshausen & Neumann 2001. Pp. 165–178. Bernd Fischer: *Das Eigene und das Eigentliche: Klopstock, Herder, Fichte, Kleist*. Berlin: Erich Schmidt Verlag 1995. Lawrence Ryan: Die 'vaterländische' Umkehr in der *Hermannsschlacht*. In: *Kleists Dramen. Neue Interpretationen*. Ed. by Walter Hinderer. Stuttgart: Philipp Reclam 1981. Pp. 188–212.
[22] This interpretation is put forward by Barbara Kennedy, who reads *Die Hermannsschlacht* as a critique of Hermann as a hero because of his failure to protect women. Barbara Kennedy*:* For the Good of the Nation: Woman's Body as Battlefield in Kleist's *Die Hermannsschlacht*. In*: Seminar* 30:1 (1994). Pp. 17–31.
[23] Both Jeffrey Sammons and Lother Bornsheuer argue that Kleist saw the function of a work of art as the exploration of an extreme response. Both can then dismiss the question of ethics from the consideration of *Die Hermannsschlacht*. Bernd Fischer also calls *Die Hermannsschlacht* an experiment, but for him the "poetischen Überschuss" ("Fremdbestimmung" 178) exceeds a foundation which is explicitly political. Jeffrey Sammons: "Rethinking Kleist's *Hermannsschlacht*". In: *Heinrich von Kleist – Studien*. Ed. by Alexej Ugrinsky. Berlin: Erich Schmidt Verlag 1980.

acknowledge to be illusory".[24] And yet, Kleist (whom I grant to be extremely puzzling) embodies this paradox. He does not avail himself of the critical potential of his analysis, but desperately embraces the violent consequences of ideology as the only alternative to a vacuum of signification. The freedom that he institutes as the highest good is the freedom from a naturalistic foundation, the freedom to bow to the construction of what then becomes one's own innermost identity.

In his manipulation of those around him, Kleist's Hermann has legitimately been compared to a playwright. But his scripting alone is insufficient to realize the nation. The martial identity that Kleist's Germans inhabit must be performed. Germania calls upon her sons not as the *Volk* per se, but as "mutger Völkerreigen", as participants in a folk dance. They quite explicitly enact their nationality, and quite suitably, do so in a theater – that of war. The theater of war is watched with admiration in the catechism by "die Kenner der Kunst" ["art connoisseurs"] (II: 355). It is a show like that of the soldier-marionettes in his *Über das Marionettentheater*. The gracefulness of this performance arises from submission to a puppet master who himself fades out of existence as an individual. While Kleist carefully delineates a performativity that grants significance to bodies constituted through their actions, he lacks Judith Butler's optimism that performance can escape or subvert patriarchy. For Kleist, performance remains firmly under the sign of the father and of the fatherland. The grace of the dance camouflages the disarticulation of the body, but the performance of nationality demands a larger stage and theater. To maintain itself, the intervention into the body must escalate. It is incompatible with peace.

Kleist's work can therefore be seen not only as a diagnosis of ideology but also as a prescription for its invention, a how-to manual of totalitarianism. Kleist reveals the process by which bodies are granted the status of authenticity which then renders them vulnerable to the role of sacrifice. The ceremonial function of the body fuses with its sacrificial function in the authorization of state power. While Kleist himself advocates this process as an antidote to the chaos of unanchored signification, he was just a little too canny about its artificiality and its violence to make his work fit comfortably with a *Volksideologie*. Only later in the nineteenth and into the twentieth century could nationalism accommodate Kleist. Once firmly naturalized, the nationalism of blood and soil could studiously overlook Kleist's jarring insistence on the artificiality of nationalism and nation itself.

The construction of a nationalistic ideology through the simultaneous aestheticization of bodies and demand for their sacrifice should sound all too familiar. The Nazi investment in the display of whole and wholesome, healthy

---

[24] Terry Eagleton: *Ideology: An Introduction*. London: Verso 1991. P. 2.

bodies which exhibit internal and communal unity through movements in unison, reveals itself as the obverse of the aesthetic war, but also as its forerunner. The horrifying potential of this configuration is augmented by the ease of combining it with other metaphorics of the body which also justify an assault on real bodies. A form of this dynamic was realized by the Nazis, who exploited an aesthetics of health to generate volunteer bodies for the cause, while employing a medical rhetoric of health to impel and justify genocide.

In an age characterized by the reimagining of the body as teleological, Kleist was a perceptive observer of the common search for a final purpose embedded in its materiality. The body's ultimate failure to produce significance endangers it. Ideologies which attempt unsuccessfully to trace their legitimacy to the body, delve into it with violence in a move which is always belated and hence insufficient, initiating an ever-escalating demand for still greater intervention into the body. The naturalizing discourses which became increasingly prevalent throughout the nineteenth century, and are certainly still with us today, attempt to obscure the body as a site of rupture by retroactively assigning meaning to material functions and by claiming that nature is therefore normative. Kleist occupies a unique position in this quest. By exposing the mechanism of this process he provides us with a critical tool, but his failure to repudiate the process demonstrates that ideology's strength lies precisely in its freedom from the demands of reason, even among the "somewhat reasonable".

Jeffrey Grossman

Fractured Histories: Heine's Responses to Violence and Revolution*

This essay explores how the study of violence can help illuminate the work of Heinrich Heine, and how, in turn, Heine's work can help illuminate the relationship between literature and violence. Drawing on the concepts of "structural violence", as articulated by Habermas, and of "symbolic violence", as presented by Pierre Bourdieu, this essay argues that Heine seeks to reveal the complex and subtle mechanisms by which such forms of violence operate. His attempts to reveal those mechanisms are manifest in works as different as the lyric poem Die Heimkehr 62 (Du hast Diamanten und Perlen) *and the journalistic reportage* Französische Zustände. *Sensitive to the changing contexts and conditions under which violence occurs, these literary attempts also help account for the shifts in Heine's positions on politics, power, and violence – something that Heine's critics often failed to note.*

Ich bin in diesem langweilgen Nest
Ein Stündchen herumgeschlendert.
Sah wieder preußisches Militär,
Hat sich nicht sehr verändert [. . .]

Sie stelzen noch immer so steif herum,
So kerzengrade geschniegelt,
Als hätten sie verschluckt den Stock
Womit man sie einst geprügelt.
(*Deutschland: Ein Wintermärchen*)

[An hour or so in this dull nest
I aimlessly wandered around;
Saw Prussian military again:
They'd changed but little, I found [. . .]

They stalk around so stiltedly,
So sprucely bolt upright,
As though they'd swallowed the whipping rod
That bloodied their backs last night.]
(*Germany, A Winter's Tale*, trans. Aaron Kramer)

I

In their recent historiographical study, *Shattered Past: Reconstructing German Histories* (2003), Konrad Jarausch and Michael Geyer oppose the

---

*I would like to thank Agnes Müller (University of South Carolina, Columbia) for her helpful comments on an earlier version of this article.

many attempts to present German history in terms of a single, unified narrative. They focus instead on the fragments, ruptures, and shattered nature of that history.[1] Although dealing with what Eric Hobsbawm has referred to as the short, but "violent" twentieth century, Jarausch and Geyer's image of a history ruptured and fragmented by violence is one which Heine, in the nineteenth century, had already come to struggle with – even if, one might assume, Heine himself would have distinguished between the excesses of the twentieth century and the events of his own times, roughly spanning the period from the French Revolution to the decade following 1848.

Heine criticism has in various ways acknowledged Heine's struggles with the question of violence, in such political writings, for instance, as *Französische Zustände*, the series of articles Heine wrote from Paris on the French Revolution of 1830, and in the more overtly historical and politically critical poetry of his middle and later periods – his satire of German nationalism in *Deutschland: Ein Wintermärchen*, his treatments of colonialism and slavery in poems like *Vitzliputzli* and *Das Sklavenschiff*, or in another context, his tribute to the Medieval Sephardic poets in the long narrative poem *Jehuda ben Halevy*. Gerhard Höhn's *Heine-Handbuch* goes so far as to entitle one of its sections "Ideenkampf und 'pacifike Mission'" ["Struggle of ideas and 'pacifist mission'"], citing Heine's efforts to forge peaceful relations between the French and Germans, a title by which Höhn seeks not least to account for Heine's use of martial imagery in describing his own project, as, for instance, when he calls himself "ein braver Soldat im Befreiungskriege der Menschheit" ["a good soldier in the war of liberation for humanity"],[2] or declares war on the remaining palaces of the *Ancien Régime* and the rising tide of German nationalism.[3] And yet, amidst the many critical works devoted to Heine's

---

[1] Konrad H. Jarausch and Michael Geyer: *Shattered Past: Reconstructing German Histories*. Princeton: Princeton University Press 2003. The following passages are indicative of their position: "There is no single master narrative to be told, no *Weltgeist* to be discovered, no national character to be indicted or, at long last, absolved" (x). "The prevarications of historiography reflect disorientation in the face of a century that will remain known for its catastrophic violence as much as for its unprecedented prosperity and creativity. German and European history encompass both excruciating violence and pain and exquisite wealth and happiness. The incommensurability of simultaneous man-made life-worlds of utter privilege, wealth, and consumption and death-worlds of utter degradation, starvation, and brutal annihilation is the sign of twentieth-century German history" (12).
[2] Heinrich Heine: *Reise von München nach Genua*. In: *Sämtliche Schriften*. Ed. by Klaus Briegleb. München: Hanser 1995. 3 rev. ed. Vol. 2. P. 382. Future references to this edition of Heine's works are given parenthetically in the text and abbreviated as B, for the Briegleb edition, followed by volume and page number.
[3] Gerhard Höhn: *Heine-Handbuch: Zeit–Prosa–Werk*. Stuttgart: Metzler 1997. 2 rev. ed. Pp. 26–29

views of revolution, politics, history, romanticism, to his conceptions of poetry and the critically engaged intellectual, pleasure-seeking Hellenes, ascetic Nazarenes, and of his own self, one seeks in vain for a study devoted specifically to the role of violence in Heine's writing.

This article marks a preliminary attempt to fill that gap in the study of Heine research while also addressing the problem of violence and literature, more generally. Its way into this question begins with a problem about Heine as a writer: how, if at all, did Heine reconcile his many conflicting impulses about writing, in general, and poetry and politics, in particular.[4] This conflict finds expression in Heine's repeatedly shifting positions, so that Heine will at times stake out a distinct position toward violence – conceived variously as violent action, structural violence, and symbolic violence – but will at other key moments alter that position.[5] As often noted, there were already critics in Heine's own time who chastised him for his unstable positions on such matters as poetry and politics. Yet, Heine undertook these re-positionings not merely for lack of a centered stance on such matters. Rather, each new position Heine stakes out points to a reconsideration of specific cases of violence – its causes and consequences, while when one steps back to take a broad view of Heine's responses to violence, his shifting positions also provide the model for an approach to the problem of violence. That is, Heine's shifting positions suggest an approach that recognizes the need to consider the changing and elusive forms violence can take under varying conditions and in differing contexts, an approach, moreover, by which Heine seeks to map out those various forms as well as the conditions that give rise to violent acts and structures, and the effects violence produces. While Heine frequently wrote about politics, he did not, as critics have often noted, offer a distinct, wholly consistent

---

[4] For an introduction to this set of problems in Heine's work, see the volume *Heinrich Heine's Contested Identities: Politics, Religion, and Nationalism in Nineteenth-Century Germany*. Ed. by Jost Hermand and Robert C. Holub. New York: Lang 1999. In this context, see especially Jeffrey L. Sammons. Who Did Heine Think He Was? Pp. 1–24; Jost Hermand: 'Tribune of the People or Aristocrat of the Spirit': Heine's Ambivalence Toward the Masses. Pp. 155–174; and Peter Uwe Hohendahl: Heine's Critical Intervention: The Intellectual as Poet. Pp. 175–196. A provocative, if to my mind not wholly convincing, argument about Heine's conversion and its consequences in this volume is Robert C. Holub: Confessions of an Apostate: Heine's Conversion and Its Psychic Displacement. Pp. 69–88. This chapter is reprinted in a (very) slightly revised version as Troubled Apostate: Heine's Conversion and Its Consequences. In: *A Companion to the Works of Heinrich Heine*. Ed. by Roger F. Cook. Rochester: Camden House 2002 (Studies in German Literature, Linguistics, and Culture). Pp. 229–250.

[5] See Hermand: 'Tribune of the People or Aristocrat of the Spirit': Heine's Ambivalence Toward the Masses. P. 157.

political program;[6] yet his recurring treatments of violence and power do point to a consistent pre-occupation with the problem, and with the question of the possibility – as well as the limits – of responding to violence and power in writing.

II

Part of the problem in addressing the subject of violence in Heine's work – or in any other context for that matter – consists in the definition of violence itself, one that varies considerably among students of the subject. The entry in the relatively recent *Routledge Encyclopedia of Philosophy* (1998) – presumably giving the standard view taken by analytical philosophy – prefers a narrow definition of violence as an act intending to do harm – such as stabbing, beating, shooting, bombing, and so forth.[7] This definition, one might note, is also close to the primary one given by Hannah Arendt in her essay *On Violence*: "Violence [. . .] , as I have said, is distinguished by its instrumental character".[8] It is a definition that raises the question of how to view the relationship between "violence", "force", or "power", – an ambiguity, which Arendt seeks to address in her essay, implied by the German term *Gewalt*. It is an ambiguity made even more complex when one seeks to account for the effects on selves and subjectivities of such phenomena as power, intimidation, and domination. Responding to Arendt's conception of violence as *action*, for instance, Jürgen Habermas offers an alternative definition, one that he detects at work in Arendt's essay, although it remains undertheorized there. It remained, *pace* Habermas, undertheorized because Arendt relied too narrowly on a theory of action deriving from Aristotelian views of praxis and of the political, and which prevent her from recognizing what Habermas calls "structural violence".[9] For Habermas,

> Structural violence is not manifest as violence; instead it blocks in an unnoticed fashion those communications in which are shaped and propagated the convictions effective for legitimation. Such a hypothesis about unnoticed yet effective barriers to communication can explain the formation of ideologies; they can make plausible how convictions are formed by which the subjects deceive themselves about themselves and their situation. Illusions that are afforded the power of common convictions are what we name ideologies. (184)

[6] Ibid. Pp. 156–157. Hohendahl emphasizes Heine's changing views of the "public" role of the writer, intervening in contemporary social and political events (176–178). Sammons, alternatively, suggests an irreconcilable conflict between Heine's "revolutionary" and "poetic" identities (16–18).
[7] C. A. J. Coady: Violence. In: *Routledge Encyclopedia of Philosophy*. Ed. by Edward Craig. New York: Routledge 1998. Vol. 10. Pp. 615–617.
[8] Hannah Arendt: *On Violence*. New York: Harcourt Brace Jovanovich 1970. P. 46.
[9] Jürgen Habermas: *Philosophical-Political Profiles*. Trans. by Frederick G. Lawrence. Pp. 178–179.

Despite his reduction of "ideology" to only one of the term's possible definitions, Habermas provides a lucid description of structural violence, one that coincides, as will be shown, with one of the views Heine articulates in *Französische Zustände* (1833). Especially important here is the idea that violence is inscribed in institutions that owe their existence to forms of violence perpetrated in another context, and that these institutions block all communications, which if transmitted would call into question the reigning convictions and the processes of institutional legitimation. They might, that is, also help subjects undeceive themselves "about themselves and their situation". In *Französische Zustände*, Heine goes beyond pointing to the role of structural violence as an underlying cause of the revolution, seeking as well to reveal in that work the kind of mechanisms by which violence and blocked or distorted communications operate.

What Habermas does not explicitly address in his discussion of structural violence is how the position one occupies in relation to a given structure or to a given communicative act further determines one's possibility of perceiving the violence that is present – by, as Habermas might say, seeing through the "ideology". Yet, precisely the problem of one's own individual social position is one that Heine will be most sensitive to. It is one, moreover, that Pierre Bourdieu seeks to address when he speaks of *symbolic violence*, a conception of violence not unrelated to the structural violence described by Habermas.

Bourdieu addresses the subject of symbolic violence in his essay *The Production and Reproduction of Legitimate Language*, suggesting, in particular, the difficulty of comprehending symbolic violence as it relates to symbolic power and domination, since its operations often remain invisible or only partially visible to those caught up in its dynamic. In response to this problem of comprehension or even recognition, Bourdieu proposes that one call into question "the usual dichotomy of freedom and constraint" by which human interaction is typically conceived and that one focus instead on the problem of social position and habitus (the set of dispositions, skills and habits, modes of conduct, bodily helix, etc., which are acquired in life and This focus becomes important since one's habitus and position determine for Bourdieu the range of choices regarding how to conduct oneself in a given

---

[10] Pierre Bourdieu: *Language and Symbolic Power*. Ed. by John B. Thompson. Trans. by Gino Raymond and Matthew Adamson. Cambridge, Massachusetts: Harvard University Press 1991. P. 51. On Bourdieu's understanding of "habitus" in relation to language, see Pp. 38–39, 81–89. See also P. Bourdieu: *Distinction: A Social Critique of the Judgement of Taste*. Trans. by Richard Nice. Cambridge, MA: Harvard University Press 1984. Pp. 169–183.

situation – for example, the adjustment of one's speech in front of "legitimate speakers". Such

> 'choices' of the habitus [. . .] are accomplished without consciousness or constraint, by virtue of the dispositions which, although they are unquestionably the product of social determinisms, are also constituted outside the spheres of consciousness and constraint. (51)

This absence of consciousness or constraint of any visible kind prompts Bourdieu to seek out and reveal the seemingly paradoxical operations of power and domination present in such situations, where many accounts would reduce (social) causes to (individual) responsibilities, so that Bourdieu concludes:

> The propensity to reduce the search for causes to a search for responsibilities makes it impossible to see that intimidation, a symbolic violence which is not aware of what it is (to the extent that it implies no act of intimidation) can only be exerted on a person predisposed (in his habitus) to feel it, whereas others will ignore it. It is already partly true to say that the cause of the timidity lies in the relation between the situation or the intimidating person (who may deny any intimidating intention) and the person intimidated, or rather, between the social conditions of production of each of them. And little by little, one has to take account thereby of the whole social structure. (*Symbolic Power* 51)

In asserting that symbolic violence "is not aware of what it is", that it masks itself, as it were, in the actual uses of language, operating "through suggestions inscribed in the most apparently insignificant things, situations and practices of everyday life", Bourdieu explains why one can only discover the presence of symbolic violence if one attends to the social positions and conditions of production of the "intimidating" and "intimidated" person. In this way, he helps elucidate a dynamic instructive for exploring the question of violence in Heine's early work. That is, by virtue of his social position and habitus, Heine seems to have been predisposed to perceive or feel the effects of symbolic violence, and, in turn, to respond to it in poetry.

III

Heine's *Buch der Lieder* (1827) – with its cycles of poems incessantly, even obsessively, reiterating in various forms and from varying angles the subject of frustrated love, whether love unrequited or physical love stifled by oppressive conventions, vapid materialism, and desiccated passions – may seem an unlikely place to begin tracing Heine's responses to violence.[11] Yet, precisely this elusive aspect of symbolic violence makes *Buch der Lieder* an ideal place to begin exploring the dynamics Bourdieu describes, particularly if one also

---

[11] S. S. Prawer: *Heine: Buch der Lieder*. London: Edward Arnold 1960. Pp. 15–19. Bernd Kortländer: *Heinrich Heine*. Stuttgart: Reclam 2003. P. 95.

takes into account the conditions – personal and social – under which Heine produced this poetry. To be sure, Heine himself opposed such historicizing gestures with regard to poetry, claiming that they would at best "deflower" the poem, or worse, disfigure it:

> Man entjungfert gleichsam das Gedicht, man zerreist den geheimnißvollen Schleyer desselben, wenn jener Einfluß der Geschichte den man nachweist wirklich vorhanden ist; man verunstaltet das Gedicht wenn man ihn fälschlich hineingegrübelt hat. Und wie wenig ist oft das äußere Gerüste unserer Geschichte mit unserer wirklichen, inneren Geschichte zusammenpassend! Bey mir wenigstens paste [sic] es nie.[12]
>
> [One deflowers the poem, so to speak, one tears off the mysterious veil of the same [poem], when that historical influence one detects is really present; one deforms the poem if one has falsely brooded it into the poem. And often how little does the external framework of our history fit together with our real inner history! In my case, at least, it has never fit.]

Not surprisingly, much Heine scholarship opposes this proscription of Heine's, although the approaches adopted toward his work vary considerably. In his still useful study of *Buch der Lieder*, dealing largely with thematic and formal questions, S. S. Prawer claimed in 1960 that while "many of the biographical facts are irrelevant to an assessment of Heine's work – others [. . .] are of vital importance, because they are reflected, directly or obliquely in his poetry, and determine its appeal" (7). Even if one might today prefer terms like "refracted" or "transformed" to Prawer's "reflected", Prawer is right to point us toward the ways in which Heine's writing responds to the conditions of his own life. In one of the better and most recent Heine biographies, Jan-Christoph Hauschild and Michael Werner conceive of the relationship between Heine's work and his life in terms of a *Trauerarbeit* for the unrequited love Heine had for his cousin Amalie:

> Amalie Heine heiratete 1821 einen ostpreußischen Gutsbesitzer und verschwand schon bald aus Heines Gesichtsfeld. Doch als *weiblicher Schatten* lebte sie, auch nach ihrem frühen Tod im Jahr 1838, unter verschiedenen Namen (*Evelina*, *Agnes*, *Bertha*, *Ottilie* und *Zuleima*) in seinen Dichtungen weiter. Die Herzblutspur der Abweisung durch die Hamburger Cousine geht durch Heines erste Lyriksammlung, die *Gedichte*, von 1822, und durch sein zweites Buch, *Tragödien, nebst einem lyrischen Intermezzo*, von 1823; von dieser Liebe künden die stark bekenntnishaften *Ideen. Das Buch Le Grand* (1827) wie noch manch anderer späterer

---

[12] Heinrich Heine: Brief an [Karl] Immermann, 10 Juni 1823. In: *Werke, Briefwechsel, Lebenszeugnisse. Säkularausgabe.* Ed. by the Nationalen Forschungs- und Gedenkstätten der klassischen deutschen Literatur in Weimar und dem Centre National de la Recherche Scientifique in Paris. Berlin-Paris: Akademie Verlag and Editions du CNRS 1970-. Vol. 20. P. 93. Except where otherwise noted, all translations are my own. Further references to this work are given parenthetically in the text with the abbreviation HSA.

Prosatext [. . .]. Es war eine Trauerarbeit, die Heine unaufhörlich beschäftigte, bis hinein in die Gedichte der Spätzeit.[13]

[In 1821, Amalie Heine married an East Prussian land owner and disappeared quite soon from Heine's field of view. Yet, as *feminine shadow* she lived on in his poetry, even after her early death in 1838, under various names (Evelina, Agnes, Bertha, Ottilie and Zuleima). The heart's blood-trace of rejection by the Hamburg cousin runs through Heine's first collection, *Die Gedichte* (*Poems*), of 1822, and through his second book, *Tragödien, nebst einem lyrischen Intermezzo* (*Tragedies, Beside a Lyrical Intermezzo*), from 1823; the strongly confessional *Ideen: Das Buch Le Grand* (*Ideas: The Book Le Grand*, 1827) bears witness to this love as does yet many another later prose text [. . .]. It was a *Trauerarbeit* (work of mourning) that occupied Heine unremittingly, into the poetry of his late period.]

In presenting Heine's poetry as "Trauerarbeit", Hausschild and Werner suggest that a wound, a sense of violation, underlies much of Heine's poetry, and it is this wound that points further to the presence of symbolic violence. That violence, in turn, comes to light only when one explores the conditions of Heine's writing. Such an exploration seeks not, as Heine would fear, to explain his poetry by reference to his "inner life" or, alternatively, to explain his "inner life" by reference to his poetry. Rather, such an exploration enables us to see in the more private and intimate sphere of personal correspondence, how in reflecting on the events and conditions of his life, Heine would, wittingly or not, point to the symbolic violence embedded within them. That is, Heine believed himself to be telling a story of unrequited love – but by revealing as well his own position and the position of his love object, he also discloses the relations that make such symbolic violence possible. His letters allow us, in turn, to relate the reflections they contain to signs of those same events and conditions in the poetry Heine produced for public consumption. A more thorough study of *Buch der Lieder* would, indeed, trace the presence and effects of symbolic violence in various poems. This essay, more modestly, seeks only to show how one might proceed toward such a project. For this reason and because of constraints of space, this essay will focus primarily on one poem in *Buch der Lieder*, poem 62, *Du hast Diamanten und Perlen* (*You've everything, pearls and diamonds*) in the cycle *Die Heimkehr* (*The Homecoming*).

Occurring three fourths of the way into the third cycle of poems in *Buch der Lieder*, *Die Heimkehr* 62 stands out for how it condenses within three strophes some of the central motifs of that and the preceding cycle (*Lyrisches Intermezzo*):

Du hast Diamanten und Perlen,
Hast alles, was Menschenbegehr,
Und hast die schönsten Augen –
Mein Liebchen, was willst du mehr?

---

[13] Jan-Christoph Hauschild and Michael Werner: *"Der Zweck des Lebens ist das Leben selbst": Heinrich Heine – Eine Biographie*. Köln: Kiepenheuer & Witsch 1997. P. 47.

Auf deine schönen Augen
Hab ich ein ganzes Heer
Von ewigen Liedern gedichtet –
Mein Liebchen, was willst du mehr?

Mit deinen schönen Augen
Hast du mich gequält so sehr,
Und hast mich zu Grunde gerichtet –
Mein Liebchen, was willst du mehr?
(Briegleb 1:137)

[You have diamonds and pearls,
Have all that humans desire
And have the most beautiful eyes,—
My love, what more could you want?

To your beautiful eyes,
I composed a whole army
Of immortal poems—
My love, what more could you want?

With your beautiful eyes,
Have you tortured me so
And ruined my life forever—
My love, what more could you want?][14]

The opposing terms established by the poem in the first two strophes – the desired woman whose beautiful eyes together with the jewels attesting to her wealth and comfort, on the one hand, and the desiring poet who composes an entire "army" of "eternal songs" to win her over, on the other – underscore the difference in power between them, a difference that places added pressure on the poetic performance itself. As the third strophe reveals, the poetry remains without effect, while the same beautiful eyes that first attracted him become a source, first, of his torment, then of his downfall. The repetition of the trope of the "beautiful eyes" and of the verse, "Mein Liebchen, was willst du mehr?" ["My love, what more do you want?"] at the end of each strophe transforms the ostensible lovesong by the end into a bitterly ironic commentary on the desired woman and the world in which she lives. The poetic voice also puts on display the effects of a symbolic violence that it remains unable to name directly, at least not if it wants to maintain the lyrical mask, for in the act of demonstrating its control of figural language it re-asserts, as it were, the *sense* of self whose downfall the poem recounts. By virtue of this mastery of

---

[14] For a translation of this poem that seeks to convey more thoroughly Heine's meter and rhyme scheme, see Hal Draper's translation (as *You've everything, pearls and diamonds*) in: Heinrich Heine. *The Complete Poems*. Trans. by Hal Draper. Boston: Suhrkamp/Insel, 1982. P. 101. Further references given in text and abbreviated as "Draper".

language, the poetic voice seeks to enhance the poet's position within what Bourdieu has called the "game of culture".[15] (At a later date, Heine would suggest his awareness of that "game" when he called baptism the "Entre Billet [sic] zur europäischen Kultur", although he actually seems to have undergone baptism because of the legal proscriptions on the employment of Jews as civil servants in the 1820s).[16] The problem is that beyond language, the poet must also seek recognition from the public – a public, moreover, whose values and conventions Heine despises, all the more no doubt because of his dependence upon it.[17] The pursuit of the potential lover by composing an "army" of poems to her reproduces this social problem in the personal sphere, even as the poem also seeks to convey the personal wound inflicted by the rejection. That the status of his poetry and hence of the poet *qua* poet depend on recognition by the desired and socially elevated woman is, however, only obliquely suggested in the poem itself. While his writing of poems seems to be ineffective, it is with her "eyes" that he tells the woman (and us): "[Du] hast mich zu Grunde gerichtet" ["You've ruined my life forever", or lit: "driven me into the ground"].

Whereas the poem presents in economically compressed form the events of a poet's rejection, the nearly nineteen-year-old Heine presents rather differently a similar event in a letter to his friend Christian Sethe. That letter stands out for the ways in which it differs from the poem – or rather, for how it addresses issues that the poem as public expression in part reveals and in part conceals. The letter begins: "Sie liebt mich nicht!" ["She doesn't love me!"]. It then proceeds to describe the power Heine finds Amalie to be exerting over him. Heine recognizes in Amalie's ["Molly's"] glances a "rätselhafte[s] Etwas" ["a puzzling something"] which first mysteriously ("auf einer unbegriefliche Art" [sic] ["in an incomprehensible way"]) repels him only then to draw him back in by force ("gewaltsam") (HSA 20:19). Her rejection produces a sense of confusion and wounding, but as his self-satire suggests, his own desire and misreading of signs, rather than any form of violence or abuse, have placed him in the position to experience her rejection in this way:

> Denn obgleich ich die unläugbarsten, unumstößlichsten Beweise habe: daß ich nichts weniger als von ihr geliebt werde – Beweise die sogar Rector Schallmeyer für grundlogisch erkennen, u kein Bedenken tragen würd seinem eignen System obenan zu stellen, – so will doch das arme liebende Herz noch immer nicht sein concedo geben, und sagt immer: was geht mich deine Logic an, ich habe meine eigne Logic. – (HSA 20:19–20)
> [For, although I have the most undeniable, irrefutable proofs: that I am nothing less than loved by her – proofs that even Rector Schallmeyer [would] recognize as

---

[15] Bourdieu: *Distinction*. P. 12.
[16] Hauschild and Werner: *"Der Zweck des Lebens ist das Leben selbst": Heinrich Heine—Eine Biographie*. P. 102.
[17] Kortländer: *Heinrich Heine*. Pp. 11, 90. Prawer: *Heine: Buch der Lieder*. P. 18.

fundamentally logical, & would without hesitation place atop his own system, – nonetheless, that poor loving heart still does not want to concede, and keeps saying: what do I care about your logic; I have my own logic.]

The sense of symbolic violence enters into the rejection only later in the account when, after wondering whether his friend Christian will now also reject him, Heine writes: "Das ist auch eine herzkränkende Sache, daß sie meine schöne Lieder, die *ich* nur für Sie gedichtet habe so bitter und schnöde gedemüthigt und mir überhaupt in dieser Hinsicht sehr häßlich mitgespielt hat" ["That is also a heart-wounding matter – that she so bitterly and contemptuously humiliated my beautiful poems, which I composed only for her, and in general treated me very nastily in this regard"] (HSA 20:21). The language by which Heine depicts this gesture suggests a gratuitously bitter and contemptuous act of humiliation and abuse ("mir überhaupt [. . .] sehr häßlich mitgespielt" ["in general treated me very nastily"]), designed, as it were, to put the aspiring poet "in his place". His depiction of the world Amalie inhabits, the home of his wealthy Uncle Salomon,[18] where "es sehr geziert und geschwänzelt zu[geht]" ["matters proceed with much affect and tail-wagging"] suggests, moreover, that this gesture remains concealed behind the formal manners and stifling cordiality that govern social interaction there – and in contrast to which "der freye unbefangene Sänger [. . .] sehr oft gegen die Etikette [sündigt]" ["the free [and] uninhibited singer [. . .] often sins against the rules of etiquette"] (HSA 20:22). Heine's depiction thus transforms the image of the rejection from something commonplace, if painful, into something operating on a level best described as symbolic violence – an "intimidation not aware of what it is (to the extent that it implies no act of intimidation)", which "can only be exerted on a person predisposed (in his habitus) to feel it, whereas others will ignore it", and which is structured by the "relation between the situation or the intimidating person (who may deny any intimidating intention) and the person intimidated" (Bourdieu, *Symbolic Power* 51)

Heine further reinforces the contrast between his own sense of position when he describes the society in which the act of humiliation (or intimidation) of the poet-suitor takes place as one peopled by "Diplomatisches Federvieh, Millionäre, hochweise Senatoren etc. etc." ["diplomatic quill-cattle, millionaires, senators most wise, etc. etc."] (HSA 20:22). He points additionally to the role that economics and social status play in that society, especially in its rituals of courtship and erotics, while also indicating how little he himself belongs there. "Der Neffe vom großen (???) Heine ist zwar überall gern

---

[18] The same uncle would later become a patron of sorts to Heine, providing him with a monthly stipend, but with whom Heine would for much of his adult life maintain a difficult relationship riddled with sometimes intense conflict, mutual explosions and recriminations, followed by emotional reconciliations.

gesehen und empfangen; schöne Mädchen schielen nach ihm hin, und die Busentücher steigen höher, die Mütter kalkulieren, aber – aber – bleib allein; Niemand bleibt mir übrig als ich selbst" ["The nephew of the great (???) Heine is, it is true, gladly seen and received everywhere; pretty girls glance sideways at him, and the corset covers climb higher, the mothers make their calculations, but – but – [I] remain alone; no one is left to me but myself"] (HSA 20:22).

When he turns to the subject of poetry, Heine draws a distinction between the private sphere of writing, a sphere that operates according to its own rules (or "muse") and the public sphere in which, if published, one's writing must contend with the social conditions of its production and reception. Thus, despite Amalie's rejection, Heine claims: "die Muse ist mir demohngeachtet jetzt noch weit lieber als je. Sie ist mir eine getreue tröstende Freundinn [*sic*] geworden" ["The muse is notwithstanding now far more dear to me than ever. She has become for me a loyal, consoling friend"] (HSA 20:21). He thus signals the role poetry plays for him when liberated from social constraints. Alternatively, when contemplating a possible book publication, Heine fears that the social field and his position within it, not the poetry itself, will determine its reception and, beyond that, his own status in the world. Ruled by the spirit of a "Schacherstadt" ["haggling city"], Hamburg lacks even "das mindeste Gefühl für Poesie" ["the least feeling for poetry"], so that beyond failing to bring recognition, publishing his "Minnelieder" ["poems of courtly love"] could even damage his reputation and hence his prospects in the world of business (HSA 20:21). Being Jewish only exacerbates the problem, placing him in a vulnerable position, especially given "die schwüle Spannung" ["the heavy tension"] between Jews and Christians in the city. Thus, Heine asks whether "die christliche Liebe die Liebeslieder eines Juden nicht ungehuldigt lassen wird" ["Christian love will not leave the lovesongs of a Jew unfavored"] (HSA 20:22). In other words, Heine explores at length in this letter how on a micrological level – in the "things, situations and practices of everyday life" (Bourdieu, *Symbolic Power* 51) – he remains subject to a power, at times even to a (symbolic) violence, that inflicts itself on his person.

Die Heimkehr 62 is, to be sure, only one of the various attempts in *Buch der Lieder* to combine social critique with the motif of unrequited or stifled love. One thinks, for instance, of the well-known *Lyrisches Intermezzo* 50, *Sie saßen und tranken am Teetisch* [*They sat and drank at the teatable*]. That poem depicts in its first three strophes a high society tea party – populated by a wizened old councilor preaching platonic love, and his frustrated wife, a vulgar canon who asserts that love must not be "rough", and a melancholy countess who, stifled by formal social convention, declares: "Die Liebe ist eine Passion! / Und präsentieret gütig / Die Tasse dem Herren Baron" ["Love is a wild passion! And graciously presents a cup to the baron"] (B 1:95). It concludes with the speaker of the poem addressing an anonymous lover in a strophe whose irony leaves indeterminate the speaker's actual attitude toward her – it leaves open, that is, the question whether she would serve to "show up" this sexually repressed and oppressive society or would herself only contribute to it:

> Am Tische war noch ein Plätzchen;
> Mein Liebchen, da hast du gefehlt.
> Du hättest so hübsch, mein Schätzchen,
> Von deiner Liebe erzählt. (B 1:96)
> [There remained one more place at the table;
> Only you were missing, my dear.
> You, my treasure, would so charmingly
> Have told of your love.]

One thinks as well of the prologue to the brief cycle of poems *Aus der Harzreise*, drawn from the partly fictionalized travel narrative about his journey through Germany's Harz region:

> Schwarze Röcke, seidne Strümpfe,
> Weiße, höfliche Manschetten,
> Sanfte Reden, Embrassieren –
> Ach, wenn sie nur Herzen hätten!
>
> Herzen in der Brust, und Liebe,
> Warme Liebe in dem Herzen –
> Ach, mich tötet ihr Gesinge
> Von erlognen Liebesschmerzen. (B 1:168)
>
> [Black frock coats and silken stockings,
> Frilled with all the tailor's arts,
> Smooth-tongued talk and suave embraces—
> Oh, if only they had hearts!
>
> Hearts that beat within their bosoms,
> In those hearts a love that glows—
> Oh, their singsong tunes will kill me
> With those bogus lovesick woes.]
> (Draper 123)

Beyond showing Heine's disillusionment with a society ruled by modes of conduct and forms he found oppressive, repressive and devoid of integrity, the tone and imagery of these poems suggests a symbolic violence, an intimidation and principle of exclusion, directed against any *subjectivity* that might actually transgress those forms. To be sure, "der freye unbefangene Sänger" may take pleasure in violating the rules of etiquette, but he makes that point in a letter that both opens and closes with laments for "Molly", that is, a letter revolving around the devastating wound he experienced when not only rejected as suitor, but also mocked as poet by a woman he believed himself to be in love with and who was positioned securely within that high society. Thus, when in *Die Heimkehr* 62, Heine abstracts from a personal "event" conveyed in the youthful letter, condensing the account of rejection into the lapidary images of pearl-and-diamond-bedecked woman and dejected poet-suitor, his act of abstraction and condensation does more than produce a biting satire of this world. It also suggests the difficulty of directly addressing in poetic form – and perhaps in any socially "respectable" form – the effects of a symbolic violence whose own nature it is to conceal itself behind the established social forms and etiquette.

IV

If *Die Heimkehr* 62 explores symbolic violence embedded within social structures, but operating on a personal level, Heine's later excursion into journalism in *Französische Zustände* (1833) turns outward, focusing on France immediately following the 1830 Revolution, and treating violence in relation to structures social and political. Although belonging to a different genre of writing and focused on a different dimension of violence, *Französische Zustände*, like the poems discussed above, does more than merely seek to address the presence of violence. It also reflects on the ways in which written works are transmitted under conditions shaped by violence and struggles for power.

This aspect of *Französische Zustände* becomes apparent if one considers the work's publication history. Like other progressive German intellectuals, Heine moved to Paris in the wake of the revolution of July 1830. Arriving in May 1831, he began in January 1832 to publish a series of long articles, followed later in the year by brief reports, for the Augsburg *Allgemeine Zeitung*. Reworking these articles and reports, Heine submitted the collection as a single volume to his publisher Julius Campe in November 1832. To this volume, Heine added a preface in which he attacked censorious measures in Germany. When the censors, not surprisingly, intervened to drastically cut down this preface, Heine, dismayed, launched a lengthy struggle with both his publisher and the censors themselves. In other words, the sense of censorship as violence done to communication accompanies not only the writing, but also the production and transmission of the work.

In the work itself, Heine begins by presenting the major figures of the revolution while continuing to report on the course of events, but he also digresses at times to comment, for instance, on such figures as Périer and Lafayette, the Republicans, the citizen-king Louis Philippe, and events related to these figures. The most important digression occurs in the sixth article where, after initially voicing his intention to address certain questions about the revolution, Heine interrupts the flow of his narrative to describe the sudden outbreak of cholera. Occurring as he writes, the cholera outbreak has begun to devastate the population of Paris, intruding as well into the political events of the day (B 3:168–169).

In digressing onto the subject of cholera, Heine underscores his effort to mediate between Germany and France, conveying to his German audience an image of French suffering in the face of natural disaster. At the same time, by digressing onto the social consequences of the cholera epidemic, Heine also points to how such disasters afflict people variously, depending on their social position, while further pointing to the – sometimes violent – dynamics that inflect the responses to those natural disasters. Yet, apart from its treatment of the cholera epidemic, the sixth article plays a central role in *Französische Zustände* for an altogether different reason. It is here, namely, that Heine begins to reflect critically on his own project – and hence to explain how he conceptualizes the relationship of his own work to the revolution and to historical understanding, more generally. Thus, as he defines it, the dual task of his own reportage consists in determining the "main idea" [*Hauptbegriff*] of the revolution and, perhaps more conventionally, in showing how this present idea has arisen out of the past. Neither of these subjects is as straightforward as it appears, not because Heine views such things as wholly unknowable, but because power and violence invariably inflect the kind of knowledge one produces about them. Further, these two concerns in his works – the revolution and the relationship of past to present – each relate to one another, and in turn, refer back to the question of violence. When, for instance, Heine turns to explicating this "main idea" of the revolution, he locates its source in a conflict inherent in the extant social and cultural conditions, while suggesting that revolution arises in response to a structural violence inhering in state institutions:

> Wenn die Geistesbildung und die daraus entstandenen Sitten und Bedürfnisse eines Volks nicht mehr im Einklange sind mit den alten Staatsinstitutionen, so tritt es mit diesen in einen Notkampf, der die Umgestaltung derselben zur Folge hat und eine Revolution genannt wird. (B 3:166)
> [When the spiritual development of a people, and the mores and needs that arise out of it, are no longer in harmony with the old institutions of state, then it [the people] enters into a struggle for survival with these [institutions], which has as a result their transformation and is called a revolution.]

The terms by which Heine presents this "main idea", like the expression itself, derive ultimately from Hegel, as does the suggestion that the "idea" of the revolution embeds itself in specific historical formations: at the same time, his quietly descriptive language notwithstanding, Heine's account also amounts to a rationale for revolution, whatever ambivalence he may express elsewhere. The image of disharmony and struggle for survival between state and people, along with the contrasting values attaching to each – the people undergoing "Geistesbildung" versus the rigidity of outmoded institutions of state – further suggests, without claiming outright, how the state seeks to accumulate and preserve power in those institutions. It also suggests how, in Habermas's terms, the state blocks those communications that would lead to its own transformation. In this sense, the state in Heine's account ultimately bears responsibility for the outbreak of violence (as action).

This analysis of the revolution's "main idea" is central to Heine's report from Paris; yet, he begins this account by addressing the problem of comprehending historical causality and the meaning of events in the first place. Thus, while his second task in *Französische Zustände* coincides with his desire to unlock the riddles of the day, Heine pauses to emphasize that, in seeking to fulfill that task, the last place one can turn is to the social sector that claims to represent "society", namely, "die Gesellschaft der Gewalthaber" ["the society of the holders of power"], as Heine calls it – or what he elsewhere refers as salon society (B 3:164). The purpose of this assertion could easily be missed for it seeks less to reveal something that is *wholly* unknown than to bring to the surface a kind of knowledge lurking below and largely unacknowledged or actively suppressed by those who dominate public discourse. In naming as problem the unreliability of these "holders of power", Heine seeks to make rifts in that discourse and to provoke debate. In one and the same gesture, Heine identifies and resists the attempts to block communication, which, as noted, also affected the publication of *Französische Zustände* itself.[19] Beyond merely providing an alternative view of things, Heine proceeds in this way to "thumb his nose", so to speak, at those forces that both seek to dominate society and to deny the fact of this domination, to prevent communication about it.

With this open assertion of that which had remained cloaked in the elliptical and ironic tropes of *Buch der Lieder*, Heine invests the critique of power in *Französische Zustände* with a clarity and visibility that was absent from the earlier lyrical work, but he does so at a cost: rather than representing from the "inside", as it were, the perspective of those subjected to the operations of undisclosed forms of power – and thus showing how one might articulate those operations even when their presence is denied – Heine's overt focus on social institutions now describes such operations from without (B 3:164). Whereas *Französische Zustände* seeks directly to inform – and provoke – its readers, *Die Heimkehr* 62 has greater potential to seduce its readers to its

---

[19] Compare Habermas's comments, cited above, on the ways in which "structural violence is not manifest as violence", but instead "blocks in an unnoticed fashion those communications in which are shaped and propagated the convictions effective for legitimation" (184).

perspective – an attempt at seduction that, in turn, risks going altogether unnoticed. This is all the more so since *Die Heimkehr* 62 seeks recognition as poetry, and hence must make its appeal in accord with the aforementioned game of culture – a game not predisposed to acknowledge the undercurrents of power the poem points to (since that would call into question the unspoken "rules" of the game).

At the same time, even if it is not able to model the dynamics of symbolic power from the perspective of those subject to it, *Französische Zustände* does at various times point in the direction of that other perspective when, for instance, Heine claims in lapidary terms: "Die Salons lügen, die Gräber sind wahr" ["The salons tell lies, the graves are true" or "hold the truth"] (B 3:164). Precisely this rejection of the "lies" propagated by *die Gewalthaber* and this desire to explore the truth of the "graves", to uncover, that is, the bodies that have been violated but also literally buried from sight, shows how subjects can become deceived "about themselves and their situation". It also suggests how for Heine determining the main idea of the revolution – the clash of state institutions with the evolving needs of the people – is directly related to the uncovering of this perspective on historical events which is "buried" out of plain sight. It is that work of historical and social archaeology that points to the violence embedded in the institutions themselves.

Yet, Heine takes the problem one step further. When attempting to explain the value of performing this kind of historical-archaeological work, Heine now claims:

> Es ist dieses ein doppelt nützliches Geschäft, da indem man die Gegenwart durch die Vergangenheit zu erklären sucht, zu gleicher Zeit offenbar wird, wie diese, die Vergangenheit, erst durch jene, die Gegenwart, ihr eigentlichstes Verständnis findet, und jeder neue Tag ein neues Licht auf sie wirft, wovon unsere bisherigen Handbuchschreiber keine Ahnung hatten. (B 3:167)
>
> [This business [of inquiry into the causes of the revolution] is doubly useful, since by seeking to explain the present through the past, it becomes clear at the same time, how the latter – the past – only finds its most actual comprehension through the former, the present, and every new day casts a new light on it, [something] about which our writers of lexica up to now have had no idea.]

This thought – that we invariably revise our view of the past in light of the present inverts the earlier view Heine himself had adopted – that the riddles of the present can be explained by uncovering the hidden past. This inversion, moreover, inflects in new ways Heine's treatment of both the revolution and violence in *Französische Zustände*. It first of all rejects any notion of teleology – or at least any notion that any future "goal" in history is humanly comprehensible – a notion found in certain kinds of historicism on both the right and left, and, more generally, in Hegel's philosophy. At the same time, it inflects in a new way Heine's discussions of revolution. Not that Heine will cease striving to unmask the violence embedded in the state's institutions. Nor will he cease to defy and openly criticize the political censors – especially in Germany – or cease, alternatively, to show sympathy, if not uncritically, for the revolutionaries. He will, however, offer a perspective on revolution that underscores the need for one to remain constantly vigilant with regard to one's social and historical position, to reflect on how one's own actions themselves alter not only the course of events in the present, but also the interpretation of the past. In other words, the conclusions one draws from the past – and which legitimize revolutionary action – depend upon the actions one takes in the present. While this point may seem a mere re-hashing of debates about "aims" and "means", it also calls into question the view that one can discover the "iron laws" of history, as Marx will later claim, even as Heine sympathizes with the Marxian ideal of ending exploitation. For Heine, long before Nietzsche and the advent of twentieth-century thought, all historical accounts ultimately achieve only partial knowledge, in both senses of the word – but one can nonetheless expose acts of manipulation, conscious or unconscious, and the interests they serve.

Thus, Heine takes the aristocracy to task for its turn to religion and claim to have abandoned its past decadence, viewing this act as an attempt by that class (or estate) to salvage the power structurally embedded in its antiquated institutions (B 3:206). Heine then re-directs his critique when he goes on to discuss the revolution of 1789:

> Ich liebe die Erinnerung der früheren Revolutionskämpfe und der Helden, die sie gekämpft, ich verehre diese ebenso hoch, wie es nur immer die Jugend Frankreichs vermag, ja, ich habe noch vor den Juliustagen [of the Revolution of 1830] den Robespierre und den Saktum Justum und den großen Berg bewundert – aber ich möchte dennoch nicht unter dem Regimente solcher Erhabenen leben, ich würde es nicht aushalten können, alle Tage guillotiniert [*sic*] zu werden, und niemand hat es aushalten können, und die französische Republik konnte nur siegen und siegend verbluten. (B 3:207)
>
> [I love the memory of the earlier revolutionary battles and of the heroes who fought them, I adore these [heroes] as much as the youth of France ever could; indeed, even before the July days [of the Revolution of 1830], I admired Robespierre and the *sactum justum* and the great mountain – but I would nonetheless not want to live under the regime of such exalted ones; I would not be able to bear it to be guillotined every day, and no one was able to bear it, and the French Republic could only be victorious and victoriously bleed itself to death.]

Even as he "loves" to recall the early struggles and heroes of the French Revolution, Heine cannot forget that when the means deployed by revolutionaries turn violent, that violence corrupts the ends in whose name they deploy it.

This problem of violence is one directly related to the uncertainty of historical knowledge – something Heine shows when in the sixth article, he reports on an event related to the cholera epidemic.

The event begins with a rumor that there is no cholera epidemic but rather that a conspiracy of killers has dispersed poison in the population. The police, knowing the rumors to be false but wanting to appear in control of the situation, issue reassurances that they are in pursuit of the killers (B 3:172). That no less an authority than the police confirm the rumor, triggers a panic in large parts of the population. The panic, in turn, results in attacks on innocent bystanders, some of whom are killed in what amount to vigilante murders. It results further in what amounts to the subversion of the idea that police authority, believing in its own "allgemeine Wissenschaft" ["general science"] knows how to use this knowledge to intervene constructively in adverse social conditions, and indeed puts into question, more generally, how well one can predict the effects of knowledge disseminated by authority (B 3:172–173).

This problem of violence and uncertainty helps explain Heine's complex stance toward the revolution, revealed perhaps nowhere more than in the Ninth article – especially when viewed in connection with his claims elsewhere. In that article, Heine recounts the debates between those who support the recently installed "Bürgerkönig" Louis Philippe, because, though a monarch, he has sympathy with the Revolution of 1789 and can bring about peace, and the convinced republicans who distrust all monarchs under any conditions. They believe themselves engaged in a "blood feud" (*Blutfeindschaft*) with the entire aristocracy of Europe. This feud, they believe, must end with the destruction of either one or the other (B 3:208). Rather than taking a stance in this debate at the outset, Heine begins by citing the hopes invested by Italian, Polish, and German republicans in the French revolutionary movement. He concludes the article with a somber image of survivors from the uprising of 5 June 1832, and the ensuing street battle at the Rue Saint-Martin. Describing the grim, serious faces of the survivors lined up at the morgue to identify the dead, Heine eventually focuses on a young woman who faints upon recognizing her dead lover, noting that she worked at a cleaning shop in his neighborhood among "acht junge[n] Damen [. . .], welche sämtliche Republikanerinnen sind" ["eight young ladies [. . .] who are all republicans"]. He concludes: "Ihre Liebhaber sind lauter junge Republikaner. Ich bin in diesem Hause immer der einzige Royalist" ["Their lovers are thoroughly young republicans. In this house, I am always the only royalist"] (B 3:221).

Heine introduces this claim to "royalist" affiliations at a moment calculated to surprise. Its introduction is further complicated by the fact that the passage reveals how Heine's views of violence and revolution are, on the one hand, bound up with the context of the events about which he writes, and, on the other, with the question of subject position, as suggested earlier by the obstacles that rise up against attempts at knowledge and understanding of the present. Here and elsewhere, Heine expresses sympathy for progressive causes and opposition to oppressive institutions of state; yet, he also held a (no doubt problematic) belief in the possibility of a "constitutional monarchy", which, though he would later revise this view, found expression in 1832 in the figure of Louis Philippe.

Beyond that, Heine cannot escape reservations about the republicans for their failure to move beyond the legacy of Robespierre, the reign of terror, and what he viewed as their cult of death.[20] He nonetheless retains his harshest language, indeed his unmitigated outrage, for the aristocracy, who bring nothing but divisiveness, antagonism, exploitation and, ultimately, "hatred and war" ["Haß und Krieg"] to the peoples of Europe.

> Wenn wir es dahin bringen, daß die große Menge die Gegewart versteht, so lassen die Völker sich nicht mehr von den Lohnschreibern der Aristokratie zu Haß und Krieg verhetzen, das große Völkerbündnis, die Heilige Allianz der Nationen, kommt zu Stande, wir brauchen aus wechselseitigem Mißtrauen keine stehenden Heere von vielen hundertausend Mördern mehr zu füttern, wir benutzen zum Pflug ihre Schwerter und Rosse, und wir erlangen Friede und Wohlstand und Freiheit. Dieser Wirksamkeit bleibt mein Leben gewidmet; es ist mein Amt. (B 3:91–92).
>
> [If we come to the point where the great majority understands the present, then the peoples will no longer let themselves be incited to hatred and war by the scribblers in the pay of the aristocracy, [and] the great people's alliance, the Holy Alliance of the Nations, will come into being[;] we will no longer need to feed out of mutual mistrust any standing armies of many hundreds of thousand of murderers[;] we will use as plowshares their swords and horses, and we will achieve peace and wealth and freedom. This activity is what my life remains committed to; it is my life's task.]

In view of the recurring violence, embedded in the institutions and practices of the aristocracy, and the failure of Republican revolutionaries to overcome it, Heine seeks – at least in his politically critical and journalistic writing – to carry out the task, however troubled, by uncovering the various forms and mechanisms that violence can assume.

V

In the German-speaking world, the political conflicts of the 1960s prompted a re-discovery of and renewed engagement with Heine's work, especially with the satirical, politically critical Heine. Beyond Germany's borders, English and American critics sought in the same period to recover a poet whose modernity and irony made him into a key figure in the transition from Romanticism to modernity, one who would address in his writings the problem of "world" explored by later nineteenth-century German realists, only to expose before their time the fallacy of the Realists' ostensibly impartial representations

---

[20] Ortwin Lämke: *Heines Begriff der Geschichte: Der Journalist Heinrich Heine und die Julimonarchie*. Heine-Studien. Stuttgart: Metzler 1997. P. 56.

of that world – while also rejecting the Romantics' withdrawal from it. In the meantime, on the basis of four decades of textual-critical, archival, and historical scholarship, critics can now work out with nuanced precision the various ways in which Heine referred to such subjects as "Volk" and "Nation", Romanticism, the restoration and revolution, Republicans, aristocrats, and the citizen-king Louis Philippe, among other things. At the same time, the sheer abundance of the research has led one critic to suggest that Heine scholarship has begun to exhaust itself,[21] something further suggested by the discontinuing of the series *Heine-Studien* published under the auspices of the Heinrich-Heine-Institut in Düsseldorf.

Yet, the twenty-first century presents its own set of questions, which may, in turn, point one way toward further inquiry into Heine's writing. In an essay composed after the events of September 11th, Martin Jay elaborates on what he calls the "agonies of the left", calling into question a tendency, found in some circles, to identify with or at least defend all acts of opposition to American neo-imperialism or global capitalism: "If there is a cardinal lesson for the left after the fall of communism, it is that compromising ideals in the service of dialectical realism is likely to turn disastrous, some hands being just too dirty to escape from the muck in which they are immersed".[22] Although the comparison with Heine is not completely adequate – French Republicanism was, for one thing, avowedly secular – Jay's suggestion is relevant here. Heine's awareness of the dynamics of violence, the various forms it could take, prefigures the analyses by later cultural or social critics and philosophers. He sought in his own time to map and respond to such violence, to provoke and, as an earlier generation might have said, to raise consciousness, even at the risk sometimes to his own reputation and status as a writer.

---

[21] Jeffrey L. Sammons: The Exhaustion of Current Heine Studies: Some Observations, Partly Speculative. In: *The Jewish Reception of Heinrich Heine*. Ed by Mark H. Gelber. Tübingen: Niemeyer 1992. Pp. 5–19. Reprinted in: Jeffrey L. Sammons: *Heinrich Heine: Alternative Perspectives 1985–2005*. Würzburg: Königshausen & Neumann 2006. Pp. 51–64.

[22] Martin Jay: Fearful Symmetries: 9/11 and the Agonies of the Left. In: *Refractions of Violence*. New York and London: Routledge 2003. P. 186.

II. Imagining the Primitive; the Return of the Repressed

Laurie Johnson

The Curse of Enthusiasm: *William Lovell* and Modern Violence

The essay reads Ludwig Tieck's novel William Lovell *(1795–1796) against the background of eighteenth-century faculty psychology in order to make a case for the existence of "male hysteria" around 1800. This is a broad personality dilemma with specific behavioral manifestations, and with parallels to contemporary conditions such as "melancholy" or "enthusiasm", with its subset of "hysteria". The combination of William Lovell's hysterical psychophysical "type" and his perceived victimization at the hands of others – lovers, friends, brothers, fathers, and secret societies – proves deadly and puts a very modern form of violence on display. At the same time, this specifically male hysteria, which is characterized by the sufferer's experience of uncanny repetitions of previously repressed, frightening phenomena, provides a model for living with and through modern violence. It also illuminates the symptoms endured by individuals in a culture collectively victimized, as it were, by modernity as a grand conspiracy.*

The latest edition of the standard diagnostic manual for psychiatrists, the *DSM-IV* (published initially in 1994), states that depression is characterized by lack of feeling as well as of affect.[1] Abnormal behaviors strongly associated with depression, such as cutting one's own flesh, stem from a sense of deadness, or what might be called a lack of enthusiasm; the sufferer desires to feel more alive, if only briefly and violently. Against the background of today's psychiatry, then, it may seem surprising to read that the protagonist of Jean Paul's sprawling novel *Titan* (1800–1803), Albano, cuts himself when he feels especially excited – in fact, too full of life, of feeling, and of love.

In a "Fieber der jungen Gesundheit" ["fever of youthful health"] and overwhelmed simultaneously by the desire to die together with his sick father, and by recurring memories of his dead mother, Albano "helps himself" by making himself bleed.[2] This self-inflicted damage, committed when he feels that "die Lunge und das Herz von Blute schwer und voll [sind]" ["the lungs and heart are heavy and full of blood"] (33), progresses over time from habitual small cuts to

---

[1] *Diagnostic and Statistical Manual of Mental Disorders, Fourth Edition (DSM-IV)*. Washington, D.C.: American Psychiatric Association 1994. Pp. 320–327, 345–349, 383–384.
[2] Jean Paul: *Titan*. Frankfurt am Main: Insel Taschenbuch 1983. P. 33. Translations are mine unless otherwise noted.

a climactic "schöne Armwunde" ["beautiful arm wound"] that bleeds enough to make Albano faint and experience mild hallucinations. Swooning, Albano

> dachte an die verschwundne Mutter, deren Liebe nun ewig unvergolten blieb – ach er hätte dieses Blut gern für sie vergossen – ; und nun quoll heißer als je in seiner Brust die Liebe für den kränklichen Vater auf: o komme bald, sagte sein Herz, ich will dich so unaussprechlich lieben, du lieber Vater! (36)
> [thought of the vanished mother, whose love now remains forever unreturned – oh, he would gladly have shed this blood for her – ; and now love for his ill father sprung up hotter than ever in his breast: O come soon, said his heart, I want to love you unspeakably, beloved father!]

In this uncanny twilight state occasioned by feeling too much (his life has become "zu warm und zu treibend" ["too warm and too active"] (35)), Albano thinks about his own past, his own parents – but simultaneously about the spirit of antiquity and about the past of Western culture. As he searches his own memory at the entrance to a grotto "voll Inschriften der vorigen Zeit" ["full of inscriptions of the past"], he feels that that cultural past will become his future ["Da wurde in Albano die fremde Vergangenheit zur eigenen Zukunft" (35)]. These perigrinations through the mythic and individual past, combined with youth and three glasses of wine, contribute to Albano's repetitive bloodletting.

When Jean Paul's characterizes self-cutting not just as a reaction to memory, but also as a prod for a productive acknowledgment of the ongoing presence of the past in Albano's adult life, this characterization is related indirectly to the belief that bleeding is basically healthy. This attitude dates back to Galen's second-century codification of earlier biomedicine, and was still persistent around 1800. Blood signifies youth and health, and its periodic expulsion is the therapeutic release of excess fluid.[3] But Albano's "self-help" also reflects the incursion of a mentalistic view of disease into the world of traditional biological medicine. While such a view has been at least an intermittent factor in medical writings since antiquity, it is modern psychology, as it develops after 1700, that will render the ancient understanding of bleeding and of the release of bodily fluids as a response to disordered states of mind

---

[3] Roy Porter: *Flesh in the Age of Reason*. New York-London: W.W. Norton 2003. Pp. 45–46. Werner Leibbrand and Annemarie Wettley summarize the significance of blood and blood-letting in ancient mythology: referring specifically to the *Iliad*, they note: "Blut bedeutet gewiß Leben, Erinnerung, Bewußtsein, aber vergossenes Blut besitzt eine eigene Dämonie. Sie treibt den Mörder außer Landes [. . .]. Das vergossene Blut verbindet sich mit der Erde, und so steht dann das ganze Land unter der Macht des Dämons [. . .]. Das Blut wird noch mehr als der Leichnam zum Agens des Wahnsinns. Blut ist Befleckung, die die Krankheit auslöst [. . .]. Vergossenes Blut is krankheitbringendes Miasma". Werner Leibbrand and Annemarie Wettley. *Der Wahnsinn. Geschichte der abendländischen Psychopathologie*. Freiburg-München: Alber 1961. P. 14.

truly multivalent.[4] By the late eighteenth century, in texts that evince a facility with the latest psychology, the release of fluids and other aberrant behaviors will be linked to new understandings of psychological maladies.

Jean Paul modeled the character of Albano in part on the protagonist of just such a psychologically informed text, a novel with an excessively emotional and even violent hero: Ludwig Tieck's *Geschichte des Herrn William Lovell* (1795–1796[5]).[6] One of William Lovell's essential problems is that he feels too much; he is, at the novel's outset, a classic eighteenth-century enthusiast (or *Schwärmer*). Like Albano, William rids himself of excess feeling by engaging in neurotic and often violent behaviors, but in William's case these behaviors do not "help" him. Compulsive sex, non-stop travel, dueling, drinking, and gambling are William's attempts to flee a past that refuses to release him.

There are different contexts for thinking about the problem of enthusiasm, of feeling too much, and about the disordered behaviors associated with it. In the late eighteenth century, enthusiasm was seen as an excess of an essentially laudable, positive quality, a quality of interest and creativity, to be found almost exclusively in young men. This positive force could become unhealthy if the young man read too much or read the wrong thing – in particular, if he internalized negative role models as a result of reading too many

---

[4] Theodore M. Brown notes: "Even in the unmistakably biological-reductionist Hippocratic Corpus, [. . .] certain mentalistic aetiological elements show through [. . .]. In the 'Sacred Disease', even epilepsy – the paradigmatic example of naturalistic, biological disease in the Corpus – is said in certain circumstances to be 'caused by fear of the mysterious.'" *Companion Encyclopedia of the History of Medicine*. Ed. by W.F. Bynum and Roy Porter. London-New York: Routledge 1997. Vol. I. Pp. 439–440. Matthew Bell reminds us that in the eighteenth and early nineteenth centuries, psychology in Germany "grew from a minor branch of philosophical doctrine into one of the central pillars of intellectual culture;" in this period, "psychology's evidential basis, theoretical structure, forms of articulation, and status both as a scientific discipline and as a cultural phenomenon took on a recognisably modern form". Matthew Bell: *The German Tradition of Psychology in Literature and Thought, 1700–1840*. Cambridge: Cambridge University Press 2005. P. 1.
[5] The novel was revised and shortened in two subsequent editions, published in 1821 and 1828.
[6] Tieck's interest in contemporary psychology is evident in his correspondence; several examples are his letters to Moritz and to William Solger: *Letters to and From Ludwig Tieck and His Circle*. Ed. by Percy Matenko. Chapel Hill: University of North Carolina Press 1967. See also *Tieck and Solger: The Complete Correspondence*. Ed. by Percy Matenko. New York-Berlin: B. Westermann 1933. For the influence of Tieck on Jean Paul and more on the relationship between these two novels, see F.J. Schneider: Tiecks *William Lovell* and Jean Pauls *Titan*. In: *Zeitschrift für deutsche Philologie* 61 (1936). Pp. 58–75.

novels.[7] And William, who is that kind of enthusiast, is also, as a character, just such a negative model. But during this same period, enthusiasm also was understood, in the context of the new faculty psychology, as an organically based and mentally exacerbated problem: as the separation of imagination from sensation.[8] While this is not precisely the same phenomenon that Freud will much later call anxiety (understood as a possible expression of the dissociation of emotion from affect),[9] the experience of enthusiasm is one of disorientation, and of estrangement from the overly-heavy body and overly-fast blood that make the experience possible.[10]

In the experience of enthusiasm as well as of its eighteenth-century companion state, melancholy, physical phenomena point to something that ultimately cannot be explained materially or mechanistically.[11] That is, if it were possible to open a person up and to see his blood circulating too quickly, an

---

[7] For a more detailed discussion of enthusiasm in the context of excessive reading, see Claire Baldwin: *The Emergence of the Modern German Novel: Christoph Martin Wieland, Sophie von La Roche, and Maria Anna Sagar*. Columbia, South Carolina: Camden House 2002. P. 9.

[8] See Bell: *The German Tradition of Psychology in Literature and Thought, 1700–1840*. P. 51.

[9] Sigmund Freud: Das Unheimliche. In: *Gesammelte Werke*. Frankfurt am Main: Fischer, 1999. Vol. 12. Pp. 229–268. Here: P. 256. This edition is abbreviated henceforth as GW. Sigmund Freud: The Uncanny. *The Standard Edition of the Complete Psychological Works of Sigmund Freud*. Trans. by James Strachey. London: Hogarth 1953–1974. Vol. 17. Pp. 219–256. Here: P. 243. This edition is abbreviated henceforth as SE.

[10] The origin of the emphasis on blood circulation as a probable contributor to mood and behavior lies in the seventeenth-century work of William Harvey, whose mechanistically oriented *Exercitation Anatomica de Motu Cordis et Sanguinis in Animalibus* [*An Anatomical Disquisition Concerning the Motion of the Heart and the Blood in Animals*] of 1628 influenced what Roy Porter calls Thomas Willis's later "rethinking of physiology at large" and the creation of the science of "neurologie", or study of the nerves, that figures prominently in eighteenth-century psychology and literature. Porter: *Flesh in the Age of Reason*. Pp. 52–56.

[11] Melancholy is much older than modernity, but, like enthusiasm, it is a changeable phenomenon occurring in a wide variety of contexts. And, like the uncanny, it proliferates in the mid- to late eighteenth century, at the peak of Enlightenment, when it is considered a disorder with physical and spiritual components. This understanding is related to, but also revises, the tradition of thinking about melancholy dating from Hippocratus, Aristotle, and the pseudo-Aristotelian *Problemata*, in which the melancholic's "black bile" contributes to his philosophical, political, or artistic exceptionalism. By the late eighteenth and early nineteenth centuries, as indicated in the research on melancholy done by Wolf Lepenies, Hans-Jürgen Schings, and Matthew Bell, among others, the melancholic can be a victim of his specific psychophysical "type", a type that may well doom him to artistic failure rather than enabling him to achieve poetic greatness.

understanding of pathological behavior would still be elusive – in William's case, an understanding of why he is addicted to sex, or feels as if he is disintegrating, or sees frightening uncanny hallucinations. Organic problems such as an overly fast blood flow instead serve as partial explanations for something perhaps best described as an excess of self, which meant at the same time an excess of the self's past, and of physically encoded traces of the past within the self. The hysterical, or hypochondriac, symptoms that could result from this problem, also and in fact especially in men, were considered manifestations of that psychosomatic excess.

Like enthusiasm, melancholy around 1800 is an organically based mood state whose behavioral manifestations signify a desire to remember and to forget. These manifestations, or symptoms, are uncanny in that they nearly always represent a dissociation of affect (as observable in the symptom: shaking, numbness, fainting, etc.) from the earlier emotional state, and from the combination of physical characteristics (such as speedy blood flow or excited nerves) and experience (including loss of love or financial ruin) that contributed to that emotional state. The mood states of melancholy and enthusiasm and their hysterical or hypochondriac consequences are uncanny, but that uncanniness signals something more and different than the intrusion of the "night side" of nature into an otherwise sunny rationalistic universe. Uncanny border experiences, represented in *Lovell* as resulting from insufficient integration of past with present, stand out from the text as moments of sharp focus in an otherwise meandering, allusive, and dense narrative. Intense descriptions of depersonalization and horrific encounters with uncanny doubles function as painful but relieving "cuts" in a text that is literally overly heavy and too full of feeling.

Men of melancholy or enthusiastic temperament, as represented in late eighteenth- and nineteenth-century literature and psychology, were prone to feel themselves at the mercy of other, uncanny men, with "special powers" akin to those to which Freud refers in his essay of 1919 on *The Uncanny*: we think of others as uncanny not only when we think of their intentions as evil, but when we believe that they have special powers (GW 12: 256; SE 17:243). These powers, however, are nothing supernatural, and in fact only exist in the mind of the melancholy man, who lives in a liminal uncanny lack-of-home and at the mercy of his own conviction that he is the victim of a conspiracy. To be sure, William is handicapped by nature; he suffers from an excess of sentiment (or of "Gemüt"). But his psychological and social doom is sealed by his perceived victimization at the hands of others – lovers, friends, brothers, fathers, and secret societies – by modernity as a grand conspiracy. This paranoia is a characteristic of "male hysteria" around 1800, a disordered manifestation of the mood states of melancholy and enthusiasm.

The use of the word hysteria may initially call to mind its deployment in the late nineteenth century as a catch-all description of a malady that was usually female and usually attributed to sexual dissatisfaction. Freud's description of a *Severe Case of Hemi-Anaesthesia in a Hysterical Male* of 1886 notes that male hysteria is very ordinary, although often overlooked.[12] However, although the origin of the term in the Greek "hystera" was indeed reactivated around 1900, eighteenth-century hysteria often was dissociated from the uterus. This dissociation happened right around the time that the concept of the uncanny was "invented" and appeared regularly in literature and aesthetic theory.[13] Hysteria however was still diagnosed in the eighteenth century more frequently in women than in men, for whom "hypochondriasis" often was the preferred diagnosis.[14]

Hypochondriasis was understood in varying ways in the eighteenth century – as manifesting merely in periodic spurts of irritability, or as a sign of "existential uncertainty" – but it often could be cured, at least in its more benign sporadic form, with the relatively simple steps of mental hygiene.[15] Both hypochondriasis and its equivalent among women in the eighteenth century, the vapors (*vapeurs*), were upper-class afflictions, and while men sought relief in mental hygiene, women pursued "fashionable" magnetic or electric treatments.[16] Hysteria, as it appears in the late eighteenth-century psychological and literary discourse, was not as simple to address. It defied mental hygiene, resisted easy classification into mechanistic or materialist categories, and was in men, I contend, a form of Romantic rebellion against the more rationally explicable and curable Enlightened disorders of hypochondriasis and vapors.

In Philipp Slavney's and Elaine Showalter's formulations, both hysteria and hypochondriasis entail "behavior that produces the *appearance* of disease, although the patient is unconscious of the motives for feeling sick".[17] Stavros Mentzos provides a succinct description of the three main categories of hysteria, in the context of a definition that includes but is not limited to

---

[12] Sigmund Freud: Observation of a Severe Case of Hemi-Anaesthesia in a Hysterical Male. SE. Vol. 1. Pp. 21–31. Here: P. 21.

[13] I describe the emergence of the term "uncanny" in the 1770's and 1780's in the second chapter of *Aesthetic Anxiety: Uncanny Symptoms in German Literature and Culture*. Amsterdam-New York: Rodopi 2010.

[14] Phillip R. Slavney: *Perspectives on "Hysteria"*. Baltimore-London: The Johns Hopkins University Press 1990. P. 16.

[15] Henri F. Ellenberger discusses hypochondriasis in *The Discovery of the Unconscious: The History and Evolution of Dynamic Psychiatry*. New York: Basic Books, 1970. Pp. 187, 197. Carl Niekerk points out that hypochondria has its own conceptual "archeology" and that it was understood in different ways in different periods. He cites Georg Christoph Lichtenberg's association of hypochondria with "existentielle[r] Verunsicherung" in *Zwischen Naturgeschichte und Anthropologie. Lichtenberg im Kontext der Spätaufklärung*. Tübingen: Niemeyer 2005. P. 129.

[16] Ellenberger: *The Discovery of the Unconscious*. P. 187.

[17] Elaine Showalter: *Hystories: Hysterical Epidemics and Modern Media*. New York: Columbia University Press 1997. P. 14.

psychoanalytic understandings of the term. Mentzos intends these features as the broadest applicable characteristics of "hysteria" as it has been understood in modernity, whether in male or female patients:

> Erstens körperliche Funktionsstörungen (Konversionssymptome), zweitens psychische Funktionsstörungen (vorwiegend dissoziative Erscheinungen) und schließlich drittens hysterische Verhaltensmuster und Charakterzüge.[18]
> [First, disruptions of physical functioning (conversion symptoms); secondly, disruptions of psychic functioning (primarily dissociative manifestations); and finally, thirdly, hysterical behavior patterns and character traits.]

The moment in which the hysterical symptom appears is a moment of dissociation between the symptom's original cause and the symptom itself. Freud describes it as a form of "Geistesspaltung" ["splitting of the mind"].[19] This dissociation is mirrored in the history of hysteria itself, specifically in its divorce from supposedly uterine origins.

Scholars including Elaine Showalter, Elisabeth Bronfen, and Paul Lerner[20] make at least some use of Freud's conviction, in his early writings on anxiety, that "die Hysterie eine Anzahl von Symptomen einfach der Angstneurose entlehnt und daß es eine innige Beziehung der Angstneurose zur Hysterie gibt" ["hysteria simply takes a number of its symptoms from the anxiety neurosis, and that there is an intimate relationship between anxiety neurosis and hysteria"].[21] Most scholars also refer at least glancingly to Freud's seduction theory of hysteria, which he himself eventually abandoned, and they adopt a much broader understanding of it as something akin to Showalter and Slavney's definition above. In pre-Freudian texts in which the uncanny plays a prominent role, the male subject's hysterical attacks are unleashed by an experience of frightening verisimilitude. That experience in turn inevitably has a strong libidinal component.

There is support for this contention historically but also more plastically across eras. In the *Versuch über die Krankheiten des Kopfes* [*Classifications of*

---

[18] Stavros Mentzos: *Hysterie. Zur Psychodynamik unbewußter Inszenierungen.* Frankfurt am Main: Fischer Taschenbuch Verlag 1989. P. 13.
[19] Josef Breuer and Sigmund Freud: *Studies on Hysteria.* SE. Vol. 2. Pp. 1–306. Here: P. 253.
[20] Elisabeth Bronfen: *The Knotted Subject: Hysteria and its Discontents.* Princeton: Princeton University Press 1998. Paul Lerner. *Hysterical Men: War, Psychiatry, and the Politics of Trauma in Germany, 1890–1930.* Ithaca, NY: Cornell University Press 2003. For Elaine Showalter see note 17.
[21] Sigmund Freud: Über die Berechtigung von der Neurasthenie einen bestimmten Symptomenkomplex als 'Angst-Neurose' abzutrennen. GW. Vol. 1. Pp. 315–342. Here: P. 342. Sigmund Freud. On the Grounds for Detaching a Particular Syndrome From Neurasthenia Under the Description 'Anxiety Neurosis'. SE. Vol. 3. Pp. 85–115. Here: P. 103.

Mental Disorders] of 1764, Kant says that hysteria happens when the otherwise normal imagination produces "allerlei Bilder von Dingen, die nicht gegenwärtig sein" ["all kinds of pictures of things not actually present"]; in the hysteric, this type of hallucination ["Hirngespenst"] is "eben so tief und zugleich eben so richtig [. . .] als eine sinnliche Empfindung nur machen kann" ["so deep and lasting, *as if* caused by an externally stimulated sensation"].[22] In Tieck's *Phantasus* (published 1812 and 1816), the character Ernst concludes similarly that all of the "Gespenster" ["ghosts"] of our imaginations have their source in nature – our minds take material from nature and convert it into hallucination.[23]

Although the intersection of imperialism and modern psychiatry that Paul Lerner demonstrates is crucial for the popularization of the category of "male hysteria" in the later nineteenth century was yet to come, many of the social and cultural conditions that prodded psychiatrists to diagnose hysteria in men around 1900 were present in 1800 as well. A century before psychoanalysis emerged, hysteria was a way of maintaining and holding onto complexity, at a time when so much of modernizing society was grasping at "solutions" to complexity, such as war.[24] Ernst Kretschmer points out that modern mobility and urbanization in particular provoked hysterical symptoms that "appear in the prehistoric forms of our ancestral existence".[25] Such anxiety permeates the fractionalized German territories in the late eighteenth and early nineteenth centuries, and psychology could only provide partial explanations for the increase in nervous disorders around this time.[26] Nevertheless, faculty psychologists attempted to specify an understanding of hysteria that was no longer strictly associated with the uterus.

In a study of hysteria and mysticism, Cristina Mazzoni notes that the male hysteric in modern Europe was inevitably marked by androgynous characteristics. Conversely, the androgyne had traits compatible with the sexual ambiguity associated with hysteria: the "image of the androgyne [. . .] represents, among other things, physical and moral ambiguity (as a hysteric, yet at the same time

---

[22] Immanuel Kant: *Versuch über die Krankheiten des Kopfes.* In: *Werke in zwölf Bänden.* Ed. by Wilhelm Weischedel. Frankfurt am Main: Suhrkamp, 1996. Vol. 2. Pp. 825–829. Immanuel Kant. *Dreams of a Spirit-Seer by Immanuel Kant and Other Related Writings.* Trans by. John Manolesco. New York: Vantage Press 1969. P. 163.

[23] Ludwig Tieck: *Phantasus.* Ed. by Manfred Frank. Frankfurt am Main: Deutscher Klassiker Verlag 1985. Pp. 112–113.

[24] Lerner calls war an "antidote to complexity" (9).

[25] Ernst Kretschmer: Hysterie. In: *Wissen und Leben: Neue schweizer Rundschau* 17 (1923). Here: P. 148. Quoted here in Lerner. P. 15.

[26] Roy Porter addresses the "'coming-out' of the hypochondriac and the hysteric" around 1800 in *Flesh in the Age of Reason.* Pp. 401–403.

also a male, he is suspended between being and having the phallus)".[27] This reading presents a more expansive view of hysteria than Freud's early understanding of anxiety as linked to sexual neuroses, and yet works with that understanding's more interesting ramifications for gender identity. Mazzoni concludes that in narrative discourse in the nineteenth-century and in other eras, hysteria was "a mimetic modality, a manipulable representational strategy, rather than a univocally referential diagnostic term" (5). Texts that feature hysterical men convert those men from desiring male subjects into feminized objects *of* desire. This is a strange form of rebellion against modern complexity, but it can be read as a rebellion nonetheless; these texts' reliance on the "masculine" maladies of melancholy (an ongoing sense of loss) and enthusiasm (too much feeling) makes the hysterical men within them representative of an anxiety that is modern and ancient at once.

No matter the gender of the sufferer, the term hysteria is vexed, and even psychiatric practitioners who have advocated keeping it as a diagnostic category have some trouble with its fluidity. Pierre Janet argues that the term hysteria "should be preserved, although its primitive meaning has much changed. Truly, it has so grand and so beautiful a history that it would be painful to give it up" (Bronfen 101). Janet here acknowledges an aesthetic component in the experience and treatment of hysteria – it has a beautiful history; it is a gorgeous concept. The conventional understanding of hysteria as self-repudiating – as a punishment of the self by the self for being inadequate – has begun to look reactionary because of its disregard for the workings of power structures and discourses.

Freud's famous patient Dora was an hysteric; her brother was a revolutionary. Along these lines, what I am calling the "male hysteria" in *William Lovell* and in *The Ghost-Seer* is in part also a reactionary move into illness as a response to victimization; these men (William, Balder, and Burton in *Lovell* in particular; the Prince in *Ghost-Seer*) are all "disempowered" by their (biological or social) fathers' old feuds as well as by their own "enthusiastic" or "melancholy" character "types". But these men are not victims in the way that Dora is; they are not disempowered or silenced in the same manner. In Schiller and Tieck, disease-like symptoms are provoked indeed by the disempowerment brought on by an ever-more instrumental rationality – a disempowerment that is a kind of emasculation – but are also provoked by bringing-to-light dark knowledge long forgotten. These hysterical symptoms are thus symptoms of a kind of rebellion that seeks to preserve that which is complicated and difficult – to preserve the enthusiastic, the melancholy. The desire to bring the outside in and move the inside out, is a very modern acknowledgement (whether conscious or not) of relatedness and of vulnerability.

---

[27] Cristina Mazzoni: *Saint Hysteria: Neurosis, Mysticism, and Gender in European Culture*. Ithaca and London: Cornell University Press 1996. P. 134.

Tieck's novel *William Lovell* consists of an extended display of uncanny encounters figured at once as psychosomatic disorders and as aesthetic revelations. In this novel, which imitates English fiction (specifically novels like Richardson's *Clarissa*) but also responds to anxieties specific to the German late Enlightenment, uncanny experience is grounded in the body and in illness. William's conviction that "the slower or faster circulation of blood [. . .] basically determines the differences in a person's inclinations"[28] influences his perception of his own moods and problems. As the novel progresses, William loses all his love objects – mistresses, friends, mentors, father – and the memory of each loss returns as an uncanny symptom that is invariably part of a psychosomatic ailment: a confluence of blood circulation and psychological orientation, of nerves and imagination, of vision and memory. Tieck uses representations of the embodiedness of mind to remind his readers that loss is not just a transcendental concept, but a material phenomenon.

In fiction from the late eighteenth century on, the uncanny dissociations between sensation and affect that occur in the presence of the strangely familiar emphasize something wrong with the interdependent relationship between body and mind; they surface in novels like *William Lovell* as part of an aestheticized portrayal of illness. When William encounters a man who bears an eerie resemblance to a portrait hanging in his father's home, a horribly burned woman who reminds him of a past mistress, or a friend whose panic attacks confront William with his own instability, then the literary tools of symbol, metaphor, and allegory are used to explore hypotheses posited in contemporary psychology as well as in aesthetic theory.[29]

William Lovell is not among the most frequently analyzed or read works of German literature.[30] Revisions that Tieck completed in 1821 and 1828

---

[28] Ludwig Tieck: *William Lovell*. Stuttgart: Reclam, 1999. P. 256. William says: "die langsamere oder schnellere Zirkulation des Blutes macht im Grunde die Verschiedenheit in den Gesinnungen des Menschen aus".

[29] I rely here in part on Lawrence Rothfield's arguments about the relationship between nineteenth-century medical and literary discourse as stated in *Vital Signs: Medical Realism in Nineteenth-Century Fiction*. Princeton: Princeton University Press 1992.

[30] *Lovell* was popular in its time, and influenced Tieck's contemporaries. *William Lovell*, says Walter Münz, "zählt zu den am zwiespältigsten beurteilten – und in ihrer [. . .] Originalfassung am wenigsten gekannten – Erzählwerken der deutschen Literatur". Münz cites Friedrich Schlegel's review in: *Athenäum*. Vol. 1.2 (1798). Reproduced in: Friedrich Schlegel, *Kritische Ausgabe*. Ed. by Ernst Behler. München: Schöningh 1967. Vol. 2. Pp. 244–245. In this review, Schlegel calls *Lovell* "einen Kampf der Prosa und der Poesie, wo die Prosa mit Füßen getreten wird und die Poesie über sich selbst den Hals bricht", and notes the general lack of response to the novel in Germanist circles. Walter Münz: Nachwort. In: Ludwig Tieck. *William Lovell*. Ed. by Walter Münz. Stuttgart: Reclam 1999. Pp. 725–726. Find the complete Schlegel review on Pp. 709–710 of the same volume.

shortened the novel (published initially in 1795–1796), but did not address all of its original inconsistencies of plot or eliminate all of its redundancy. But while the *Bildungsroman, Franz Sternbalds Wanderungen* commands far more attention, *Lovell* is arguably Tieck's most psychologically compelling text. This effect is related to its uncanniness, which in turn both motivates and reveals a high level of anxiety. In this novel, the difficulty or even impossibility of containing various kinds of emotional and physical excess is represented in compulsively repetitive ways, and all of the factors Freud eventually identifies as the constitutive elements of the uncanny are present in multiple settings: "Animismus, der Magie und Zauberei, der Allmacht der Gedanken, der Beziehung zum Tode, der unbeabsichtigten Wiederholung und dem Kastrationskomplex" (GW 12:256) ["animism, magic and sorcery, the omnipotence of thoughts, man's attitude to death, involuntary repetition and the castration complex" (SE 17:219)]. As in contemporary psychological literature, these uncanny elements surface during the experience of psychic disorder – disorder occasioned either from within the self or from the community without, and with an impact on both the self and others. The uncanny encounters suffered by *Lovell*'s anxious men are often symptoms of psychosomatic illness.

Viewing enthusiasm and melancholy and their hysterical consequences against the backdrop of faculty psychology allows us to shift our understanding of subjectivity and violence around 1800, and not necessarily only inward. A psychological viewpoint is not restricted to introspection. It also can signify the medicalization and objectification of the self, which in turn expands the subject outward; the world then becomes what Victoria Nelson calls a "psychotopography" in which "interior psychic regions" are "projected onto an outer landscape".[31] *William Lovell*, which although written in 1795–1796 resembles in many respects a work of psychological realism, is such a psychotopography.

I wish to argue first, that William and other male characters in the novel suffer from a kind of hysteria (which is in turn a subset of "enthusiasm", the broad category in empirical psychology as well as in aesthetic theory); secondly, that hysteria is marked by the uncanny (which is in fact a defining characteristic of this hysteria); and, finally, that it is this uncanny neurosis which, while violent and deadly in the novel, actually points to one way of living with and through the tensions of Enlightenment, and of a violent period. My argument therefore runs counter to the most prevalent contemporary understanding of the uncanny as "the toxic side effect of the Enlightenment's

---

[31] Victoria Nelson: *The Secret Life of Puppets*. Cambridge-London: Harvard University Press 2001. P. 110.

rationalist project",³² to quote Terry Castle's important study on the invention of the uncanny in the eighteenth century. Relying on that understanding, Elisabeth Bronfen envisions a retreat into uncanny repetition as something that happens at a time in philosophical and social history when "the Other – be this people or the external world – came to be reduced more and more to a mental effect, devoid of corporeality, valued as an internalized image, a mental phantom, until these phantasmatic objects had come to seem increasingly real" (140). I want to argue, however, that Tieck's novel opens the path to an opposed understanding of the uncanny. In this novel, the neurotic symptom of uncanny repetition (which occurs in the context of an hysteria caused by an organically based enthusiasm) reminds us of the inescapability of others and of the inevitability of Enlightenment (literally, of the past coming to light), even as we try to escape it into a sort of Romantic phantom world. The "psychotopography" of *William Lovell* actually resists spectralization; the projection of an interior domain onto the external landscape is different from the reduction of the world to a mental effect. Uncanny repetition becomes a way of resisting modern alienation and reification, though it does not and cannot bring about the actual return of the real. Rather, it stands as a reminder of what is lost. In William's case, uncanny encounters are occasioned primarily by his relationship to and rebellion against his dying father; as his rebellion acts itself out against other societal structures, the potential of the uncanny to both trap and liberate is revealed. To support this argument, I will first turn to the creative condition and context in which Tieck penned *Lovell* in order to connect the faculty psychology to an analysis of the text itself.

Tieck was preoccupied with how issues prevalent in the psychological literature and practice of his time might intersect with aesthetic concepts. A desire to understand his own disordered moods most certainly underscored this preoccupation, but Tieck also was interested in how the biological and mentalistic explanations of disease and the concerns of a philosophically-oriented psychology could be worked together in the interest of more effective and better poetry. In 1790, he attempted to distinguish between emotional states that are useful for poets and those that are not, by catagorizing the emotions. Each emotion manifests itself in three possible stages, in increasing order of intensity; for instance, an initial state of "goodwill" can progress from there to "tenderness" and ultimately to "love". "Melancholy" may intensify into "madness" and finally to "insanity". "Cowardice" moves on to "fear", and then to "anxiety". Tieck calls the final stage of each emotional state "sublime", meaning that a precarious balance between philosophical and psychological elements has been struck. However, once passion progresses beyond that third stage of

---

³² Terry Castle: *The Female Thermometer: Eighteenth-Century Culture and the Invention of the Uncanny*. Oxford: Oxford University Press 1995. P. 8.

expression, it is "ganz für den Dichter unbrauchbar, weil es ganz körperl. ist und hier gar keine Illusion" ["completely useless for the poet, because it is completely physical and there is no illusion"].[33] A complete enslavement to the body prevents the poet from applying imagination.

William Lovell manifests this concern with emotional states, their relation to each other, and their level of dependence on the body. Tieck's contemporaries viewed his representation of such relationships with a mixture of skepticism and concern. Rudolf Haym in 1870 saw in *Lovell* a "Geist der skeptischen Melancholie" ["spirit of skeptical melancholy"], but concluded that that skepticism never amounts to more than a repetition of the same questions about the extent to which the mind is trapped at the mercy of the body's whims, a repetition that "in langnachhallendem, vielgebrochem Echo unbeantwortet zu dem Frager zurückkehrt[]" ["return[s] unanswered to the questioner in a long resounding, much-broken echo"].[34] The Dutch statesman Jan Rudolf Thorbecke also found a form of repetition in the novel troubling, but simultaneously promising, when he called *Lovell*

> ein sich Bewegen in der nichtigen Welt der Erscheinung, nachdem man einmahl das Wesentliche in sich selber zerstört hat, und es nun auch außer sich nicht wiederfinden kann. Dann entsteht ein Schwanken und eine Willkür, worin der Mensch geradezu untergehn müsste, wenn nicht ein Gespenst des Wahren, womit er nie fertig wird, ihn unablässig verfolgte und hielte.[35]
>
> [a movement in the trivial world of appearance, after one once has destroyed that which is most essential in oneself, and cannot find it again in the external world. Then a fluctuation and arbitrariness arise in which one would have to go under, if the ghost of the True, with which one is never finished, were not in ceaseless pursuit.]

A letter from Tieck to a close friend, the philosopher and aesthetic theorist Karl Wilhelm Ferdinand Solger, reveals that the author himself also saw *Lovell* in ghostly, but also corporeal, terms, and as engaging in an act of preservation, if not of repetition. He compares the novel to a physical home for the dead, a "Mausoleum vieler gehegten und geliebten Leiden und Irrthümer" ["mausoleum of many closely kept and beloved passions and errors"]. However, he goes on to say that once this mausoleum was constructed,

> war der Zeichner und Arbeiter schon von diesen Leiden frei, ich war fast immer sehr heiter, als ich dies Buch schrieb, nur gefiel ich mir noch in der Verwirrung.

---

[33] Ludwig Tieck: *Schriften 1789–1793*. Ed. by Achim Hölter. Frankfurt am Main: Klassiker Verlag 1991. P. 651.
[34] Rudolf Haym: *Die Romantische Schule*. Pp. 49, 50. Quoted here in Percy Matenko: *Tieck and Solger*. P. 143.
[35] Letter from Jan Rudolf Thorbecke to Ludwig Tieck of December 7, 1821. Quoted here in Matenko: *Letters To and From Ludwig Tieck and His Circle*. P. 49.

Etwas von dieser Sucht wird mir gewiß immer anhängen bleiben, auch hängt es wohl mit meinem Besten wieder zusammen. Wie Alles.[36]

[the sketch artist and worker was already free of this suffering; I was almost always very cheerful when I was writing this book, but I was still pleased with myself in this confusion. Something of this mania certainly will always cling to me, and it has to do with my best qualities. Like Everything.]

By the time he had finished *Lovell*, Tieck believed he had reached a sort of compromise solution to a problem that had haunted him since adolescence: that of which personality type was best suited to living with and through agonizing and inevitable anxiety about the meaning of existence. The genius-poets of the Storm and Stress epoch displayed the "Sucht" ["mania"] to which Tieck refers above – they were madly productive, or productively mad, but Tieck suspected that their passion was hyperbolic, and in any event it could not be sustained. The alternative personality type found among artists and intellectuals of the time as Tieck saw it, was a type the editor of his letters, Percy Matenko, calls the "calmer, colder, simpler, and truer people, who had definitely bidden farewell to all illusions and lived therefore in a narrow parochial world where none could envy their lot".[37] In *William Lovell*, Tieck presents both types, and they occur along a spectrum in the characters of Balder, William himself, Mortimer, Karl Wilmont, and Eduard Burton. He asserts that this exploration of character and of various psychosocial disorders has permitted him to reach a point at which the "mania" that will always be part of him (and in fact helps make him successful) can be integrated with a more cheerful ["heiter"] and balanced disposition.

Karl Solger was not quite persuaded by Tieck's insistence that, while *Lovell* indeed represented a difficult phase in his own life, he had used it successfully to represent and work through that phase and then to move on. Solger was troubled in particular by the text's lack of irony, which he held responsible for his "uncanny" concern as a reader about the author's, rather than the characters', well-being. For Solger, the "Schwanken und Willkür" ["fluctuation and arbitrariness"] of the "sich Bewegen in der nichtigen Welt der Erscheinung" ["movement in the null world of appearance"] identified by Thorbecke could well signal recurring problems from Tieck's own past. The lack of a leveling irony in the novel leads Solger to fear that Tieck may be stuck in a melancholy cycle. At the same time, he praises Tieck's poetic abilities, but does not make the connection that Tieck implies, in the poetic theory of 1790

---

[36] Letter from Ludwig Tieck to Karl Wilhelm Ferdinand Solger on March 31, 1815. Quoted here in Percy Matenko: *Tieck and Solger*. Pp. 167–168.
[37] Ibid. P. 65.

referred to above, between melancholy emotion and aesthetic achievement. In a letter to Tieck, Solger writes:

> Den *Lovell* habe ich mit großem Interesse gelesen, vorzüglich weil er gewiß eine bedeutende Periode Ihres Lebens bezeichnet. Ich kenne diesen Zustand, in welchem man sich in gewissen Jugendperioden befindet, und welcher nach und nach schwächer sich auch späterhin wohl zuweilen wieder meldet. Man sieht, daß Sie selbst in den Gegenständen und Gefühlen befangen sind, und daher erscheint manches beinah willkürlich, weil es zu sehr an Ironie mangelt. Deshalb war mir oft unheimlich dabei zu Muthe, nicht gerade weil mich der Zustand der handelnden Personen ängstigte, denn diesen übersah ich dann am meisten, wie er von dem Verfasser gedacht war, sondern eben um des Verfassers und seiner persönlichen Stimmung willen. Wenn ich darauf sehe, so muß ich um so mehr die Kraft und Bildung der Darstellung bewundern, die nur dem so eigen sein konnte, der zum Meister bestimmt war.[38]
>
> [I read *Lovell* with great interest, primarily because it certainly represents an important period in your life. I know this condition, in which one finds oneself in certain youthful periods, and which later occasionally shows up again in weaker form. One sees that you yourself are caught up in these subjects and feelings, and therefore some of this appears almost arbitrary, because there is not enough irony. This is why I often had an uncanny feeling; not because the characters' situation made me fearful – I usually could understand how that was thought up by the author – but rather I feared for the author and his personal mood. Considering this, I must admire the power and composition of the presentation all the more, which could only belong to one destined to be a master.]

Tieck's friends knew that he, like Karl Philipp Moritz, suffered intermittently but repeatedly from depressed moods as well as from an excess of emotion. *William Lovell* was, on the one hand, an attempt to imitate and improve upon English epistolary fiction; Richardson's *Clarissa* is the most commonly mentioned model.[39] But it was simultaneously a working-through – a therapeutic replaying, as well as a repetition – of Tieck's own reading of and reactions to Carl Grosse's monumentally popular novel *Der Genius* [*The Genius*] of 1791. More successful among intellectuals of the period than either *Lovell* or Schiller's *Geisterseher* (1787/1789), *Der Genius* was also powerful enough to send Tieck into delirium and then a temporary nervous collapse.[40] But

---

[38] Ibid. P. 163. Letter from Karl Wilhelm Ferdinand Solger to Ludwig Tieck on March 18, 1815.
[39] In a letter to Solger, Tieck expresses a strong and searing criticism of the "undeutsches" German theater of the time, then immediately admits that his reactions are perhaps extreme and that something can be learned from other cultures. Matenko: *Tieck and Solger*. P. 168.
[40] Münz in *Lovell*. P. 727. Here Münz cites as evidence a letter of June 12, 1792 from Tieck to Wackenroder, saying that *Der Genius* had occasioned "Delirium und die wahrscheinlich schwerste Nervenkrise seines (Tiecks) Lebens".

although reading a novel was responsible for a neurotic outbreak, Tieck believed that he treated himself effectively by writing one in response. This confirmed his conviction that aesthetic creation ultimately rescued him from the potentially deadly dilemma of personality choice – specifically, the choice between overly enthusiastic genius and cold rationality.

Faculty psychologists of the late eighteenth century, including Tieck's friend Karl Philipp Moritz, saw a close connection between the prevalence of certain psychosomatic disorders and psychophysical "types" such as William Lovell's. Moritz asserts that melancholy, an excess of imagination, and enthusiastic fanaticism are interdependent problems, and quotes one Daniel Jenisch's assertion that these problems "kindle" one another "like electric sparks". Moritz's piece in the *Erfahrungsseelenkunde* [*Journal of Empirical Psychology*] entitled *Über die Schwärmerey und ihre Quellen in unseren Zeiten* [*On Enthusiasm and its Sources in Our Times*] is an attempt to explain why such behavior persists in an enlightened age, and includes the following testimony from Jenisch:

> Noch muß ich anmerken, daß [. . .] Schwärmerey, Enthusiasmus, Fantasterey und Fanatismus durch einen sehr feinen Organismus zusammenhängen, und wie electrische Funken, wenn leichtere Ideen nicht ins Mittel treten, sich eins an dem andern entzünden.[41]
>
> [I must also note, that [. . .] rapture, enthusiasm, phantastery and fanaticism are associated via a very fine organism, and like electric sparks, if more sober ideas do not intercede, will kindle one another.]

When William spends too much time in what Tieck calls the "unnatural realms of fantasy" (101), such experiences "kindle" one another within him as well, until he repeatedly experiences an uncanny anxiety: he feels that he is disintegrating or dissociating; his unnatural imagination provokes a sick response in his physical nature.[42]

William's uncanny anxiety, provoked by enthusiasm, manifests as hysterical symptom, which is a violent affect. And the dissociation between the affect (the symptom) and the initial enthusiasm is what is uncanny. That is, the hysterical affect is the return of the repressed enthusiastic feeling, which is not welcome in the rapidly modernizing society in which William and his acquaintances find themselves. In this society, in England as well as on the

---

[41] Karl Philipp Moritz: *Gnothi sauton oder Magazin zur Erfahrungsseelenkunde als ein Lesebuch für Gelehrte und Ungelehrte*. Ed. by Petra and Uwe Nettelbeck. Nördlingen: Franz Greno 1986. Vol. 5. P. 219.

[42] The existential psychologist Leon Salzman aligns this kind of anxiety with the uncanny emotion "resulting from the abrupt appearance of intense anxiety in situations in which a person suddenly comes close to a realization of the dissociated components in his personality". Uncanny Feeling. In: *Psychiatry* 17 (1954). Pp. 100–102. Here: P. 100.

continent, the landed gentry is clearly in an irrevocable process of decay – it is literally being buried alive by urbanization and by a recently empowered middle class, whose assertion of power in finance and industry creates immense anxiety for the increasingly impotent aristocrats as well as for members of the middle class themselves.

William is not the only male character who evinces a potentially harmful enthusiasm with hysterical symptoms: he can be seen as occupying a position along a spectrum of men with varying degrees of symptoms, with his friend and eventual nemesis Eduard Burton positioned at one end and Balder at the other extreme. If we see William in the middle of this group, we can also see his male acquaintances and their symptomology as representing facets of William's own personality, or different possible courses that any male protagonist or reader could also take. In any and in every case, enthusiasm or excessive feeling (itself a response to an excess *of* feeling), is acted out in compulsively repetitive ways in and on the external landscape; all of these behaviors are violent, or at least have a violent component. They include addictive sex, compulsive travel, fighting or duelling, and the frightening experiences of horrific uncanny visions.

All of this acting out is performed by a set of male characters who alternately occupy positions of victims and persecutors. Cosimo/Waterloo is perhaps the novel's only clear villain (that is, he is only a perpetrator and never a victim), and his appearances and disappearances in the novel are examples of the operation of revealing-and-withdrawing that Hélène Cixous has called *the* mechanism of the uncanny.[43] Cosimo represents the past coming back in a familiar but strange form, with violent consequences. This uncanny mechanism of revealing and withdrawing does not happen on a discursive level alone; it happens around 1800 in the context and course of psychological illness, with its physical symptoms that, repetitively, come and go.

In the following passages from the novel, at least one of the three hysterical behaviors or symptoms identified above occurs: dissociation (from oneself), phobia (specifically of women), and paranoia (fear of manipulation at the hands of secret societies or dark unseen forces) – all of these hysterical instances are uncanny, and all are the consequence of too much enthusiasm. And yet all can also be read as methods of living with loss – of moving forward while remembering, and of taking part in progress while resisting it.

Near the end of the novel's first volume, William's friend Balder relates his experience of a classic neurotic anxiety attack with uncanny characteristics:

> Ich schlafe nicht und kann nicht erwachen [. . .] ich fahre erbleichend zusammen, wenn ich meine Hand aufhebe: wer ist der Fremdling, frag' ich erschrocken,

---

[43] Hélène Cixous: Fiction and its Phantoms: A Reading of Freud's *Das Unheimliche*. In: *New Literary History* 7 (1976). Pp. 525–548.

der mir den Arm zum Gruße entgegenstreckt? – Ich greife ängstlich darnach und ergreife schaudernd meine eigene, leichenkalte Hand, wie ein fremdartiges Stück, das mir nicht zugehört. (174)

[I do not sleep, and I cannot wake up [. . .] I shudder and turn pale, when I raise my hand: who is this stranger, I ask, shocked, who reaches out his arm to me in greeting? – I grasp for it anxiously and grab, in horror, my own corpse-cold hand, like an estranged thing that does not belong to me.]

During these repeated attacks, the familiar is strange – Balder feels that he is observing his own body from a distance; he is alienated from himself. He repeatedly experiences what the existential psychologist Leon Salzman calls the uncanny emotion "resulting from the abrupt appearance of intense anxiety in situations in which a person suddenly comes close to a realization of the dissociated components in his personality" (100).

The above passage, and Salzman's description of the quintessentially uncanny emotion of anxiety created by dissociation, echo Tieck's narration of his own experience after he spent a night reading the first two parts of Carl Grosse's horror novel *Der Genius* aloud to friends. In a much-cited letter to Wilhelm Heinrich Wackenroder, Tieck writes that, when trying to sleep in the early-morning hours,

> war mir als schwämme ich auf einem Strom, als löste sich mein Kopf ab und schwämme rückwärts, der Körper vorwärts, eine Empfindung die ich sonst noch nie gehabt habe, wenn ich die Augen aufmachte war mir's, als läg ich in einem weiten Totengewölbe, drei Särge nebeneinander, ich sehe deutlich die weißen, schimmernden Gebeine, alles dehnte sich in eine fürchterliche Länge, alle meine Glieder waren mir selbst fremd geworden, und ich erschrak, wenn ich mit der Hand nach meinem Gesicht faßte.[44]
>
> [it was as if I were swimming in a stream, as if my head detached and swam backwards, my body forwards, a sensation I had never had before, when I opened my eyes it was as if I lay in a large mausoleum, three coffins next to one another, I see clearly the white, gleaming bones, everything expanded to a dreadful length, all of my limbs had become foreign to me, and I jumped when my hand touched my face.]

In the case of Balder's letter to William, as well as in the context of Tieck's reading of *Der Genius* together with friends, an experience of horrifying dissociation and disorientation leads to a need to connect and communicate with others. For Balder, however, this attempt is ultimately hopeless; like his namesake, the Norse god Baldur,[45] he dies in a kind of exile, that of madness.

---

[44] Wilhelm Heinrich Wackenroder: *Werke und Briefe*. Heidelberg: Lambert Schneider 1967. P. 325 Tieck's letter is from June 12, 1792.

[45] Heather Sullivan notes and expands upon the reference to Norse mythology. In: *The Intercontextuality of Self and Nature in Ludwig Tieck's Early Works*. New York: Peter Lang 1997. Pp. 171–172n25.

Balder's attacks, experienced in a kind of "twilight state", or "Dämmerzustand" ("Ich schlafe nicht und kann nicht erwachen" ["I do not sleep, and I cannot wake up"]), also can be read as a response to his own enthusiastic excess and as the expression of a desire to die at least a little. This is reminiscent of Moritz, who documents a number of similar real-life cases in his *Erfahrungsseelenkunde*, and who refers to this desire in himself as the wish to "nicht mehr seyn" ["be no more"].[46] These attacks also blur the distinction between inside and outside, as Freud puts it: "bei Entfremdung sind wir bemüht, etwas von uns auszuschließen" ["in alienation [or derealization] we are busy trying to shut something out of us"].[47] But there is an equally uncanny experience of *fausse reconnaissance* or *déjà vu*, in which, according to Freud, we want to bring something in that does not really belong there ["wir [wollen] etwas als zu unserem Ich gehörig annehmen" ["we want to take something in as if it belonged to us"]).[48] And this phenomenon of "fausse reconnaissance" [false remembering] is what happens when William's object relations are most obviously distorted: in his exploitation of and re-encounters with the women he really despises.

When William encounters a former lover, Louise, now horribly disfigured by contagious disease, she is a strange, yet familiar, reminder of the beautiful temptress she once was, as well as an uncanny replication or externalization of William's own desires. She is his desires' outward manifestation, their psychotopography, and her disfigurement reveals how degenerate his desires truly are, and therefore how degenerate he is. His increasingly wayward and abusive sexual life is the reality that her disfigured face and sexually repulsive body represent. Louise's face also is analogous to Freud's understanding of Medusa's head, which is (for Freud) apotropaic: it takes the place of

---

[46] Marianne Thalmann contends: "Tiecks Menschen leben mehr im Dämmerzustand als im Traum. Der Übergang vom Wachzustand in den traumhaftesten ist ein rascher und häufiger. Tieck selbst legte großen Wert auf seine eigenen Träume, deren Gequältheit sich ihm besonders einprägte. Er betrachtete den Traum an sich als Offenbarung verhemmter Tagesseiten der menschlicher Natur. Er wird ihm daher zum Ausdruck unserer höchsten Philosophie". Marianne Thalmann: *Probleme der Dämonie in Ludwig Tiecks Schriften*. Hildesheim: Gerstenberg 1978. P. 47. She refers to R. Köpke: *Ludwig Tieck. Erinnerungen aus dem Leben eines Dichters*. Leipzig: Brockhaus 1855. Vol. 2. P. 126.
[47] Freud: Brief an Romain Rolland (Eine Erinnerungsstörung auf der Akropolis). GW. Vol. 16. Pp. 250–257. Here: P. 255. Freud: Letter to Romain Rolland (A Disturbance of Memory on the Acropolis). SE. Vol. 22. Pp. 237–248. Here: P. 246. For more on this phenomenon, see Freud: Über Fausse Reconnaissance (Déjà raconté) während der psychoanalytischen Arbeit. GW. Vol. 10. Pp. 115–123. Freud: Fausse Reconnaissance (Déjà raconté) in Psycho-Analysis. SE 13. Pp. 199–207.
[48] Freud: GW. Vol. 16. Pp. 250–257. Here: P. 255. Freud: SE. Vol. 22. Pp. 237–248. Here: P. 246.

a representation of the female genitals, which provokes horror and hysteria in "the enemy" (in this case, in William, who panics).[49] Louise is also not unlike the uncanny dolls of nineteenth- and twentieth-century fiction and aesthetic theory, in that she fulfills what Wilhelm Stekel calls a "sexually aberrant" function.[50] When William agrees to have sex with her in exchange for her arranging a meeting with Amalie, the true love of his youth, he agrees to become Louise's object, to be used; his already decidedly ambiguous morality transmutes into the kind of physical ambiguity that Mazzoni contends characterizes the male hysteric. William possesses the phallus that Louise desires, but he must to an extent relinquish it in order to attain the object of his own desire. This act is not only symbolic; it carries with it the risk of real disease. In a letter to mentor-figure Rosa, William writes that Louise's husband, the Count Melun, died soon after their marriage; another lover, the Chevalier Valois, has shot himself.

In this same letter, William writes that Louise's disease has merely revealed

> dies Ungeheuer [, das] doch schon damals verlarvt in dem schönen Weibe lag [. . .], das ich umarmte, – bei jedem Weibe und Mädchen fällt mir jetzt der Gedanke ein: Die Alte, die mit grauen Haaren, abgefallen, mit roten Augen und auf einer Krücke vorüberhinkt, war auch einmal jung und hatte ihre Anbeter, sie dachte damals nicht daran, daß sie sich ändern könne; ihrem begeisterten Liebhaber fiel es nicht ein, über sich selbst zu lachen, denn er kannte die Gestalt nicht, gegen die er seine Deklamationen richtete. – O hinweg davon! – Aber was sind alle Freuden dieser Welt? – Es ist mir ein widriger Anblick, wenn ich ein Paar gehn sehe, das zärtlich gegeneinander tut. In der Kindheit wünschen wir uns Glasperlen, dann Liebe, dann Reichtum, dann Gesundheit, dann nur noch das Leben; auf jeder Station glauben wir weitergekommen zu sein und fahren doch im Kreise herum. (472–473)
> [the monster that already lay inside the beautiful woman [...] I embraced – now, with every woman and girl the thought comes to me: the old crone, who limps by on a crutch, with gray hair, stooped, and with red eyes, she was once young and had suitors; she did not think then that she could change; it did not occur to her enraptured lover to laugh about himself, because he did not know the real figure to whom he addressed his declarations. – O, away from all of that! – But what are all the joys of this world? – It is a disgusting sight to me, when I see a pair being

---

[49] Freud writes: "If Medusa's head takes the place of a representation of the female genitals, or rather if it isolates their horrifying effects from the pleasure-giving ones, it may be recalled that displaying the genitals is familiar in other connections as an apotropaic act. What arouses horror in oneself will produce the same effect upon the enemy against whom one is seeking to defend oneself. We read in Rabelais of how the Devil took to flight when the woman showed him her vulva". Freud. Medusa's Head. SE. Vol. 18. Pp. 273–274. Here: P. 273. Freud. Das Medusenhaupt. GW. Vol. 17. Pp. 47–48. Here: P. 48.
[50] Wilhelm Stekel: *Sexual Aberrations*. New York: Liveright Publishing Corp. 1930. P. 54. Quoted here in Mike Kelley: *The Uncanny*. Exhibit catalogue, with essays by Mike Kelley, John C. Welchman, and Christoph Grunenberg. Cologne: Verlag der Buchhandlung Walther König 2004. P. 16.

tender to one another. In childhood we wish for glassy beads, then love, then riches, then health, then only for life; in every phase we think we have come further, but we are going around in a circle.]

William's description of the meaninglessness that accompanies transience echoes Balder's view of nature. In a letter William writes before his own downward spiral begins, he recounts a conversation he has had with Balder while on a walk. William encourages Balder to enjoy himself: "Sieh die reizende Schöpfung umher, redete ich ihn wieder an, sieh wie sich die ganze Natur freut und glücklich ist!" ["Look at the beautiful creation all around us, I said to him, see how happy all of nature is!"] But Balder answers:

> Und alles stirbt und verwes't; – vergissest du, daß wir über die Leichen von Millionen mannichfaltiger Geschöpfe gehn, – daß die Pracht der Natur ihren Stoff aus dem Moder nimmt, – daß sie nichts als eine verkleidete Verwesung ist?" (139)
> [And everything dies and decays; are you forgetting that we are walking over the corpses of millions of varied beings, – that nature's majesty takes its material from rot, – that it is nothing but disguised decomposition?]

When William pleads with him to at least enjoy nature's beautiful disguise – "so laß uns doch wenigstens den Betrug für wahr anerkennen, der uns glücklich macht" ["let us at least recognize that betrayal, which makes us happy, as true"] – Balder refuses to relent: "*Deine* Täuschung macht mich nicht glücklich, die Farben sind für mich verbleicht, das verhüllende Gewand von der Natur abgefallen, ich sehe das weiße Gerippe in seiner fürchterlichen Nacktheit" ["*Your* deception does not make me happy; for me the colors are faded, the cloaking garment has fallen from nature, I see the white skeleton in its frightful nakedness"] (140).

Although in this early part of the novel he is still able to condemn Balder's "schreckliche Kälte" ["terrible coldness"] and to suggest that he surrender to cheerfulness, "daß dein Blut schneller durch die Adern fließt" ["so that your blood will flow faster in your veins"] (140), William eventually will fall prey to the same types of psychic and physical disorders that plague Balder, and will come to the same conclusion about life's transience and about the permanence of death. Although other factors contribute to William's increasing neuroses and eventual downfall, his contact with Balder is crucial; here Tieck references contemporary faculty psychology's acknowledgment that mental disorders could be contagious.[51]

---

[51] It is possible that Tieck's speculation about the contagious nature of mental disorders comes directly from his friend Karl Philipp Moritz, whose *Erfahrungsseelenkunde* includes this characteristic in an enumeration of the many facets of psychosomata; volume 4:31. I examine this aspect of the *Erfahrungsseelenkunde* in more detail in *Aesthetic Anxiety: Uncanny Symptoms in German Literature and Culture*. Amsterdam-New York: Rodopi 2010."

William's melancholy also is occasioned in part by a disrupted relation to his mother, who is portrayed in some letters as dead, in others as alive (probably due to Tieck's lack of revision), but always as absent. But while Oedipal conflicts are not absent from the novel, *William Lovell* is inspired by the existential dilemmas and disturbed object relations of the male subject, and not ultimately by the mother. That is, the mothers and female lovers are proximate factors rather than the real causes of William's problems.[52]

In contrast to Louise, Amalie, William's first love (and his English, "heimliche Liebe") remains beautiful throughout the novel. But she never really is an object of desire; she functions as a means towards William's initial end, that is, to modify his overly enthusiastic and sentimental character in a rational direction, in the direction of his close male friend Eduard. But William's vulnerability to external manipulation, along with his own innate excess of sensuality, doom him to repetitive re-exploitations of woman after woman, and there really is no way out of this cycle. Louise is a horrifying uncanny apotropaic projection, and Amalie is not what he wants; by the time he does try to reunite with her, it is much too late.

Similarly, William's encounters with Cosimo/Waterloo, the man who reminds him of and in fact is the subject of the frightening painting in his childhood home, are uncanny and frightening, but the fact that the encounters propel William into hysterical behavioral excesses (panic, insomnia, and nymphomanic episodes) is due to his growing sense of paranoia that secret, dark forces must be manipulating him. However, what is truly uncanny about the painting is the fact that ultimately it reveals that there is no supernatural force at work in William's downfall; his desire to believe that a hidden evil is at work results from his desire to deny his dependence on his own participation in a community of

---

[52] Here I rely on the premise of Martha Helfer's research that, at least in several significant cases, "the metaphysical ground of the Romantic project – presumed to be the maternal, eternal feminine embodied in the form of the beloved – proves to be the self-positing male subject". Martha Helfer: The Male Muses of Romanticism: The Poetics of Gender in Novalis, E.T.A. Hoffmann, and Eichendorff. In: *The German Quarterly* 78.3 (2005). Pp. 299–319. Here: P. 300. Helfer's work in no way excludes a psychoanalytic understanding of essential complexes and disorders, but it illuminates a competing and prevalent paradigm of the "male muse" in Romantic cultural production that challenges by-now standard readings of "woman (as) the idealized, unattainable 'other' against which the male poet defines himself in a gesture of wish fulfillment, (as) the priestess and source of enlightenment for the male poet [. . .] (as) 'the discursive production of the Mother as the source of discursive production'" (299). The embedded quotation is from David Wellbery: Foreword. In: Friedrich A. Kittler: *Discourse Networks 1800/1900*. Trans by Michael Metteer with Chris Cullens. Stanford: Stanford University Press 1990. P. xxiii.

frail, finite beings.[53] The painting, placed in William's childhood home, brings the Other in – it is a rendering of a supposed foreigner whom William later comes to know, in Italy, as an Italian. The appearance of Cosimo in Italy later brings the "inside", William's childhood past, out into the foreign environment. The painting functions as a kind of "ghost" in the novel – dead, but unburied. S. S. Prawer argues that the "uncanny portrait" in horror fiction and in film acts like an uncanny double, similar to the robot in *Metropolis* or the wooden doll Olympia in *Der Sandmann*. This double in turn has a ghostly function: "In the end the portrait seems to take (the protagonist) over altogether, marrying ancient fears of the dead 'possessing' the living with more modern fears on which the terror-film constantly plays: fears about the degree to which men can be manipulated, individually or collectively, by their fellow-men".[54]

William is attracted to and also repelled by Rosa, a chilly Italian atheist who has a similar function to the Armenian in Schiller's *Geisterseher* or to father-like figures in other secret-society novels. William finds Rosa compelling precisely because Rosa's cold nature and the secret world he represents seem to offer strategies to contain and master the uncanny manifestations of William's hysterical excess. Secret societies offer a refuge from modernity, but they also entrap in further conspiracy and manipulation. The mysterious and threatening male figures William encounters, as well as his male friends (Karl and Eduard) who (justifiably) turn against him, all can be read as re-representations of his father, whose voice follows and haunts him in letters throughout his continental tour. He never manages to rebel or even to differentiate himself sufficiently, and will ultimately end up paying for the father's past.

William and Balder, but also their seemingly rational counterparts Eduard and Karl, are all men in trouble: men manipulated – ultimately by themselves, by their own unconscious choices – into at least partly uncanny existences, and trapped in endless melancholy by their uncanny experiences. But the uncanny could, were these characters gifted with more insight, also point to the way out of their dilemmas. And to a certain extent it does just that, by presenting readers with an early version of what will much later be known as

---

[53] As Heather Sullivan puts it: "Despite the deceptive usage of seemingly supernatural tricks, the only 'evil' present in *William Lovell* is the disturbing feelings arising with the realization of the necessary dependency on other human beings" (55). She points to William Lillyman's reading of *Lovell* as a novel that attests that there "is no penetrating, expansive view possible, no apprehension of the beyond, no extension of the boundaries of existence, no transformation of the world and the novel into a fairy tale; instead there is merely deceit and contrived illusion". William Lillyman: *Reality's Dark Dream: The Narrative Fiction of Ludwig Tieck*. Berlin: de Gruyter 1979. Pp. 37–38. Quoted here in Sullivan, pp. 169–170n17.

[54] S.S. Prawer: *Caligari's Children: The Film as Tale of Terror*. Oxford: Oxford University Press 1980. P. 57.

existential dread and awareness, and with an emphasis on the need to, if not escape, then acknowledge and live with repetitive psychological and social dilemmas via insight – and thus to live more authentically.

In *William Lovell*, the nameless but implicitly present secret society re-represents the tension between regress and progress that is part of the uncanny, and this tension produces and is part of hysterical symptoms, manifested by male characters; these symptoms also have uncanny characteristics. By the later nineteenth century, the domination of secret societies in the literary and cultural imagination is over. Already by the time *William Lovell* was first published, the role of the society as containing strategy is in serious question, as is the potential for the secret society to act as an antidote to the supposedly "toxic effects" of the Enlightenment – the uncanny it produces. The society no longer functions as a space for the experience of "fausse reconnaissance", allowing the subject to take something in, to make something external and potentially dark a part of himself. William is certainly not a positive role model: he has become a victim of external forces as well as of his own uncanny perceptions. But, the novel *William Lovell*, the literary text, assumes in part the role the secret society can no longer play. It provides a set of codes for living with, if not mastering, what is essentially unmasterable – and ultimately for sustaining loss and its concomitant complexity, darkness, and "enthusiasm" as well.

Lynne Tatlock

Communion at the Sign of the Wild Man

In this rereading of Wilhelm Raabe's Zum wilden Mann *(1874) I argue that the author invented in the guise of a universal fable an alternative story to the self-congratulatory visions of Germany current after unification in 1871. Furthermore, by choosing to re-publish the tale in 1885 in Reclam's Universalbibliothek, he afforded this alternative story wide circulation and canonical status. The juxtaposition in this text of the choleric executioner-mercenary, who in the role of the wild man tends to communal well-being in the name of the state, with the melancholy apothecary, who blindly and ineffectually tends to communal health, reveals that the social and economic order preserved in the new Reich is constituted and maintained by violence. With this harrowing insight the story thus launches its own violent address to its reading public by leaving readers in an unclosed narrative frame in the apothecary shop, vainly awaiting solace and healing.*

> Was ist solch ein unbedeutendes Gemetzel wie bei Cannae, Leipzig oder Sedan gegen die fort und fort um den Erdball tosende Schlacht des Daseins? (Wilhelm Raabe, 8 March 1875)[1]
> [What is a bloodbath like that in the case of Cannae, Leipzig, or Sedan in comparison with the slaughter of existence that rages unceasingly around the globe?]

> It is not the perversions of others that render our homespaces dangerous. It is those ritualized, moralizing, "elevated", "innocent", pathological responses that grant purified self-definition to our "ordered worlds" by locating the "demon" in others and exorcizing them from our midst.[2]

In 1885 the short novel *Zum wilden Mann* entered the literary marketplace for the third time, this time as volume 2000 of Reclam's *Universalbibliothek*. Its author, Wilhelm Raabe, had carefully selected it from his many works, excising it from the anthology *Krähenfelder Geschichten*, where it had been republished in 1879 following its initial serialized publication in *Westermanns Monatshefte* in 1874. This universal library in fact constituted a potentially significant venue for *Zum wilden Mann*, for it held out the promise of wide circulation in a series established to democratize literature by making it affordable

---

[1] Wilhelm Raabe: *Sämtliche Werke. Im Auftrage der Braunschweigischen Wissenschaftlichen Gesellschaft*. 20 vols. in 21. ed. Ed. by Karl Hoppe et al. Göttingen: Vandenhoeck & Ruprecht 1960–70. Ergänzungsbände. 5 vols., 1970–1994. Here: Ergänzungsband 5. P. 335. All subsequent parenthetical references in the text will be to this edition of Raabe's works. All translations are mine unless otherwise noted.
[2] Wendy Hamblet: *The Sacred Monstrous. A Reflection on Violence in Human Communities*. Lanham, Maryland: Lexington Books 2004. P. 100.

even as it conserved Germany's better literature as national literature. While Reclam included a wide range of fiction in this series, many volumes of which corresponded more to ephemeral popular taste than to a program of *Bildung*, each thousandth publication constituted a special place of honor dedicated to "den führenden Schriftstellern der Zeit, den Lieblingen eines literarisch anspruchsvollen Publikums" ["the leading writers of the time, the darlings of an audience with literary pretension"].[3] When in 1910 Reclam celebrated the publication of the 5000th volume of the Universalbibliothek, Raabe counted himself, not without a show of pride, among the signatories.[4]

This choice of text for Reclam's widely circulating series was a striking, even aggressive one, for, as has often been observed, *Zum wilden Mann* had met with criticism even from those otherwise disposed to praise Raabe's work. Wilhelm Jensen for one had asserted in a lengthy review of Raabe's entire oeuvre that *Zum wilden Mann* should be "polizeilich verboten" ["banned"].[5] In his view and that of others, the piece presented a shockingly bleak and disparaging – and thus misguided – vision of humankind, inappropriate to better literature. Indeed, *Zum wilden Mann* violated contemporary expectations of the function of literature as affirming reality, as providing a picture of a harmonious world (Otto Ludwig's "poetic realism"), as offering Fontane's "humoristische Verklärung" ["humorous transfiguration"], even an ideal world.[6] The piece was, furthermore, difficult to read and thus hardly the stuff of popular consumption. The journalist Fritz Hartmann asked Raabe outright why he selected a work that could really only engage "an intellectual readership" for the mass distribution of the universal library. Raabe's blunt answer, "Weil sie zu meinen besten Sachen gehört" ["Because it's one of my best pieces"] (Ergänzungsband 4:242),[7] in turn led Raabe editor Hans Butzmann to conclude that quality alone determined Raabe's choice (11:480). While Butzmann may

---

[3] Annemarie Meiner: *Reclam. Eine Geschichte der Universal-Bibliothek zu ihrem 75. jährigen Bestehen*. Leipzig: Philipp Reclam 1942. P. 187.
[4] *Widmungsblätter an Hans-Henr.-Reclam beim Erscheinen der No. 5000 von Reclams Universal-Bibliothek*. Leipzig: Philipp Reclam Jr. 1910. P. 763.
[5] Wilhelm Jensen: Wilhelm Raabe. Zur Würdigung des Dichters. In: *Westermann's Monatshefte* (October 1879). Pp. 106–123. Here: P. 119.
[6] Stephan Kohl: *Realismus: Theorie und Geschichte*. Uni-Taschenbücher 643. München: Wilhelm Fink 1977. Pp. 111–115. For a recent discussion of *Zum wilden Mann* and realism, see Søren Fauth: Tranzendenter Fatalismus: Wilhelm Raabes Erzählung *Zum wilden Mann* im Horizont Schopenhauers und Goethes. In: *Deutsche Vierteljahrsschrift für Literaturwissenschaft und Geistesgeschichte* 78 (2004). Pp. 609–645.
[7] Thaddäus Abitz-Schultze similarly recounts that he once asked Raabe why he had chosen "die so niederdrückende Novelle" and received the answer "Weil ich den 'Wilden Mann' für eine meiner besten Novellen halte" (Ergänzungsband 4. P. 294).

not be wrong to stress Raabe's feelings about the artistic achievement of *Zum wilden Mann*, this provocative selection of a book for the people nevertheless merits further consideration, for the placement in Reclam's universal library meant de facto canonization and easy access to the German reading public that had increasingly disappointed Raabe.[8] Indeed, Reclam enabled him to position himself strategically as German author and intellectual and thus effectively to renew his verbal assault on his German readers. This assault, as I shall explain in this interrogation of violence and community, lay at the heart of the matter.

Raabe's Fable of the Wild Man

The improbable plot of *Zum wilden Mann* can be quickly summarized. One night sometime in the 1860s[9] on the thirtieth anniversary of his purchase of the apothecary shop "Zum wilden Mann", the apothecary Philipp Kristeller, aided by the punch prepared by his sister, reveals to his most intimate friends, the village worthies, the long-kept secret of his reasonably comfortable material and professional circumstances. His account runs as follows.

Long ago, in despair because he had been told that he had to relinquish his fiancée whom he could not support, he set out on an herb-gathering expedition where he encountered a peculiar friend whom he had met in the forest some time earlier. This time he finds his friend in turmoil at the so-called "Blutstuhl" ["bloody seat"] a site named for a rock formation that had once served as a sacrificial altar, a symbolic landscape to which we shall return below. Refusing to shake Kristeller's hand, the man declared that he now stood apart from all humankind and that he had to quit this place forever. The following day Kristeller received a letter, wherein the man declared that he had left Kristeller and his fiancée all of his money; he planned to start over and wished to be free of anything tying him to the past. Kristeller, who now had the material means for a happy life, piously determined at the urging of his fiancée to keep an empty chair ready for him should he ever return, this chair serving as monument to

---

[8] See Ulrike Koller, Eckhardt Meyer-Krentler, and Jeffrey L. Sammons on Raabe's fraught relationship with his readers. Ulrike Koller: "Vom Lesepöbel" zur Leser-"Gemeinde". Raabes Beziehung zum zeitgenössischen Publikum im Spiegel der Leserbehandlung. In: *Jahrbuch der Raabe Gesellschaft* (1979). Pp. 94–127. Eckhardt Meyer-Krentler: "Gibt es nicht Völker, in denen vergessen zu werden eine Ehre ist?" Raabe and German Unification. In: *1870/71–1989/90. German Unifications and the Change of Literary Discourse*. Ed. by Walter Pape. Berlin-New York: Walter de Gruyter 1993. Pp. 144–168. Jeffrey L. Sammons: *Wilhelm Raabe. The Fiction of the Alternative Community*. Princeton: Princeton University Press 1987.

[9] The decade in which Kristeller recounts his life story to his friends must be the 1860s, given that the letter leaving him the money is dated 30 October 183-, which, he emphasizes quite pointedly, was from thirty-one years previously (11:196, 11:198).

his generosity and as sign of gratitude. Kristeller can point on this evening to that very chair.

Even as Kristeller relates this story, a knock at the door disrupts the male communion around the punch bowl and heralds the return of the stranger. Kristeller's long-lost benefactor has become a mercenary soldier, who calls himself Colonel Dom Agostin Agonista. Agonista now fills in the missing details of the story. As August Mördling, the scion of a family that had for generations served the state as executioners, he was one day called upon to perform a public execution with the approval and support of the state and church, a duty such as no one in his family had been called upon to fulfill for over a generation.[10] Having been raised by his father in the spirit of Weimar humanism, he recoiled from violence but nevertheless reluctantly fulfilled his obligation to the state and beheaded a miscreant before ten thousand onlookers for which he was praised by the authorities, the newspapers, and the gawking mob. In the hope of taming what he sees as his inherited "bad blood" by avoiding any future perpetration of violence, he fled Germany. Instead of eschewing violence as intended, however, Mördling has made his living as the mercenary Agonista by means of unspeakable violence in service of several South American governments. An education under the auspices of Weimar humanism clearly counted for nothing once his bloodthirstiness had been aroused. Now, no longer young but still filled with zest for life, he wishes to

---

[10] As improbable as this plot element may seem, Raabe did in fact set this part of the story in the 1830s before public executions had been abolished in the German territories. Public executions such as the kind that Mördling describes had been terminated throughout the German territories in the 1850s and 1860s, however – before Raabe's own time. See Richard J. Evans: *Rituals of Retribution: Capital Punishment in Germany 1600–1987.* Oxford: Oxford University Press 1996. Pp. 305–317. Executions took place instead behind prison walls, witnessed only by a select audience (Evans. P. 305). Evans, like Foucault in *Discipline and Punish: The Birth of the Prison* (New York: Pantheon Books 1977), observes a shift in the nineteenth century from ritualized public executions intended in the early modern period to serve state power to a new secrecy surrounding punishment. In Evans's view the concealment of punishment stemmed from the fear that public executions aroused violence in those who viewed them, that is, a violence that could have had revolutionary potential (305, 315–316). I have not found evidence of Raabe's participation in the debate centered on capital punishment in the 1860s and early 1870s, but *Zum wilden Mann* suggests that he was aware of this debate at some level. In 1870 the liberals who favored abolition of capital punishment were outvoted, and capital punishment was thus included in the new Reich Criminal Code. As Evans points out, "National unification had been grounded on a series of compromises on human rights issues, of which the retention of the death penalty, given its symbolic role in the politics of 1848, was perhaps the most striking" (346). In point of fact, however, no executions occurred in Prussia from 1868 to 1878 (356).

settle down and marry, to join civil society as it were, and he needs the means to do it.

Eventually Mördling lays claim to all of Kristeller's wealth as if foreclosing on a loan with interest, although over thirty years after the fact, the reader should note, Mördling cannot be considered to have a legal case. Nevertheless, with hardly a struggle, Kristeller sacrifices everything to pay off the alleged debt, including the patent for the "Kristeller", the bitters to which he has given his own name. Meanwhile the villagers ignore the ruthless expropriation that is occurring before their very eyes, even though they well know that Agonista has an extraordinarily violent past and would be capable of almost anything. Agonista finally departs on the twenty-third of December amid sentimental urging from well wishers that he stay at least for Christmas. In an uncanny anticipation of twentieth-century events, the villagers, even the "liebe, gute, treue Freunde und Nachbarn" ["the dear, good, loyal friends and neighbors"] (11:177) to whom Kristeller told his story suffer a collective blindness concerning the nature of the evil fortune that has befallen him, simply shaking their heads in bewilderment when he must auction off his property, piece by piece. Occasionally they profit from his loss by buying an item that is up for auction, even as they make the condescending and – in the main – incorrect assumption that he has come into such financial straits as a result of bad speculation. The villagers' pious assumptions about speculation on the final page thus tie one of many slender threads to contemporary German history – in this case, the period immediately following the stock market crash of 1873.[11] The tale closes with the villagers' puzzlement that Kristeller stubbornly fails to follow their advice to enlist the aid of Agonista. The story, with its echoes of a demonic pact although no such pact was actually made, ultimately has the feel of a fable without the requisite moral, or at the very least, of a fable with an opaque one.[12]

The narrative itself is, on the surface of it, sedate if relentless. Although it alludes to physical violence, it does not depict it in any detail. Even Jensen conceded in his critical commentary that there were no passages in *Zum wilden Mann* that were in and of themselves objectionable and thus worthy of censorship.[13] As Raabe scholar Jeffrey L. Sammons has pointed out, the

---

[11] Raabe derived material for the story from a visit to Bad Harzburg in July 1873. He had begun work on the piece by late July and completed it in October of the same year (11:472–474). The Vienna Stock Exchange collapsed on 9 May 1873, halting the mad speculation of the so-called *Gründerzeit*.

[12] On the echoes of the demonic pact in *Zum wilden Mann*, see Volker Hoffmann: *Zum wilden Mann*: Die anthropologische und poetologische Reduktion des Teufelpaktthemas in der Literatur des Realismus am Beispiel von Wilhelm Raabes Erzählung. In: *Jahrbuch der Schillergesellschaft* 30 (1986). Pp. 472–492.

[13] Jensen: Wilhelm Raabe. Zur Würdigung des Dichters. P. 119.

source of the outrage of a critic like Jensen and other contemporaries appears to have stemmed largely from the lack of poetic justice in the face of overt cruelty in the fictional world of this tale. Sammons focuses in contrast on what he argues is the more shocking element, namely the revelation that Kristeller's life "has been on loan" (232). Morality makes no difference; good fortune is merely a matter of contingency not of desert. In both of these understandings, the text betrays reader expectation of an inherently orderly and just world. The betrayal of such reader expectation is, however, not the whole story, for *Zum wilden Mann* potentially delivers a still more unsettling vision when read at the sign of the wild man, a pessimistic vision that, in questioning the nature of social order itself, confronted Raabe's late-century readership where they lived – in post-unification Germany.

The Emblematic Wild Man

Raabe's title for this work, *At the Sign of the Wild Man*, invokes a well-known figure. Indeed, while the sign itself is never described and no character ever remarks on it, the wild man was, as I shall explain, visible enough in Raabe's times to serve as a prompt to the imagination – and particularly visible in the provinces that make up "Mitteldeutschland", the geographical heart of the new empire.

Alert readers will likely take the titular sign to refer simply and obviously to Agonista under whose auspices Kristeller acquired the apothecary shop – and readers are certainly not wrong to do so. Yet because the work is not entitled *The Wild Man* but rather *At the Sign of the Wild Man*, merely equating Agonista with the wild man does not take a full account of what *could* meet the eye at the sign of the wild man. Sammons, who takes Agonista to be the namesake of the pharmacy, is himself not entirely content with this narrow interpretation and puzzles that "the symbol, as so often, seems to hang in the air somewhat without being fully integrated" (235). Of course the sign literally hangs in the air, and as is his wont, Raabe belabors the phrase "Zum wilden Mann" in this story, thus forcing it on the reader's attention.[14]

The meaning of the phrase "Zum wilden Mann" comes more readily into focus if we consider the possibility that Agonista constitutes but one instantiation of the sign under which the story unfolds. He becomes the most obvious wild man of this particular story, because in his case the state has overtly instrumentalized the human will to violence. In other words, the sign at which we gather for this story points not merely to the unchecked violence of an individual, but to the relationship of the violence he embodies to human community and social order.

---

[14] Sammons asserts that "Raabe was much given to label naming, and we are inclined to suspect that the image is not arbitrary" (*Wilhelm Raabe*. P. 234).

In his analysis of *Zum wilden Mann* Sammons alludes to the proliferation of images of the wild man in the Harz region and in the duchy of Braunschweig-Wolfenbüttel, the North German territory to which Raabe had recently returned when he wrote *Zum wilden Mann* in 1873.[15] Butzmann also identifies a tale from the Harz Mountains of a wild man and buried treasure that may have served as one of Raabe's sources (11:474). Raabe scholarship has, however, not yet considered more deeply and fully the meanings of these German wild men as they ramify in Raabe's short novel. A brief look at the historical significance of displays of the wild man, particularly as regards state power, thus proves illuminating for a rereading that takes into account the broader social significance of this image.

While the wild man emerges in diverse iterations in early modern Europe, those meanings and functions most pertinent to interpreting Raabe's fable concern the wild man's part in court festivals and appearance on coins and in heraldry as a symbol of state power and authority.[16] The wild man, as a legendary creature displaying both human and bestial qualities, marked the boundary between civilization and wildness, borders to be demarcated and guarded by the state. The wild man in service to the state lived at, indeed, personified these liminal spaces.

A well-known legend from the Harz region tells of a wild man who was caught after putting up fierce resistance and who then expired in captivity because the loss of freedom did not suit him.[17] But capturing and subduing the wild man was, according to legend, desirable, inasmuch as an able captor could exploit wild men, known for their strength and ferocity, as warrior-guardians. The tamed and subdued wild man, like Cybeles with her lion-drawn chariot, thus emblematized civilization: violence held in check by, but simultaneously at the disposal of, human community and sovereign power.[18] The appearance of revelers dressed as club-wielding wild men in court festivals, for example, celebrated the ruler's power, a power so great that it could command the

---

[15] Ibid. P. 234.
[16] The "wilde Mann", a 1/8 Taler from seventeenth-century Braunschweig-Wolfenbüttel, for example, featured a wild man with an uprooted fir tree. Deutschland. See, Braunschweig-Wolfenbüttel. August d. J., 1635–1666. *Medieval-Modern E-Shop. LHS Numismatik*. http://www.lhs-numismatik.com/. Downloaded 5.1.2006. See also Wilder Mann. In: *Anumis. Münzen Lexikon*. http://www.anumis.de/lexikon/index.html. Downloaded 5.1.2006.
[17] *Sagen aus Niedersachsen zwischen Harz, Heide und Meer*. Ed. by Ulf Diederichs and Christa Hinze. Düsseldorf: Eugen Diederichs Verlag 1977. P. 27.
[18] Bartra similarly points out that the heraldic wild man "symbolically transmitted his virility to the coat of arms' owner." Roger Bartra: *Wild Men in the Looking Glass. The Mythic Origins of European Otherness*. Trans. by Carl T. Berrisford. Ann Arbor: U of Michigan Press 1994. P. 87.

service of these violent creatures.[19] In short, the wild man embodied the force required to create and maintain order.

More explicit to Raabe's life and times, in many North German provinces including Braunschweig and Brandenburg-Prussia the wild man circulated as the bearer of the heraldic shield. In the great crest of Braunschweig and Lüneburg, two bearded wild men, dressed in a loin cloth of oak leaves and with their customary weapons, large wooden clubs, turned to the earth, stand on either side of the shield supporting it with their free hand.[20] Similarly the crest of the Kingdom of Prussia of 1701 displays two wild men, leaning on the shield, their clubs resting on the ground. By Raabe's day these heraldic wild men had acquired the Prussian and Brandenburg banners in place of the clubs.[21] As a heraldic figure, the wild man embodies, as he did in early modern festivals, the brute strength and potential for violence that supports and serves the state. Yet another version of the Prussian crest depicts the shield flanked by a wild man on one side of the Prussian eagle and a knight in full armor on the other, thus making the link between brute force and military service to the state explicit. On 3 August 1871, William I established by decree the crest of the new Reich; when actually worked out, it too included two wild men supporting the shield in keeping with the Prussian crest.[22] Likewise two wild men holding flags upright were to be seen in a version of the Prussian crest on the masthead of the widely circulating *Vossische Zeitung*. In every case the heraldic wild men perform their assigned duty visually on the margin, outside the shield and the territories and power it represents. One can easily see an

---

[19] On the presence of wild men at court pageants and ceremonies, see Kevin Salatino, Alan St. H. Brock, and Eberbard Fähler. Kevin Salatino: *Incendiary Art: The Representation of Fireworks in Early Modern Europe*. Los Angeles: Getty Research Institute for the History of Art and the Humanities 1997. (Bibliographies & Dossiers: The Collection of the Getty Research Institute for the History of Art and the Humanities 3.) P. 14. Alan St. H. Brock: *A History of Fireworks*. London: George G. Harrap 1949. P. 32. Alan St. H. Brock: *Pyrotechnics: The History and Art of Firework Making*. London: Daniel O'Connor 1922. P. 17. Eberhard Fähler: *Feuerwerke des Barock. Studien zum öffentlichen Fest und seiner literarischen Deutung vom 16. bis 18. Jahrhundert*. Stuttgart: J. B. Metzler 1974. P. 27.

[20] *Wappen und Flaggen des Deutschen Reiches und seiner Bundesstaaten*. Ed. by Jürgen Arndt. Dortmund: Harenberg Kommunikation 1979. P. 59.

[21] Preußisches Wappen. *Preußen. Chronik eines deutschen Staates*. http://www.preussenchronik.de. Downloaded 5.1.2006.

[22] Arndt. Pp. 10–11. See also Maximilian Gritzner and Ottfried Neubecker. Maximilian Gritzner: *Landes- und Wappenkunde der Brandenburgisch-Preußischen Monarchie, Geschichte ihrer einzelnen Landestheile, deren Herrscher und Wappen*. Berlin: Carl Heymanns Verlag 1894. P. xiv. Ottfried Neubecker: *Das Deutsche Wappen 1806–1871*. Diss. Friedrich-Wilhelms-Universität Berlin, 1931. Görlitz-Biesnitz: Hans Kretschmer 1931. Pp. 15, 36.

analogy between such wild men in the service of the state and the executioner-mercenary Mördling/Agonista.

While these heraldic wild men may seem unremarkable *because* ubiquitous, an engraving by Albrecht Dürer – to whom we shall return below – reveals the potential for injury and disorder when the wild man bursts the bonds of his narrowly defined role and thus suggests by analogy the impact of this figure in Raabe's work. In his well-known *Coat of Arms of Death* from 1503, which Richard Bernheimer identifies as "in a sense a marriage print", the wild man steps out of his role as shield-supporter to force his attentions on a young maiden. Bernheimer proposes that Dürer's wild man embodies the commonplace theme of the intrusion of death into the marriage feast.[23] Germane to Raabe's story, however, is the simple fact of the transgression of boundaries by Dürer's wild man, his breaking out of his circumscribed role and his growing into ever greater mayhem. The very crossing over of Dürer's wild man brings the menace of death into life – death is thus no longer memorialized, contained, and separate as it is in the artistry of the shield, but part and parcel of human affairs.

Raabe's story likewise concerns itself with a crossing of boundaries and stepping out of roles that painfully uncover the underpinnings of human society. The Mördling men try to transcend their roles as executioners who serve state power to become part of the culture and civil society protected by this penal system. But in the German territories, the executioner who also served as torturer had traditionally and systematically been excluded from civil society and the rights accorded to its members by the very government whose penal authority he upheld.[24] In early modern Germany his marriage choices, his living space, and his place of burial were regulated and restricted. Often he was forced to live outside the city walls, or if within the city, he dwelt among other excluded groups. He was banned from entering certain spaces, and most people scrupulously avoided contact with him, dead or alive, or with any of the tools of his trade. In short, his trade belonged to the dishonorable ones, and thus he bore the stigma of what Günter Voß calls the classic "Tabuperson des Mittelalters" ["tabooed figure of the middle ages"] (101). Raabe, writing in so-called modern times in the new Reich, alludes lightly to these age-old restrictions when he refers to executioners as the "anrüchigsten Geschlechter

---

[23] Richard Bernheimer: *Wild Men in the Middle Ages: A Study in Art, Sentiment, and Demonology*. Cambridge: Harvard University Press 1952. Pp. 183–185.
[24] According to Voß, the rights of the executioner and the restrictions on him varied from territory to territory. He points out that in Braunschweig the executioner did not have the rights of the citizen (96) and that his dwelling place was next to the bordello, cater-corner from the parsonage. Günter Voß: Henker, Tabugestalt und Sündenbock. In: *Randgruppen der spätmittelalterlichen Gesellschaft*. Ed. by Bernd-Ulrich Hergemöller. Wahrendorf: Fahlbusch 1990. Pp. 86–114. Here: P. 94.

Deutschlands" ["most disreputable classes of men in Germany"] (11:209) and when he describes the Mördling household as located "natürlich außerhalb der Stadt" ["naturally outside the city"] (11:211). Early in the story Mördling himself will come only to the edge of the forest, never into the communal space of the town. The family name of course expresses the stigma of the trade more blatantly.

Mördling senior improbably manages in his solitude to gain at least intellectual entry into the humanistic culture of his day simply because the state never calls upon him to serve his inherited social function; Mördling junior meets a different and less benign fate, and even as he struggles with what he believes to be his inborn violence, unleashed by his inherited social role, he pulls the unwitting Kristeller into its vortex. Kristeller in fact founds his bourgeois success at the sign of the wild man without understanding its full meaning, that is, that his civil society and the new economic order depend on violence, its energy and its coercive power; violence is therefore always present, even if not always visible.[25] The empty chair held ready among the carefully assembled artifacts of civilization for communion with the wild man, underlines Kristeller's lack of comprehension. What, then, happens when the paid purveyor of state-sanctioned violence takes a seat at a domestic table as Agonista now intends to do?

By returning to Germany years later after organizing his life around his aroused will to violence and living as mercenary on the margins of civil society and beyond the purview of Europe in South America, Agonista explicitly renews his effort to force entry into civil society as bridegroom and businessman – and rather successfully at that. "Ich will es doch wenigstens einmal noch behaglich im deutschen Vaterlande haben" ["I really want to be nice and comfortable at least for once in [our] German Fatherland"], he declares after asking for a dressing gown and a pair of slippers (11:220). He cannot, however, merely sit down contentedly at the table. His destabilizing transgression of implicit boundaries leaves havoc in its wake: the ruin of Kristeller and the disruption and dissolving of the community into its own petty violence, a state of things that enables its members so easily to ignore Agonista's violation of

---

[25] Marshall remarks as well on Kristeller's failure to understand his situation; her reading, however, concerns itself with the perennial interpretation of the text as an indictment of capitalism. See Jennifer Cizik Marshall: Wilhelm Raabe's Apothecary. Two Texts Tracing the Pharmakology of the Wild Man. In: *Colloquia Germanica* 34 (2001). Pp. 27–40, esp. Pp. 29–30. Citing Nicholaas Cornelis Adrianus Perquin on Raabe, Sammons too asserts that Kristeller shares some blame for his misfortune (234). For an additional reading that focuses on *Zum wilden Mann* as an indictment of the new economic order, see Wilfried Thürmer: Entfremdetes Behagen. Wilhelm Raabes Erzählung "Zum wilden Mann" als Konkretion gründerzeitlichen Bewusstseins. In: *Jahrbuch der Raabegesellschaft* (1976). Pp. 151–161.

Kristeller and his sister. What are we to make of this story? Has Raabe simply left us with a morality tale?

No Shelter at the Sign of the Wild Man

The faint echo of the heraldic crest of the Second Empire notwithstanding, *Zum wilden Mann* does not at first glance readily connect with the moment in which it was written. A closer examination yields evidence, however, that even a story that has the air of a timeless morality tale broods on the immediate culture from which it emerged. We recall, for example, the aforementioned reference to speculation. But Raabe's text overtly invokes recent history and post-1871 Germany in its opening pages when it refers to the narrator and the friends, "die er aus dem deutschen Bund in den Norddeutschen und aus diesem in das neue Reich mit sich hinübergenommen hat" ["whom he brought over with him from the German Confederation into the North German Confederation and from the latter into the new Empire"]. Together the narrator and his friends seek shelter under the roof "dieser neuen Geschichte" ["of this new story/history"] (11:162). The locution is ambiguous – is this "Geschichte" the shelter of Raabe's newest story, ostensibly a form of escapism in literature, or is it the shelter of the new history, that is, the new times, the new empire? Those seeking shelter in either sense of the word are doomed to disappointment, because, as we quickly learn at the sign of the wild man, violence inheres in both meanings of the word "Geschichte" in the very structure of the fragile edifice.

A jotting in Raabe's notebook from 17 March 1875 obliquely raises the question of art with respect to the German present, that euphoric era following the defeat of France and the founding of the empire. It suggests a preoccupation on the author's part not merely with what art should have to do with the present, but with what the public expects of an artist in that respect. "Ein ächter Dichter sage *Ich*!" Raabe complains,

> Dieses heißt: Die Gebilde seiner Phantasie haben eine solche Wirklichkeit, dass sie die Gebilde des Tages ihm vollständig zurückdrängen, oder sich sublimieren – nachher spricht die Nation von Vaterlandslosigkeit und dergleichen. (Ergänzungsband 5:337)
> [A true poet *I* say! This means that the products of his imagination are so real that they completely repress the products of the day in his mind, or [the products of the day] are sublimated – later on the nation speaks of [his] lack of patriotism and such things.]

To paraphrase Raabe, the poetic imagination wields – and should wield – greater power than present experience per se, but the writer who surrenders himself to such vision runs the risk of having the public accuse him of ignoring the present and in the particular case of post-unification Germany of failing to affirm the achievements of that present. A month earlier on 25 February 1875, Raabe had disdainfully observed how public art had responded to the times. In this note he aimed his scorn at the ubiquitous kitschy self-congratulatory nationalist monuments to the victory over France: "Einige hundert Siegesdenkmäler und auf jedem eine Germania mit einem Kranz oder einer Palme in der Hand. Man würde sich wirklich freuen, mal etwas Neues zu sehn z.B. das hehre Weib auf dem Kopfe stehend" ["Several hundred victory monuments and on each of them a Germania-figure with a wreath or a palm frond in her hand. One would really be happy to see something new, for example, the sublime wench standing on her head"] (Ergänzungsband 5:336). Where, in fact, were the Raabian works celebrating the German people and their new empire?

Although a fervent nationalist in his Stuttgart years and the author of such blatantly sentimental and affirmative literature as *Im Siegeskranze* (1866) or *Des Reiches Krone* (1870),[26] Raabe had, so it appears, withdrawn at the very moment when he had reason and occasion to produce affirmative art in service of the new German empire. He moved his family from bustling Stuttgart to the backwaters of Braunschweig in the midst of the Franco-Prussian War as if turning his back on the present. *Der Dräumling* (1872), his first Braunschweig publication and most overt tribute to the times from the period immediately following the *Reichsgründung*, tends more toward ridicule of provincial celebration of German culture and nation than enthusiastic expression of patriotism or allegiance to the new empire. Indeed, Eckhardt Meyer-Krentler, noting *Der Dräumling* and other works including *Zum wilden Mann*, states outright,

> after 1871 Raabe wrote and spoke differently about the 'German people' in general and about the series of crucial events in 1859, 1860, 1864, 1866, and 1871. Again and again his literary works took up the theme [. . .] but never again to promote the national idea. His intention now was to heap scorn and mockery upon its failure. (151–152)

This is not to say that Raabe was uninterested in the new Germany, whether conceived culturally or politically. Although Meyer-Krentler categorically asserts that "Raabe had no interest in articulating a concrete political critique", he also maintains that Raabe was interested in a critique of sorts: "what he found important was the crass transformation of the social milieu and of the modes of behavior of the 'Gründerzeit' " (166–167). In the end, the social and the political are perhaps not so easily separated as Meyer-Krentler would have it. In any case, Raabe, the writer, observed the present with eyes different from those of the political activist, the patriot, or the journalist. His take on

---

[26] Meyer-Krentler. P. 156.

his historical moment is diffused rather than explicitly reflected in his literary work as he ponders social relations as he saw them carried over into and *preserved* in the edifice of this new German Reich. Raabe most certainly did wish to speak to a German nation of readers and with *Zum wilden Mann* he did so in the context of a series of stories that took up themes of violence.

Disease and Melancholy: Violence in the Wake of the *Reichsgründung*

Zum wilden Mann was the first of six stories serialized in *Westermanns Monatshefte* from April 1874 through August 1876 that were collected and published together in book form in 1879 as the *Krähenfelder Geschichten*, named for the Braunschweig suburb where Raabe wrote them. In keeping with their label, they number among the first fruits of his return to Braunschweig. As Butzmann explains, however, the publisher chose the title of the collection, not Raabe, who wished instead to name the collection for its oddest piece, *Vom alten Proteus*, an allusion, according to Butzmann, to the powerful and changeable life force that does not submit to human intellect or will (11:478–479; 12:524).

With the title *Krähenfelder Geschichten*, as with the list of contributors to *Westermanns Monatshefte* itself, where the physical location of each author is meticulously listed, the Braunschweig publisher stressed the regional – and perhaps homey-sounding and thus emotionally assimilable – origins of a literature that he marketed to a newly created empire. While these Krähenfeld stories are for the most part situated in real German regional localities – and largely in towns and villages near Braunschweig – the provincial and harmless ring of "Krähenfeld" belies the tragic and violent marbling of the works in the collection. Indeed, the stories in this anthology depict a world shaped by violence.[27]

Höxter und Corvey, the second of the *Krähenfelder Geschichten*, concerns the continued religious strife in the devastated town of Höxter on the Weser River around twenty-five years after the Peace of Westphalia. It recounts mob violence resulting in the pillaging of the few Jews remaining in Höxter. *Frau Salome* is set in the Harz mountains and tells the story of a girl abused by

---

[27] Baasner stresses in his analysis of *Zum wilden Mann* that these stories appear in the middle of Raabe's career and mark a transition between his early and late work. Rainer Baasner: "Sie konnten zusammen nicht kommen". Wilhelm Raabes Erzählung *Zum wilden Mann*. In: *Sinn und Symbol. Festschrift für Joseph P. Strelka zum 60. Geburtstag*. Ed. by Karl Konrad Polheim. Paris: Lang 1987. Pp. 179–199. Here: P. 180. He points out that one finds experimental innovation in their formal aspects and a preoccupation with eccentric cases that, overall, exhibits not so much pessimism as a search for a tolerable compromise in place of the harmony typically sought in German realism (198).

her mad artist father, who himself comes to a bad end in a violent scene of iconoclasm. *Die Innerste*, named for a wild river that runs through the Harz, takes place during the Seven Years War when the Harz was "bei weitem mehr als heute der wilde Harz" ["by far more the wild Harz than [it is] today"] (12:160) and involves a protagonist who has been recruited to the army of Frederick the Great as a mercenary only to desert later and try to lead a civilian life as a miller; he meets a bitter end when the mill is raided by three marauders wearing scraps of uniforms from several opposing armies. The text ironically calls the historical moment "die gute alte Zeit des Siebenjährigen Krieges" ["the good old days of the Seven Years War"] (12:105).[28] *Eulenpfingsten* concerns a family that was split apart by politics and betrayal in the 1830s. This work with its forced and lightly ironicized happy ending suggests with its title, which could be translated as "once in a blue moon", that happy endings are rare. Indeed, in *Eulenpfingsten*, set in Frankfurt, Arthur Schopenhauer himself tips his hat with deliberate politeness, after nearly bumping into the story's male protagonist (11:390–391). Finally, *Vom alten Proteus*, a peculiar ghost story that also exhibits some of the features of a fairy tale, a specifically "Germanic" one, as the narrator notes (12:202), comically – and grotesquely – plays with the haunting of the present by the pettiness and stupidity of the past, while depicting characters – both living and ghostly – deformed, as it were, by common everyday cruelty. The suggestion of cruelty behind domestic facades is made concrete by the plot element of a ghost who claims to have died of a broken heart and who has been trapped for thirty years behind the wallpaper in the living room of the very man who had broken her heart. The marriage plot, on the other hand, which in another work might have provided the happy ending, recedes in the face of a final dream. As the narrator cryptically asserts, "der alte Proteus entschlüpft wieder einmal unsern haltenden Armen; er behält nur zu gern all sein Wissen des Vergangenen, Gegenwärtigen und Zukünftigen für sich allein" ["once again old Proteus escapes our embrace; he is only too happy to retain all of his knowledge of things past, present, and future for himself alone"] (12:289).

All six stories, from *Zum wilden Mann* to *Vom alten Proteus*, have in common their close work with German settings, folk legends, history, politics, and cultural heritage. Furthermore, these variations on a theme, these literary probes into the "Innerste", that is, not the river per se but the innermost workings of the domestic – the German nation and the home – and its attendant

---

[28] For an in-depth examination of violence in *Die Innerste*, see Lynne Tatlock: Resonant Violence in *Die Innerste* and the Rupture of the German Idyll after 1871. In: *Wilhelm Raabe: Global Themes – International Perspectives*. Ed. by Dirk Göttsche and Florian Krobb. Oxford: Legenda, 2009. Pp. 126–137.

and ritualized violences, are at times as opaque in language and outlook as they are illuminating. Yet it is clear enough that in these stories Raabe, once the purveyor of sentimental literature, palpates what he now sees as something like a German heart of darkness. An odd detail in *Zum wilden Mann* underscores the idea of a literary probe of the body politic.

As is well known, *Zum wilden Mann* owes much to Raabe's biography. In July of 1873, while vacationing in Bad Harzburg, Raabe had to make repeated journeys on foot to an apothecary shop in a neighboring village – an apothecary shop that finds its literary counterpart in *Zum wilden Mann* – to retrieve medicine for his ten-year-old daughter Margarethe. Margarethe was suffering from "rote Ruhr", a form of dysentery that begins with diarrhea and devolves into a disintegration of the lining of the lower intestine (Butzmann 11:472). The salient symptom of this disease is bloody flux, "Blut im Stuhl". This "Blut im Stuhl" circulates in *Zum wilden Mann*, that is, in the very name conferred on the site of the ancient Germanic sacrificial altar, that is, the site of the critical scene between Kristeller and Mördling/Agonista.

The text contains two clues that suggest that the designation "Blutstuhl" serves a cryptic invocation of the core of the body. The first of these is the description of the site itself as labyrinthine; the second is Agonista's account of the ventriloquism of his first victim. Agonista relates how he had to remove the body of the man he had just beheaded from the scaffold and how he then imagined himself having dragged to the "Blutstuhl" this headless "patient" (as those condemned to death were termed in German), whom he had spent three weeks preparing for execution (11:215). Upon reaching the spot, Agonista fell on his face with the headless scoundrel on his back, who sang a song of triumph as a "Bauchredner sondergleichen" ["incomparable ventriloquist"] (11:216). This imagined ventriloquism in this symbolically charged Germanic landscape bespeaks a malaise of the body politic that, I propose, stands at the core of Raabe's fable. I shall explain.

"Blutstuhl" in its several connotations links the wild man Mördling's policing, that is, his so-called "healing" occupation as executioner, with Kristeller's healing profession and his minor claim to fame, the "*Magen*bitter" [literally: "*stomach* bitters"; my italics], the Kristeller that bears his name.[29]

---

[29] Stuart has demonstrated that in the German territories, despite the many taboos associated with him, the executioner often functioned as healer and purveyor of medicines well into the eighteenth century; his skill as healer derived from his intimate knowledge of the body as executioner, torturer, and knacker. Kathy Stuart: Des Scharfrichters heilende Hand. In: *Ehrenkonzepte in der Frühen Neuzeit. Identitäten und Abgrenzungen*. Ed. by Sibylle Backmann, Hans-Jörg Künast, Sabine Ullmann, and B. Ann Tlusty. Berlin: Akademie Verlag 1998. (Institut für Europäische Kulturgeschichte der Universität Augsburg Colloquia Augustana 8.) Pp. 321–347.

It connects this site of ancient sacrifice and the executioner's despair, an uncanny liminal space, to the liminal space occupied by the melancholy apothecary and his shop on the edge of the village with its "terrible bench" (with its obvious echoes of the rack, the "Folterbank") where those seeking healing medicine wait. In their respective professions, both the executioner and the apothecary tend, sometimes painfully, to communal health from the margins, as it were. The awful truth of the matter is, however, that the uncanny wielder of state-sanctioned violence exudes far more vitality because violence forms the community in the first place.

At the time of his meeting Mördling, Kristeller suffers from a depression that none of the drugs in the pharmacopeia aid. He lives his life in vicissitudes "zwischen Hypochondrie und gutem Lebensmut" ["between hypochondria and zest for life"] (11:180). While he wishes to help his forest friend, in the end that friend helps him. The narrative suggests, however, that despite the reversal of fortune his depression and lack of vitality persist. Even before Mördling's return, the story signals that Kristeller is not well; the narrator introduces him to us as "hager" and "gelb" ["gaunt" and "yellow"] (11:166).[30]

The very prominence of Dürer's master engraving *Melencolia I* (1514) in the interior of the shop attracts attention (11:166). Readers familiar with this famous piece, which like the sign of the wild man is only named and not described, may recall that a fair-haired, dark-faced Melancholia (dark faced because melancholic) sits paralyzed with thought and surrounded by

---

[30] I am by no means the first to draw attention to this melancholic aspect of Kristeller. Fauth's recent interpretation of Kristeller in the vein of a Schopenhauerian withdrawal from the world for the purpose of avoiding suffering reviews the copious textual evidence for Kristeller's melancholy. The color yellow, with its well-known associations with disease, may belong to an even more complex network of meaning. It is worth noting in any case that in the humoral medicine that had long dominated Western thought, yellow bile is associated with choler (not melancholy), Agonista's leading characteristic, while black bile is associated with melancholy. Choler and melancholy were in fact not so far apart as might appear; Hippocrates believed that the choleric ran the risk of becoming dried up and falling into melancholy sicknesses. See Raymond Klibansky, Erwin Panofsky and Fritz Saxl: *Saturn and Melancholy. Studies in the History of Natural Philosophy, Religion, and Art*. New York: Basic Books 1964. P. 12. Indeed, black bile was long "considered a noxious degeneration of the yellow bile" (14). Raabe's color coding may in the end be intended to underline the connection between the disposition of the two characters as two sides of a coin as it were. See Klibansky, Panofsky, and Saxl on the doctrine of the four humors as they pertain to melancholy. Pp. 3–15.

the props of geometry, the evidence of creative activity.[31] Kristeller, likewise surrounded by his medicines and the props of civilization, is also paralyzed. His invention, his tonic, as every reader must know, does not possess curative powers but merely mildly stimulates the appetite, a poor substitute for innate vitality. The "Kristeller" in fact offers humankind nothing to match or combat the radical cure meted out by the executioner.

Although Kristeller is initially unaware of the origins of his good fortune in violence, the text also provides ample evidence that he later deliberately avoids discovering this knowledge. He never returns to the "Blutstuhl", never inquires after the family name of his benefactor, and merely accedes to this fortunate turn of fate. Moreover, he even claims initially to have forgotten the anniversary of his purchase of the apothecary that bears the sign of violence. Even the empty chair, which should serve as a mnemonic device, has become such a familiar part of his domestic life that it is easy to overlook its significance. Furthermore, when Mördling returns as Agonista and fills in the gaps in the story, Kristeller, like the rest of the village, remains willfully blind to the depravity of Agonista's nature and its consequences for brother and sister – despite the sister's repeated warnings. His gratitude to the unknown man is so ritualized as to block insight. Yet at some level, the perennially depressed Kristeller must have an inkling of the "mystery" encrypted in the wild man.

A review that appeared in a Braunschweig newspaper on 23 July 1885 understands Raabe's wild man to incorporate the naked will to survive

---

[31] See Klibansky, Panofsky, and Saxl on the black or dark face (289–290) and on associations of melancholy with creativity and idleness as well as on *Melencolia I* as a fusion of an "ars geometrica" with a "homo melancholicus" (284–365): "[Dürer] was bold enough to bring down the timeless knowledge and method of a liberal art into the sphere of human striving and failure, bold enough, too, to raise the animal heaviness of a 'sad earthly' temperament to the height of a struggle with intellectual problems" (317). They assert further that here Melancholia's inactivity has "changed from the idler's lethargy and the sleeper's unconsciousness to the compulsive preoccupation of the highly-strung" (317–318). The authors also point out that Dürer's *Melencolia I* displays some traditional motifs of the figure of melancholy, namely the association of melancholy with avarice and wealth. Indeed, Dürer himself noted that the purse signified riches and the keys hanging from Melancholy's belt, power (284). Klibansky, Panofsky and Saxl point furthermore to Nicholas of Cusa's assertion of "the melancholic's ability to attain 'great riches' even by dishonest means" as a "symptom of 'avaritiosa melancholia'" (284). Since the narrator only mentions the engraving, we cannot know to what extent Raabe was familiar with the complex iconographic tradition of melancholy as rendered here. The combination of melancholy, riches, and power is certainly suggestive of the issues that stand at the center of *Zum wilden Mann*.

(11:477), a notion that resonates with the popular Darwinism of the period.[32] Agonista's vitality compared with Kristeller's melancholy might well suggest a Darwinian competition of the fittest for survival, one that Kristeller is certain to lose even if readers see him as the morally superior character. In any case, as types, melancholic and choleric, Kristeller and Agonista, the apothecary and the executioner, may in the end be less interesting in psychological terms than as products and determinants of social relations. If so, what then do they have to do as signs of social relations with the community of readers whom Raabe addresses at the sign of the wild man?

Narration and Communion at the Sign of the Wild Man

The novel places in the foreground the encounter between reader and narrator when it commences on a stormy night with a meeting of the narrator and the reader at the sign of the wild man, thus to launch a reflection on human brutality. In this opening meeting of reader and narrator, it therefore concerns itself with community and violence not merely as an element of plot but also as a feature of narration.

The opening pages of the story comprise a protracted description of entry into narrative, a narrative that cannot unfold until the frantic travelers, an unidentified "we", reach an apothecary's shop that stands at the outermost end of the village highway. Narrator and reader meet on the staircase leading to the door to the apothecary shop, and the narrator pulls the reader through that door and across the threshold into the house where they find themselves "in dem Hause sowohl wie in der Geschichte vom *Wilden Mann!*" ["in the house as well as in the story/history of the *Wild Man!*"] (11:163). Pages later after what the narrator calls a setting of the stage, namely a thorough description of the museum-like interior of the apothecary shop, which the text refers to as a "Bildergalerie" ["picture gallery"] (11:166), and the arrival of intimate friends, Kristeller finally takes up his story but not before the forester makes the ostensibly incongruous remark "Endlich ist das Wild los!" ["Finally the hunt has begun!" literally: "Finally the wild game is loose!"] (11:177) that obliquely references the novel's title. The remark also recalls the stuffed and contained "Wildkatze" ["wild cat"] in the glass case (11:165) that numbers among the many carefully noted artifacts of civilization meticulously arrayed in the apothecary shop, the product of thirty years' careful accumulation.[33]

---

[32] Butzmann believes that Raabe approved or may even have influenced this review. Hans Butzmann: Zum wilden Mann. In: Wilhelm Raabe: *Sämtliche Werke*. Vol. 11. Göttingen: Vandenhoeck & Ruprecht 1956. Pp. 472–491. Here: P. 477.

[33] Fauth makes the important point that the art that Kristeller has collected in fact depicts some of the defects of the world outside, that is, the world of Agonista (614). In art violence is contained.

At the very moment when the forester imagines that storytelling figuratively lets loose wild things to be hunted down, we enter into the history that has devastating consequences for Kristeller's present, and judging from Jensen's and others' reactions to this story, for the reader's peace of mind. Is the narrator a taxidermist? Is narrative supposed to stuff wild things and put them in a glass case, that is, should it like taxidermy display violence but hold it in check for its readers, or does it rather run the risk of causing permanent disruption by unleashing wildness? The text explores this question overtly, for Raabe not only meticulously sets up the narrative situation in *Zum wilden Mann*, but also records the impact of a narration of violence on those who hear it.

The apothecary shop at the sign of the wild man is the fully realized setting of the narration of Kristeller's and Agonista's past. The description of this interior space and the narration of the past within that space take up nine of seventeen chapters of the short novel. As suggested by Kristeller's cap embroidered with acorns and oak leaves and his pipe adorned with a *Maikäfer*, the village worthies around the punch bowl initially invoke the "Behaglichkeit" ["comfortable coziness"] sought by many German realists, that is, "Behaglichkeit" as a feature of their writing, of a particular German brand of realism, and "Behaglichkeit" as a specific national characteristic to be depicted and cherished.[34] The "Behaglichkeit" of this story, however, is evoked only to be unmasked as illusory. This is not the nature of the community that Raabe depicts here. Nor is it the kind of narrative that he is prepared to offer his German readership in 1874.

Despite the punch bowl, the setting quickly undercuts any feelings of comfort the reader may initially have or seek, for it provides frequent reminders of sickness and the pressing need for drastic treatment; among other things, customers continue to ring the bell late into the evening.[35] Moreover, while

---

[34] The works of Gustav Freytag, the proponent of so-called "programmatic realism", offer perhaps the most striking examples of the idea of "Behaglichkeit" as a German characteristic. Not only does Freytag frequently employ the word but he cites the quality as specifically German. See Lynne Tatlock: Realistic Historiography and the Historiography of Realism: Gustav Freytag's "Bilder aus der deutschen Vergangenheit". In: *German Quarterly* 63 (1990). Pp. 59–74; Lynne Tatlock: Regional History as National History: Gustav Freytag's *Bilder aus der deutschen Vergangenheit*. In: *Searching for Common Ground: Diskurse zur deutschen Identität 1750–1871*. Ed. by Nicholas Vazsonyi. Cologne: Böhlau 2000. Pp. 161–178; and Lynne Tatlock: "In the Heart of the Heart of the Country": Regional Histories as National History in Gustav Freytag's *Die Ahnen* (1872–80). In: *A Companion to German Realism (1848–1900)*. Ed. by Todd Kontje. Rochester, New York: Camden House Press 2002. Pp. 85–108.

[35] The general undercutting of expectations of "Behaglichkeit" in Raabe's later works, expectations raised in part by Raabe's early works, has been addressed by, among others, Sammons: *Wilhelm Raabe* and William Hanson: Raabe's Region. In: *Seminar* 12 (1986). Pp. 277–298.

it presents itself externally at the sign of the energetic wild man, inside, at its core, Dürer's paralyzed *Melencolia* reigns, hanging, as Sammons remarks, significantly between two street scenes from 1848 (101).[36]

The text does not allow the reader to forget the questionable nature of the space where the story is being told, a place where medicine is dispensed to the desperate. At the moment when the narrator officially declares the reader and the narrator to be in the story of the wild man, he interjects that the smell of the place reminds us that we are in an apothecary shop. Furthermore, the narrator notes the aforementioned "schreckliche Bank" ["terrible bench"] where those seeking medicine must wait. If it were not for this bench, he adds, "hätte das Werkzeug und Geräte der hohen Kunst [. . .] jedermann das höchste Vertrauen einflößen müssen" ["the tools and equipment of the lofty art would have had to fill everyone with the greatest confidence"] (11:163). The "böse Bank! Der abgeriebene, schlimme Stuhl" ["evil bench! The awful chair, worn smooth"] recalls the suffering not just of the sick, but of those who come there, frantic with grief and seeking aid for patient and caregiver (11:163–164).[37] What then does the narrative at the sign of the wild man offer patients, those who hear or read it?

The men actually listening to Agonista's story are initially dumbstruck. Their confused helplessness persists when Agonista goes on to recount his violent past in South America in still more detail and toasts Kristeller and his apothecary shop. Yet on their homeward journey the doctor preens himself for having brought Agonista into the village, and he and the forester eagerly make plans to entertain this splendid fellow. Only the pastor, sensing a diabolic foundation to Kristeller's present existence, is alarmed by Agonista's parading of his violent past. The narrator insists that if a million others had been in this situation, they would not have noticed more than did the pastor and the forester (11:225). The reader, however, cued by Kristeller's alarmed sister, must view the situation differently.

The village in any case takes up Agonista with alacrity. Soon his deep bass voice resounds within the walls of the village church and the villagers line up ceremoniously to pay their respects to the old mercenary soldier, as if he were a conquering hero. This paid executioner in fact stirs up the entire village; the doctor later tells him that he awakened everyone's imagination, leading to widespread sleeplessness (11:251). Rather than condemnatory of his violent career, the obscure community is, as we learn, enthralled by visions of conquest

---

[36] Raabe leaves unstated the fact that street scenes from 1848 refer to revolutionary fighting. The placement of melancholy between two such pictures may reflect sadness over the failed mid-century struggle for freedom and unity and perhaps discontent over the form that unity has taken in the 1870s.

[37] Note the affinity of this "Stuhl" to the "Blutstuhl".

and exotic lands, consumed by a will to colonize. The story of Agonista's vital brutality has awakened the inherent brutality of the community, and at precisely this disruptive and disorderly moment it openly allies itself with the executioner and mercenary, turning its back on the apothecary. We can further infer that this now overtly brutal society, one made so by narrations of violence in this story set in the 1860s, will be conserved in the new Reich.

But what of the impact of *Zum wilden Mann* on its *readers*? The text describes readers' entry into the apothecary shop and into the story, but does not characterize their exit. Raabe never closes the frame so laboriously established in the opening pages and in effect leaves his imagined readers vainly waiting on the torturous bench for a medicine that is not forthcoming. One of Raabe's much later works, namely *Stopfkuchen*, offers a clue as to how we might understand the impact on the reader of this novel. Indeed, it suggests how the bitter medicine doled out through narration at the sign of the wild man could prove salutary for Germans readers in late nineteenth-century Germany.

A Cannonball in a Domestic Frame

Why then did Raabe choose this disturbing and curiously unresolved story for mass circulation and de facto canonization? I return to the question that opened this essay by way of the late work *Stopfkuchen*, which appeared in 1891, seventeen years after the initial serialized publication of *Zum wilden Mann*. With the character Heinrich Schaumann, aka Stopfkuchen, Raabe again took up themes of violence and community sounded in *Zum wilden Mann*. In *Stopfkuchen* the eponymous hero sets up his household in an old military fortification, the red redoubt, which like the apothecary shop occupies a marginal space on the edge of the community. From this vantage Schaumann solves a murder that itself grew out of the social injustice around which this putatively respectable town is organized, that is, what Johan Galtung terms "structural violence".[38] In identifying the killer, the perennially angry Schaumann performs what has been called the cultural "policing function" of anger.[39]

We can recognize in the voracious Heinrich Schaumann, the inveterate talker, the expansive ego of the intellectual who desires to be heard, and thus we can also understand the author's well-known – although perhaps ironic – sympathy with this character, whether or not we share it. Despite his belligerent address to the outside world, and particularly to the community from which he emerged, Schaumann has sublimated his own will to violence. As Sammons points out, he has, as it were, civilized his own immediate

---

[38] Johan Galtung: Violence, Peace, and Peace Research. In: *Journal of Peace Research* 6 (1969). Pp.167–191.
[39] Carol Tavris: Uncivil Rites – The Cultural Rules of Anger. In: *Anger. The Misunderstood Emotion*. Rev. ed. New York: Touchstone 1989. Pp. 48–69. Here: P. 3.

environment; he has put a stop to the domestic abuse within the confines of the walls of the red redoubt as well as tamed his wife, the "wild cat" Tinchen Quakatz.[40] He has, furthermore, transformed himself from the child, whom everyone bullied and who might himself have eventually been capable of murder – like everyone else in the community, Schaumann implies (18:22) – into the aggressive talker who is prepared to confront his entire community. In the end, his own heart of darkness enables him to suspect even the ostensibly harmless Störzer and thus to solve a murder. Unlike the quiescent Kristeller who suffers privately leaving the village its platitudes and illusions, the choleric Schaumann unmasks injustice leaving his community – and particularly the narrator, Eduard – in turmoil.

The particular impetus for Schaumann's life plan to conquer the red redoubt and thereby to position himself strategically to turn the tables on his brutal community throws light in retrospect on Raabe's selection of a harrowing tale that should have been "polizeilich verboten" as food for the German people. This inspiration inheres in the very facade of the house in which Schaumann was born. Unlike Kristeller, however, Schaumann can read the sign on his own home and thus takes up a policing position at the edge of the community with an active aggression more reminiscent of the choler of an Agonista than the melancholy of a Kristeller.

This sign and inspiration is a cannonball fired on the town during the Seven Years War and suspended in a domestic facade. Raabe refashioned here a historic impromptu monument known to him from Wolfenbüttel to produce a device for stirring up Schaumann's imagination.[41] Schaumann, insisting on the power of this improvised commemoration of a civil war of sorts, wonders pointedly whether his interlocutor has in colonial Africa anything better than this cannonball for instructing his boys (11:68).

The cannonball suspended in a domestic wall opens Schaumann's eyes to more than the mere facts of the Seven Years War. On the one hand, it displays the inherence of violence in this community. On the other, it suggests to Schaumann the possibility of liberating himself from and confronting that community. Most important for our context, it may be seen to figure the import and impact of the tale at the *sign* of the wild man, the canonized story in which the violence that Raabe portrays as endemic to German community is evoked and interrogated, yet suspended, because here it is after all only fiction.

By excising *Zum wilden Mann* from the *Krähenfelder Geschichten* for publication in Reclam's *Universalbibliothek*, Raabe challenged the German nation to read what some contemporaries considered a dangerous book. The

---

[40] Sammons: *Wilhelm Raabe*. P. 290.
[41] Hans Oppermann: *Wilhelm Raabe in Selbstzeugnissen und Bilddokumentation*. Reinbek bei Hamburg: Rowohlt 1970. P. 119.

highly visible placement of the novel made it a public monument of sorts akin to the cannonball in the domestic facade in Wolfenbüttel, that is, it appeared as a surprisingly explosive piece in a disarming setting. Forced, literary, and removed from the present as it may appear on its surface, Raabe's story – at the sign of the wild man – probes German communal life, alluding obliquely to the violent underpinnings of a modern social formation, indeed, one founded in a series of wars. Raabe thus invented and in the end had canonized an alternative, although cryptic, story for the Germans to tell themselves about themselves. In other words, with the elusive sign of the wild man that conceals a fair-haired, dark-faced Melancholia within – and significantly one engraved by the artist touted by Hermann Grimm in 1866 as the embodiment of Germany and the Fatherland[42] – Raabe offers a Germania standing on her head, so to speak, one that, as he once quipped, might make a good alternative to the self-congratulatory commemorations springing up all over Germany.

---

[42] Ute Kuhlemann: The Celebration of Dürer in Germany during the Nineteenth and Twentieth Centuries. In: *Albrecht Dürer and His Legacy*. Ed. by Giulia Bartrum. Princeton: Princeton University Press 2002. Pp. 39–60. Here: P. 39. As Kuhlemann maintains, by the 1870s Dürer and his works had been taken up by German nationalists. Four months after the declaration of the German empire in January 1871, Dürer's 400th birthday (21 May 1471) was celebrated in Nuremberg with among other things a torch-light procession to the Dürer monument, led by Turners (50).

Carl Niekerk

Constructing the Fascist Subject: Violence, Gender, and Sexuality in Ödön von Horváth's *Jugend ohne Gott*

This interpretation reads Ödön von Horváth's novel Jugend ohne Gott *(1937) in the context of the critique of modern subjectivity as dependent on "trans- or pre-subjective foundational powers", articulated among others by Horkheimer and Adorno in their seminal* Dialectic of the Enlightenment *(1947). The paper asks to what extent fascism was successful at colonizing this dependence for its totalitarian purposes. While Horváth published his novel with a prominent exile publishing house, he had repeatedly spent longer periods of time in Germany after 1933 and his novel therefore offers a unique "inside" view of fascist Germany. Horváth's novel demonstrates that in particular "sexuality" and "violence" are key areas in which the fascist regime sought to tie its subjects to its totalitarian and racist agenda. The novel, however, also suggests that any attempt to mobilize its subjects for this agenda can only be imperfect, and hints at strategies of resistance, leaving open the question of their success.*

One of the most influential philosophical texts that seeks to understand the origins of the Third Reich has been Max Horkheimer and Theodor W. Adorno's *Dialektik der Aufklärung* [*Dialectic of the Enlightenment*], written in California during the Second World War and first published in book form by Querido in Amsterdam (1947), and republished, in a second edition, by Fischer in 1969. Even though the *Dialektik* has a coherent thesis, it is a very diverse book; it contains a number thematically focused chapters on the concept of Enlightenment, the culture industry, and anti-Semitism respectively, but also two lengthy excurses on Homer's *Odyssey* and the Marquis de Sade, and concludes with a number of aphoristic fragments on a wide range of topics. One of the key images used by Horkheimer and Adorno to explain the book's central thesis – the idea that the Enlightenment runs the risk of turning into what it claims to oppose, namely myth – is that of Odysseus escaping the seductive songs of the Sirens. Odysseus has his men tie him to the mast of his ship, in such a way that he can barely move his head to indicate when the danger has passed. He simultaneously forces the men themselves to put wax into their ears so that they will not be distracted by the songs of the Sirens from rowing their ship to safety (the source of this story is the twelfth book of Homer's *Odyssey*).[1]

---

[1] Max Horkheimer and Theodor W. Adorno: *Dialektik der Aufklärung. Philosophische Fragmente*. Frankfurt am Main: Fischer 1988. Pp. 38–41. In the following this volume will be cited as *DA*.

This is an intriguing image. It raises the question of the foundations of human agency in a totalitarian state. It is this question that I would like to pursue in this essay in relation to fascism. In the following, I will contrast a reading of the Odysseus-references in the *Dialektik* with a reading of Ödön von Horváths novel *Jugend ohne Gott*, first published in 1937 by Allert de Lange in Amsterdam and almost immediately a bestseller in pre-war Europe.[2] What interests us here is the extent to which the type of agency Horkheimer and Adorno attribute to Odysseus is viable when dealing with the Third Reich, not on a philosophical level, but as an every-day reality. *Jugend ohne Gott* is very much a novel about power structures and the limits they place on human agency. Moreover, in this novel Hitler's Germany is not an abstract entity, something seen from a distance, but rather is described from the "inside" and very much based on what Horváth himself saw and experienced during his visits to Germany between 1933 and 1937.

While the deliberations on Odysseus in Horkheimer and Adorno's *Dialektik der Aufklärung* certainly answer some questions about the book's underlying ideas, they also evoke others, in particular concerning the presuppositions underlying Horkheimer and Adorno's project. For the two authors of the *Dialektik*, Odysseus is one of the figures personifying the Enlightenment. The Sirens represent for Horkheimer and Adorno the danger of getting lost in the past (*DA* 39), or, one could say, the irrational seductions of mythological knowledge, presented in an aesthetically pleasing form. At the same time the lure of the Sirens, not only in Homer's text, but also in Horkheimer and Adorno's interpretation, is a sexual one. The scenario is a highly gendered one: the very masculine Odysseus is to reject the temptations represented by female sexuality in order to save the Enlightenment.[3] It is as if Horkheimer and Adorno are saying that the human need for mythological models to make sense of life is similar to other basic human drives like sexual desire. This point is not unique to Horkheimer and Adorno, but also resonates with Fritz Lang's *Metropolis*, made a decade earlier, in which a hyper-sexual robotic Maria-figure is designed to tie workers to a highly technological, totalitarian

---

[2] Ödön von Horváth: *Jugend ohne Gott*. In: *Gesammelte Werke*. Ed. by Traugott Krischke and Susanna Foral-Krischke. Frankfurt am Main: Suhrkamp 1983. Vol. 13. All page numbers in the text refer to this edition. All translations are mine unless otherwise noted.

[3] This gendered dimension of Horkheimer and Adorno's reconstruction of the *Odyssey* has been criticized in scholarship on the *Dialektik*; see Helga Geyer-Ryan and Helmut Lethen: Von der Dialektik der Gewalt zur *Dialektik der Aufklärung*. Eine Re-Vision der *Odyssee*. In: *Vierzig Jahre Flaschenpost*. Dialektik der Aufklärung *1947 bis 1987*. Ed. by Willem van Reijen and Gunzelin Schmid Noerr. Frankfurt am Main: Fischer 1987. Pp. 41–72. Here: Pp. 46–48 and 67.

regime.[4] Through its analysis, the *Dialektik* participates in a trend within modern German thinking that critiques human autonomy by pointing to the subject's dependence on what Manfred Frank has called "trans- oder vor-subjektive Ursprungsmächte" ["trans- or pre-subjective foundational powers"].[5] Human autonomy, according to this line of thinking, is endangered, because the subject has to rely on what is beyond its powers; this realm of the "beyond" is projected onto female sexuality. Surprisingly, in spite of the *Dialektik*'s clear indebtedness to Freud's thinking, Horkheimer and Adorno have a predominantly negative view of human sexuality and advocate a repressive model that is highly gendered in that it favors "male" repression over what it sees as "female" indulgence. It is especially problematic that in the *Dialektik der Aufklärung*, "sexuality" functions as a metaphor for the anti-subjective tendencies in fascism as a whole.

In their choice of imagery, Horkheimer and Adorno conflate in Manfred Frank's terminology the "trans-" and "pre-subjective" dimensions exerting pressure on the self-conscious and self-critical Western subject. Manfred Frank bases his thinking here on Jürgen Habermas's *Der philosophische Diskurs der Moderne* [*Philosophical Discourse of Modernity*], first published in 1985 – a book that thematized the contradictory nature of the subject criticism in the work of some of the main critics of modern subjectivity (Nietzsche, Heidegger, Derrida, Foucault, and also Horkheimer and Adorno) and their inability to provide a normative framework for modern society.[6] While Frank on the one hand feels the need to distinguish between "trans-" and "pre-subjective" powers in summarizing Habermas's text, he does little on the other hand to explain this distinction. While one may assume that pre-subjective foundational powers are those drives that are part of the subject before it became a self-conscious being (in a Freudian sense), and trans-subjective powers may be conceived to be those technological, institutional, and discursive powers existing independent of subjectivity, Frank gives few concrete examples of such powers. His abstract formulations include the "will", the "unconscious", "being", "différance", and the "naked will to power" (12). This is in part the case because Habermas and Frank's main sources do not make a clear distinction between both categories either, a lapse which could be taken as indicative of a lacuna inherent to the philosophical discourse they analyze.

[4] See Andreas Huyssen: *After the Great Divide: Modernism, Mass Culture, Postmodernism*. Bloomington: Indiana University Press 1986. Pp. 70–72.
[5] Manfred Frank: *Die Unhintergehbarkeit von Individualität. Reflexionen über Subjekt, Person und Individuum aus Anlaß ihrer "postmodernen" Toterklärung*. Frankfurt am Main: Suhrkamp 1986. P. 12. Frank bases his deliberations here on Jürgen Habermas's *Philosophical Discourse of Modernity*.
[6] See Jürgen Habermas: *Der philosophische Diskurs der Moderne. Zwölf Vorlesungen*. Frankfurt am Main: Suhrkamp 1988. P. 31.

It is perhaps this need for the Odysseus-metaphor to represent many diverging things that makes Horkheimer and Adorno's attitude toward him as a figure for their philosophical enterprise ambiguous. In the excursus on the *Odyssey* in the *Dialektik*, Odysseus figures as the prototypical bourgeois, capitalist citizen (*DA* 50, 69). This is different, however, in the passage referred to above that is part of the introductory chapter on the concept of Enlightenment. In this particular context, Odysseus does not represent any specific collective, but rather the person who thinks for the collective, the artist-intellectual. While Horkheimer and Adorno's attitude toward Odysseus is rather dismissive in the excursus, this does not seem to be the case in the earlier passage. In fact, this is one of the few passages in the *Dialektik* where the authors suggest a successful strategy of resistance against the Enlightenment's enemies: Odysseus outsmarts the Sirens by temporarily limiting his men's (and his own) autonomy. What remains unclear though is where exactly in this specific passage the authors position themselves in the conflict between Enlightenment and mythology. While in general there is no doubt about Horkheimer and Adorno's commitment to the Enlightenment's goals of (relative) autonomy, knowledge, and a fairer society for all, here they seem to suggest that abandoning the Enlightenment's goals temporarily might be a smart thing for the artist-intellectual to do, if it is in the interest of the Enlightenment's longer-term goals. It is remarkable to note (and often overlooked) that for Horkheimer and Adorno "tricks" and "cheating" ["List" / "Betrug"] are constitutive components of Enlightenment thinking (see for instance *DA* 55, 56), and therefore also permitted tactics, one could conclude, if in the cause of defeating the Enlightenment's reactionary enemies (i.e. fascism), as the passage about Odysseus's encounter with the Sirens appears to suggest. This too points to a gap at the core of the *Dialektik*: a fundamental, but mostly unreflected ambiguity toward some of its key ideas, in particular to the figure of the artist-intellectual.

That the *Dialektik* became a key text for the generation of 1968 has a lot to do with the critical potential of the *Dialektik*'s central ideas. It allowed the '68 generation to view the Third Reich not as the results of the actions of a madman (Hitler), or at most a small group of criminally minded demagogues, but made it possible to understand the crimes of the Third Reich as the result of long-term processes and power structures at work in German society that were beyond the control of the subject (the "trans- or pre-subjective foundational powers" mentioned above). In fact, this generation perceived these authoritarian power structures as still at work in German society in the late 1960s, since the generation of their parents, it was stipulated, had done little to work through its past, and fascism, one could assume, had not just suddenly disappeared in 1945. Developments after 1968 however proved that a perspective which was employed critically at that specific point in time could all-too-easily be co-opted to explain (and maybe even legitimate) participation in the Third Reich. Much of the debate about Heidegger and his work in the 1970s and 1980s asked whether there is a connection between a trans-/pre-subjective critique of modernity and Heidegger's naiveté in dealing with those in power in the Third Reich. The *Historikerstreit* of the 1980s can be understood as the response to the work of one historian who claimed that the crimes of the Nazis were by no means unique, but rather merely reproduced what Stalin and the Soviets had done before them. The real provocation of Daniel Goldhagen's *Hitler's Willing Executioners*, in contrast, was that it forced Germans to turn away from structural explanations that depended on institutional powers beyond individual control and face the question of the extent to which the crimes of the Third Reich needed the participation and decision-making of ordinary German citizens.[7] Ideas that had been perceived to be highly critical around 1968 represented a consensus around the mid-1990s. What is critical at one point can be a nearly irrelevant observation in another historical context.

In the following, I hope to contribute to an answer to some of the questions raised by my reading of the Odysseus-myth in Horkheimer and Adorno's *Dialektik der Aufklärung*. In my view, Ödön von Horváth's novel *Jugend ohne Gott* is important because it was written before the beginning of the Second World War at a point in time when there was still little consensus about the sociological, psychological, and ideological roots of fascism, and by an author with, in every respect, rather unorthodox ideas, who had not only observed Germany's transition to a fascist state from close by, but had also lived in Nazi Germany. My analysis of *Jugend ohne Gott* will focus on the role of the intellectual and his functioning in a totalitarian state. In particular, I am interested in the question of human autonomy, keeping in mind not only Horkheimer and Adorno's views in the *Dialektik der Aufklärung*, but also how post-war discourse on this issue in relation to the Third Reich has veered between opposing positions. *Jugend ohne Gott* is a text about how technology, media, and discourse can serve to indoctrinate a population (the trans-subjective

---

[7] For a summary of the debate on Heidegger, see the contributions to two special issues on Heidegger of the *New German Critique:* 45 (1988) and 53 (1991). For a discussion of the *Historikerstreit*, see *"Historikerstreit". Die Dokumentation der Kontroverse um die Einzigartigkeit der nationalsozialistischen Judenvernichtung*. München-Zurich: Piper 1987, and *Ist der Nationalsozialismus Geschichte? Zu Historisierung und Historikerstreit*. Ed. by Dan Diner. Frankfurt am Main: Fischer 1987. Regarding the debate on Daniel Goldhagen's book, see *Ein Volk von Mördern? Die Dokumentation zur Goldhagen-Kontroverse um die Rolle der Deutschen im Holocaust*. Ed. by Julius H. Schoeps. Hamburg: Hofmann and Campe 1996, and *"The Goldhagen Effect": History, Memory, Nazism – Facing the German Past*. Ed. by Geoff Eley. Ann Arbor: Michigan University Press 2000.

element in Horkheimer and Adorno's analysis). With the help of modern media (the radio), an authoritarian regime seeks to create cultural homogeneity through a mythical language full of gendered and racist stereotypes that in particular thematize "violence" and "sexuality". In *Jugend ohne Gott*, violence and sexuality are however also thematized as pre-subjective foundational powers, as basic drives in human nature. As part of the Freudian heritage in Horváth's novel, both are seen as basic human drives. The question I want to answer in the following is how an untangling of these super- and pre-subjective foundational powers can help us to come to a more differentiated and complex reading of German fascism than Horkheimer and Adorno's *Dialektik*, with its predominantly repressive view of power, would suggest. Horváth's text, on the contrary, thematizes the friction between an ideological mobilization of violence and sexuality on the one hand, and Freud's insight that these drives are beyond rational control on the other. Only if we understand violence and sexuality as basic elements of human nature we can understand the psychological origins of fascism.

As an author, Ödön von Horváth does not easily fit any of the established paradigms with which we approach German-language literature published between 1933 and 1945, and yet he does in many respects exemplify the dilemmas of the intellectual under a totalitarian regime. He published his last two novels, *Jugend ohne Gott* and *Ein Kind unserer Zeit*, with Allert de Lange, the prominent publishing house of German-language texts in Amsterdam for authors who could no longer publish in Germany. But to categorize him therefore as a (typical) representative of exile literature is problematic; at the very least his trajectory in the 1930s is not typical of those who went into exile. Horváth was born as the son of a diplomat on December 9, 1901, in Fiume,[8] a city that at the time was part of the Austrian-Hungarian Empire; today it is called Rijeka and part of Croatia. He spent his childhood in Belgrade, Budapest, Munich, Preßburg, and Vienna where he graduated from high school in 1919. From 1923 to early 1933, Horváth divided his time between Berlin and Murnau, a small town in southern Bavaria bordering on the Alps where his parents owned a villa. Horváth attempted to become a German citizen, but at the beginning of the Third Reich was still in possession of his Hungarian nationality. National Socialism was popular in Murnau, and Horváth observed this with growing concern.[9] On February 1, 1931, Horváth witnessed

---

[8] The following factual information about Horváth's biography is based on Traugott Krischke: *Ödön von Horváth. Kind seiner Zeit*. München: Wilhelm Heyne 1980.
[9] The following biographical information is taken from Elisabeth Tworek-Müller: Am Rande der weißblauen Kalkalpen – Ödön von Horváth und Murnau. In: *Horváth und Murnau, 1924–1933*. Ed. by Elisabeth Tworek-Müller. Vienna: Löcker 1988. Pp. 40–63. Here: Pp. 41–45.

a battle between Nazis and SPD members in Hotel Kirchmeier that caused considerable damage; asked about it by two different courts later that same year, he gave a report that was rather unflattering for the Nazis.[10] A second incident happened on February 10, 1933, when a radio in Horváth's favorite bar, Hotel Post, played a speech by Hitler from the Berlin Sport Palace. When Horváth asked for the radio to be turned off, the waitress did so but this action led to fierce protests from members of the SA present. What happened next is not entirely clear, but eventually two SA members escorted Ödön von Horváth home. He left Murnau the next day; his parents' house was searched soon thereafter.

On the basis of this and a number of texts published by the author that were highly critical of the Nazis – among them in particular *Sladek* (1928) and *Italienische Nacht* (1930) – one would have expected that Horváth would be one of strongest critics of the Third Reich from the very beginning. Initially, however, Horváth decided otherwise. In spite of the fact that the Nazi-press agitated against him, that his books were no longer sold and his plays no longer performed in Germany, he spent most of 1934 and 1935 in Berlin – from March 12, 1934, to September 20, 1935, to be precise, when he was again officially registered as an inhabitant of Vienna.[11] In Berlin, his initial intention was to write for the theater, but he ended up making a living as a screenwriter (under the pseudonym H.W. Becker, even though it is not clear whether he is the only person who used this pen name).[12] To be allowed to do so, on July 11, 1934, he became a member of the *Reichsverband Deutscher Schriftsteller*, the Nazi organization that controlled all publishing in the Third Reich – although he only paid his member fees for a short time, and was for that reason officially expelled in 1937.[13] Equally problematic is that in May 1933, Horváth decided to withdraw his signature from a protest telegram by antifascist authors to the PEN conference in Ragusa. Also after initially agreeing to contribute to *Die Sammlung*, edited by a number of prominent exile authors and published by Querido in Amsterdam, he later withdrew his offer of cooperation (September 1933) with the argument that he did not want to publish

---

[10] See the reports on the trials about the incident in the *Weilheimer Tageblatt*. 22.7.1931 and 23.7.1931. The articles are reprinted in: *Materialien zu Ödön von Horváth*. Ed. by Traugott Krischke. Frankfurt am Main: Suhrkamp 1970. Pp. 23–31, esp. P. 27.
[11] Krischke: *Ödön von Horváth*. P. 216. See also Heinz Lunzer, Victoria Lunzer-Talos, and Elisabeth Tworek: *Horváth. Einem Schriftsteller auf der Spur*. Salzburg-Vienna-Frankfurt am Main: Residenz 2001. P. 112.
[12] Lunzer, Lunzer-Talos, and Tworek: *Horváth*. P. 121.
[13] Krischke: *Ödön von Horváth. Kind seiner Zeit*. Pp. 186, 187. Lunzer, Lunzer-Talos, and Tworek: Lunzer. P. 112.

in political publications.[14] It has also been documented that Horváth visited Germany for shorter periods in July 1936, and again in March and September 1937.[15]

How are we to interpret all of this? Scholars have gone through a great amount of trouble to reconstruct what went through Horváth's mind when he decided to return to Germany in 1934 and to make Berlin his principle residence. It is possible that financial needs or the belief that Hitler's regime would perhaps only be a very temporary thing may have played a role in Horváth's decision to return to Berlin. Immediately before 1933 Horváth's plays had been exceptionally successful in Berlin; interest in his work outside of Germany in contrast, had been only marginal. Understood this way, Horváth's actions from 1934–1935 easily might be construed as opportunistic. Keeping the harshness of the author's criticism of German fascism before 1933 and after 1935 in mind, however, it may also have been that Horváth naively hoped to resist or reform Hitler's regime from within. I believe however that a third explanation is more probable: Horváth had a literary interest in staying in Germany; he was, in other words, interested in the stories that he might be able to tell on the basis of his experiences in the Third Reich. While his text *Jugend ohne Gott* avoids using the term "fascism" or any specific references to historical material, it is necessary to import these terms for any analysis, since the text is so clearly written as a response to the Third Reich.

Horváth's experiences in Germany during the Third Reich exemplify many of the dilemmas that intellectuals faced after Hitler came to power. Horváth could examine the seductive powers of Hitler's totalitarian approach to politics first hand. It is therefore, in my view, no coincidence that Horváth also chose as the main protagonist of his novel *Jugend ohne Gott* an intellectual who in some respects resembled him. The anonymous 34-year old principal character of the novel is a high school teacher who shows little resemblance to the idealized author-intellectual imagined by Horkeimer and Adorno. In the figure of the teacher, *Jugend ohne Gott* problematizes the intellectual's socio-economic status and also his masculinity under a totalitarian regime. On the teacher's mind are his job, his pension – it is important to him that he has "eine sichere Stelle mit Pensionsberechtigung" ["a secure job with pension benefits"] (11) –, and his aging parents who are in need of his financial support. Because of his need for job-security, he is highly dependent not only on those in charge, but also on the goodwill of his students whose intellectual and psychological development he watches with concern, even though initially he does not appear to have made up his mind about the new regime. He appears to be

---

[14] See Krischke: *Ödön von Horváth. Kind seiner Zeit.* Pp. 175, 176. Lunzer, Lunzer-Talos, and Tworek: *Horváth.* Pp. 108, 110.

[15] Krischke: *Ödön von Horváth. Kind seiner Zeit.* Pp. 222, 230 and 242.

guided by a sense of "moral panic" – the idea that a young generation was growing up without values – an idea which conservative and (proto-)fascist groups sought to capitalize on in the interbellum.[16] The teacher's position in a society ruled by totalitarian politics is one of insecurity. His masculinity is constantly challenged or threatened by his students' aggressive and militaristic behavior fostered by the new regime. The highly ambiguous status of the intellectual under an authoritarian regime is mirrored in the teacher's ambiguous sexuality that defines itself in conflict with conventional middle-class norms. The teacher likes to hang out in bars and occasionally wakes up next to women whose names he does not remember (30). He also develops a sexually tainted crush on Eva, a homeless girl suspected of theft and murder (74, 75, and 123), and diagnoses in himself a "Sehnsucht nach der Verkommenheit" ["desire for depravity"] (122).[17]

Jugend ohne Gott shows society in the grip of trans-subjective powers. Fascism is explained socio-economically through the economic pressures on the middle class and its desire to move up in society, to conform to those in power. The parents of the protagonist's students, who personify for the teacher the new political class, belong without exception to the middle or upper classes: "Arbeiter war keiner darunter" ["There were no workers among them"] (17). They are driven by economic self-interest: "es regiert einzig und allein das Geld" ["money alone reigns"] (21). For the teacher, the prototypical fascist is the "Bäckermeister N." ["Master Baker N."], the father of one of his students, who accuses him among other thing, of "Sabotage am Vaterland" ["sabotaging the fatherland"] and "Humanitätsduselei" ["humanitarian patter"] (19) – terms that indicate how aware Horváth was of the rhetoric of German fascism. In a conversation between the teacher and the school director (20, 21), the novel describes the social model underlying fascism by drawing a parallel to pre-imperial Roman society, in which plebians (middle class) overtook power from the patrician class (upper class). In this process a small group of rich plebians played a key role, by allying themselves with those who had been in power until then (decadent patricians). Horváth here follows standard Marxist explanations according to which economic interests of the middle classes were the backbone of fascism.

Horváth's text is less conventional in pointing to other trans-subjective powers in order to explain the new regime's functioning. In the eyes of the

---

[16] See John Alexander Williams: *Turning to Nature in Germany: Hiking, Nudism, and Conservation, 1900–1940*. Stanford: Stanford University Press 2007. Pp. 141, 148–156.

[17] For an analysis of the literary tradition of the figure of the "creature" in German literature of the 1920s and 1930s, for which Eva is representative, see Helmut Lethen: *Verhaltenslehren der Kälte. Lebensversuche zwischen den Kriegen*. Frankfurt am Main: Suhrkamp 1994. Pp. 247, 248.

teacher, modern media are to be blamed for what he sees as his students' moral decline. "Die Zeitung. Das Radio" ["The Newspaper. The Radio"] were incidentally the very first words Horváth wrote down when he started to plan *Jugend ohne Gott* (153). The novel starts with the report of an incident directly related to the role of the media in society. The teacher is in the process of correcting his students' essays on the question of why the country needs colonies (not a topic chosen by himself, but assigned by those higher up). When one of the students, N., writes that "Neger" ["negroes"] are "hinterlistig, feig und faul" ["deceitful, cowardly, and lazy"] (13), the teacher's initial intuition is to call this a generalization that makes no sense, but he then realizes that this is something that is being told on the radio, and that it might be problematic to criticize it. Nevertheless he cannot hold his opinion back and tells the student that "Auch die Neger doch Menschen [sind]" ["Negroes are humans too"] (17). Because of this incident the teacher is not only threatened by the father of N., the master baker, but the students also write a collective letter stating that they no longer wish to receive instruction from him (21, 22). From this moment on, the teacher's nickname, we learn, is "der Neger" ["negro"] (120). Later in the text, during the murder trial integral to the novel's plot, it becomes clear that the power of radio even limits juridical power. The court's president, for example, hesitates to ask one of the suspects, Z., who is accused of murder, a question, because, the teacher interprets, he felt he would "ein Gebiet betreten [. . .], wo das Radio regiert" ["enter a realm, where radio reigns"] (90). These two examples show that *Jugend ohne Gott* is very much about how citizens internalize power structures beyond their control, and that technical media play a key role in this process.

It should be no surprise that the students, all around 14 years old (12) and incidentally also the first generation that grew up with radio, have internalized a self-image shaped by society's technology while de-emphasizing individual responsibility, subjective agency, or empathy. In the analysis of the teacher, his students – all boys – identify completely with technology: they hate to think; they want to be "Maschinen" ["machines"] instead, preferably "Munition: Bomben, Schrapnells, Granaten" ["ammunition: bombs, shrapnel, grenades"]; their dream is to have their names eternalized on a "Kriegerdenkmal" ["war memorial"] (24). Technology, nationalism, and gender stereotypes, all trans-subjective foundational powers, work together in shaping the ideal of a new citizen for a new world. Hidden behind the students' fascination with technology is, in other words, an educational goal that emphasizes aggressive masculinity in the service of the fatherland.[18] It becomes clear later in the book that not all of the teacher's

---

[18] For a detailed analysis of the ideal of aggressive masculinity in the Third Reich, see George L. Mosse: *Nationalism and Sexuality: Respectability & Abnormal Sexuality in Modern Europe.* New York: Howard Fertig 1985. Pp. 170–173.

students agree. It turns out that one of them, Z., keeps a diary, something some of his fellow students frown upon; in the words of the student R., "Das Tagebuchschreiben ist der typische Ausdruck der typischen Überschätzung des eigenen Ichs" ["To write a diary is the typical expression of the typical overvaluing of one's own ego"] (61). In *The Authoritarian Personality*, first published in 1950, but based on research going back to the final years of the Second World War, Adorno and a group of co-authors claimed that "*Anti-intraception*", defined as "Opposition to the subjective, the imaginative, the tender-minded", is one of the key psychological characteristics of those harboring anti-democratic leanings and also of Nazi ideology.[19] It is traced to a fear of loss of control and seen as leading to an objectification of humans; it explains how material, inanimate objects are invested with emotions, while living beings are not.[20]

While *Jugend ohne Gott* emphasizes fascism's infatuation with technology, it also shows that Nazi ideology paradoxically lives off an idealization of its opposite, the idea of a return to nature – another form of trans-subjective foundational power –, as well. Fascism picked up on trends in Germany before fascism, in particular the popularity of nature movements that were often affiliated with youth movements.[21] In *Jugend ohne Gott*, all students are required to participate in a 10-day "Zeltlager" ["tent camp"] under the guidance of the teacher and a former soldier, the goal of which is to provide them with a pre-military training in what the teacher calls "sogenannte freie Natur" ["so-called free nature"] (34). That the teacher speaks of "so-called free nature" indicates that he is well aware of the concept's ideological overtones. The tent camp – the description of which strikes one as very realistic – is where the most important part of the plot of *Jugend ohne Gott*, the murder of N., takes place. The assumption is that Horváth used a so-called "Hochlandlager" ["high land camp"] of the *Hitler-Jugend* that took place in 1934 in the vicinity of Murnau as his model, and that he probably also relied on knowledge of a sport festival of the *Bund Deutscher Mädel*, the female counterpart to the *Hitler-Jugend*, that took place in Munich on September 23, 1934. Details about both events were widely published, but Horváth may also have relied on information provided to him by acquaintances in Murnau.[22] The dark side

---

[19] T.W. Adorno, Else Frenkel-Brunswick, Daniel J. Levinson, and R. Nevitt Sanford: *The Authoritarian Personality*. New York-London: Norton 1982. P. 157; see also Pp. 163, 164.
[20] Ibid. P. 164.
[21] Gert Gröning and Joachim Wolschke-Bulmahn: Landschafts- und Naturschutz. In: *Handbuch der deutschen Reformbewegungen 1880–1933*. Ed. by Diethart Kerbs and Jürgen Reulecke. Wuppertal: Peter Hammer 1998. Pp. 23–34. Here: P. 28.
[22] See Alexander Fuhrmann: Der historische Hintergrund: Schule – Kirche – Staat. In: *Horváths* Jugend ohne Gott. Ed. by Traugott Krischke. Frankfurt am Main: Suhrkamp 1984. Pp. 129–146. Here: P. 140.

of this idolizing of nature is personified by those living without the means to support themselves: the "Räuberbande" ["band of robbers"] (42) consisting in reality of a small group of homeless teenagers (among them Eva, the lover of Z.) who live in the caves around the tent camp. While its own "back-to-nature" sentiments were firmly inscribed within an adherence to social hierarchies, fascism forced certain groups back into nature literally, reducing them to living in a state of nature.

Both technology and nature provide Nazi thinking with an anti-subjective bias. Within fascist ideology, such visions of technology and nature relieve the subject of a responsibility for its own actions. And yet, while it may be that some people have no choice, the text makes a radical point by arguing that the idea that one lives in the power of totalitarian forces is, to some extent, a subjective construction, an interpretation, in particular when intellectuals are concerned. It is here that the text problematizes the role of the intellectual most outspokenly. The teacher and others in a situation similar to his have in principle a freedom of choice left, even if at moments they would prefer not to acknowledge this. After the negro-incident, the teacher has to appear before his school's director, a man who used to be in his own words a pacifist (20). The director is sympathetic toward the teacher's situation, but points out to him that neither one of them is forced to do anything: "es gibt keinen Zwang. Ich könnte ja dem Zeitgeist widersprechen und mich von einem Herrn Bäckermeister einsperren lassen" ["there is no force. I could contradict the spirit of the times and let myself be locked up by a master baker"] (20). The result would probably be dismissal and the loss of one's pension (20). The point the text makes here, relatively early, is that power does not necessarily function through repression alone, but rather by making certain modes of behavior attractive. By doing so, it limits the intellectual's agency, even though in principle the intellectual can make a choice. This is important, in particular if one keeps one of the novel's intended audiences in mind: it was not Germany, where the text certainly would be blacklisted, but the citizens of its neighboring countries where Horváth's texts could still be read (the text was almost immediately translated into a number of European languages).[23] To those readers Horváth explains how fascism changes society's structures and puts psychological pressures on the citizens of these societies.

---

[23] Horváth's correspondence shows that he indeed saw countries under the threat of fascism as his primary audience for the text, even though as late as November 1937 he also takes into consideration the possibility of his books being sold within the Third Reich. See Jürgen Schröder: Das Spätwerk Ödön von Horváths. In: *Odön von Horváth*. Ed. by Traugott Krischke. Frankfurt am Main: Suhrkamp 1981. Pp. 125–155. Here: P. 129. *Jugend ohne Gott* was translated into Czech, Dutch, English, French, and Polish within two years from its first publication in German. See editor's note, *Jugend ohne Gott*. Pp. 153, 181.

Jugend ohne Gott complicates its contemporaries' view of totalitarianism and the role of the individual in it. In an exceptionally direct way, the novel does not just address the criminal nature of the new German regime, but also visualizes everyday life under a totalitarian regime. "War" and "violence" are at the core of the agenda of the new regime. Even though anti-Semitism is not mentioned explicitly, the novel emphasizes, already at its very beginning, the role of racist discourse in fascist ideology.[24] But does it also offer strategies of resistance? The book leaves no doubt about the trans-subjective powers of fascism's ideology at work in society. While theoretically there is space left for agency as the result of rational deliberation (for example in the conversation between the director and the teacher), in practice, as the text shows, not much is to be expected from such a model of agency founded on the subject's rational powers. Instead, as I hope to show in the following, the text promotes as more effective a model of agency that is not located in the rational subject, but rather in pre-subjective drives – sex and violence – that can be at odds with the trans-subjective power structures on which fascism hopes to capitalize. Something in the subject's pre-subjective drives resists colonization by trans-subjective power mechanisms; there is a potential for conflict between the two. While violence is seen as a negative, yet fundamental aspect of the human psyche, Horváth's text has a more positive view of sexuality than Horkheimer and Adorno in *Dialektik der Aufklärung.*

Remarkably little has been written on the *Jugend ohne Gott*'s very explicit thematization of sexual matters. At the center of the text is the (sexual) encounter between Z. (Adam) and the homeless girl Eva; this relationship is the catalyst for many of the events that follow. Horváth's text also offers its own concise theory of the history of sexuality, albeit in the words of "Julius Caesar", nickname of a former colleague and a friend of the teacher who was dismissed because of (sexual) relations with an underage female student (27). The reader is not necessarily meant to take this figure very seriously – one of his trademarks is a fake miniature skull on his tie with a little light bulb that he can illuminate with the help of a battery in his pocket. Nonetheless, his analysis is revealing. To understand the society of his time, Julius Caesar points to its division in different generations. His own generation, around sixty in the 1930s, lived through a puberty marked by repression on the one hand and masturbation including the "völlig sinnlose Angst vor gesundheitsschädigenden Konsequenzen" ["totally senseless fear of its health-damaging consequences"] (28) on the other. The puberty of the teacher, in contrast, who, we assume, was born around 1900, started during the First World War and was characterized by far more liberty. For the teacher's generation "war

---

[24] I would argue that the debate about the humanity of "negroes" at the beginning of the book is a metonymic representation of the Third Reich's anti-Semitic agenda.

das Weib keine Heilige mehr" ["women were no longer saints"] (28).[25] The problem of the students' generation is that there are no "wahrhaftige" ["real"] women anymore; exemplification of the new woman is the "rucksacktragende Venus" ["backpack-carrying Venus"] (29). At first sight, this could be read as a rather reactionary view of gender relations articulated by Julius Caesar, and possibly Horváth. Maybe this is implied. More important within the context of the novel's critique of fascism is that the text also articulates here that not just masculinity, but also femininity is the target of society's ubiquitous militarization. This is very much in conflict with the popular stereotype that the Third Reich was especially interested in promoting traditional family roles. Elsewhere the text makes explicit that it is men who force upon women their new role in society (44).

Julius Caesar's line of thinking does not remain without a critical response in *Jugend ohne Gott*; the teacher calls him an "Erotomane" ["obsessed with Eros"] and believes it typical for his generation to view everything from a sexual angle (28). The teacher's stance in this matter, I would say, is not unproblematic. In fact, in *The Authoritarian Personality* Adorno and his co-authors identify an "exaggerated concern with sexual 'goings-on'" as one of the characteristics of the fascist mindset.[26] Fascism claimed to critique the "pansexual" attitudes that were, for example, part of psychoanalysis, but at the same time fascism was itself obsessed by the supposed existence of sexual subdiscourses. Julius Caesar appears to confirm fascism's stereotypes about the sexual fixation of intellectuals, and the teacher seems to share the fascist point of view. The point the text makes here is that the teacher, as a true antihero, is far less distanced from fascist ideology than a naïve reading of the text might assume. What is important about Julius Caesar's reconstruction of the history of sexuality is that this history is not linear, but veers back and forth between repression and liberation; it is, in other words, subject to ideology. Fascism's attitude toward sexuality is characterized by a double bind. On the surface it seems to maintain middle-class morals in sexual matters. The novel certainly also illustrates a "new repression" of sexuality under fascism – most visible in the new military ideals of masculinity and femininity – but that is not the main point of what Julius Caesar intends to say. It is rather that

---

[25] During the Weimar Republic, the notion of a "rampaging wartime sexuality" among adolescents was a major topic in debates focusing on youth movements, in particular in conservative and fascist circles (see Williams 136–140). In general I have the sense that many of the cultural-political issues to which Horváth's novel refers are situated in the context of debates on youth movements and youth culture in the 1920s and 1930s.

[26] Adorno, Frenkel-Brunswick, Levinson, and Sanford: *The Authoritarian Personality*. P. 157. See also Pp. 169, 170.

the "innigsten Gefühle" ["most inner feelings"] of students have been mobilized too often "für irgendeinen Popanz" ["for some kind of bugaboo"] (29). Sexual feelings, what I earlier called the domain of the "pre-subjective", are used or colonized for political purposes, to exert power. This is in line with newer research by historians who, consciously breaking with an approach that emphasized the Third Reich's repression of sexuality, have pointed out that the Nazis' sexual politics sought to exploit "popular liberalizing impulses and growing occupation with sex" for their own racist and homophobic agenda.[27] While the Nazis' attitudes toward sexuality were contradictory, part of fascism's appeal for young people was that it "mocked Christian efforts to defend the sanctity of marriage, and aligned itself with young people's impatience with traditional bourgeois mores".[28]

Jugend ohne Gott quite explicitly thematizes this spirit of rebellion associated with sexuality as a pre-subjective force, but it simultaneously questions whether it can be functionalized in the service of fascism. It is precisely in their sexuality that human beings show that they will not always do what they are being told. Z. (whose first name, it is suggested, is Adam) rebels against the spirit of the time in general, and his own middle-class upbringing in particular, by falling in love and having a sexual relationship with Eva, the leader of the *Räuberbande* he meets while at the tent camp. His mother, facing Eva for the first time in court, calls her a "dreckiges Weibsbild" ["dirty hussy"] and "verkommenes Luder" ["degenerate slut"] (98). Z. denies this: "Das ist kein Luder" ["She is not a slut"] (98), and at the same time reminds his mother how poorly she treated the servant girls she employed who had to work long days for her, but received little food (98, 99). This exchange between mother and son shows how the spirit of rebellion, fostered by his stay in the youth camp, leads Z. to question his mother's typical middle-class morality. But the exchange also demonstrates that Z. realizes that sexuality is tied to important social issues which the fascist regime would rather ignore. Eva may very well be one of the people affected by the high unemployment in the village close to the tent camp after the local factory has been closed (35, 36). She and the servant girls belong to the lower classes and are therefore, as the text shows, virtually without rights. Z.'s mother implies a sexual liaison between her former husband and the servant girls she used to employ (98). One could say that the repressive attitude of the middle classes is based on a double standard: it seeks to repress what it cannot live without. This also goes for the teacher who in spite of his position of social responsibility likes

---

[27] Dagmar Herzog: Hubris and Hypocrisy, Incitement and Disavowal: Sexuality and German Fascism. In: *Sexuality and German Fasicism*. Ed. by Dagmar Herzog. New York-Oxford: Berghahn 2005. Pp. 1–21. Here: P. 4.
[28] Ibid. P. 11.

to visit prostitutes and falls head over heels for Eva himself, even though he barely knows her. But fascism's attempt to capitalize on an agenda of anti-bourgeois sexual morals fails as well; in fact it makes Z. aware of the class-structure and economic policy underlying its politics. In spite of the book's seemingly romantic plot, *Jugend ohne Gott* is also not a classical Romeo-and-Juliet-story that suggests the potential existence of an alternative world of innocence and love. In court Eva confesses that she does not love and has never loved Z. (104, 105; see also 107). Z.'s infatuation with Eva is generally viewed with cynicism by the other characters. The teacher, after the trial, believes that Z. has already started to hate Eva (107) and the defense attorney states to the teacher that Z. has already been cured of his love for Eva (119). The teacher's own attraction to Eva is primarily sexual, and he claims not to know whether that means that he loved her (123; see also 74). At the end of the novel when he visits her in prison, he only notices that she has "Diebesaugen" ["the eyes of a thief"] (149).

Sexuality and violence are comparable in that both are the target of trans-subjective power mechanisms, but also part of the realm of the pre-subjective. *Jugend ohne Gott* makes the point that the rhetoric of war and violence was very much part of the ideology of the Third Reich. It is significant that the book (written in 1937!) contains a chapter entitled "Der totale Krieg" that in its final lines asks the questions "wo ist die Front?" ["where is the frontline?"] (38). In fact, I would claim that at its initial publication one of the book's primary functions (and also the author's intention) may have been to alert its audiences outside Germany to the presence of this rhetoric and the militarization of society in general in the Third Reich. The book also shows, however, that it is naïve to think that violence can be the subject of ideological control. In his classical essay *Zur Kritik der Gewalt* (1921), Walter Benjamin objects against such a mode of thinking that in reality the opposite is often the case: inherent to violence is a tendency to create the law, rather than that to serve merely at the disposal of the law.[29] Violence, in other words, is not just a matter of ideology (theory), but also of a practice that creates ideology. Violence turns into a trans-subjective force that develops its own dynamic.

In the novel, the question of how the practice of violence originates in the group of 14-year-olds which the teacher is assigned to supervise, is tied to T.'s motives for murdering N. On the surface there is no motive for T. to murder N. (106). After returning from the summer camp, the teacher arranges a "coincidental" meeting with T. and tries in the ensuing conversation to figure out T.'s possible motive. He does not get very far: T. confesses (or affirms)

---

[29] Walter Benjamin: Zur Kritik der Gewalt. In: *Gesammelte Werke. Aufsätze. Essays. Vorträge.* Ed. by Rolf Tiedemann and Hermann Schweppenhäuser. Frankfurt am Main: Suhrkamp 1991. Pp. 179–203. Here: P. 185.

that he likes to spy on other people, claims to know no fear, and comments on the teacher's ability to observe without showing emotion (109–111). The teacher's nickname is for that reason according to T. "the fish" (111). This characterization stuns the teacher; T. attributes to him traits the teacher himself sees as typical for his students. Again, the text makes the point here that the teacher's attitudes may be closer to fascist ideology and practice than a naïve reading of the text might assume.[30] In his conversation with the teacher, Julius Caesar had spoken of a new age of coldness, for which the "fish" is a metaphor: "Es kommen kalte Zeiten, das Zeitalter der Fische" ["Cold times are coming, the age of the fish"] (30). The teacher later repeats this diagnosis verbatim (118). "Coldness" is an important motive in Horváth's later works,[31] but interestingly the "cold persona" was already an object of fascination for many German writers of the 1920s and early 1930s as well.[32] Indirectly, one could argue, Horváth here also criticizes the cult of coldness among his fellow authors of the Weimar Republic and thereby their complicity in the Third Reich. It is possible to read the figure of the "cold persona" as a symptom of social disintegration.[33]

T. models his behavior after the ideal of "coldness" promoted (consciously) by fascism and (unconsciously) by figures like the teacher. This is reinforced by the circumstances in which he grew up. T. has been neglected by his mother and father, the director of a major company, who always have too many other things to do to be able to pay attention to him (130). Interestingly, earlier Z. complained about being neglected (by his mother) as well (98). From this the reader may infer that emotional neglect is typical for this generation as a whole. Some of T.'s motives for murdering N. have however deeper roots. After T.'s suicide has been discovered, the teacher attempts something of an explanation for his behavior, picking up on a remark by B., one of T.'s fellow students, that T. once told him that he would like to see how someone dies or how a child is born (115). The teacher integrates this piece of information into a more comprehensive picture of T.'s personality:

> Geburt und Tod, und alles, was dazwischen liegt, wollt er genau wissen. Er wollte alle Geheimnisse ergründen, aber nur, um darüberstehen zu können – darüber mit seinem Hohn. Er kannte keine Schauer, denn seine Angst war nur Feigheit. Und seine Liebe zur Wirklichkeit war nur der Haß auf die Wahrheit. (146)

---

[30] I think however that it would be a mistake to call T. the teacher's "Doppelgänger" ["double"], as Jürgen Schröder does (Das Spätwerk Ödön von Horváths 136). The point the text makes in my opinion is that the teacher naively and unwillingly functions as a model for his students because of this emotional detachment; i.e., he is complicit in the origins of their fascist attitudes.
[31] See Schröder: Das Spätwerk Ödön von Horváths. Pp. 133, 141–142.
[32] See Lethen: *Verhaltenslehren der Kälte*. Pp. 133–215.
[33] Ibid. Pp. 139, 140.

[He wanted to know about birth and death, and everything in between. He wanted to comprehend all secrets, but only to be able to stand above them – with his sarcasm. He knew no fright, because his fear was only cowardice. And his love of reality was only hatred of truth.]

Nowhere does *Jugend ohne Gott* come closer to a psychological explanation of the origins of fascism. In the teacher's explanation of T.'s behavior, sexuality and violence are closely linked as elementary forces in the human psyche. The desire to know about sexual matters and death are recognized as primary – or, one could say, pre-subjective – drives in human nature that very well may be common to all. What is specific for T.'s psyche, is that the drive to know about them is linked to a profound cynicism and sarcasm. This may have something to do with his individual upbringing, but it is certainly also linked to trans-subjective forces: fascism's "opposition to the subjective, the imaginative, the tender-minded",[34] and its cult of coldness. Fascism simultaneously utilizes and would like to make humans forget about this double dependence on the pre- and trans-subjective in order to mask the workings of its own ideology. *Jugend ohne Gott*, in contrast, exposes this double dependency precisely to expose fascism's workings. The novel certainly does not defend humans' violent nature. But it does argue that a better insight into humans' (pre-subjective) sexual and violent drives can help to understand their functioning better.

Scholarship has signaled in Horváth's work after 1933 a tendency to return to the old idealistic and individualistic concepts, often typically middle-class, that he had been battling in the period immediately before 1933.[35] If there exists such a "conservative" turn in Horváth's work, one would have to say that it is not a naïve one. The text is informed by Marx and Freud's criticism of such bourgeois ideals. It is highly critical of the idea that humans are in charge of their own destiny. Although *Jugend ohne Gott* is in part a love story, love is certainly no panacea, as I have shown. Even the teacher's ultimate decision to leave for Africa (149) has been critiqued earlier in the text. When the suggestion to work as a teacher and missionary in Africa first came up, the teacher responded with the remark that he does not believe in such a mission because bringing God to Africa's blacks is a "schmutziges Geschäft" ["dirty business"] (126); missionary work and the church in general are driven by financial interests. The text shows the limited power of intellectuals to have an impact on a totalitarian regime. One question to ask the text is whether it offers strategies of resistance different from the self-chosen "exile" of the

---

[34] See Adorno, Frenkel-Brunswick, Levinson, and Sanford: *The Authoritarian Personality*. P. 157.
[35] See Schröder: Das Spätwerk Ödön von Horváths. P. 134.

teacher? To what extent does the text offer an effective approach for resisting violence?

On the surface, *Jugend ohne Gott* may be about a group of teenagers in the age of fascism. At the beginning of the novel these 14-year olds are portrayed as an anonymous and seemingly homogenous group. This is certainly how the teacher sees them; he refers to his students only by the first initials of their last names. Scholarship has pointed out that (at least initially) the teacher is by no means free of the type of fascist language that is criticized in the novel, for instance when he compares his students to "weeds" ["Unkraut"] that need to be "exterminated" ["vertilgt"] (73) explicitly highlighting the aspect of the biological and pathogenic connotations of the term, the aspect of contagion.[36] Here, Horváth certainly problematizes the role of the intellectual protagonist of his text. He most certainly also reflects on his own experiences as an intellectual living in the Third Reich, and illustrates how easy the transition from critical observer to fellow traveler ("Mitläufer") can be. Nevertheless, the novel functions also as a primitive sort of Bildungsroman; the teacher undergoes a change of attitude and eventually recognizes his students' individuality.[37] Parallel to this change of the teacher's perspective, the students themselves also appear to go through a transformation. While initially all of them signed the letter asking for the teacher's removal from the class after the "negro"-incident (21), eventually a small group of students become sick of marching and being bossed around. They found a club to read what is forbidden (116, 117), and also decide to help sort out the events surrounding N.'s death with the goal of assisting the innocent Eva, who has been accused of the crime (119). That makes it difficult to see the students as a homogenous group, even though the lure of fascism's anti-individual agenda is still powerful.

The club members trust the teacher because of his decision to tell the truth at the trial, even though this was against his own interests (118). The teacher decided to do so after a voice that may belong to either the cigar-store owner or God advises him to tell the truth (95, 96). How are we to understand this religious subtext of *Jugend ohne Gott* that is so prominent in the text (and to which the title alludes as well)? I am particularly interested in whether it is possible to reconcile the text's "religious turn" with the Marxist / Freudian view of fascism mentioned above and its insistence on the subject's dependence on trans- and pre-subjective powers. In his essay *Zur Kritik der Gewalt*, Walter Benjamin attempts to break through conventional thinking about violence as a legitimate means for a legitimate goal, and asks whether it is

---

[36] See also Franz Kadrnoska: Sozialkritik und Transparenz faschistischer Ideologeme in *Jugend ohne Gott*. In: *Horváths* Jugend ohne Gott. Ed. by Traugott Krischke. Frankfurt am Main: Suhrkamp 1984. Pp. 69–91. Here: Pp. 75–77.
[37] See Kurt Bartsch: *Ödön von Horváth*. Stuttgart-Weimar: Metzler 2000. P. 164.

possible to conceive of violence in other ways. Interestingly, for Benjamin "God" functions as a metaphor for a position that legitimates another way of understanding violence, one that is critical of existing modes of viewing violence and their ideological legitimation.[38] It is significant (and certainly no coincidence) that his deliberations on the divine nature of violence immediately follow a passage in which he discusses non-violent forms of protest.[39]

The teacher's decision in the cigar store to tell the truth at the trial is not rationally motivated: it goes very much against his own interests and it has no impact on determining who is guilty of N.'s murder, but it does make the teacher in the public's eyes seem an unethical person. Here too, "God" functions as a metaphor. That the teacher associates his decision with a divine principle (the voice of God) is meant to be indicative of the fact that sometimes our actions defy rationalization and yet are guided by an ethical principle. I would be inclined to de-emphasize the element of revelation in this decision. The decisively religious connotation is already questioned by the fact that the teacher is quite possibly motivated, at least in part, by his sexual feelings for Eva. On the one hand, the teacher makes an intuitive choice for something that he believes is right (whatever his exact motives may be). On the other hand, the teacher's decision is much less a momentary event than a superficial reading of the text may suggest. Earlier the teacher had already announced: "Ja, Gott ist schrecklich, aber ich will ihm einen Strich durch die Rechnung machen. Mit meinem freien Willen" ["God is terrible, but I will thwart his intentions. With my free will"] (72, see also 78). In this context too, "God" functions as a metaphor. By phrasing the choice he intends to make as a matter of "free will", the teacher stays within the religious imagery he has chosen. While here and elsewhere in the text "God" is an equivalent for the lawlessness (80) of the world, the teacher asserts his agency through his "free" decision to interfere with this chaos. This move is highly critical of the status quo, in spite of its lack of a clear motivation. It reinstates human agency, but a form of agency that privileges the pre-subjective or intuitive over rational forms of agency. It is only consistent with this interpretation that the teacher later claims that he believes in God, but does not like him (94).

Invoking God as a metaphor for a legitimating source, not unlike Benjamin in *Zur Kritik der Gewalt*, is one function of the religious imagery in *Jugend ohne Gott*. There is in my opinion a second reason why Horváth modeled his story after a religious conversion story ["Bekehrungsgeschichte"], as one

---

[38] Benjamin: Zur Kritik der Gewalt. Pp. 196 and 199–201. For this aspect of Benjamin's theory see also Beatrice Hanssen: *Critique of Violence: Between Poststructuralism and Critical Theory*. London-New York: Routledge 2000. Pp. 20–22.
[39] Benjamin: Zur Kritik der Gewalt. Pp. 194–195.

scholar has claimed.[40] In particular in Austria and Switzerland one can speak of a "Renaissance konservativ-religiöser Denkweisen" ["renaissance of conservative and religious ways of thinking"][41] during the Third Reich. For a conservative or religious audience, the title *Jugend ohne Gott* is a provocation.[42] One motive for Horváth could have been that the church was one of the few social institutions that had remained somewhat intact under Nazism and therefore would have the potential to overthrow the Nazi regime or similar fascist regimes in neighboring countries. But Horváth also sought other means to interest a broad audience. Through his work for film in the Third Reich, he was acutely aware that the fascist regime was quite skilled at using popular culture and mass media to mobilize the masses. This may explain why *Jugend ohne Gott*, in spite of its title, is first and foremost not a conversion story, but a suspenseful detective novel about a murder case.[43] The story has also many traits of a romance novel and, as mentioned before, may also be read as a *Bildungsroman*, which, in spite of the aura associated with it, was no longer an example of "high", but of "low" culture in the twentieth century.

Ultimately, *Jugend ohne Gott* does not offer *one* clear strategy of resistance or counter-violence, but *several*. At its roots is the question of how to save agency, while acknowledging human dependency on pre- or trans-subjective powers beyond its control. The teacher's decision to speak the truth at the trial encourages several other characters to do so too, but remains short-lived and does not turn into a permanent intention of being truthful (this too speaks against reading *Jugend ohne Gott* as a conversion story).[44] In fact, the text more than once makes the point that for strategic reasons, one may decide not

---

[40] Adolf Holl: Gott ist die Wahrheit oder: Horváths Suche nach der zweiten religiösen Naivität. In: *Horváths* Jugend ohne Gott. Ed. by Traugott Krischke. Frankfurt am Main: Suhrkamp 1984. Pp. 147–156. Here: P. 150.
[41] Wolfgang Müller-Funk: Faschismus und freier Wille. Horváths Roman *Jugend ohne Gott* zwischen Zeitbilanz und Theodizee. In: *Horváths* Jugend ohne Gott. Ed. by Traugott Krischke. Frankfurt am Main: Suhrkamp 1984. Pp. 157–179. Here: P. 175.
[42] For some countries maybe a little too provocative. The title of the Dutch translation from 1938 is *Er is een moord begaan* [*A Murder has been committed*] – perhaps because a literal translation of the title was seen as too offensive?
[43] See Bernhard Spies: Der Faschismus als Mordfall. Ödön von Horváths *Jugend ohne Gott*. In: *Experimente mit dem Kriminalroman. Ein Erzählmodell in der deutschsprachigen Literatur des 20. Jahrhunderts*. Ed. by Wolfgang Düsing. Frankfurt am Main: Peter Lang 1993. Pp. 97–116, esp. Pp. 103–105.
[44] As I hope to have made clear, I believe Horváth's interest in religion is purely pragmatic. Nevertheless some scholarship has tried to read his work (and *Jugend ohne Gott* in particular) as indicative of a religious conversion of the author. See for instance: Peter Baumann: *Ödön von Horváth:* Jugend ohne Gott – *Autor mit Gott?* Bern: Peter Lang 2003. Pp. 545–548.

to act truthfully and adopt one's opponents' attitudes. In spite of his "conversion" and the fact that he has been suspended from his job (and knows that he will be dismissed; 108), the teacher flies a flag to celebrate the birthday of the "Oberplebejer" ["first among the plebians"], i.e. Hitler, the evening before his birthday: "Wer mit Verbrechern und Narren zu tun hat, muß verbrecherisch und närrisch handeln, sonst hört er auf" ["He who deals with fools and criminals, will have to act criminally and foolishly, otherwise it is over with him"] (112). Eventually, the teacher opts for exile (to work as a missionary and teacher in Africa). The text's point is that there are many ways to resist totalitarian regimes. None of the strategies proposed, incidentally, endorses violence as a means to combat violence. With that, one could say that the novel propagates a pacifist agenda.[45]

Jugend ohne Gott problematizes the position of the intellectual under a totalitarian regime, by showing his multiple dependencies, rather than conceiving of him as a heroic individual. The text in fact shows that it is precisely the kind of heroic masculinity exemplified by Horkheimer and Adorno's Odysseus that lends itself to ideological abuse. All indications are that the author Horváth, as a historical person living in- and outside the Third Reich, faced fascism with a certain helplessness. His novel *Jugend ohne Gott* acknowledges this through its main character, but, in the end, it also articulates an anti-fascist program that is testimony to Horváth's intellectual slyness. The strategies of resistance in Horváth's novel in some respects are not unlike those of Horkheimer and Adorno's Odysseus in his encounter with the Sirens. They include the willingness on the part of the artist-intellectual to compromise (temporarily) with those in power, to accept a limitation of one's own freedom and autonomy (and that of others) in the interest of realizing the Enlightenment's program in the longer term. One needs to be aware, however, that Odysseus, in Horkheimer and Adorno's interpretation, while expecting his inferiors to blindly submit to his will, seeks to repress his sexuality along with the pull of totalitarian politics. Through this equation of the lure of fascist ideology with that of humans' sexual drives in the image of Odysseus and the Sirens, the authors demonize sexuality and the realm of the pre-subjective in general. Horváth's *Jugend ohne Gott* instead dissociates trans-subjective from pre-subjective endangerments of the subject and is therefore more successful at integrating the Freudian legacy – sexuality and aggression ("Eros" and "Thanatos") as two poles of the unconscious – than Horkheimer and Adorno in the *Dialektik*. By untangling the trans- from pre-subjective, *Jugend ohne Gott* allows for a more complex reading of fascism. Neither sexuality nor violence is seen as positive in *Jugend ohne Gott*, but they are acknowledged to be

---

[45] Regarding Horváth's pacifism, see also Müller-Funk. P. 163.

constitutive elements of humans' psychic life. "Violence" can only be controlled up to a point; to some extent it resists rational control and may very well turn itself against those who hope to profit from it. This is how I would interpret not only the fact that it is N., the son of the prototypical fascist, the *Bäckermeister* N., who is the victim of a violent crime in *Jugend ohne Gott*, but also that N's murderer, T., hangs himself because he knows that the teacher has figured out his guilt. The novel certainly does not defend humans' violent nature, but it does note that violence ultimately may turn against itself.

In exploring fascism, the novel cautions us not to be too reductive or monolithic in our search for its origins. Ideology, racism, the economic concerns of the middle-class, economic profiteering, repression of the working class, the media, the rhetoric of violence and war, the militarization of society, a rigid ideal of masculinity together with a repression of what is considered "feminine", humans' so-called "lower" instincts, the failure of intellectuals – all of these factors are identified in *Jugend ohne Gott* as linked to the emergence of German fascism, but none of them can explain its origins exclusively. Fascism is neither the product of trans- nor of pre-subjective forces alone.

It is a merit of Horváth's *Jugend ohne Gott* that it reminds us of the need to understand the origins of totalitarian regimes and how intellectuals function under such regimes, while simultaneously offering a complex view of totalitarianism. What makes *Jugend ohne Gott* unusual, if not unique, is the inside perspective on the Third Reich the text offers. In part certainly because of Horváth's own experiences within the Third Reich, the text succeeds in asking uncomfortable questions about the complicity of individuals in totalitarian structures and, to some extent also, whether the readers' own values, then and now, are compromised by their proximity to those of the Third Reich.

III. Violence in the Age of Globalization;
  German Culture and Its Others

Barbara Fischer

From the Emancipation of the Jews to the Emancipation from the Jews: On the Rhetoric, Power and Violence of German-Jewish "Dialogue"

This essay examines the problematic relationship of Jews and Gentiles during the period of Jewish emancipation in Germany that began during the Enlightenment and concluded with the legal achievements that accompanied the establishment of the German nation-state. Through the analysis of nineteenth-century responses to two literary icons of central importance to Jewish-German dialogue, Lessing and Goethe, my study seeks to ascertain whether this "dialogue" was marked from the beginning by an innate impossibility and violence. These two canonical authors received, for different reasons, much attention from Jewish recipients, and had a tremendous influence on Jewish audiences, on their participation in a German-Jewish "dialogue", and subsequently on their assimilation into German Bildungsbürgertum. *Yet in return, the Jewish participation in German cultural production paradoxically led to resentments against the acculturated intellectuals who had provided their own "Jewish" interpretations of "German" national culture. "Fighting for emancipation from the Jews", was the final call of openly violent anti-Semitic rhetoric.*

One of the more violent threats on the German stage is to be found in a drama generally known for its message of humanism and tolerance. In *Nathan der Weise* [*Nathan the Wise*], published by the Enlightenment author Gotthold Ephraim Lessing in 1779, the Christian patriarch, who regards it as a sin against the Holy Spirit to raise a Christian child as a Jew, knows only one remedy for the "guilty" Jewish stepfather Nathan. The ecclesiastical despot exclaims repeatedly "Der Jude wird verbrannt" ["The Jew will be burned"].[1] The post-Shoah audience knows that this threat staged in an eighteenth-century play turned into reality for six million Jews in twentieth-century Nazi Germany.

Late twentieth-century stagings of Lessing's drama tended no longer to concentrate on the universal or humanist message delivered by the wise Jewish protagonist in his parable of the three rings, but to focus on the inadequacy, and even emptiness, of the play's message of tolerance. Nathan is either represented as an anachronistic fiction, which the recent history of the Shoah has rendered tragically irrelevant, or he is reduced to a puppet-like showman, reciting someone else's words mechanically and without conviction. While the

---

[1] Gotthold Ephraim Lessing: *Werke und Briefe in zwölf Bänden*. Ed. by Wilfried Barner a.o. Frankfurt am Main: Deutscher Klassiker Verlag 1993. Vol. 9. P. 578. In subsequent citations as Ba. Unless otherwise indicated, all translations are my own.

debate over the success or the failure of the message of tolerance dominated much of the discussion about the play during the past centuries, the potential of violence in Lessing's plot has – with a few exceptions – been generally overlooked.[2] Yet violence dominates the action from the beginning until the end. The drama begins with the fire in Nathan's house. We hear of the murder of Nathan's family, of the templar's planned execution, and of Nathan's projected fate: death from burning. We hear of oppression, treachery, blackmail, and genocide. Lessing's choice of setting, Jerusalem, symbolizes the potential for violent action due to its multi-cultural and multi-religious population with numerous conflicting interests. The play ends with the despotic ruler's, the Sultan's, final words directed at his newly found nephew, the templar, when he utters: "Wart!" ["Just wait!"][3]

The Hungarian-Jewish playwright George Tabori, who was born on the eve of the First World War, translates the undercurrent of violence in Lessing's play *Nathan der Weise* into "real", literal violence, which becomes the central element in his collage *Nathans Tod* [*Nathan's Death*] in 1991. By focusing on the numerous scenarios of underlying violence in the Lessing text and on the intertwined role of language, rhetoric, and dialogue between majority and minority culture, Tabori provides us with the most revealing *Nathan* interpretation to date. He attempts to show how ideals of Jewish emancipation which were proclaimed in such a promising way by the Lutheran Lessing, and were further personified in Lessing's exemplary friendship with the Jewish philosopher Moses Mendelssohn, led in the twentieth century to persecution, expulsion, and in its last consequence, murder of the Jews. This path is the darkest of all the possible turns to which Lessing's original multi-faceted eighteenth-century text points.[4]

Tabori calls his *Nathan* adaptation *Nathan's Death*. This title refers not only to the actual death of the Jewish protagonist, who dies of a heart attack, but also to the death of dialogue, of language, to the death of meaning and

---

[2] An important contribution on this topic is Christiane Bohnert: Enlightenment and Despotism: Two Worlds in Lessing's *Nathan the Wise*. In: *Impure Reason: Dialectic of Enlightenment in Germany*. Ed. by W. Daniel Wilson and Robert C. Holub. Detroit: Wayne State University Press 1993. Pp. 344–363.
[3] This translates into: "I'll get even with you" or "You'll pay for this". Ba 9. P. 627.
[4] In Tabori's stage adaptation, Lessing's Middle-Eastern location under palm trees has become a killing field. The world is in chaos; violence, rape, torture, burnings, and beatings dominate the dramatic action without interruption. The barbarism and power structures of the past and the present meet on stage and are interchangeable, as are those in power who make sure that the hierarchies remain in place. Tabori, by dissecting the text, by bending it, by adding other Lessing material to his twentieth-century work, shows the audience what has taken place between Nathan's first steps onto a German stage and the Shoah.

the death of the never-ending search for meaning.[5] Tabori points to a world which has "progressed" historically from domination to domination. Domination stood at the beginning of the Jewish-German (Christian) dialogue, and domination is at its end. Knowledge and wisdom, the instruments of liberation from despotic church domination in the eighteenth century, have had to step aside for new forms of power represented by the state. As Tabori's killing fields show, Lessing's "love free of prejudice" (Ba 9:559) or Walter Benjamin's "nonviolent resolution" discussed in his *Zur Kritik der Gewalt* [*Critique of Violence*][6] were not able to claim victory. The Jewish-German dialogue did not reach the age of love and friendship, but the age of genocide.

While the path from advocacy for Jewish emancipation to the desire for an emancipation from the Jews is mapped artistically by George Tabori in 1991, literary scholar Jeffrey Librett attempts in 2000 his own rhetorical-philosophical rereading of the relationship between Jews and Germans in *The Rhetoric of Cultural Dialogue: Jews and Germans from Moses Mendelssohn to Richard Wagner and Beyond*.[7] In this study, Librett first sketches the notion of ideal dialogue, and concludes that all dialogical relations hold a paradoxical mixture, a struggle over which side assimilates to the other side's signification.[8] He introduces the rhetorical framework of dialogical relationship:

> On the one hand, dialogue is *impossible* because each of its monological building blocks, the translative movements of understanding and response, without whose conjunction or synthesis dialogue cannot take place, is undone insofar as it occurs. Yet, on the other hand, dialogue is *necessary* for the same reason. (6)

---

[5] Nathan's parable of the rings, the most prominent message of tolerance and non-violent dialogue in German literature, is completely divested of its centrality in this collage.

[6] Walter Benjamin: Critique of Violence. In: *Walter Benjamin. Reflections: Essays, Aphorisms, Autobiographical Writings*. New York-London: Harcourt Brace Jovanovich 1978. Pp. 277–300. Here: P. 289.

[7] Jeffrey S. Librett: *The Rhetoric of Cultural Dialogue: Jews and Germans from Moses Mendelssohn to Richard Wagner and Beyond*. Stanford: Stanford University Press 2000. Librett examines the Jewish-Christian relation as fraught by the tension between what is perceived as the dead letter on the one hand and as the fulfilled spirit on the other. Through his discussion of cross-cultural translation in general and an analysis based on specific texts by Moses Mendelssohn, Friedrich and Dorothea Schlegel, Karl Marx, Richard Wagner, Friedrich Nietzsche, and Sigmund Freud, Librett shows that it is the figural-literal distinction which determines the power hierarchy of cross-cultural translation.

[8] My use of the term "signification" refers to the process of providing an interpretation of the space between signifier and signified. This space is filled with differing meaning by various participants in a dialogical relationship.

Librett proceeds to analyze how relationships of violent domination, oppression, and elitism stem from "non-violent" rhetoric. This rhetoric aims first to persuade the other to change. The second step consists of the use of clear rhetorical force on the minority culture to change. In its final stages the rhetoric sets the justification for physical violence, which at this point aims to eliminate the other by expulsion, or in its last consequence aims at physical elimination.

While Librett's study provides an extended reading of texts reaching from Paul to Martin Walser, I would like to focus primarily on his model of dialogue. It serves as the basis for my further discussion of nineteenth-century Jewish-German responses to two literary icons of central importance to Jewish-German dialogue, Lessing and Goethe. These two canonical authors received much attention from Jewish readers and audiences over the centuries. Lessing, the author of *Die Juden* [*The Jews*; written in 1749 and published in 1754], and *Nathan der Weise*, and the great private and public friend of Moses Mendelssohn, was seen as one of the most important promulgators of Jewish emancipation. Goethe, whose anti-Jewish sentiments have been analyzed by many, nevertheless had through his concept of *Bildung* [educational self-cultivation], as developed in his novel *Wilhelm Meisters Lehrjahre* [*Wilhelm Meister's Apprenticeship*] (1795/1796), a tremendous influence on his Jewish audiences in Germany. My study will focus on the following questions: If indeed all dialogue remains marked by a certain impossibility (dialogue of mutual understanding and recognition is, if at all, only found within the sphere of true friendship), and consists of the disfiguration of the other's intention, as Librett claims, what does this mean for the dialogical structure of the Jewish-German emancipation discourse? What does this tell us about interpretations of literary texts in general and about the Jewish-German reception of Lessing and Goethe in particular? Which effects did non-Jewish literary and non-literary texts have on Jewish emancipation in Germany? In return, which consequences did the Jewish response to these texts and their producers have for Jewish emancipation?

The dialogue about Jewish emancipation originated during the age of Enlightenment, when the Jew who had been the century-long stigmatized other of Church-dominated societies became for rationalist philosophers and liberal political theorists the symbol of the suffering for which those retrograde and superstitious societies stood. Such discrimination and victimization was an affront to those intellectuals arguing in favor of Enlightenment ideals. The German-Jewish dialogue began during the time when initial ideas regarding the future German nation-state also slowly found their way into official discourse. The emancipation period extended from the first public deliberations concerning the possibility of granting full civil status to the Jews around 1780 to the actual granting of this right during Bismarck's Empire in 1869. In their longing for a geographic and political "home", the German-Jews became strong supporters of the "myth" of the nation.[9] Timothy Brennan applies this term in all its multivalence: myth as legend, as tradition, myth as distortion, as lie, and myth as fiction, as literature. The process of Jewish emancipation clearly demonstrates various sides of this "myth", and the Janus-face of nationalism. The German Jews were eager consumers of the myth of the nation, and they also collaborated in writing it.

In 1779 Lessing's *Nathan* was published, and his advocacy for the Jews brought him much respect by those who favored Jewish emancipation and integration into a primarily German-Christian society. Two years later, in 1781, statesman Christian Wilhelm von Dohm deliberated in his treatise *Über die bürgerliche Verbesserung der Juden* [*On the Civil Amelioration of the Jews*] on the possibility of including the Jews as citizens of a future German state.[10] While we are aware of the fact that some of the better known public statesmen and thinkers, including Dohm, had no interest in or sympathy for individual Jews, as I have discussed elsewhere,[11] the logic of their arguments about individual freedom within a secular state had to apply to all subjects of a new society and therefore to Jews as well. The close connection between an interest in nation building and civil rights for all citizens (and this would include German-Jewish citizens) had been reiterated by many. Or as Moses Mendelssohn wrote in his preface (1782) to the German translation of *Vindiciae Judaeorum* [*Vindication of the Jews*] by Manasseh ben Israel: "Ein Glück für uns, wenn diese Sache auch zugleich die unsrige wird, wenn man auf die Rechte der Menschheit nicht dringen kann, ohne zugleich die Unserigen zu reclamiren" ["It is our fortune that this issue turns also into an issue concerning us, that one cannot proclaim human rights without at the same time reclaiming our rights"].[12] Both Lessing and Dohm were greatly interested in the role identity should play in the national project of the future. The notion of identity revolved around religion and citizenship, and led to an active participation in German (Christian) and Jewish dialogue from both sides.

---

[9] I have borrowed the term from Timothy Brennan: The National Longing for Form. In: *Nation and Narration*. Ed. by Homi Bhabha. London-New York: Routledge 1990. Pp. 44–70.
[10] Christian K. Wilhelm von Dohm: *Über die bürgerliche Verbesserung der Juden*. (1781) 2 Teile in einem Band. Hildesheim-New York: Georg Olms Verlag 1973.
[11] Barbara Fischer: Residues of Otherness: On Jewish Emancipation during the Age of German Enlightenment. In: *Insiders and Outsiders: Jewish and Gentile Culture in Germany and Austria*. Ed. by Dagmar C. G. Lorenz and Gabriele Weinberger. Detroit: Wayne State University Press 1994. Pp. 30–38.
[12] Moses Mendelssohn: *Gesammelte Schriften. Jubiläumsausgabe*. Orig. ed. by I. Ellbogen, J. Guttmann, E. Mittwoch. Cont. by A. Altmann together with H. Bar-Dayan et al. Stuttgart-Bad Cannstatt: Frommann 1971-. Vol. 8. P. 5.

For Lessing, the lover of theology,[13] the Jewish-German dialogue of the eighteenth century was still a Jewish-Christian dialogue that needed to accompany any debate about citizenship. His interest in respectful exchange and peaceful admission into a German nation differed substantially from that of Dohm, Wilhelm von Humboldt,[14] and others. For Lessing, Judaism stood at the heart of the genesis of the Christian religion. Consequently, as long as this nexus was not acknowledged, Christianity and the emerging German nation based on Jewish-Christian traditions was denying its very essence. The genealogical link required a change in attitude towards the Jews. Lessing, according to Willi Goetschel, and I share his reading, propagates a dialogue between the Jews and the Christians based on their common century-old tradition, a dialogue personified in Lessing's synecdochic friendship with Moses Mendelssohn.[15] In various writings Lessing argues for the imperative recognition of Jewishness as a valid, productive and promising culture that enriches an already inherently multi-ethnic make-up of the German "nation".[16] Seen in this perpective, his attitude towards Jews is thus no longer simply to be viewed as a token of good will. Lessing shares with his audience the project of rethinking both the claims of Christianity and groundwork of modern national identity:

> As [*Nathan der Weise*] frames its concern as one of delimiting the juridico-political claim of religious groups in the interest of a modern, emancipated understanding of religion, the paradigm of tolerance is abandoned. Instead, it is replaced by a model of full legal equality whereby the state (Saladin) recognizes the necessity of granting its citizens the same rights regardless of their religious affiliation. [...] At the end of the drama, Nathan no longer needs to pose as typical Jew or its opposite, as traditional or assimilated. Instead, he now – like everybody else – is able to be himself, be just a man for himself in all his particularity, that is, a Jew who has to explain and to legitimate himself as little as anyone else. (Goetschel 201)

Lessing's fundamental reconsideration of the dialogic relationship of Jews and Christians directs critical attention to the construction of Christian identity, an identity based on the Judeo-Christian tradition. The particular religions – both

---

[13] See Arno Schilson: Lessing and Theology. In: *A Companion to the Works of Gotthold Ephraim Lessing*. Ed. by Barbara Fischer and Thomas C. Fox. Suffolk-Rochester: Boydell and Brewer-Camden House 2005. Pp. 157–184. Here: P. 157.

[14] The interventions and writings by such high state officials as Wilhelm von Humboldt, Director of Culture and Education for the Prussian Ministry of the Interior, were influential in policy terms.

[15] Willi Goetschel: Lessing and the Jews. In: *A Companion to the Works of Gotthold Ephraim Lessing*. Pp. 185–208.

[16] Lessing repeatedly stages minorities in his plays, and hereby frequently shows a heterogeneous society to his readers/audience. He himself grew up in a region where Saxons and Sorbs lived peacefully next to each other.

based on this one tradition – then find themselves connected by a new, future common denominator, a new identity of solidarity.

This view differed substantially from the ones held by many other Christian commentators, both then and now. For them the Judeo-Christian tradition equals a "prefiguration-fulfillment" model, a practice of scriptural interpretation which starts with the apostle Paul and acknowledges the Old Testament not as the law and history of Israel, but as the promise and prefiguration of Christ. Consequently, as Jeffrey Librett points out in his reading of Erich Auerbach, the Old Testament has "no definitive meaning [endgültige Bedeutung], but only a prophetic meaning [Vorbedeutung]".[17] Therefore the Jewish scriptures were to be subsumed under the Christian interpretation. As we see in the following, not only the scriptures, but also those who adhered to them, the Jews, were to be subsumed under the Christian exegesis of the upcoming German national project.

Two years after the publication of *Nathan*, the first part of *Über die bürgerliche Verbesserung der Juden* appeared. It attempts to define the parameters of Jewish integration into German bourgeois society. The second part of Dohm's work followed in 1783. The effects Dohm's writings had on the political debates, on subsequent writings, and on reform policies should not be underestimated. At the same time, as Dohm himself conceded, he was not interested in the Jews as an oppressed minority, or, as was Lessing, in a modern emancipated understanding of religion which acknowledged the genealogical link between Judaism and Christianity. He was further not interested in the unconditional protection of Jewish cultural and religious identity, but in the assimilated bourgeois subjects into whom German Jews had to be transformed in the interest of the nation-state.[18]

The German Jews became the strongest promulgators of this new concept of national acculturation. Yet the Jewish-Christian dialogue, after a promising start between Mendelssohn and Lessing, turned into an unevenly balanced enterprise.[19] The Jewish longing for inclusion into a national form led to their participation with full energy, while their Christian counterparts based the political emancipation of the Jewish minority on the terms of a mercantile exchange. It became a commodity to be "purchased" with services rendered to the state. The Jewish sociologist and philosopher Gershom Scholem analyzed this unwillingness of the gentile side to enter into an equally balanced dialogue of mutual understanding and recognition. Scholem announced his

---

[17] Erich Auerbach quoted in Librett. P. xvi.
[18] Dohm II. P. 17.
[19] Their true friendship had allowed an exceptional dialogue as close to mutual understanding and recognition as possible between two independent subjects – in contrast to what came later.

famous refusal to contribute to a publication in honor of German-Jewish dialogue with the denial that it ever existed:

> I deny that there has ever been [. . .] a German-Jewish dialogue in any genuine sense whatsoever, i.e., *as a historical phenomenon*. It takes two to have a dialogue, who listen to each other, who are prepared to perceive the other as what he is and represents, and to respond to him. Nothing can be more misleading than to apply such a concept to the discussions between the Germans and Jews during the last 200 years. This dialogue died at its very start and never took place. [. . .] Where Germans ventured on a discussion with Jews in a humane spirit, such a discussion, from Wilhelm von Humboldt to Stefan George, was always based on the expressed or unexpressed self-abandonment [Selbstaufgabe] of the Jews.[20]

According to Scholem, for the German Jews the inclusion into a German nation came at the price of a "Selbstaufgabe", a violent transformation of the other, the Jew, to a Christian-German norm imagined as primary. Dohm, Humboldt, and other promulgators of Jewish inclusion into a German society and nation expected this self-abandonment which entailed full assimilation and acculturation.

Basing his study on Scholem's well-known and often criticized passage, Jeffrey Librett claims, as briefly mentioned above, that all dialogue remains marked by a certain impossibility and that there is never an undisfigured translation of the other's intention. Librett states: "there is no understanding that does not pass by way of violence, the violence of the reduction of the other to the self, the reduction of the different to the self-same, which is always an effect of force" (xvii). In *The Rhetoric of Cultural Dialogue* Librett bases his discussion of cross-cultural translation on this model, and examines the Jewish-Christian relation as the tension between what Christians perceived as the dead letter and the fulfilled spirit, between figural and literal, between the (Jewish) prefiguration and the (Christian) literal fulfillment. Librett concludes: "From the point of view of the Christian discourse, then, the Jews are figures, the Christians the literal truth" (12). A few sentences later he points out what will be of importance to the second part of our discussion here: "The passage from figural to literal is always reversible and hence the Jewish influence a threat" (12).

If the Enlightenment made Jewish emancipation and inclusion into a future German state possible, it also proclaimed an already inherent Jewish ideal of educational self-cultivation, of *Bildung*. Moses Mendelssohn introduced the term in 1784 in his essay *Über die Frage: Was heißt aufklären?* [*On the Question: What does 'to enlighten' mean?*], which appeared in the *Berlinische Monatsschrift* in September 1784. Mendelssohn employed *Bildung* as his central concept, and concluded that "Bildung of the nation" represented the most

---

[20] Translation of Gershom Scholem in Librett. P. xi.

noble task.[21] As Ehrhard Bahr points out in his essay "Goethe and the Concept of Bildung in Jewish Emancipation", statistics confirm that *Bildung* in the Mendelssohnian sense formed the basis of a reform movement that founded schools that educated Jewish students to become members of the dominant culture, to become interpreters of the meaning of cultural processes and products.[22]

A substantial percentage of German Jews assimilated into German "Bildungsbürger", educated, self-cultivated citizens. This is not surprising, taking into account the educational element in Jewish tradition. While the concept of a modern nation-state was unknown to the ancient Hebrews, a strong consciousness of a cultural and educational mission was always prominent within Jewish culture and continued throughout the centuries. Consequently, the German Jews in the first half of the nineteenth century accepted the "offer" of sociopolitical assimilation and acculturation.

It was within the realm of German letters where an innate potential for "Jewish" signification was possible. The cultural historian George Mosse, who himself contributed to the Jewish-(Christian-)German dialogue in many scholarly studies, points out in his *German Jews beyond Judaism* that the concept of *Bildung* became part of a new Jewish identity, if not a substitute for religion, an *Ersatzreligion*, for the Jewish *Bildungselite* in German lands:

> Man must grow like a plant, as Herder put it, toward the unfolding of his personality until he becomes a harmonious, autonomous individual exemplifying both the continuing quest for knowledge and the moral imperative. Goethe's *Wilhelm Meister's Apprenticeship* (1795/96) summed up this ideal in one phrase – "the cultivation of my individual self just as I am" ["mich selbst, ganz wie ich da bin, auszubilden"].[23] Such self-education was an inward process of development through which the inherent abilities of the individual were developed and realized. [. . .] *Bildung* and the Enlightenment joined hands during the period of Jewish emancipation; they were meant to complement each other. [. . .] Surely here was an ideal ready-made for Jewish assimilation, because it transcended all differences of nationality and religion through the unfolding of the individual personality.[24]

---

[21] Moses Mendelssohn: Über die Frage: Was heißt aufklären? In: *Was ist Aufklärung? Thesen und Definitionen.* Ed. by Ehrhard Bahr. Stuttgart: Reclam 1996. Pp. 3–8. Here: P. 4.
[22] Ehrhard Bahr: Goethe and the Concept of Bildung in Jewish Emancipation. In: *Goethe in German-Jewish Culture.* Ed. by Klaus L. Berghahn and Jost Hermand. Rochester, New York: Camden House 2001. Pp. 16–28. Here: P. 23.
[23] Goethe's contemporaries, nineteenth-century recipients, as well as Mosse himself in the twentieth century interpreted this phrase in terms of a program of *Bildung*. What is surprising is that George Mosse showed himself to be an admirer and participant of the concept of Goethean *Bildung* and to a certain extent became himself a representative of the problematic systematics he deconstructed. See Bahr. P. 25.
[24] George Mosse, *German Jews beyond Judaism.* Cincinnati: Hebrew Union College Press 1985. P. 3.

The old Jewish-Christian "prefiguration-fulfillment model", which in Scholem's opinion led to Jewish *Selbstaufgabe,* was complemented by a new German-Jewish "prefiguration-fulfillment model" that featured an aesthetic ideal of self-formation. If *Bildung*, as Mosse puts it, transcends all cultural, ethnic, and religious differences "through the unfolding of the individual personality", *Bildung* was turned into the *sine qua non* of Jewish integration.

Without doubt the general emancipation and freedom discourse of Lessing and Schiller matched the Jewish emancipation discourse more than anything in Goethe's writings.[25] Nevertheless, it was Goethe's concept of self-cultivation that had a tremendous influence on the Jewish elite in the German-speaking lands. First signs of the Goethe "cult" were to be detected in Berlin's Jewish salon culture (1780–1806). Rahel Levin, later Varnhagen von Ense, one of the salon hostesses, is perhaps the most famous admirer of Goethe. She was joined by Henriette Herz and Dorothea Veit Schlegel, the latter the oldest living daughter of Moses Mendelssohn. While the Jewish salon culture established a cult of Goethe admiration, it was not until the later years of the nineteenth century that personalized enthusiam gave way to institutionalized fame with important Jewish contributions to Goethe philology.

On the one hand the "bourgeoisification" of the German Jews can be seen as one side of the dialogical structure of German-Jewish emancipation. On the other hand, there was an active Jewish subscription to patriotism, to the "myth of nation", to bourgeois morality, and *Bildung*, that occurred with much enthusiasm and paved the way for the minority to enter into a "secularized" majority culture of a German national society. Not only in the German-speaking West, but also and especially in the Yiddish-speaking East, Lessing and Schiller became icons of cultural and political liberation. Both authors were translated into Hebrew and Yiddish, and they became the most read poets in the ghetto. The first translation of Goethe into Hebrew was of *Herrmann und Dorothea* in Warsaw in 1857.[26] All over the German lands, the veneration of the German men of letters also led to active Jewish participation in anniversary celebrations. These anniversaries resembled pseudo-national holidays, especially the Schiller anniversary, which was celebrated in 1859, and the Lessing anniversaries, which fell in the newly united German nation-state and were celebrated in 1879 and in 1881.[27]

---

[25] While Goethe's work and his concept of *Bildung* had a tremendous influence on the Jewish audience, there has been extensive discussion of Goethe's resentments against Jews. One of the fiercest critics of Goethe was Ludwig Börne.

[26] See Wilfried Barner: *Von Rahel Varnhagen bis Friedrich Gundolf: Juden als deutsche Goethe-Verehrer*. Göttingen: Wallstein 1992. P. 21.

[27] The Goethe anniversary in 1849 fell into a period when the general interest in Goethe in comparison to Schiller was somewhat restrained. It took another two decades for scholarly interest in Goethe to boom. See Barner: *Von Rahel Varnhagen*. Pp. 18–21.

It would go far beyond the scope of this essay to discuss the wide array of Jewish reactions to the German poets of the classical age, but I would like to concentrate in the following pages on a selection of Jewish responses to Lessing and Goethe in the second part of the nineteenth century. Not only did changes within the socio-political sphere of the late eighteenth century and nineteenth century bring many new opportunities for the Jews within German lands, a major transformation process took place for society in general in the sphere of *Bildung*, primarily in the second part of the nineteenth century. German Jews adopted models presented by non-Jewish statesmen and intellectuals in the knowledge that humanist-educational representations like the ones constructed by Lessing in *Nathan der Weise* or by Goethe in *Wilhelm Meisters Lehrjahre* provided them with an additional prospect of participation in a cross-cultural interaction. The active Jewish inscription into the "German" sphere of letters, the Jewish signification within the path of transformation from figural to literal was not welcomed by those who were eager to provide their own "German" signification of the Jews.

The *Nathan* veneration celebrated by the Jewish-German *Bildungsbürgertum* of the nineteenth century led to the celebration of his creator as well. Emil Lehmann, active member of the Jewish community in Dresden and elected representative of the Saxon parliament, announced in the *Lessing-Mendelssohn-Gedenkbuch* (1879) that Lessing was the most prominent proponent of Jewish emancipation, who had paved the way for the integration of the Jews into a German national state. Lehmann considered *Nathan* the point of departure into a new time period and assured the reader of God's involvement: "Ja, dies Buch hat Gott gegeben durch seinen Propheten Lessing" ["Yes, this book was given by God through his prophet Lessing"]. A few sentences later the Germans were turned – thanks to Lessing's *Nathan* – into the chosen people: "Kein andres Volk wie das deutsche hat solch ein Werk" ["No other people besides the Germans has such a work"].[28]

Gabriel Riesser, a Jewish lawyer from Hamburg and vice-president of the first national assembly, the Frankfurt parliament (1848–49), stated that it was his duty to thank Lessing, the fighter for light and freedom. He considered his rights as a German citizen a consequence of his rights as a German native:

> Wir sind nicht eingewandert, wir sind eingeboren, und weil wir es sind, haben wir keinen Anspruch anderswo auf eine Heimat; wir sind entweder Deutsche, oder wir sind heimatlos. Wer mir den Anspruch auf mein deutsches Vaterland bestreitet, der bestreitet mir das Recht auf meine Gedanken, meine Gefühle, auf die Sprache, die

---

[28] Emil Lehmann: Lessing – Mendelssohn – Nathan. 1729. 1754. 1779. In: *Lessing – Mendelssohn – Gedenkbuch*. Ed. by Deutsch-Israelitischer Gemeindebunde. Leipzig: Verlag von Baumgärtner's Buchhandlung 1879. Pp. 3–26. Here: Pp. 4, 5.

ich rede, auf die Luft, die ich atme; darum muß ich mich gegen ihn wehren, wie gegen einen Mörder.[29]

[We did not immigrate, we are natives of Germany, and this is why we cannot lay claim to another homeland; we are either Germans, or we have no homeland. He who contests my claim to my German fatherland also contests my right to my thoughts, my feelings, to the language I speak, to the air I breathe; therefore I have to defend myself against him, as against a murderer.]

This form of placeable and geographic bonding, according to Riesser, is essential to the human experience. The late twentieth-century British cultural historian Raymond Williams points out: "'Nation,' as a term, is radically connected with 'native.' We are *born* into relationships, which are typically settled in a place".[30] While much contemporary research is available on the problematic nature of this association, from Benedict Anderson to Homi Bhabha, for intellectuals like Riesser, who had struggled to move from the periphery to the center, this very connection was essential in their argument for inclusion within a new German nation.

The Leipzig Rabbi Abraham Meyer Goldschmidt asserted in his speech on the occasion of a Lessing celebration in Leipzig, where Lessing went to university and wrote some of his most important early plays, that *Nathan*, together with Goethe's *Faust*, was a historical sensation, a historical deed. He seemed certain that what Lessing had anticipated would be turned into reality by the grateful fatherland.[31] The nationalist doctrine supplanted religion's social role: The sense of belonging, the sense of community and obedience to the Law were shifted into the secular realm. According to Hans Kohn, nationalism was messianic in its European origins, modeled on the patterns of Judeo-Christianity. In his study *Nationalism* he states that modern nationalism took three concepts from Old Testament mythology: "the idea of the chosen people, the emphasis on a common stock of memory of the past and

---

[29] Riesser quoted in H.G. Adler: *Die Juden in Deutschland. Von der Aufklärung bis zum Nationalsozialismus*. München: R. Piper Verlag 1987. P. 71.

[30] Raymond Williams: *The Year 2000*. New York: Pantheon 1983. P. 180.

[31] "Durch ihn (Nathan) hat Lessing nicht nur die deutsche Literatur mit einer ihrer schönsten Zierden beschenkt; er hat eine ganze, numerisch nicht unbedeutende Klasse – die Juden Deutschlands – mit dem deutschen Vaterland beschenkt! Das deutsche Vaterland wird, kann nicht einem seiner edelsten Söhne, kann nicht sich selbst untreu werden. Was jener als ein heiliges Vermächtnis zurückgelassen, es wird, es muss gepflegt werden, und was er im Geiste ahnend geschaut, das dankbare Vaterland wird's zur Tat gestalten". Abraham Meyer Goldschmidt: Rede zur Lessingfeier in Leipzig (1860). In: *Lessing – ein unpoetischer Dichter: Dokumente aus drei Jahrhunderten zur Wirkungsgeschichte Lessings in Deutschland*. Ed. by Horst Steinmetz. Frankfurt am Main-Bonn: Athenäum Verlag 1969. Pp. 346–348.

of hopes for the future, and finally national messianism".[32] The German Jews took refuge in the hopes of a "messianic" mission, and the secular idea of historical progress contained much religious force. All hopes were projected onto the "fatherland", the "nation", the post-religious community. "Placeable" bonding once again attained a level of fundamental importance for a representative of the Jewish people, a people who had been without a *patria* for centuries. Lessing and Nathan, Goethe, Wilhelm Meister and Faust were turned into guarantees of belonging. As signifiers of a German future they reached mythic dimensions.

As a contrast let us turn now to the voices of non-Jewish nationalists and gauge their reactions to the Jewish subscription to a German national project. The Bismarck empire had succeeded in establishing the first German state in 1871. Eight years later, shortly after Lessing's 150th birthday and one-hundred years after the publication of *Nathan der Weise*, in March 1879, journalist and political agitator Wilhelm Marr published his book titled *Sieg des Judenthums über das Germanenthum. Vom nicht confessionellen Standpunkt aus betrachtet* [*Victory of the Jews over the Germans. Examined from a Non-Confessional Perspective*].[33] This book was the beginning of a new wave of anti-Lessing and anti-Semitic publications. It was in this document that the term "Antisemitismus" was introduced in printed form for the first time. Marr, who identified himself as an admirer of Lessing,[34] was deeply disturbed by the impact of Lessing's *Nathan* on the German-Jewish dialogue. It becomes clear that it was not so much the content of the drama that Marr criticized, but more the effect of the translation of Lessing's work by Jewish recipients into their own cultural context. By usurping *Nathan*, a representative work of German literature, the German Jews as translators/interpreters of this literature gained power over the German literary product, over German culture, over Germany and its "natives", Marr claimed. This led, as he continued, to "Herrschaft des jüdischen Realismus auf Kosten alles Ideellen" ["domination of Jewish realism over all idealism"] (21). Later in the text Marr went so far as to claim that "in allen Branchen des Lebens geht der Weg zum Ziel durch die *jüdische Vermittlung*" ["in all spheres of life, the path to the goal leads through *Jewish mediation*"] (27). Marr directed his strongest critique at the concept of Jewish *mediation*, at the Jewish interpretation of not only German literary products, but of "all spheres of life". Here we recall Libretto's discussion of cross-cultural translation and his analysis of the early tension between what Christians

---

[32] Hans Kohn: *Nationalism: Its Meaning and History*. Princeton-New York-Toronto-London: D. van Nostrand Company 1955. P. 11.
[33] Wilhelm Marr: *Sieg des Judenthums über das Germanenthum. Vom nicht confessionellen Standpunkt aus betrachtet*. Bern: Rudolph Costenoble 1879.
[34] Ibid. P. 17.

perceived as the dead letter and the fulfilled spirit, between figural and literal, between the (Jewish) prefiguration and the (Christian) literal fulfillment. Marr reversed this model, asserting that the Jews had subsumed everything from all spheres of life under their interpretation, under their Jewish "literal truth", and the result was, according to Marr, the domination of "Jewish realism".

Marr's publication appeared at a time when Jewish-German scholars and citizens regularly gave Lessing speeches and published commemorative essays in order to celebrate the specific Lessing anniversaries and to cultivate the Lessing heritage. Yet, Jewish Germans were living in an atmosphere of growing anti-Jewish sentiments, and Marr's writing did not remain without consequences. It was followed by numerous attacks against Lessing and *Nathan*, the more prominent ones by Richard Mayr, Adolf Bartels, and Eugen Dühring, to name just a few. The exaggerated assumption that the Jews would take over German culture, that they would put their "Jewish" signification upon German cultural heritage and assets, formed part of a violent turn in the rhetoric on Jewish and German identity.

We can detect similar systematics of cross-cultural rhetoric when we analyse the Jewish Goethe veneration and non-Jewish reactions to it. As mentioned above, Jewish salon culture had already established a Jewish community of Goethe enthusiasts in Berlin and Vienna. The decades following the founding of the German nation-state in 1871 saw this adoration of the "national" poet translated into institutionalized fame.[35] Michael Bernays, who had embraced Christianity at an early age, and Ludwig Geiger, son of German Rabbi Abraham Geiger, initiated critical Goethe philology. Geiger edited the influential *Goethe Jahrbuch* [*Goethe Yearbook*], for more than thirty years, from 1880–1913. The first president of the *Goethe Gesellschaft* [*Goethe Society*; founded in 1885 in Weimar] was the baptised Jew Eduard Simson, who had, like the above mentioned Gabriel Riesser, been a member of the first national assembly – the Frankfurt parliament – from 1848–49. Jewish Germans indeed were major players in Goethe representation during the period of the Wilhelminian Empire, among them also Karl Heinemann, Eugen Wolff, Richard Moritz Meyer, Albert Bielschowsky, Georg Witkowski, Emil Ludwig, Georg Simmel, Eduard Engel, and Friedrich Gundolf.[36] Their frequent contributions to Goethe philology and biography, often with an emphasis on a wider distribution for popular audiences, led the scholar Victor Hehn to describe the period as a "Jüdisches Zeitalter" [a "Jewish age"].[37] Unlike Lessing, Goethe

---

[35] Barner provides an excellent study of this topic in *Von Rahel Varnhagen bis Friedrich Gundolf.*

[36] Ibid. Pp. 33–42.

[37] Hope Hague, Brenda Machosky, and Marcel Rotter: Waiting for Goethe: Goethe Biographies from Ludwig Geiger to Friedrich Gundolf. In: *Goethe in German-Jewish Culture*. Pp. 84–103. Here: P. 84.

had only marginally been interested in the emancipation of the Jews, to which he had in fact objected. But Goethe's *Bildungskonzept* allowed for a common denominator between Christian and Jewish Germans, a common denominator of educated Germanness, of a personal identity beyond religion. Albert Bielschowsky's Goethe biography was printed in forty-two editions and sold over 80,000 copies between 1896 and 1922.[38] As Hope Hague, Brenda Machosky, and Marcel Rotter point out in their study of Goethe biographies: "Bielschowsky's *Goethe* borders on the mythic. In his preface he draws Goethe as the 'most human of all human beings,' even as an 'Übermensch'" (92, 93). Comparable to the Lessing venerations, scholars and biographers like Bielschowsky, Gundolf, and others transform Goethe in their "biographies" into "the highest potential of humanity", "the eternal savior", a "superhuman",[39] into their own "truth", putting their own views in the place of the individual poet.

In his paradigmatic biography of 1916 Friedrich Gundolf allegorizes the individual Goethe and elevates him to the status of "eternal savior". This led Walter Benjamin to a vehement critique of mythologizing tendencies. Benjamin was like Gundolf a representative of the emancipated and acculturated German Jewry, and his critique of Gundolf needs to be read as an analysis of Gundolf's act of translation which turns the historical individual into a mythical hero within the genre of historical biography. In his essay fragment *Comments on Gundolf's 'Goethe'* (written ca. 1917), Walter Benjamin calls Gundolf's work "a veritable falsification of knowledge",[40] and sees in it "the falsification of a historical individual, namely Goethe, by transforming him into a mythical hero" (98). Hague, Machosky, and Rotter concur with Benjamin's analysis:

> Gundolf writes the Gospel of Goethe, treating his life and works as an absolute existence, complete and autonomous, and infusing that existence with meaning. He begins with the assumption that in the representation of Goethe's completed figure the greatest unity of the German spirit has embodied itself.[41]

The human Goethe is turned into something divine. Gundolf translates the dead letter of biographical data into fulfilled spirit. Benjamin's critique refers to the signification process as such, a process which we also find with Goethe himself in his *Dichtung und Wahrheit*. Benjamin rightly pointed out the danger

---

[38] Ibid. P. 92. Compare also Barner: *Von Rahel Varnhagen*. P. 33.
[39] See Barner: *Von Rahel Varnhagen*. Pp. 27–29. See also Hague, Machosky, and Rotter. P. 97.
[40] Walter Benjamin: Comments on Gundolf's *Goethe*. In: Walter Benjamin: *Selected Writings. Volume 1, 1913–1926*. Ed. by Marcus Bullock and Michael W. Jennings. Cambridge: Harvard University Press 1996. Pp. 97–99. Here: P. 99.
[41] Hague, Machosky, and Rotter. P. 97. Again, one should compare this with Librett's cultural translation model in Librett. P. 12.

of turning an individual, an artist, the one who produces, into an absolute product, into a closed system of reference. To emphasize this notion further I refer to another admirer of Goethe who participated in this signification process: Houston Stewart Chamberlain. He admired the work and politics of his father-in-law Richard Wagner, and was himself a systematic racist. As Wilfried Barner rightly stresses, a detailed comparison of Gundolf's and Chamberlain's veneration of Goethe would reveal that Chamberlain's heroicizing and idolatrous attitudes toward Goethe lead in substance to the same type of "biography" as Gundolf's.[42]

While in Benjamin's analysis of Gundolf, it was the questionable quality of the biography which was under attack, *not* the ethnic or religious background or the political agenda of the biographer, most attacks on Goethe biographers of Jewish background focused on the perceived Jewishness of their interpretations. At a time when Jewish-Germans considered Jewish emancipation a *fait accompli* and could finally establish themselves as German citizens, institutional rejection of Jewish-German academics within circles interested in Goethe scholarship took place. No historical figure demonstrates the tension between inclusion in the majority culture and rejection by it better than the *Goethe Yearbook* editor Ludwig Geiger.

Geiger considered himself a German citizen of Jewish faith, and was a noted Lessing and Goethe scholar. For Geiger, Goethe promised a German culture in which being Jewish was not an identity, but an attribute. Throughout his professional life Geiger was the target of anti-Semitic attacks, from demagogues like Adolf Bartels, but also from pioneering scholars like Victor Hehn. The literary historian, Goethe scholar, and director of the Goethe archive, Erich Schmidt also argued in 1894: "Das Jahrbuch ist nicht in rechten Händen" ["The Yearbook is not in the right hands"]; he later succeeded in having Geiger removed as editor of the *Goethe Yearbook*.[43]

Richard Wagner, known for his ardent anti-Semitism, had already in the middle of the nineteenth century employed inflammatory rhetoric in his essay *Das Judentum in der Musik* [*Judaism in Music*] (1850; reprinted with changes and appended explanations 1869).[44] Wagner argued that the Jews do not belong within the space of art, and complained that they have come not

---

[42] Barner: *Von Rahel Varnhagen*. P. 36.
[43] See Christoph König: Cultural History as Enlightenment: Remarks on Ludwig Geiger's Experiences of Judaism, Philology, and Goethe. In: *Goethe in German-Jewish Culture*. Pp. 65–83. Here: P. 75.
[44] An excellent study of Wagner's essay and his anti-Semitism is provided by Jens Malte Fischer: *Richard Wagners "Das Judentum in der Musik"*. Frankfurt am Main: Insel 2000.

only to reside in it, but to control this space.⁴⁵ Schmidt's response to Geiger's work, Hehn's term "jüdisches Zeitalter", and Marr's criticism of Jews "usurping *Nathan*," were all based on the same fear of "Jewish" signification. The anxiety that the non-Jewish "German" side would assimilate to this signification provided the basis for the agitative rhetoric of the anti-Semites. They called on "Germans" to resist a perceived take-over by the "Jews". As Wagner forwarned the "Germans": "da *wir* vielmehr uns in die Notwendigkeit versetzt sehen, um Emanzipation von den Juden zu kämpfen" ["it is much rather *we* who are shifted into the necessity of fighting for emancipation from the Jews"].⁴⁶ The anti-Semites based their arguments for the "necessity" of the reversal of Jewish emancipation not only on the need to remove "Jewish control" from financial sectors. They further argued for this "necessity" under the assumption that the "Jewish control" over the "German" *Bildungs- und Kulturgut*, over "Germannness", would lead to an assimilation of "Germans" to "Jewish" interpretation and signification. An almost unqualified, tenacious adherence to the ideals of humanism and *Bildung* among acculturated Jewish-German intellectuals persisted into the period of Nazi dictatorship. Only the Zionists, who sought to reclaim their Jewish identity, refused integration into a German majority culture. Finally, as nineteenth-century ultra-nationalists put forward an increasingly racial and exclusionary notion of German citizenship, they represented Jewish assimilation invariably as a threat to the ethnic purity of the "national family". Thus they accused acculturated Jews of "disguising" themselves as "real" Germans.

A few decades later, as soon as state despotism had the legal power to turn this rhetoric into a legal contract, which, as Benjamin points out, holds the potential of "recourse to violence in some form against the other",⁴⁷ Jewish Germans perished in millions – like Tabori's protagonist – in the concentration and death camps of the Nazis. We find the endnote to the cult of *Bildung* in George Tabori's memoirs and in Victor Klemperer's diaries. When Tabori moved to Berlin in 1932 his aunt told him: "Wenn dieses Stück nicht wäre [*Nathan der Weise*], würde ich Dich nicht nach Deutschland gehen lassen, ich würde mich vor Deinen Zug schmeißen" ["If we didn't have this play [*Nathan der Weise*], I wouldn't let you go to Germany. I would throw myself in front

---

⁴⁵ Richard Wagner: Das Judentum in der Musik. In: Jens Malte Fischer. Pp. 139–196. Here: P. 153. Richard Wagner: Judaism in Music. In: Richard Wagner: *Judaism in Music and Other Essays*. Lincoln-London: University of Nebraska Press 1995. Pp. 75–122. Here: P. 87.
⁴⁶ Richard Wagner: Das Judentum in der Musik. P. 146. Richard Wagner: Judaism in Music. P. 81.
⁴⁷ Walter Benjamin: Critique of Violence. P. 288.

of your train"].[48] Victor Klemperer describes in his diaries of June 1942 a woman from the Jewish community in Dresden, Frau Hirschel, as "deutsch, betont nichtzionistisch, betont ästhetisch, goethedeutsch", ["German, emphatically non-Zionist, emphatically aesthetic, Goethe-German"] who insisted on Jews becoming the saviour of German high culture: "[W]ir werden Goethe retten!" ["We shall save Goethe [from the Nazis]"].[49]

This exclamation exemplifies that the national identity searched for by Jewish Germans was in diametrical opposition to the national identity searched for by Wagner, Houston Stewart Chamberlain, by the Nazis and their supporters. While the first group inscribed itself into nation building based on the premise that this German nation would define as its common denominator a common language, culture, history, and education, the second group "created" as their common denominator a national "myth" of a people of common "race". This mythical construct upheld by ultimately meaningless higher-case signifiers like "Deutsches Volk, Deutsches Blut [blood] und Deutscher Boden [soil]" excluded, persecuted, and exterminated those who had helped to bring together a construct called "Germany", and who had been strong promulgators of a common cultural and educational identity, the Jewish Germans. As soon as authority was given to the national construct, and as long as its authority stayed uncontested, it was clearly open for manipulation by those groups interested in abusing this inclusionary concept for exclusion. Jewish citizens who were instrumental in nation building were violently expelled by that very concept.

But the (non-)dialogue of Germans and Jews did not end in Auschwitz. The united Germany has struggled while searching for new forms of communicating about Auschwitz. Finally, in 2005, the national monument to German dishonor was unveiled and dedicated to the German nation. It is situated in the middle of Berlin, near a more traditional national monument, the Brandenburg Gate. It covers a wide area, and the silence between Peter Eisenman's gravestones points not only to the murdered six million Jews, but also to the shattered German-Jewish dialogue. And yet by its very presentation of this silence, a first new rapprochement may be occurring.

---

[48] George Tabori: *Unterammergau oder die guten Deutschen*. Frankfurt am Main: Suhrkamp 1981. P. 34.
[49] Victor Klemperer: *Ich will Zeugnis ablegen bis zum letzten: Tagebücher 1942–1945*. Ed. by Walter Nowojski with assistance from Hadwig Klemperer. Berlin: Aufbau 1995. Vol. 2. P. 135. See also Ehrhard Bahr. P. 25.

Mark Christian Thompson

The Negro Who Disappeared: Race in Kafka's *Amerika*

This essay examines how Kafka's Amerika, *also known under the title* Der Verschollene, *presents a landscape in which the protagonist, Karl Roßmann, can become an artist by acts of racial appropriation and mimesis via the misprision of African American "blackness". Kafka conflates an "aesthetics of becoming" with Negro identity as a way for* Amerika's *Karl Roßmann to take a subject-position as artist. In* Amerika, *Kafka's Roßmann performs his own minstrel show, his own blackface: in effect, becoming black is the only way to become a white artist.*

Describing his grandfather's frustration over unsuccessful attempts to collect his war pension due to a lack of legitimating papers, African American author Richard Wright observes in his 1945 autobiography, *Black Boy*, that, "Like 'K' of Kafka's novel, *The Castle*, [my grandfather] tried desperately to persuade the authorities of his true identity right up to the day of his death, and failed".[1] On the offensive against what he perceived as Wright's tendency toward two-dimensionality in fiction, and what he considered to be Wright's inadvertent complicity with America's racially repressive Christian morality, James Baldwin wrote in a withering 1949 critique of Wright: "In America, now, this country devoted to the death of the paradox which may, therefore, be put to death by one – [the African American's] lot is as ambiguous as a tableau by Kafka".[2] Regardless of the specifics of Baldwin's and Wright's developed antipathy toward one another, both call upon Kafka to describe the contradictory, paradoxical position of African Americans in the United States.

Perhaps then Wright and Baldwin would not have been surprised to have learned that Kafka, in his unfinished novel *Amerika*, likens his own aesthetic to the life of blacks. Nowhere are the deterritorializing effects of Kafka's use of language more on display than in his suspiciously Prague-like America. In this essay I analyze Karl Roßmann's self-identification as "Negro", and demonstrate what this has to do with Karl's ultimate disappearance. *Avant la lettre*, I suggest, Kafka understands Karl's disappearance as bound up with race, and compares stylistic disruption of language to the performative aspect of a fetishized black culture. *Amerika* presents Kafka with a landscape in

---

[1] Richard Wright: *Black Boy*. (1945) New York: Harper Collins 1998. P. 140.
[2] James Baldwin: Everybody's Protest Novel. In: *The Norton Anthology of African American Literature*. Ed. by Henry Louis Gates and Nellie Y. McKay. New York: Norton 1997. Pp. 1654–1659. Here: P. 1658.

which his Karl Roßmann can become an artist, not simply through America's "sameness" and "otherness" in comparisons with Europe, but also through America's "others". Kafka exploits an image of blackness as open to invasion and habitation by *Der Verschollene*'s Karl Roßmann for the purpose of his taking a subject-position, that of the artist, otherwise unavailable to him. In *Amerika*, Kafka's Roßmann performs his own minstrel show, his own blackface, to the effect that becoming black is the only way to become a white artist.

Begun in 1912, *Der Verschollene* – the title Kafka gave to his unfinished first novel, as opposed to *Amerika*, the name selected by Max Brod – traces the movements of Karl Roßmann, a German-speaking Prague-native who has been exiled to the US by his family for impregnating his governess. Unexpectedly greeted directly off the boat by his wealthy uncle, Karl's life seems ideal, until his troublingly mercurial uncle kicks him out of the house, forcing Karl to fend for himself. What follows is a carefully mapped out, bizarrely picaresque journey through a deterritorialized American landscape, which ends, sort of, with Karl landing a job with a vast theater group called the Theater of Oklahoma.

Karl finds his new show business career by answering an advertisement that reads: "Jeder ist willkommen! Wer Künstler werden will, melde sich!" (295) ["All welcome! Anyone who wants to be an artist, step forward!"] (202).[3] The advertisement for the great Theater of Oklahoma is deceptively clear. Mentioning nothing of wages, activities, working conditions, etc., the theater promises training. The troupe's self-representation on the surface frustrates the very expectation one expects to have met in a job listing, namely the nature of the job. By insisting that the theater seeks workers to fill various unnamed positions, the poster Karl sees in fact promotes not so much an occupation as a transformation. The usual prerequisites – experience, education, and training – mean, or at least seem to mean, nothing here. The work at-hand will be a process of becoming, of metamorphosis, into Artist. There is in fact only one requirement for employment at the Theater: the desire to be an artist. One must want to become an artist to be taken on as a hired hand in the Oklahoma Company. Therefore, if Karl is to be accepted into the Theater's ranks, which he will be, he must tacitly or unconsciously already possess the desire to be an artist.

In exile, Karl awaits the ecstasy of being an out-of-place, or ek-statos (standing out of place) artist, a feeling Kafka knew well. Max Brod records in

---

[3] All citations to Kafka in the original German will be taken from Franz Kafka: *Der Verschollene*. (1927) Frankfurt am Main: S. Fischer Verlag 1994. (Kritische Ausgabe.) All English translations are taken from *Amerika (The Man Who Disappeared)*. Trans. by Michael Hofmann. New York: New Directions 2004. Future citations will be parenthetical.

a diary entry of September 9, 1912: "Kafka is in ecstasy, writes whole nights through. A novel set in America". And Brod writes on October 1: "Kafka in unbelievable ecstasy".[4] Walter Benjamin believes that Kafka was plagued by a "great sadness", and that Kafka's ecstasy over *Amerika* fed off of, as it annihilated, this deep sorrow. "The ardent 'wish to become a Red Indian,'" Benjamin surmises, referring to Kafka's short piece *Wunsch, Indianer zu werden*, "may have consumed [his] great sadness at some point [. . .]. A great deal is contained in this wish. Its fulfillment, which he finds in America, yields up its secret".[5] Benjamin draws attention to the fact that becoming racially other provided Kafka not only with the means to escape the self and the material conditions that invoke great sadness in the suffering subject. For Benjamin, Kafka's racial charade also creates a "purity of feeling". "No matter how one may convey it intellectually", Benjamin asserts, "this purity of feeling may be a particularly sensitive measurement of gestic behavior; the Nature Theater of Oklahoma in any case harkens back to the Chinese theater, which is a gestic theater" (120). At one moment American Indian, at another a member of a Chinese Theater Company, America offered Kafka a landscape in which to people his racial others, positioning them at various checkpoints in the deterritorialized zone of the desire to become an artist. These figures embody nothing less than Kafka's process of aesthetic rebirth and de-birth. When Karl Roßmann identifies himself to the Theater of Oklahoma as "Negro", he performs his own minstrel show, his own blackface, as if becoming black were the only way to become a white artist.

Kafka was not unfamiliar with *Ausstellungsneger*. In a diary entry of 15 December, 1910, Kafka observes that "Kein Wort fast, daß ich schreibe, paßt zum andren, ich höre, wie sich die Konsonanten blechern aneinanderreiben, und die Vokale singen dazu wie Ausstellungsneger" ["Scarcely a word that I write suits the next, I hear the tinny grating of the consonants, and the vowels sing along like minstrels"].[6] By his own estimation, Kafka's writing produces a literary text that emits a cacophonous noise, one that clangs as the consonants rub together and as the vowels carol like exhibition Negroes performing a minstrel show. Absolutely dissimilar to the music produced by Grete Samsa in *Die Verwandlung*, the clamber Kafka's prose emits sounds closer in tenor to

---

[4] Max Brod: *Franz Kafka: A Biography*. (1937) Trans. by G. Humphreys Roberts and Richard Winston. New York: Schocken 1963. P. 128.
[5] Walter Benjamin: Franz Kafka. In: *Illuminations: Essays and Reflections*. Trans. by Harry Zohn. New York: Schocken 1969. Pp. 111–140. Here: P. 119.
[6] Franz Kafka: *Tagebücher: 1909–1912*. Ed. by Hans-Gerd Koch. Frankfurt am Main: S. Fischer Verlag 1994. (Kritische Ausgabe.) Vol. 1. P. 27. Translations are mine when not otherwise noted.

the noise Gregor Samsa makes while he speaks.[7] As repellent as the "music" of Kafka's prose sounds, it is no wonder that the task of being an artist in Kafka's oeuvre is an ostensibly abhorrent one.

Indeed, Kafka's Karl Roßmann seems the last person to want to become an artist. After reading the Oklahoma Theater's advertisement for work, Karl affirms that "Künstlerwerden wollte niemand, wohl aber wollte jeder für seine Arbeit bezahlt werden" (295) ["No one wanted to be an artist, but everyone wanted to be paid for his work" (202)]. To be an artist and to be paid for one's work are here at odds. The tacit assumption operative in Karl's proclamation on the viability of the artist's life is that art does not pay. Karl also assumes that the production of art is, categorically, a form of work. Although no one wants to become an artist, and everyone wants to get paid for her work, the two statements are not mutually antagonistic to each other in this context; nor do they have a relation to each other beyond the purely grammatical. It could very well be that one is an artist despite having lacked the desire to become one *precisely* because one gets well-paid for one's art. It could be, in other words, that no one wants to become an artist, but that one does so anyway because, in a given situation, it pays well. The list of permutations, or eradications, of the seemingly easy logic of Karl's assertion is quite long, and in fact ends only at the limits of imagination. What we find on the border of implied sense and the aporias opened up by the deception of the apparent grammatical ordering of meaning in Kafka's text is ambivalence. Where Karl appears to deny absolutely the insurmountable precondition of becoming an artist, namely desire, he negatively affirms the probability of the artist-instinct within him. Lack of desire cannot position itself between Karl and his becoming-artist. Instead, it is Karl's inability to concede that he possesses such as desire in the first place that leads to the tension and ambiguity that holds *Amerika* together as it breaks it apart.

Throughout his journey across *Amerika*, Karl deploys various strategies of denial that do not subvert so much as distort and defer the teleological end of this novel without end. Palpable in his piano playing, Karl desires to admit to his desire to become an artist. But he cannot do so without first performing a series of evasions, misrecognitions and misrepresentations which cause him to disappear at the moment he seeks to affirm his identity. In fact, Karl must disappear in order to circumvent his own desire and present himself to himself as artist. The Oklahoma Theater offers Karl not merely the ability to train as an artist (assuming he has the desire to do so), but to fulfill a logical requirement of becoming other. The annihilation of the self in terms of a past that would hinder his metamorphosis into an artist must occur before the

---

[7] Franz Kafka: Die Verwandlung. (1915) In: *Ein Landarzt*. Ed. By Hans-Gerd Koch. Frankfurt am Main: S. Fischer Verlag 1994. (Kritische Ausgabe.) Pp. 91–158.

positive transformation can take place. If it is the case the Oklahoma Theater welcomes anyone and everyone, then "Alles was er bisher getan hatte, war vergessen, niemand wollte daraus einen Vorwurf machen" (295) ["Everything he had done up until now would be forgotten, no one would hold it against him" (202)].

Working with a clean slate, Karl believes that he can no longer be held responsible for his past sins. In becoming artist, Karl must first become innocent. "Innocence" here does not mean free of sin, but free from reproach. Having forgotten past behavior that may have impugned his character, those who will stand in judgment of Karl, should they pick up the trace of crime of banal character flaw, will not want to admonish him for his indiscretions and transgressions. Therefore, becoming an artist necessitates both the desire to be an artist, and a support structure that allows for this becoming by providing a space in which the various transformations mandated by this trial of becoming-artist take place. This space does not create a value-free environment but one amenable only to the strictures of art itself. In other words, the seemingly endless, and endlessly permutable, Oklahoma Theater provides a stage upon which only the laws of art apply. Against this backdrop of endless referentiality, the Theater stages no referent. In the absence of a referent, everything would be forgotten, would disappear without a trace, and almost unbelievably so. This is why "Karl las das Plakat nicht zum zweitenmale, suchte aber noch einmal den Satz: 'Jeder ist willkommen' hervor" (296) ["Karl didn't read the poster through again, he just looked out the sentence 'All Welcome' once more" (203)]. "Everyone is welcome" means here that anyone can disappear, dissolve into someone or something else.

Given that the only artistic talent Karl shows in the novel is musical in nature, it is not surprising that his first impression of the theater comes from the music of trumpets: "Als er in Clayton ausstieg, hörte er den Lärm vieler Trompeten. Es war ein wirrer Lärm, die Trompeten waren nicht gegeneinander abgestimmt, es wurde rücksichtslos geblasen" (296) ["When he got out in Clayton, the sound of many trumpets greeted his ears. It was a confused noise, the trumpets weren't playing in tune, there was just wild playing" (203)]. Like the atonal music generated in *Forschungen eines Hundes*, and *Josefine*, the blast of sound that greets Karl lacks form and contour, this quality of lack signaling all the more in Kafka's work the presence of the work of art.[8]

---

[8] Franz Kafka: Forschungen eines Hundes (1931). In: *Das Ehepaar und andere Schriften aus dem Nachlaß.* Ed. by Hans-Gerd Koch. Frankfurt am Main: S. Fischer Verlag 1994. (Kritische Ausgabe.) Pp. 48–93. Franz Kafka: Josefine, die Sängerin oder Das Volk der Mäuse (1924). In: *Das Ehepaar und andere Schriften aus dem Nachlaß.* Ed. by Hans-Gerd Koch. Frankfurt am Main: S. Fischer Verlag 1994. (Kritische Ausgabe.) Pp. 223–244.

The music of the trumpets evades its audience as it imposes itself upon it; it transforms itself instantaneously and constantly, as to deny access to a central axis point and point of reference. Karl is greeted by symphonic cacophony, by the music of the angels. Indeed, the trumpets are played by "hundrete Frauen als Engel gekleidet" (297) ["hundreds of women dressed as angels" (203; translation modified)].

By dressing his musicians as angels, Kafka displaces the scene of the theater, or at least distorts it to such an extent that the music being played is not entirely sublunary. Never forgetting that this angelic music is played by women dressed as angels, the illusion of a celestial orchestra is made all the more complete by the fact that "die Gestalten der Frauen riesenhaft aus[sahen]" (297) ["the forms of the women looked gigantic" (203; translation modified).] Seen here are the *forms* of the women, the angels, not the women themselves. Kafka removes from the women any attribute beyond a formal one, creating in the process a vision of the angelic as pure form. Forms without the possibility of knowable contents, or without representable contents, name not merely the celestial, but the negative aesthetic. The music being blown out by the heavenly trumpet players is, like the many forms of the angels, fragmented and without content. No demonstrable sense can be made of the noise Karl hears except to say that it announces itself within the realm of the aesthetic, and that it is self-referential, or reflexive, insofar as it speaks of nothing except its own self-referentiality or reflexivity.

Perhaps it is because of this self-referentiality that Kafka employs musical Negroes in his diaries as similes for his art. As Adorno asserts,

> It is not for nothing that Kafka, like no writer before him, should have assigned a place of honour to music in a number of memorable texts. He treated the meanings of spoken, intentional language as if they were those of music, parables broken off in mid-phrase.[9]

Kafka himself confirms this belief in a letter to his lover, Milena. Describing *Das Urteil* to Milena, who was translating the story into Czech, Kafka wrote: "In jener Geschichte hängt jeder Satz, jedes Wort, jede – wenn's erlaubt ist – Musik mit der 'Angst' zusammen" ["Each sentence in this story, each word, each – if I may say so – *music* is connected with fear"].[10] The description Kafka gives of his writing begins with the sentence, and ends in music. The meaning, the materiality, of Kafka's writing is composition in the musical

---

[9] Theodor W. Adorno: Music and Language: A Fragment. In: *Quasi una Fantasia*. Trans. by Rodney Livingstone. New York: Verso 1998. Pp. 1–6. Here: P. 3.
[10] Franz Kafka: *Briefe an Milena*. Ed. by Jürgen Born and Michael Müller. Frankfurt am Main: S. Fischer Verlag 1983. (Erweiterte Neuausgabe.) P. 235. English version quoted in Nicholas Murray: *Kafka*. Abacus: London 2004. P. 127.

sense. Writing is music. This is why, when asked by the Oklahoma Theater for his name, Karl Roßmann "antwortete nicht gleich, er hatte eine Scheu, seinen wirklichen Namen zu nennen und aufschreiben zu lassen" (306) ["didn't reply right away, he was reluctant to give his real name and have that entered" (210)]. Afraid to reveal his true identity and as if attempting to test, negatively, the theater's policy of accepting everyone, even a no one, or a false name, Karl

> nannte daher, da ihm im Augenblick kein anderer Name einfiel, nur den Rufnamen aus seinen letzten Stellungen: "Negro". "Negro?" fragte der Leiter, drehte den Kopf und machte eine Grimasse, als hätte Karl jetzt den Höhepunkt der Unglaubwürdigkeit erreicht. Auch der Schreiber sah Karl eine Weile prüfend an, dann aber wiederholte er, Negro, und schrieb den Namen ein. (306–307)
>
> [Therefore, as nothing else came to mind just then, he gave what had been his nickname on his last jobs: "Negro". "Negro?" asked the boss, turning his head and pulling a face, as though Karl had now reached the height of preposterousness. The secretary too looked at Karl awhile, but then repeated 'Negro' and wrote it down. (210)]

In the critical work that has treated Karl Roßmann's self-proclaimed negritude, this identification with African American blackness as he applies for a job at the great Theater of Oklahoma is consistently seen in an overwhelmingly negative light. "Enrolling himself as 'Negro'", Anne Fuchs laments,

> he now aligns himself with the most stigmatized and oppressed group in American history [. . .]. Karl's grotesque categorization as "Negro, technical worker" underlines once more the loss of his social status, true history, name, and voice.[11]

Although the label is unfortunate, it is not grotesque. Fuchs labors under the assumption that to be a Negro is a bad thing, that it is totally undesirable, and that it entails solely stigmatization and oppression. Two deeply erroneous assumptions condition Fuchs's argument: that the black experience in America (and *Amerika*) outlines a purely negative position; that Kafka limited himself to such a rigorously undialectical attitude. As a corrective, I submit that the appearance of a "Negro" in *Der Verschollene* is so shocking that it blinds us to the rhetorical potential Kafka deploys when introducing us to his allegory of race.

Thus I disagree with Rolf J. Goebel that "Negro" is here "a deeply emblematic signifier for [Karl's] hybrid position between cultures", and that, "Karl comes to shed the pretenses of theatrical artistry for the stereotypical affiliation of

---

[11] Anne Fuchs: A Psychoanalytic Reading of "The Man Who Disappeared". In: *The Cambridge Companion to Kafka*. Ed. by Julian Preece. Cambridge: Cambridge University Press 2002. Pp. 25–41. Here: P. 38.

minority status with menial labor".¹² My reading moves irrevocably in the opposite direction in large part to remedy the preponderance of critical views that cannot imagine the (albeit false) self-selection as "Negro" as positive in any way, dialectically speaking or otherwise. Also, Goebel's understanding of the type of labor Karl will perform as part of the Oklahoma Theater, namely "technical worker", forgets what the theater designates itself as, namely an organ for the production of artists *and nothing else*.

Perhaps if someone had simply gone back and read *Der Verschollene*'s Urtext, namely Holitscher's *Amerika: Heute und Morgen*, this Negro problem would have been solved a long time ago. We know Kafka read Holitscher because Kafka indirectly quotes Holitscher's photo of a lynched African American, "Idyll aus Oklahama" (Figure 9.1), and because the book was among those in Kafka's library. Aside from the Oklahoma connection, *Amerika: Heute und Morgen* is crucial to understanding *Der Verschollene* for at least

Idyll aus Oklahama

Figure 9.1 From *Amerika Heute und Morgen* (1912) by Arthur Holitscher, p. 367.

---

¹² Rolf J. Goebel: *Constructing China: Kafka's Orientalist Discourse*. Columbia, SC: Camden House 1997. P. 196.

two reasons. First, in the opening pages of *Amerika: Heute und Morgen*, Holitscher describes his arrival, by ship, in New York Harbor. Of the poor who had to travel in squalid conditions deep in the bowels of the ship, Holitscher writes:

> Diese Armen da unten, die Leute "aus der Tiefe", heut noch fünf Tage lang dürfen sie sich Menschen nennen. Sie sind nicht von ihrer Scholle losgerissen, denn wer unter ihnen hat denn heut noch seine Scholle? Was heisst denn das heute: Scholle?
>
> [These poor people below deck, the people "out of the deep", for the last five days they were still able to call themselves human. They weren't yet torn from their homes, for who among them has a home today? What does that mean today: Home?][13]

This rhetorical bombast, found in *Amerika: Heute und Morgen*'s opening, introductory pages, becomes the main question that Holitscher's, and Kafka's, book seeks to answer. The German noun "die Scholle" is the root of "Der Verschollene", the title Kafka gave to his unfinished novel. "Der Verschollene" means literally, "the lost one", or, "the one who went missing", and is translated as the title of Kafka's novel as, "The Man Who Disappeared". The word is of particular importance aboard ships because it also indicates those who have gone overboard and are considered lost at sea. "Scholle" commonly translates as a flatfish or plaice, and a clump of earth or clod. The related English word, important for the nautical context we find ourselves in, is "shoal". Holitscher uses "Scholle" as a way, within his nautical context of fish and shoal, to question the advanced and at the same time barbaric state of economic exploitation aboard his ship of passage. Deep below decks, "aus der Tiefe", Holitscher hears the cry of the poor and wonders how they can bear their state of homelessness. They are homeless because, Holitscher tacitly assumes, most who would travel in this manner and endure such hardship are attempting to escape an even greater hardship, to immigrate to America, to the land of opportunity. Relying on the many traces to be followed in the word Scholle, Holitscher silently equates the poor with fish in a barrel (fish that come "aus der Tiefe" and must remind themselves that they are human). The immigrants below have no shoal of their own, no oasis from the sea poverty on which they live.

America promises "eine Scholle" as much for Karl Rossmann as for Holitscher's poor. Fleeing not poverty but certain shameful circumstances, Karl immigrates. While aboard ship, in between lives, homeless, Karl lives among the lowly deep in the belly of the boat as he takes his own middle passage. Both Karl and Holitscher arrive in New York Harbor. Although Karl seeks an oasis in the United States, a home among the homeless, Kafka edits

---

[13] Arthur Holitscher: *Amerika Heute und Morgen* (1912). Berlin: S. Fischer Verlag 1919. Pp. 14–15.

Holitscher in at least one important way. Whereas Holitscher maintained the hope that home could be found in America, Kafka's opinion was, if not pessimistic, then characteristically elliptical. Karl has gone overboard and remains, by the book's end, lost at sea.

The second clue we can follow in Holitscher's text, in a chapter entitled "Der Neger" ["The Negro"], is to be found directly opposite the page on which the lynching in Oklahoma is depicted. Here, Holitscher offers this interpretation of why so many Jews are sympathetic to the plight of blacks in America:

> Tatsächlich finden sich unter den Wohltätern und Förderern der Neger-Emanzipation auffallend viele Juden. Tatsächlich haben Juden und Neger in manchen Punkten der Einschätzung gleicherweise zu leiden, im öffentlichen Leben, in der Verwaltung, im Heer. (Die Neger stärker als die Juden, selbstredend, aber das Prinzip bleibt dasselbe.)[14]
>
> [In fact, among the supporters and activists working toward the emancipation of the Negro are a striking number of Jews. Indeed, Jews and Negroes in many ways suffer in the same way, in public life, in business, and in the armed forces. (Negroes more strongly than the Jews, to be sure, but the principle remains the same.)]

For Holitscher, blacks and Jews share significantly in the ways in which they are oppressed, the ways in which they suffer. By commonality of suffering, Holitscher establishes an essential link between blacks and Jews. Jews can sympathize with blacks because they identify with the plight of blacks, seeing it as, if not literally, then *essentially* their own. Kafka's Negro is a Jew, with some slight modifications. One difference is that the Negro, according to Holitscher, is stronger and more self-aware than the Jew. The Negro would then be not merely the representative of Jewish suffering, albeit in metamorphosed, aestheticized form, but also the telos of Jewish self-awareness and power. Paradoxically, the lynched Negro becomes, through aesthetic-allegorical reconstruction, the self-empowered Jew. If seen in this light, as allegorical and not as emblematic or symbolic, then the positive element of Kafka's Negro is that it holds at least the potential for a Jewish voice. It offers, in any event, a closer understanding of how Kafka's texts proceed about the business of racialized signifying. According to Adorno,

> In its striving not for symbol but for allegory, Kafka's prose sides with the outcasts. [. . .] It expresses itself not through expression but by its repudiation, by breaking off. It is a parabolic system the key to which has been stolen; yet any effort to make this fact itself the key is bound to go astray by confounding the abstract thesis of Kafka's work, 'the obscurity of the existent, with its substance. Each sentence says 'interpret me,' and none will permit it.[15]

---

[14] Ibid. P. 352.

Foreclosing on the possibility of wresting meaning even from meaninglessness in Kafka's writings, Adorno notes Kafka's elliptical opacity while, of course, denying he does so. Without recourse to the vocabulary with which to translate the muteness of Kafka's mode of signification, the almost self-annihilating movement of Adorno's negative dialectic speaks for both Adorno and Kafka through a critical silence. Giorgio Agamben, however, does not hesitate to inscribe the arc described by the journey one takes while reading Kafka. "One of the peculiar characteristics of Kafka's allegories" Agamben writes, "is that at their very end they offer the possibility of an about-face that completely upsets their meaning".[16] Admitting that Kafka's figures are allegorical in nature, Agamben explains their effect as essentially iterative; where one's reading of Kafka's allegories ends, a fresh reading begins. As Blanchot notes, each successive allegorical reading is the progression of a common search by the author and reader for an existential affirmation:

> Kafka's entire work is in search of an affirmation that it wants to gain by negation, an affirmation that conceals itself as soon as it emerges, seems to be a lie and thus is excluded from being affirmation, making affirmation once again possible.[17]

There can be no affirmation in Kafka's work without a radical, and in this case racial, negation of the thing to be affirmed, and vice versa. Blanchot sees the extreme limit of this as the "death" that permeates Kafka's writings, which, at the end (beginning) of Kafka's rigorous dialectic, would be an absolute commitment to life (death).

This is precisely the paradoxical logic of boundaries Derrida reads in Kafka:

> If we subtract from [Kafka's texts] all the elements which could belong to another register (everyday information, history, knowledge, philosophy, fiction, and so forth – anything that is not necessarily affiliated with literature), we vaguely feel that what is *at work* in this text retains an essential rapport with the play of framing and the paradoxical logic of boundaries, which introduces a kind of perturbation in the "normal" system of reference, while simultaneously *revealing* an essential structure of referentiality.[18]

---

[15] T.W. Adorno: Notes on Kafka. In: *Prisms*. Trans. by Samuel and Shierry Weber. Cambridge, Massachusetts: Massachusetts Institute of Technology Press 1997. Pp. 243–271. Here: P. 246.
[16] Giorgio Agamben: *Homo Sacer: Sovereign Power and Bare Life*. Trans. by Daniel Heller-Roazen. Stanford, California: Stanford University Press 1998. P. 58.
[17] Maurice Blanchot: Reading Kafka. In: *The Work of Fire*. Trans. by Charlotte Mandell. Stanford, CA: Stanford University Press 1995. Pp. 1–11. Here: P. 7.
[18] Jacques Derrida: Before the Law. In: *Acts of Literature*. Ed. by Derek Attridge. Trans. by Avital Ronell and C. Roulston. New York: Routledge 1992. Pp. 181–220. Here: P. 213.

The revelation of the essential structure of referentiality marks the allegorical imperative of Kafka's oeuvre, and maps out Deleuze and Guattari's concept of the deterritorialized literary text in general and *Amerika* in particular. They theorize that Kafka's paired down "Prague German is a deterritorialized language, appropriate for strange and minor uses. (This can be compared in another context to what blacks in America today are able to do with the English language)".[19] Common to Kafka as a Prague German speaker and what African Americans do with the English language is the capability to cultivate the fertile linguistic terrain at which "*Language stops being representative in order to now move toward its extremities or its limits*".[20] At the extreme limits of language's referentiality, the representative symbolic order implicit in the linguistic utterance subverts itself and in so doing becomes deterritorialized.

This theory of linguistic deterritorialization that Deleuze and Guattari identify in Kafka bears a striking resemblance to the work Paul de Man believes allegory generally performs in the literary text. De Man sees allegory as "an immaterial shape that represents a sheer phantom devoid of shape and substance".[21] Opposing it to the untroubled symbolic logic of identification between the subject of an utterance and its object, de Man's "phantom proxy" (191) – allegory – is the ghost of a ghost. This "phantom proxy" circulates throughout, and indeed makes the effect of Kafka's language possible. Playing the part of the phantom proxy, Kafka's Negro serves as an allegory of the process of becoming artist, and as an allegory of allegory, or the very mechanism of Kafka's prose.

One thing is certain, Kafka's Negro does not, as one critic would have it, allude to "Schwarzarbeit", the type of work Karl undertakes at the great Theater of Oklahoma. The term was not in use as such at the time Kafka writes.[22] Another interpretation sees Negro as foreshadowing Karl's dealings with gangsters, even though there are no gangsters in *Amerika* as it stands, no suggestion of gangsters, and as if all African Americans were easily and readily identified as gangsters at this time or any time, which they were and are not.[23]

Following a dialogue in the diaries and offering a more credible reading of Negro, Wolfgang Jahn invests in the fact that "Negro" was changed from "Leo", a name that would have vaguely invoked via Löwe, Kafka's mother's maiden

---

[19] Gilles Deleuze & Félix Guattari: *Kafka: Towards a Minor Literature*. Trans. by Dana Polan. Minneapolis: University of Minnesota Press 1986. P. 17.
[20] Ibid. P. 23.
[21] Paul de Man: The Rhetoric of Temporality. In: *Blindness and Insight: Essays in the Rhetoric of Contemporary Criticism*. Minneapolis: University of Minnesota Press 1983. Pp. 187–228. Here: P. 192.
[22] Heinz Politzer: *Franz Kafka: Parable and Paradox*. Ithaca, NY: Cornell University Press 1966. Pp. 159, 161.
[23] Hartmut Binder: *Kafka-Kommentar zu den Romanen, Rezensionen, Aphorismen und zum Brief an den Vater*. München: Winkler 1976. P. 148.

name, "Löwy", and so Kafka himself.[24] It might also somehow call to mind the exaltation of "Lion" in general. This possible alteration leads Ralf R. Nicolai to suggest that

> Was Kafka dazu bewog, den Namen "Leo" zu "Negro" zu ändern, wird dunkel bleiben, doch unbedingt der Wechsel der Richtung, die der Handlungsverlauf zu nehmen hat. Der Name "Leo" läßt auf die Entwicklung zum höchsten Bewußtsein und dem von Brod erwähnten versöhnlichen Ausgang schließen; Negro drückt das Gegenteil aus und führt in die Stagnierung.[25]
>
> [What possessed Kafka to change the name from "Leo" to "Negro", and the vast difference this change made to the possible way in which the novel could have unfolded, will remain forever unknown. Whereas "Leo" would have allowed for a teleological reading leading to the highest form of self-awareness and, as Max Brod believed, redemption, "Negro" has the exact opposite effect, one of stagnation.]

Again, Kafka's association with the word Negro is seen as overwhelmingly negative, as if to be a Negro in America can only lead to no good. As Gerhard Loose assumes with partial accuracy, "Ein völlig neues Leben will er beginnen und wechselt daher den Namen. Negro bezeichnet die Schicht, um deren Entrechtung und gesetzlose Behandlung auch Kafka wußte" ["Karl changes his name because he wishes to start a completely new life. Negro describes a level of abuse and lawless treatment that Kafka knew"].[26]

In point of fact, Kafka did not know "die Entrechtung und gesetzlose Behandlung" African Americans experienced on a daily basis. What he did know was Holitscher's reproduction of a photograph of a lynched African American male entitled "Idyll aus Oklahama" (Figure 9.1).[27] Nothing accompanied the photo aside from the caption, not even a brief explanation. Oklahoma was misspelled ("Oklahama"), a mistake Kafka retains throughout the text of *Der Verschollene*.[28] But the caption, or label, of "Idyll" is just as important as the misspelling of "Oklahama". Defining, however ironically or cruelly, a scene of lynching as an idyll transforms the act into romantic, pastoral poetry. In other words, abject suffering becomes cause for poetic inspiration and execution; it becomes aesthetic. Robbing the gruesome image of its historical content leads to its transformation into mythopoeia.

For *Amerika*'s critics, then, Karl's endless process of transformation (and not becoming) reaches the apex of abjection, if one can speak of such a thing,

---

[24] Wolfgang Jahn: *Kafkas Roman "Der Verschollene" ("Amerika")*. Stuttgart: Metzler 1965. P. 100.
[25] Ralf R. Nicolai: *Kafkas Amerika-Roman "Der Verschollene". Motive und Gestalten*. Würzburg: Königshausen & Neumann 1981. P. 240.
[26] Gerhard Loose: *Franz Kafka und Amerika*. Frankfurt am Main: Klostermann 1968. P. 69.
[27] See Arthur Holitscher: *Amerika Heute und Morgen*.
[28] Loose: *Franz Kafka und Amerika*. P. 239.

when he calls himself "Negro". Unlike the passage from Kafka's diary (*Ausstellungsneger* has been falsely translated as "Minstrel show"), there is no problem of translation here. The word Kafka uses is neither *Neger* nor *Schwarzer*, but "Negro". The strong current of disbelief that runs through the theater's Registrar cannot go unnoticed and surpasses mere doubt as to the veracity of Karl's name in terms of its legal validity. At issue for the Registrar is precisely the applicability of the racial designation Karl gives as he submits his name. In order to determine if Karl has misrepresented himself racially, the Registrar does not ask him questions, but instead looks at him, as if to say that the truth of Karl's status as a "Negro" is written on his face. Karl takes the name itself from the "title" given either to him or workers at more than one of the many menial jobs he has performed but which did not find its way into Kafka's text. Translated by Michael Hofmann as "nothing else came to mind just then, he gave what had been *his* nickname on his last jobs" (210). In Kafka's German it is, more precisely, grammatically unclear if the nickname "Negro" belongs entirely to Karl. Kafka writes "den", not "seinen". Although "den" in this context generally means "seinen", or "his", the substitution allows for slippage, if in no other sense then the purely grammatical.

Amerika's early translators, Willa and Edwin Muir, sought to solve the "Negro" problem by eliminating the plurality of jobs to which Kafka refers: "[Karl] gave the nickname he had had in his last post".[29] Even though the idea that Karl was named "Negro" at only one job makes for a smoother, more logical narrative progression, this is absolutely grammatically false. Kafka writes "aus seinen letzten Stellungen". The plurality of jobs is clear. Nowhere does Kafka indicate that Karl has ever called himself by this name before. Indeed, the novel is scrupulous on this point: asked several times throughout the narrative what his name is, each time Karl emphatically gives his name as simply "Karl". If, then, he was spontaneously called Negro at several jobs, then the disbelief of the Theater workers makes no sense, as there would be something *self-evident in coloring or demeanor* about the appropriateness of this designation vis-à-vis Karl's appearance. Instead, we must maintain the indeterminacy produced by Kafka's lack of grammatical clarity, and understand that the nickname was in use at several of Karl's menial jobs, and indicates the otherwise phantom presence of Negro co-workers, and African Americans in *Amerika* in general, with whom Karl was lumped. Karl was named "Negro" because he worked with Negroes.

In other words, the meaning, or at least the origin, of "Negro" is one of the only unequivocal, unambiguous aspects of *Der Verschollene*. So much so, in

---

[29] Franz Kafka: *Amerika*. Trans. by Willa and Edwin Muir. New York: Schocken 1996. P. 286.

fact, that it ruthlessly destroys any sense that can be made of the scene, indeed the entire fictive ground, in which Kafka plants it. The one thing of which one can say something concrete reveals itself to be not just complicit with, but determinative of, an aesthetic system of indeterminacy. When Karl names himself "Negro", he gives birth to Kafka's racialized phantom proxy.

Karl's self-selection as Negro, however, does not go totally unchallenged in the text:

> "Sie haben doch nicht Negro aufgeschrieben", fuhr ihn der Leiter an. "Ja, Negro", sagte der Schreiber ruhig und machte eine Handbewegung, als habe nun der Leiter das Weitere zu veranlassen [. . .]. Der Leiter bezwang sich auch, stand auf und sagte: "Sie sind für das Theater von Oklahoma". Aber weiter kam er nicht, er konnte nichts gegen sein Gewissen tun, setzte sich und sagte: "Er heißt nicht Negro". [. . .] Er [Der Herr des Theaters] stellte an Karl zunächst gar keine Fragen, sondern sagte zu einem Herrn, der mit gekreuzten Beinen, die Hand am Kinn neben ihm lehnte: "Negro, ein europaeischer Mittelschüler". (307–08)
>
> ["You didn't write down Negro, did you", the boss shouted at him. "Yes, Negro", said the secretary placidly, and gestured to the boss to conclude the formalities [. . .]. The boss restrained himself, stood up and said: "I hereby proclaim that the Theater of Oklahoma – " But he got no further, he could not violate his conscience, sat down, and said: "His name is not Negro". [. . .] [H]e [the head of the theater] asked Karl no questions to begin with, but merely observed to another gentleman who was leaning next to him, with feet crossed, and his chin cupped in his hand: "Negro, a secondary schoolboy from Europe".] (210–211)

Despite being certain that Karl's name is not "Negro", and so that Karl is not a Negro, the Registrar and the theater group's leader accept Karl as Negro. But Karl's new identity as Negro does not come without qualification. He is Negro, the European intermediary school student. As if to set him partially within his "proper" national and racial milieu, the Registrar situates Karl's origins somewhere between Africa, African America, and Europe, but also still within the process of becoming. As a student, Karl is not yet formed. Of mixed race, Karl, like *Amerika* itself, can never truly be formed as anything other than hybrid, a crossbreed, a figure of which Kafka was quite fond.

But unlike the crossbreed in Kafka's very short story *Eine Kreuzung*, Karl is not doomed to the butcher's block.[30] With a new name and a new job title, Karl is off to Oklahoma:

> Während Karl hinunterstieg wurde zur Seite der Treppe auf der Anzeigetafel die Aufschrift hochgezogen: "Negro, technischer Arbeiter". Da alles hier seinen ordentlichen Gang nahm, hätte es Karl nicht mehr so sehr bedauert, wenn auf der Tafel sein wirklicher Name zu lesen gewesen wäre. (312)

---

[30] Franz Kafka: Eine Kreuzung. (1931) In: *Beim Bau der chinesischen Mauer*. Frankfurt am Main: S. Fischer Verlag 1994. (Kritische Ausgabe.) Pp. 92–93.

> [As Karl climbed down the stairs, next to him the scoreboard was pulled up, and on it the words: "Negro, Technical Worker". As everything had gone so well, Karl wouldn't have minded too much if it had been his real name up on the board. (213–214)]

Karl's professional moniker is "technical worker", which here, once again, could mean anything. Like Negro, the tag of "technical worker" distorts the representation of Karl's identity in order to forge it anew as that which it always was. Where the name "Karl" obeys a strange racial morphology in order to become Negro, "Künstler" transforms into "technischer Arbeiter". Karl becomes artist by first becoming a Negro technical worker. And it is right after this, and because of this, metamorphosis that Karl can and does get on the bus, this time to Oklahoma, where they accept everyone, even a Negro European middle school student, so long as he or she desires to become a Negro, which is to say an artist.

Claudia Breger

Performing Violence: Joe May's *Indian Tomb* (1921)

The article investigates the productivity of performance-theoretical approaches for the study of violence in German cultural history. My case study for this undertaking is Joe May's popular Das Indische Grabmal *[The Indian Tomb] (1921), through which I connect the theoretical argument to film-historical debates on Kracauer's genealogies of fascist violence in Weimar cinema. Different approaches subsumed under the "performative turn" concur in the notion that performance wins its critical force by subverting narrative and representation. My close reading of the film begins by discussing two epistemologically divergent versions of this argument (performance as the presencing of the real vs. performance as the theatricalizing of representation). While building on the latter argument, my own reading of* Das Indische Grabmal *nonetheless demonstrates that the complex workings of performance are better understood by reconceptualizing it as a force of (critical) re-contextualization, acting not necessarily against, but in and through narrative. Analyzing the film's aesthetic of narrative performance ennables a reading of it as an artistic "Kritik der Gewalt" ["critique of violence"] (Benjamin), which, however, remains equivocally embedded in trans/national discourses of imperialist and racist violence.*

With roots in theater studies, linguistics, and anthropology as well as the aesthetic discourses of twentieth century avant-gardes, notions of performance have taken center stage throughout the humanities in the last decades. Perhaps too neatly summarized as "the performative turn", this shift has foregrounded theoretical paradigms associated with diverging disciplinary as well as epistemological and political ideas; arguably, the notion "performance" can be defined only as an "essentially contested concept".[1] Throughout this heterogeneous field, however, a prominent theoretical motif is the idea that performative forms of articulation – be it linguistic or bodily – present a challenge to representation and narrative. In various ways, performance has thus been conceptualized as a force of critique or subversion vis-à-vis the coherence of ideology, hegemonic discourse or socio-symbolic regimes of discipline.

In this article, I investigate the theoretical productivity of several of these performative approaches for the historical analysis of violence in German culture. My case study is the 1921 film *Das Indische Grabmal* [*The Indian*

---

[1] Marvin Carlson: *Performance: A Critical Introduction*. New York: Routledge 1996. P. 1. (in reference to Mary S. Strine, Beverly Whitaker Long, and Mary Frances Hopkins.) See also Shannon Jackson: *Professing Performance: Theatre in the Academy from Philology to Performativity*. Cambridge: Cambridge University Press 2004. Pp. 8–15.

Tomb], a two-part epic directed by Joe May and written by Fritz Lang in collaboration with Thea von Harbou, based on her novel of the same title.[2] This choice leads us onto charged terrain with respect to national histories of violence. Weimar film in general, but especially its expressionist scenarios for which Lang and Harbou stand in as representative figures,[3] have been closely associated with the rise of fascism ever since Siegfried Kracauer's famous verdict regarding the link between Caligari and Hitler. To be sure, Kracauer himself discusses *Das Indische Grabmal* only briefly as a film of "secondary importance", an example of the sensational adventure genre marked by imperialist fantasy without the "introvert tendency" of expressionism.[4] But one could certainly make a case for fully including the film's Orientalist narrative, with its motifs of charismatic tyranny and unconditional submission, into Kracauer's filmic "procession of tyrants" (77), be it based on Lang's and Harbou's involvement in the film[5] or on more general critiques of the dichotomy between popular and art film in Weimar Germany. Furthermore, we could highlight the central importance of imperialist scenarios for the violent, anti-democratic figuration at stake in Kracauer's account of a cinema "[r]eplete with authoritarian figures" and "fables that offered protofascist solutions".[6]

Arguably more relevant, however, are questions about the validity, and continued relevance, of Kracauer's larger point. Throughout the last decades, film scholarship has seriously challenged his verdict on Weimar film, taking issue with the underlying assumptions about the national character of film history, as well as Kracauer's methodological strategies for establishing it.[7] In an article specifically relevant to my context, for example, Christian Rogowski

---

[2] Decades later, Lang directed a post-war remake which is quite radically different in both aesthetics and plot: *Der Tiger von Eschnapur* [*The Tiger of Eschnapur*]. *Das Indische* Grabmal [*The Indian Tomb*]. Dir. Fritz Lang. CCC Filmkunst [Berlin], Rizzoli Editore, Régina, Critérion Film [Paris] 1959. DVDs 2003 Fantoma Films. For biographical information on May, see *Joe May: Regisseur und Produzent*. Ed. by Hans-Michael Bock and Claudia Lenssen. München: edition text + kritik 1991.
[3] Thomas Elsaesser qualifies this misperception, emphasizing that Lang never identified himself as an expressionist filmmaker. Thomas Elsaesser: *Weimar Cinema and After: Germany's Historical Imaginary*. New York: Routledge 2000. P. 145.
[4] Siegfried Kracauer: *From Caligari to Hitler: A Psychological History of the German Film* Ed. by Leonardo Quaresima. Princeton, NJ: Princeton University Press 2004. (Rev. and exp. edition.) Pp. 56–57.
[5] See Thomas Elsaesser: Filmgeschichte – Firmengeschichte – Familiengeschichte. Der Übergang vom Wilhelminischen zum Weimarer Film. In: *Joe May*. Pp. 11–30.
[6] Elsaesser: *Weimar Cinema*. P. 145.
[7] For a summary of these criticisms see Leonardo Quaresima: Introduction, Rereading Kracauer. In: *From Caligari to Hitler: A Psychological History of the German Film*. By Siegfried Kracauer. Ed. by Leonardo Quaresima. Princeton, NJ: Princeton University Press 2004. (Rev. and exp. edition.) Pp. xv–xlix.

argued for "Challenging Kracauer's Demonology with Weimar Popular Film", the transnational character and cosmopolitan orientation of which he outlines with reference to another early Weimar film by Joe May, *Die Herrin der Welt* [*The Mistress of the World*].[8] As the first German-American co-production on the local market,[9] *Das Indische Grabmal* doubtlessly invites a similar re-investigation in the light of broader transnational turns in film historiography. If the notion of "national cinema" still has a place in contemporary scholarship, it may acquire its relevance only "as a category of contestation".[10] As we have begun to understand, collective identities are not only multiply fractured at the intersecting differentials of race, class, gender and sexuality, but their ongoing imaginative (re-)articulation only emerges from the transnational traffic in art, technology, science and politics. Investigating these transnational processes complicates established narratives about the national character of violence. While it may lead us to abandon Kracauer's simple answers, however, this does not imply that we also have to abandon the critical questions about the political significations of art forms for which his study does remain pioneering.[11]

My chapter pursues this task of revisiting the aesthetics of violence in Weimar culture. Performative approaches win their particular relevance for this endeavor as an ensemble of concepts which has informed the methodology of recent critical challenges to Kracauer's thesis in film studies. As suggested above, one of the few motifs uniting almost the entire spectrum of performative concepts is the belief in the "subversive" force which the performative act can unfold by breaking the coherence of cultural narratives. In sections one and two of this article, I look more closely at two competing versions of this argument, as they have been developed within as well as beyond film studies.

The first of these versions finds its current theoretical articulation most prominently in the work of the German performance scholar Erika Fischer-Lichte, but also informs much scholarship on early film. According to this argument, the aesthetics of performance develops its critical force by providing direct ("unmediated") experiences of the "real" of body and nature. In contrast, the second argument for performative subversion locates the critical potential in the ways in which performance, here more closely aligned with linguistic concepts of performativity, theatricalizes, and thereby offers to

---

[8] Christian Rogowski: From Ernst Lubitsch to Joe May: Challenging Kracauer's Demonology with Weimar Popular Film. In: *Light Motives: German Popular Film in Perspektive.* Ed. by Randall Halle and Margaret McCarthy. Detroit, Michigan: Wayne State University Press 2003. Pp. 1–23.
[9] Jürgen Kasten: "Veritas Vincit" und "Das Indische Grabmal": Dramaturgie des Monumentalen. In: *Joe May.* Pp. 73–79. Here: P. 77.
[10] Sabine Hake: *German National Cinema.* New York: Routledge 2002. P. 3.
[11] Quaresima: Introduction, Rereading Kracauer. P. xxxv.

a reflective gaze, the act of mediation which constitutes representation. The general epistemological development of this argument is closely associated with scholars like Judith Butler and Jacques Derrida.

Interestingly for our context, Derrida specifically discussed the performative constitution of authority – as violence – through a reading of Walter Benjamin's essay *Zur Kritik der Gewalt* [*Critique of Violence*], an essay which dates back to the same year as May's film, and thus shares its early Weimar context. Discussing analogies between Benjamin's philosophical text and *Das Indische Grabmal*, I pursue the question of discursive resonances across disciplinary discourses and media in this specific spatio-temporal context. At the same time, I look more closely at the specific *aesthetic* dimensions of *Das Indische Grabmal* by drawing on the ways in which film scholarship, in particular that of Thomas Elsaesser, has developed the argument that performative forms subvert cultural narratives by theatricalizing the act of representation.

My own reading of the film, as unfolded in section three of this chapter, draws on this second version of the argument about the critical potential of performance, which I find epistemologically more convincing than the first. However, I also emphasize the limits of its usefulness for the discussion of our film. I challenge the opposition between narrative and performance which informs both versions of the "performance as subversion" argument, as both share an insistence on the performative act's break with context. Instead, I argue that a closer look at the film's techniques of *narrative* performance allows us to more fully grasp the ways in which performance functions both critically *and* affirmatively in the film, as a practice of theatrical "re-contextualization" rather than simply as "break".

By developing these twofold workings, I conclude by returning to Derrida's ambivalent evaluation of Benjamin's theoretical work in a manner enabled by my media-specific investigation. In "furchtbar zweideutige" ["terribly equivocal"] ways, Derrida claims, Benjamin's *Zur Kritik der Gewalt* both transcends its historical context through its critical argument regarding the performative constitution of authority and, haunted by the theme of "radikaler Zerstörung" ["radical destruction"] also participates in the anti-democratic thinking of the 1920's that we associate with the rise of fascism.[12] In its own, specifically filmic ways, *Das Indische Grabmal* presents itself as an analogously "furchtbar

---

[12] The quotes are from the German edition of Derrida's text which translates a reworked version of the original English paper. Jacques Derrida: *Gesetzeskraft. Der mythische Grund der Autorität*. Trans. by Alexander García Düttmann. Frankfurt am Main.: Suhrkamp 1991. P. 60. This German edition is at times substantially different from the English edition. See Jacques Derrida: Force of Law: The "Mystical" Foundation of Authority. Trans. by Mary Quaintance. In: *Deconstruction and the Possibility of Justice*. Ed. by Drucilla Cornell, Michael Rosenfeld and David Gray Carlson. New York: Routledge 1992. Pp. 3–67.

zweideutige[r] Text". To a degree, it does fit within established narratives about the violent trajectories of German culture, even while it clearly transcends the monolithic articulation that one finds, for example, in Kracauer's work.

1. Roaring Tigers and the Spectacle of the Despot: Orientalist Attractions

As suggested by Kracauer's quick dismissal, *Das indische Grabmal* did not quite make it into the canon of German art cinema. The 2000 DVD edition, which brought the film back into popular as well as critical circulation after decades of neglect, advertises its offerings in terms of its "spectacular" character. "Made in Germany, this lavish two-part adventure thriller takes place in an atmospheric India of romantic imagination, replete with elaborate temples and palaces, mystical yogis and dancing girls, roaring tigers and hissing cobras".[13] At the turn of the twenty-first century, the film's return into cultural memory may have been eased by the fact that such a "cinema of attractions" has begun to resonate with film production again in this era of digitally composited floods and dinosaurs. At the same time, such an aesthetic has been associated with the very first days of film culture. Thus, critics have debated in which ways the spectacles designed in Hollywood's contemporary "postclassical" phase should be seen in analogy with "pre-classical" cinema, for which Tom Gunning first coined the notion of a "cinema of attractions".[14] As he outlines, the early development of cinematic entertainment in the institutional context of the vaudeville (or the varieté in the German context) was characterized by an aesthetic organized around the "act of showing and exhibition", creating "pleasure through an exciting spectacle".[15] Emphasizing bodily acts of various kinds, from parades and sporting events to slapstick gags, juggling, acrobatic and dances, early cinema worked with surprise and shock rather than suspense. Thus, it rendered its attractions in (presumably) immediate form; its temporality was an "intense form of present tense".[16]

---

[13] *Das Indische Grabmal* [*The Indian Tomb*]. Dir. Joe May. Screenplay: Fritz Lang, Thea v. Harbou. May-Film, EFA 1921. DVD 2000 Water Bearer Films. Back cover.
[14] Tom Gunning: The Cinema of Attractions: Early Film, Its Spectator and the Avant-Garde. In: *Early Cinema: Space – Frame – Narrative*. Ed. by Thomas Elsaesser with Adam Barker. London: British Film Institute 1990. Pp. 56–62. See also Geoff King: *Spectacular Narratives: Hollywood in the Age of the Blockbuster*. New York: St. Martin's Press 2000. Here: specifically P. 30.
[15] See Gunning: The Cinema of Attractions. Pp. 56, 58. For the German context see Joseph Garncarz: Vom Varieté zum Kino. Ein Plädoyer für ein erweitertes Konzept der Intermedialität. In: *Intermedialität. Theorie und Praxis eines interdisziplinären Forschungsgebiets*. Ed. by Jörg Helbig. Berlin: Erich Schmidt 1998. Pp. 244–256.
[16] Tom Gunning: Now You See It, Now You Don't: The Temporality of the Cinema of Attractions. In: *The Silent Cinema Reader*. Ed. by Lee Grieveson and Peter Krämer. London: Routledge 2004. Pp. 41–50. Here: P. 44; see also P. 42. First published in: *The Velvet Light Trap*. 32 (1993). Pp. 3–12.

In short, the aesthetics of early cinema was *performative* in the sense in which this notion has been developed in much later 20th-century performance theory.[17] Foregrounding the presence of the body, influential German performance scholar Erika Fischer-Lichte suggests, the *Ästhetik des Performativen* highlights materiality. Taking bodies, gestures and objects out of context, it disrupts the logic of motivation, action and psychology.[18]

The gradual development of film into a "respectable" medium with artistic potential has been closely associated with its development beyond these early performative forms. As Gunning also emphasizes, however, spectacle and performance did not cease to play a role in the age of classical narrative cinema. While narrative integration became dominant, the "cinema of attractions" went "underground, both into certain avant-garde practices and as a component of narrative films, more evident in some genres (e.g. the musical) than in others".[19] Building on the latter argument, we can interpret the foregrounding of attractions in *Das Indische Grabmal*, even in the overall frame of narrative integration, by including it in the equally "spectacular" genre of adventure.[20] Resonating with the regime of pleasures in early cinema, the film unfolds its Indian world as a world of sensational sights. At generally extremely slow speed, we are invited to visually indulge in a series of exoticist "tableaux". Compared to Fritz Lang's 1958 remake of the Indian tomb story, the spectacle of dancing girls advertised on the DVD cover is actually not very developed; arguably, the spectacle of its effeminized, alluringly cruel "Indian despot" presents a sexually more titillating thrill. Overall, *Das Indische Grabmal*

---

[17] Traditionally, the aesthetics of early cinema has been discussed in terms of early film as not yet liberated from "borrowed" theatrical form. Gunning qualifies this account, emphasizing not only that this early "theatricality" was already the effect of properly filmic practices, but also that early cinema's viewing experiences relate more to those of the "fairground than to the traditions of the legitimate theatre" (Gunning: The Cinema of Attractions. P. 58.) See also: Now You See It. P. 42; and Gunning: "Primitive" Cinema: A Frame-up? Or the Trick's on Us. In: *Early Cinema*. Pp. 95–103. With reference to these qualifications, the attribute "performative" offers itself as an alternative to the notion of theatricality, insofar as it reflects the distance vis-à-vis institutionalized theater that has been articulated in performance studies.
[18] Erika Fischer-Lichte: *Ästhetik des Performativen*. Frankfurt am Main: Suhrkamp 2004. Here: particularly Pp. 243–248.
[19] Gunning: The Cinema of Attractions. P. 57.
[20] Reflecting on his own practice as a film director in 1928, May described his recipe for success in terms of striving for an ideal "mixture" of "spannende Handlung" ["suspenseful plot"] with "starken Sensationen" ["strong sensations"]. Hans-Michael Bock: Ein Instinkt- und Zahlenmensch. Joe May als Produzent und Regisseur in Deutschland. In: *Joe May*. Pp. 125–144.

offers primarily the kind of attractions this volume as a whole investigates – spectacles of violence. Intermittently speeding things up, chase and fighting sequences dominate significant parts of the film. Even more impressively, lengthy takes present us with roaring (and, in fact, attacking) tigers, crocodiles and deadly snakes, often in close-ups from diegetically impossible positions. As "inserts" rather than point-of-view shots, these takes ambiguously function within both a narrative and the "de/monstrative" logic of early cinema.[21]

While this affinity with the aesthetics of attraction certainly contributed to the long-term devaluation of May's "merely" popular film, it presents a critical promise from the vantage point of today's scholarly orthodoxy. Thus, recent early cinema scholarship has described its performative nature as a resource for subversion.[22] The central point of comparison for these accounts is classical Hollywood cinema where, according to Laura Mulvey's account (still canonical in spite of multiple revisions), the disturbing power of feminine, or feminized, spectacle is subjected through the smoothness of its narrative integration.[23] In contrast and as suggested by the concerns of early twentieth-century reformers, the predominance of spectacle in early cinema presents a form of bodily excess which disturbed the bourgeois order of sexual repression and moral discipline, as well as its hegemonic gender codes.[24] Our Indian prince, for example, might function as such a "subversive" spectacle. The role is cast with the actor Conradt Veidt, who was known to contemporary audiences not only as Cesare, the sleepwalker, but also as the homosexual protagonist of *Anders als die anderen* [*Different from the Others*, 1919]. Feminized through dress as well as gesture (for example the posture of arms akimbo that has become associated with a lack of masculinity and queerness in the modern imaginary),[25] the presence of his male body is highlighted as a focal point in the spectacular tableaus captured by the camera. Most notably in a scene in which he impersonates a god in "full drag", the gaze of the audience is presented with the spectacle of his adorned physicality, complete with jewelry and a cantilevered headdress, naked legs and belly (see Figure 10.1). The lines of his costume run parallel to those of his similarly dressed

---

[21] See Thomas Elsaesser: *Filmgeschichte und frühes Kino: Archäologie eines Medienwandels*. München: edition text + kritik 2002. P. 78. (in reference to Noel Burch.)

[22] See Hake: *German National Cinema*. P. 8.

[23] Laura Mulvey: Visual Pleasure and Narrative Cinema. In: *Screen* 16.3 (1975). Pp. 6–18.

[24] See Heide Schlüpmann: *Unheimlichkeit des Blicks: Das Drama des frühen deutschen Kinos*. Basel: Stroemfeld/Roter Stern 1990. Pp. 13–18.

[25] See Thomas A. King: Performing "Akimbo": Queer Pride and Epistemological Prejudice. In: *The Politics and Poetics of Camp*. Ed. by Moe Meyer. New York: Routledge 1994. Pp. 23–50.

Figure 10.1 From *Das Indische Grabmal* [*The Indian Tomb*]. Dir. Joe May. Screenplay: Fritz Lang, Thea v. Harbou. May-Film, EFA 1921. DVD 2000 Water Bearer Films.

up, but less spectacular female partner in this scene, the fiancé of the European architect, Irene. Through these techniques of foregrounding the body of the prince, the film potentially caters to a variety of female and queer desires.

Meanwhile, the dominance of violent spectacles in *Das Indische Grabmal* may suggest that it mostly serves to gratify, as film critic Walter Serner put it already in 1913, "Lust an der Grausamkeit" ["lust for cruelty"].[26] In several close-up shots, we indulge, for example, in the sight of a tiger, frontally looking at us while devouring a meal. In conjunction with the long duration of these shots, their diegetically impossible angle may background the narrative context at least momentarily. If we wanted to transfer Fischer-Lichte's discussion of contemporary performance art to our performative film, we could argue that the (apparently immediate) presence of the animal in *Das Indische Grabmal* enacts an "Einbruch des Realen in das Fiktive" ["invasion of the real into fiction"], or even "'ursprüngliche', 'geheimnisvolle', unberechenbare' Natur"

---

[26] See Schlüpmann: *Unheimlichkeit des Blicks*. P. 299.

["'primal', 'mysterious', and 'volatile' nature"].²⁷ The latter wording is significant because it highlights an epistemological premise which Fischer-Lichte's argument shares with Serner's and, more or less explicitly, many other claims for performative subversion qua "immediate" presence (effect), namely its foundation in a narrative of civilization. Thus, the argument suggests that the "primal power of the attraction" arouses desires which have been repressed by civilization;²⁸ in making the body (whether animal or human) present, performance recovers what is lost in the process of enlightenment through dominance over nature.²⁹

Importantly, however, the grand narratives of human nature and development which underwrite these descriptions of promise have formed precisely the critical focus of other investigations into performance, namely those informed by performativity theory. Long before the latter's deconstructive elaboration in Derrida and Butler, Benjamin's "Kritik der Gewalt" already cautioned against performative gestures of naturalization, which may lead to the championing of violence as "ursprüngliches und allen vitalen Zwecken der Natur allein angemessenes Mittel" ["the only original means [. . .] appropriate to all the vital ends of nature"].³⁰ Fischer-Lichte risks performing such gestures of affirmation as she approvingly quotes René Girard's naturalizing analysis of violence in terms of universal taboo.³¹ What remains untheorized in such an

---

[27] Fischer-Lichte: *Ästhetik des Performativen*. P. 185. It should be noted that Fischer-Lichte herself would not apply her concept to film since she deems the actual physical co-presence of actors and spectators in a shared space to be crucial for the subversive workings of performance. In her view, media (re)productions of performative events do not equally address all senses and cannot create the same experiences of physical intimacy, aura, etc. (125). However, film and other media scholars have cautioned us not to underestimate the power of mediated presence and aura effects. As suggested by the above summary, early film's specific modes of spectator address tended to produce a sense of physical presence. Beyond "merely theater-like" effects, the particular technological possibilities of the medium (for example through close shots) enabled experiences of intimacy precisely not afforded by the theater. See Hake: *German National Cinema*. P. 16.
[28] Gunning: The Cinema of Attractions. P. 61.
[29] Fischer-Lichte: *Ästhetik des Performativen*. Pp. 174–175, 315.
[30] Walter Benjamin: Zur Kritik der Gewalt. In: *Gesammelte Schriften*. Vol. II.1. Ed. by Rolf Tiedemann and Hermann Schweppenhäuser. Frankfurt am Main: Suhrkamp 1977. Pp. 179–203. Here: P. 180. Walter Benjamin: Critique of Violence. In: *Selected Writings, 1913–1926*. Ed. by Marcus Bullock and Michael W. Jennings. Trans. by Edmund Jephcott. Cambridge-Massachusetts-London: The Belknap Press of Harvard University Press 1996. Vol. 1. Pp. 236–253. Here: P. 237.
[31] Fischer-Lichte: *Ästhetik des Performativen*. P. 266. See René Girard: *Violence and the Sacred*. Trans. by Patrick Gregory. Baltimore: The Johns Hopkins University Press 1977.

account are the ways in which the "real" of, for example, an Indian tiger in early twentieth-century European film – or for that matter later twentieth-century European performance art – is constituted by processes of cultural signification, including the ways in which the "nature vs. civilization" dichotomy has categorically supported imperialist frames of reference throughout European modernity.

Fischer-Lichte brackets these questions by subordinating semiotic perspectives to phenomenological ones. According to her argument, the decontextualization inherent in performative aesthetics "de-semanticizes" its elements, at least "in gewisser Weise" ["in a certain way"].[32] Performative acts are self-referential in the sense that they mean "nothing but what they effect[ed];" in the terms of speech act theory, they are Austin's "original performatives",[33] which have, in Fischer-Lichte's account, a "magical" quality unfolding at the margins of language. Thus, the sudden appearance of a phenomenon can endow perception with "eine ganz besondere Qualität" ["a very special quality"] which excludes questions about possible meanings "beyond" materiality; the objects "geben ihre 'Eigenbedeutung' preis" ["reveal their 'very own' meaning"] (246). In this context, Fischer-Lichte draws on Benjamin's philosophy of language, connecting the performative act to Benjamin's notion of the symbol as an artistic expression which discloses its meaning in the same way objects disclosed their god-given meanings in the state of (linguistic) paradise.[34]

As Fischer-Lichte's quotation marks around the notion "Eigenbedeutung" may indicate, however, her theoretical move of bracketing the play of difference in signification seems precarious in the (post-)deconstructivist epistemological landscape of the early twenty-first century. Consequently perhaps, Fischer-Lichte herself introduces a second mode of signification operative in performance, that of "allegory" in Benjaminian terms, in which the appearance of the phenomenon invites a multiplicity of associations: concepts, memories, feelings, thoughts.[35] While Fischer-Lichte privileges the first mode of self-referential signification, suggesting that it is in fact the primary one operative in performance, this second, "allegorical" mode resonates with the ways in which critics like Derrida, Butler or also Homi Bhabha have theorized the performative as an act of citation, that is, an act which quotes previous speech and bodily acts, be it intentionally or inadvertently. In discussing her second mode of signification in performance, Fischer-Lichte emphasizes the subjective dimension of these associations; however, she also points to the role of intersubjective cultural codes in this context (248).

---

[32] Fischer-Lichte: *Ästhetik des Performativen*. P. 243.
[33] Ibid. Pp. 26–27, see also Pp. 31–33.
[34] Ibid. P. 251.
[35] Ibid. P. 247.

In pursuing precisely this role, Butler and Bhabha have conceptualized the performative as a fundamentally two-sided mode of cultural productivity, which virtually undoes, but also (more or less phantasmatically) constitutes social identities through discourses of gender, nation or race.[36] Relating these epistemological models back to the realms of artistic performance, Elin Diamond argues that performance "is the site in which performativity materializes in concentrated form, reiterating "'concealed and dissimulated conventions.'"[37] Following these conceptualizations, we need to reckon with the ways in which cultural narratives co-constitute signification in performance, for example the ways in which cultural associations of "Oriental violence" or "bestiality" haunt the screen- or stage-presence of an Indian tiger. As I would critically emphasize vis-à-vis Fischer-Lichte, even a radical aesthetics of decontextualization, as developed in the later 20th-century performance art she focuses on, does not entirely erase these imperialist implications in modern Europe's representations of nature. For our context, however, in which the tiger's narrative embedding is only momentarily disrupted by the film's spectacular aesthetics, these questions are even more crucial. The film plot actualizes the virtual Orientalist narratives which haunt even the single shot. When a cut finally interrupts our close encounter with the hungry animal, we are reminded that the prince, albeit from a different, more distant angle, is watching his "darlings" as well; their "natural" force functions as a metonymy of his violence. In the larger frame of imperialist discourse, the "other" culture tends to be presented as a spectacle of primitivism which contrastively confirms "European history". Thus, our tigers may predominantly function as a "specular seduction" which interpellates spectators into hegemonic ideology.[38]

Similarly, the spectacle of the prince itself cannot be separated from the topical evocation of "diabolic despots" in almost all cinematic imaginations of the Orient in the Weimar period.[39] As highlighted by the "Oriental" ornamentation, his screen body is already inscribed with cultural narratives. His

---

[36] Judith Butler: *Gender Trouble: Feminism and the Subversion of Identity.* New York: Routledge 1990. Judith Butler: *Bodies That Matter:On the Discursive Limits of Sex.* New York: Routledge 1993. Judith Butler: *Excitable Speech: A Politics of the Performative.* New York: Routledge 1997. Homi Bhabha: *The Location of Culture.* New York: Routledge 1994.
[37] Elin Diamond: *Unmaking Mimesis.* London-New York: Routledge 1997. P. 47. (in reference to an earlier text by herself).
[38] The quote is from Elsaesser: *Weimar Cinema.* P. 151. For *Das Indische Grabmal*, see Wolfgang Kabatek: *Imagerie des Anderen im Weimarer Kino.* Bielefeld: transcript 2003. Pp. 117–147.
[39] Wolfgang Kabatek: Projektionen der Askese im Kino der Weimarer Republik. In: *Askese. Geschlecht und Geschichte der Selbstdisziplinierung.* Ed. by Irmela M. Krüger-Fürhoff and Tanja Nusser. Bielefeld: Aisthesis 2004. Pp. 145–165. Here: P. 145.

feminization is congruent with that of "Orientals", as well as aristocrats, in the modern European imagination in general;[40] and his ethnic identity is filmically articulated not least through the language of racist physiognomy, that is, his dark make-up in conjunction with often distorted features, signifying his violent schemes. Emphasizing these connections, however, might bring the specter of Kracauer's reading back into the foreground. Does the film's performance of violence, as embodied by well-known figures from the topical inventory of Western Orientalism such as the "despot" and his tigers, manifest another instance of the peculiarly "German" "compulsion of hate-love" for the mysterious, if evil authority of "tyrants"?[41]

2. The Yogi's Gaze, or: Self-reflexive Poses

Of course, the very play of signification which embeds performance in cultural narratives has also been described precisely as its subversive force by deconstructivist critics. As Derrida argued in *Force of Law*, Benjamin's *Zur Kritik der Gewalt* wins its theoretical significance from the fact that it demonstrates the violently performative origin of law and authority. First of all, this means that violence is not located in nature here, but in the process of re-presenting authority, for example through the staging of "Oriental despots" on screen. Secondly, the fact that only reiteration creates authority implies that the acts of asserting it are subject to essential instability, in Derrida's words the force of *différance*.[42] With reference to Austin's development of linguistic performativity beyond his notion of "original" performatives, Butler suggests in *Excitable Speech* that the perlocutionary dimension of the speech act, that is, the fact that it is precisely not identical with its effects,[43] creates the space for countering the violence of (hegemonic) representation with the critical force of (other) speech acts.

Striving to concretize these philosophical interventions in aesthetic terms, Diamond returns to the theatrical metaphors employed in Butler's early works, including the model of drag as a de-naturalizing and de-normalizing theatricalization of gender identity. By materializing performativity in "concentrated form", performance has the potential of investigating and reimagining the otherwise concealed conventions it reiterates.[44] For the context of Weimar art film, Elsaesser has developed an argument which builds on this second

---

[40] See my own *Szenarien kopfloser Herrschaft – Performanzen gespenstischer Macht. Königsfiguren in der deutschsprachigen Literatur und Kultur des 20. Jahrhunderts*. Freiburg im Breisgau: Rombach 2004.
[41] Kracauer: *From Caligari to Hitler*. Pp. 77, 79.
[42] See Derrida: Force of Law. Pp. 6–7, 14.
[43] Butler: *Excitable Speech*. P. 3.
[44] Diamond: *Unmaking Mimesis*. P. 47.

articulation of the claim to performative subversion. In film-historical terms, this argument also refers back to the cinema of attractions, although Elsaesser casts the process as a reflexive appropriation rather than "retention of early film form": Weimar art film "reinvent[ed] certain aspects of a cinema of non-continuity and spatial coherence".[45] While these wordings stress expressionism's avant-garde character, the argument proceeds not least by positing similarities and exchange processes between Weimar art cinema and popular film of the 1910s,[46] namely the work of Davi Wark Griffith. While Griffith became known as the (mythical) "father" of classical narrative cinema, he may, Elsaesser suggests, be better described as a transitional figure whose complex stylistic legacy is more visible in the European art film of the 1920s than in classical Hollywood cinema.[47] As Sabine Hake summarizes, Griffith's stylistic influence in German expressionist film can be observed in the emphasis on frame composition, the "relative disregard for narrative continuity" as well as the "theatricalization of performance through exaggerated gestures, dramatic costumes and heavy make-up".[48]

Setting out to re-evaluate Kracauer's reading, Elsaesser specifically reads Lang's films, with a focus on his *Dr. Mabuse der Spieler,* in terms of "self-reflexivity".[49] Unlike Fischer-Lichte's self-*referentiality*, self-reflexivity here does not describe the erasure of linguistic difference in the performance of the body. Instead, it designates the way in which the process of representation is theatricalized with the effect of loosening the signifiers' grip on the objects it purports to represent. These gestures of "showing" have their predecessors in early cinema features like the actors' looking at the camera, or the use of an extra-diegetic "commentator", which explicitly acknowledges the viewer. These nods to the viewer evoke an "exhibitionist" rather than the "voyeuristic" regime of classical narrative cinema.[50] As Elsaesser postulates, Lang's cinema makes artifice triumphant. By staging the "detail as disruption" (through, not least, the use of the insert shot) and in general "concentrating on the individual image", his cinema emphasizes narrative incoherence, "shock and surprise".[51] The obsession with the gaze and technologies of vision, too, highlights the act of representation as interference, thus suspending "unmediated access to the

---

[45] Elsaesser: *Weimar Cinema.* P. 165. Thomas Elsaesser and Adam Barker: Introduction, The Continuity System: Griffith and Beyond. In: *Early Cinema: Space – Frame – Narrative.* Pp. 293–317. Here: P. 313.
[46] See Elsaesser: *Filmgeschichte.* P. 224.
[47] Elsaesser and Barker: Introduction. P. 294. See also Elsaesser, *Filmgeschichte.* Pp. 190–223.
[48] Hake: *German National Cinema.* Pp. 30, 28.
[49] Elsaesser: *Weimar Cinema.* Pp. 149, 151.
[50] Ibid. P. 166. See also Gunning: Now You See It. Pp. 43–44.
[51] Elsaesser: *Weimar Cinema.* Pp. 163, 160.

real".[52] In this way, Lang's cinema dramatizes the violence of representation; in fact, Elsaesser suggests that the "extraordinary climate of violence that emanates from Lang's films" is created precisely through this insistence (163).

Not only Lang, but also Joe May was influenced by Griffith, and in some respects, Elsaesser's analysis resonates for *Das Indische Grabmal* as well, inviting us to re-evaluate the distinction between Weimar popular and art film.[53] For example, the film participates in a dramatization of gaze structures typical of early Weimar film, through the character of the yogi. Sent to Europe with the task of luring to India the architect Herbert Rowland, whom the prince wants to build a tomb for his "lost love", the yogi performs a series of violent "magic" interventions into European technologies. In order to prevent Herbert from communicating with his fiancé, whom the prince wants him to leave behind, the yogi not only fakes a phone call, but also cuts a phone cord and disconnects a cab tire specifically through the force of his gaze. The latter act is presented in a series of frontal shots culminating in a close-up, with the yogi directly looking at, and possibly hypnotizing, the spectator, before the targeted car is blended in (see Figure 10.2). Thus, the spectator is momentarily positioned in a direct, diegetically not fully mediated relationship to the yogi's violent performance. Still more than the analogous tiger intermezzo, this thematization of the gaze lends itself to being read as a mise-en-abyme of the technical apparatus which empowers the yogi's destruction of modern communication technology.[54] Staged as the magic of film trick, the yogi's acts might thus function as playful nods to the violence of filmic representation rather than to that of "Indian nature and myth". In fact, a comparison with Thea von Harbou's novel suggests that the theme belongs specifically to cinematic, rather than generally Orientalist discourses of the time: in the literary text, the motif of yogi magic is not at all developed.[55]

However, such moments of self-reflexivity do not yet necessarily undo a film's fantasy in the minds of actual spectators, and in this particular case, the overall case for self-reflexivity is not as strong as with respect to *Dr. Mabuse*. Those interested in upholding the difference between film art and popular entertainment would be correct in pointing out that as a whole, *Das Indische Grabmal* is less obsessed with the intricacies of perception and that, by balancing moves of narrative discontinuity and continuity, its regime of spectatorship is comparatively less exhibitionistic and more voyeuristic. In fact, Wolfgang Kabatek has argued that May's film can be analyzed in terms of its overall

---

[52] Ibid. P. 153.
[53] On parallels between Lang and May, see Elsaesser: Filmgeschichte – Firmengeschichte. Pp. 25–26.
[54] See also Kabatek: Projektionen der Askese. P. 154.
[55] Thea von Harbou: *Das indische Grabmal. Roman*. Berlin: Müller 1921.

Figure 10.2 From *Das Indische Grabmal* [*The Indian Tomb*]. Dir. Joe May. Screenplay: Fritz Lang, Thea v. Harbou. May-Film, EFA 1921. DVD 2000 Water Bearer Films.

realist agenda, showing the crucial role of authentication strategies through a detailed analysis of marketing and reception as well as mis-en-scene.[56] The prevalent praise for the film's visual and atmospheric verisimilitude, which contemporary critics saw effected not least through its slow, presumably "Oriental" speed, suggests that the film effectively interpellated spectators into its Orientalist fantasy, in close formal alliance with contemporary ethnography.[57] In other words, the "extraordinary climate of violence" in May's film may overall reflect less on the "violence of enunciation"[58] than, after all, on the spectacular visibility of its Indian threats.

As I argue in the remaining part of this chapter, this does not yet mean that the case "against" Kracauer's coherent narrative, as developed here through arguments of performative subversion, is altogether lost with respect to

[56] Kabatek: *Imagerie*. P. 117–147. See also Kabatek: Projektionen der Askese.
[57] Kabatek: *Imagerie*. P. 124. In general see also Assenka Oksiloff: *Picturing the Primitive: Visual Culture, Ethnography and Early German Cinema*. New York: Palgrave 2001.
[58] Elsaesser: *Weimar Cinema*. P. 165.

Das Indische Grabmal. In order to make this case stronger, however, we need to develop the concept of performance a bit further. As outlined above, the citational character of the performative means that it has to be read in its socio-symbolic context: the performative's break with the past is itself "legible only in terms of the past from which it breaks".[59] However, the notion of break – or decontextualization – remains nonetheless decisive for Butler's theorizing of the performative as well. To be sure, she critically distances herself from the ways in which Derrida's linguistic-philosophical account fetishizes this break. Butler qualifies Derrida's account, which locates the performative force of the utterance in the relative autonomy of the sign's operation, by insisting that "contexts inhere in certain speech acts in ways that are very difficult to shake".[60] But for Butler herself, this role of context remains a primarily negative one. While context is acknowledged as a restraining force, the critical *potential* of performance remains located in the hope of shattering contextual bonds.

Without elaborating on the theme, however, Butler herself also hints at a more positive function of context: performativity, she suggests, "remains *enabled* precisely by the contexts from which it breaks".[61] Against the dominant tendency of isolating the moment of break in performance, I believe it is promising to emphasize the productivity of context for the cultural work of performance, including its affirmative, but also its critical workings. Looking at performance as a force of critical re-contextualization, that is, as a force not exclusively operating against narrative, but also in and through narrative, I submit, enables a stronger claim for the critical complexity of *Das Indische Grabmal*.

3. Narrative Performance, or: *Zur Kritik der Gewalt*

Rather than working in opposition to the argument about theatrical self-reflexivity, my concept of narrative performance unfolds by integrating this moment of break into a larger process of de- and recontextualization, which re-assembles significations. Thus, I suggest that we study gestures of theatrical excess in context by focusing on the ways in which the film embeds its performative acts both within individual shots and through the succession of shots, that is through mis-en-scène and editing. This argument can proceed by re-emphasizing, and further pursuing, Elsaesser's discussion of Griffith's stylistic legacy in Weimar film. This legacy, Lang submits, includes the emphasis on alternation both within and in-between shots. Within shots, the theatricality of the dominantly frontal, complex images, combined with the stylized

---

[59] Butler: *Excitable Speech*. P. 14.
[60] Ibid. P. 161.
[61] Ibid. P. 40. My italics.

acting,[62] allows relations of symmetry and doubling between characters to aesthetically unfold. Similarly, dramatic situations are connected in terms of repetition, echo and counterpoint, for example through a use of cross-cutting (also known as parallel editing) which functions more explicitly as an agent of causality than in classical cinema.[63] As a result, the film develops its narrative through "an orgy of metaphor;" in excess of clear-cut ideological boundaries, it unfolds a realm of similarity (beyond identity) where "everything can be combined with everything else, stand for everything else".[64] Closely linked to the concept of performance as an instance of linguistic performativity, metaphor has been theorized "as a semiotic principle of rupture", which suspends reference and breaks up the narrative.[65] As I would emphasize, however, it not only undoes, but also *re*does meaning. Establishing new connections, metaphor assumes its productive function in establishing non-linear narrativity, or the "formal complexity" by which emplotting is worked out.[66]

This complication of narrative does not equal "subversion" per se. However, I argue that in *Das Indische Grabmal*, it balances the unfolding of Orientalist fantasy with counter-moves that investigate European desires for and within this world of evidently charismatic tyranny and unconditional submission. To use Benjamin's and Derrida's terms, the film deconstructs (all) authority as a performance of violence. Through the ways in which the spectacle of the despot is contextualized in the film, the film's Orientalist stage becomes a stage for a modern critique of authority in general.

The starting point of this critique, however, is precisely this Orientalist trope of the despot, who is *per definitionem*, that is, through discursive reiteration, a figure of violence without legitimation, acting excessively and brutally based on his personal desire and (thus) "inner" weakness. As the film plot has it, our Maharajah's desire for a tomb is based on lust for revenge; he wants to build it for a woman who is not yet dead, presumably with the intent of either killing her or burying her alive, after she betrayed him with an English officer, whom the film identifies in racial language as a "white" man. In order to accomplish this goal, we are informed by a long introductory intertitle, the Maharajah awakens the yogi from the "sleep of death" induced by his ascetic practice, which culminates in having himself buried alive. In other words, the prince usurps the performative power of religion, for the yogi's ascetic practice enables him to transcend laws of nature through "the ecstasy of willpower".

---

[62] See Ben Brewster and Lea Jacobs: *Theatre to Cinema: Stage Pictorialism and the Early Feature Film*. Oxford: Oxford University Press 1997.
[63] Elsaesser: *Weimar Cinema*. Pp. 155, 174–175.
[64] Elsaesser and Barker: Introduction. Pp. 301–302.
[65] Here: Elsaesser: *Weimar Cinema*. P. 155.
[66] Elsaesser and Barker: Introduction. P. 307.

In developing this configuration, the film introduces an account of the performative origins of authority à la Benjamin and Derrida as what seems to be, first of all, a point regarding the nature of Oriental authority. The introductory intertitle embeds the film's specific story in a more general condition of religious law, thus suggesting, in accordance with Derrida, that the relationship between (religious) law and (royal) force established by the plot is not one of accidental "service", but rather one of structural implication.[67] Even while the yogi's adherence to religious law makes him disapprove of the prince's violent schemes, the "duties imposed by sacred commandments" force him to subject himself to the prince's despotism, as he is required to fulfill "the deepest wish" of whoever awakens him.

This structural implication of religious law into royal violence is developed through the theatrical mis-en-scène of various encounters between prince and yogi, which positions them next to each other in the frame, balancing themes of conflict and association. The series of encounters begins with the prologue, in which the constitutive "impurity" of religious law is visualized as the dirty, intensely physical and abject work of purification. During the process of uncovering the buried yogi from the earth, from which he is virtually indistinguishable at first, the camera cuts back and forth between this spectacle and that of the waiting prince in his elegant, adorned costume. A little later in the temple, the contrasting figures are united in one frame. The elegant prince has become spatially associated with the dirty work of the priests who try to force a milky liquid into the yogi's mouth, which ends up soiling his face. In a later scene, the tables seem to have turned. Now clean and properly dressed, the yogi admonishes the prince for his transgressive usurpation of God's exclusive right to revenge. While succeeding close-ups contrast the light, stern face of the yogi with the darker, distorted features of the prince, their costumes, including their almost identical headwear, make a counter-point of similarity. In yet another scene, their parallel poses visually dramatize the dialogue reminder that the yogi is "chained" to the prince "by holy law".

While on a first level, this diagnosis of the structurally violent character of Indian religious law articulates the film's Orientalist fantasy, the process of association is not confined to the contrary figures of prince and yogi. Through their re-contextualization in the film's diegetic world, its performances of Oriental despotism are thus displaced; at least implicitly, the film also articulates a radical critique of authority in general (as "despotism"). The key to this argument is the circumstance that the film's world does not provide any counter-images of non-violent ("Western") authority. If Kracauer was right to critique Wiene's *Caligari* for its glorification of institutional authority (qua added frame story), *Das Indische Grabmal* evades such glorification by

---

[67] Derrida: Force of Law. P. 13.

leaving the respective structural space blank.[68] Neither images nor dialogue provide us with any representation of government or legal order in Europe. With respect to the Indian world, the public dimensions of colonial power are almost entirely elided; for all practical purposes, the prince seems to be politically sovereign.[69]

The only colonial representative who plays a significant role in the film is the love interest of the princess, a British "officer" who, for all we can see, leads an essentially private life of leisure in India. Crucially, this lack of explicitly political legitimation is narratively bound up with the fact that his identity, or personal authority, is based on violence as well. Simply put, the officer, who will become the prey of the prince when the latter sends his tiger hunters after this competitor, is himself a tiger hunter. Importantly for our context, these structures of reversal, or contiguity and similarity in contrast, are established through the film's aesthetic of narrative performance. Through cross-cutting, the British officer is first introduced parallel to the tigers, which the prince spoils as "his darlings". The intertitle, which provides spectator orientation in this process of association, balances motifs of contrast and parallel: "At a hunting lodge some distance away, the English officer MacAllan hosts his friends". Announcing simultaneity and (some sort of) narrative connection, the link established by the montage is ambiguous. Looking at MacAllan with his more benign friends (human, horses and dogs), we can read it as a gesture of foreshadowing which introduces him as the future victim of the prince and his darlings. At the same time, the cross-cutting also establishes an analogy between the prince and the officer, whose "unmanly" fascination with (Oriental) adornment is emphasized in this introductory scene, as he vainly shows off the large ring that the princess gave him. The analogy is developed in subsequent scenes, as we watch MacAllan prepare for a tiger hunt and later turn his rifles against human beings. To be sure, he officially acts in self-defense against the black, iconographically "savage" tiger hunters sent by the prince. However, the repeated, lengthy takes of his shooting performance not only implicate the spectator in the violent process;

---

[68] Kracauer makes his point about *Caligari* by contrasting the "revolutionary" original script, which identified the lunatic with the asylum director, with the version that was actually shot; here, narrative closure converts that identification into the fantasy of the lunatic.

[69] To be exact, British presence in India is marked by the office of a "consul", a term which may trigger historical associations of Empire (Rome), but in the modern world designates a diplomatic representative in intergovernmental affairs. A "military airport" is shown on the occasion of Irene's travels to the province, but unlike the prince, who commands large armies of soldiers and elephants, the British are not presented as a significant military force, and the film gives no indication of their actual territorial sovereignty.

through the use of physiognomy and gesture, they also highlight that the officer takes vivid pleasure in this violence.

Of course, the film's staging of British colonial authority as a cruel, pleasure-based hunting endeavor does not yet necessarily mean that it develops an anti-imperialist message.[70] Despite the international co-operation and marketing involved, we may be tempted to instead read the 1921 production in terms of national competition intensified by the treaty of Versailles, which forced Germans to hand over "their" colonies to their victorious European neighbors. For its German spectators, the film may very well offer a revenge fantasy by both downplaying and morally compromising the actual British domination over the region in which it is set. In any case, *Das Indische Grabmal* resonates with the fantasies of *cultural* imperialism which shaped German life and letters in the absence of actual colonial authority both before the late 19th century and after World War One.[71] The European architect is summoned by the Indian prince because he would be able to give "soul" to "stone", and the epilogue of the film presents us with the tomb that Herbert has eventually built for the – now in fact dead – princess, showing him and his fiancé visiting the completed work of art. On their way out, they walk by the prince who has become a ragged penitent, and probably madman, creeping on the impressive staircase leading up to the tomb. Kracauer's reading of staircases as symbols of authority in mind, we may conclude that the film thus does, after all, develop a counter-image of *cultural* authority: European-animated art has conquered Indian despotism.

In this vein, Kabatek has argued that the European couple is presented as a benign, humanistic counterforce opposing "Oriental" violence.[72] Intriguingly, Benjamin's *Zur Kritik der Gewalt* analogously develops the idea that, in the absence of public alternatives to violence, the private realm may offer a counterforce. In a brief interlude, his text calls upon the "Kultur des Herzens" as an earthly alternative to law's necessary violence.[73] In that very spirit, Herbert and Irene embark on the mission to rescue both the princess and her loyal servant upon discovering the "dark" schemes of the prince. However, the film's aesthetics of narrative performance deconstructs this opposition between "European humanism" and "Oriental violence" as well. Establishing relations between the apparently contrary characters, the film's theatrical tableaus

---

[70] For such a reading of Joe May's *The Mistress of the World*, see Rogowski: From Ernst Lubitsch.
[71] See Susanne Zantop: *Colonial Fantasies: Conquest, Family, and Nation in Precolonial Germany, 1770–1870*. Durham, North Carolina: Duke University Press 1997.
[72] Kabatek: *Imagerie*. P. 144.
[73] P. 191. The notion is translated as "a civilized outlook;" literally, it is "culture of the heart" (Critique of Violence 244).

develop an irresolvable interplay of contrast and association. For example, there is the crucial scene in which Herbert is led by the prince to the mountain location where he is to build the tomb. During this scene, in which he first understands the implications of this project, mis-en-scène and shot succession emphasize that he cannot disengage from the planned act of violence to which the prince now confesses. To be sure, a number of shots primarily contrast Herbert as a figure of upright masculinity with the cringed figure of the prince who is tormented by his violent desires. At the same time, even these primarily contrastive shots still present parallels, as both of the men are dressed similarly (the prince wears a white suit in this scene) and stand on the mountainous slope at identical angles, holding scepter and hiking stick or whip plus hat in the same hand. Meanwhile, other shots suggest primarily analogy by highlighting their parallel poses with arms akimbo and angled legs in their identical boots (see Figure 10.3).

As unfolded in the larger film narrative, the background of Herbert's implication in "Oriental violence" is that he is subject to dangerous desires himself. It is useful to draw on Lang's 1959 remake in comparison here. In that later version, the architect is called upon as the stereotypical bearer of the burden

Figure 10.3 From *Das Indische Grabmal* [*The Indian Tomb*]. Dir. Joe May. Screenplay: Fritz Lang, Thea v. Harbou. May-Film, EFA 1921. DVD 2000 Water Bearer Films.

of civilization, with a mission of constructing hospitals and schools. In contrast, the 1921 version explicitly situates its Orientalist spectacle as (co-)constituted in the architect's desire. Before the yogi's arrival in his house, we are introduced to Herbert as he melancholically contemplates a representation of the Taj Mahal on his desk. In the following conversation with Irene, he explicates his longing: "To have such a commission – once – in a lifetime!" More precisely, it is the modern European concept of masculinity as (artistic) sovereignty which makes him subject to "Oriental despotism" and implicates him in murder through art. "As man and artist", Herbert later writes apologetically to his fiancé, "I cannot refuse this commission". The later scene in the mountains aesthetically unfolds these plot-indications. Confounding its ethnic oppositions through its analysis also of European masculinity, the film universalizes the "ethnic" realm of despotic desire into a generalized "human" condition. In the mountain panorama of shared melancholy and guilt, Herbert looses his innocence in compassionately acknowledging the desires of the prince (as his own).

In the corresponding relationship between the prince and Irene, the film develops the theme of (hetero-)*sexual* desire. Determined to find her fiancé, Irene has made her way to the palace. Initially outraged by the news, the prince immediately turns mellow when he sees her. Irene's openness to his seduction, that is, the developing relation of similarity in mutual attraction, is established by the mis-en-scène during this initial encounter. Positioned next to each other in the theatrical frame, their light clothes have the same color, and the scepter of the prince corresponds to Irene's umbrella. Later, when the prince's refusal to allow her to see Herbert begins to seriously worry Irene, another encounter begins on a note of contrast: her white, spot-lighted face and Madonna pose are opposed to his dark face, which shows a spark ambiguously signifying desire or cunning. Faced with her love for her fiancé, however, his features melt into melancholy, and when she reads this physiognomic message of "human" sadness and longing, she melts down as well, asking compassionately: "Are you unhappy, Prince?" The scene ends with her approaching and touching him.

Thus, *Das Indische Grabmal* suggests that the "human" call of the heart is compromised by implication into the violent spheres of "despotic" desire. Perhaps not surprisingly then, humanistic intentions fail to provide a non-violent resolution. In the course of the action, the couple make themselves complicit in the Maharajah's revenge by usurping a pose of sovereignty vis-à-vis the servant of the princess who pleads for their help. Ignoring her concerns while boastfully promising to protect her, they deliver the servant to the spectacle of her public death as she dances for the European guests. Afterwards, we see how the couple, attempting to flee with the princess, violently shoots and stabs their way out of the palace. While Herbert's face does not show the same pleasure in killing exhibited by the officer, there is no reluctance, either; from one moment to the next, the melancholy artist is transformed into a resolute action hero delivering a "proper" showdown. In tribute to hegemonic gender norms, Irene's face shows an expression of shock as she finds herself using the gun which her fiancé handed to her, but arguably, this move of differentiation only underscores the narrative point that no one can escape his or her implication in violence.

4. Epilogue: Violent Resolutions

By undoing its oppositions through the diffusion of violence, however, the film does not exactly suggest an optimistic conclusion. Only a sacrifice will eventually bring the spread of violence to a halt: when the fleeing heroes get trapped in the mountains, the princess throws herself into a canyon, transforming the prince's lust for revenge into mourning and providing the architect with the legitimation needed for building his tomb. This narrative resolution resonates with Girard's anthropological theory of (mimetically spreading) violence. In the absence of a protective judicial system, he suggests, "sacrifice has a "purifying" function, serving "to protect the entire community" from the "unending process" of vengeance.[74]

With its conclusion in sacrifice, the "radically destructive" course of the film brings Derrida's ambivalent evaluation of Benjamin's *Zur Kritik der Gewalt* back to mind. A concluding look at Derrida's argument regarding the text's "terribly equivocal" politics can help us to specify the ways in which the film's aesthetic critique of violence remains trapped in a larger discursive figuration, which may have allowed for the deconstruction of authority to unfold only through the proliferation of violence. According to Derrida's argument, it is Benjamin's critique of representation – as mediation, the arbitrary play of difference and similarity – that is to blame for the text's resonances with contemporary anti-democratic thinking. In the realm of politics, the notion of the "fall" of language, which pervades Benjamin's philosophy of language, turns into a critique of parliamentary democracy. While *Zur Kritik der Gewalt* does not explicitly develop Benjamin's philosophy of language, its interference may explain the overall "radically destructive" course of the text, which remains unchanged by the excursus on the culture of the heart. For it is precisely mediation which allows the imagining of non-violent means of human interaction here. The means of the heart, Benjamin suggests, are never "solche unmittelbarer [. . .] Lösungen" ["never those of direct [literally, *immediate*] solutions"], but rather regularly *mediated* through objects or "Technik im weitesten Sinne" ["technique in the broadest sense"], including

---

[74] Girard: *Violence and the Sacred*. Pp. 8, 17, 49.

"die Unterredung als eine Technik ziviler Übereinkunft" ["conference" (in the sense of "discussion") "considered as a technique of civil agreement"].[75] This description remains in an unresolved tension with the overall prevailing rhetoric of immediacy in Benjamin's text, including his designation even of the means of the heart as "pure".[76] Consequently, Benjamin abandons the heart and concludes by highlighting the "pure, immediate" force of "rechtsvernichtende" ["law destroying"], "göttliche" ["divine"] violence as a messianic counterforce to the structural presence of "mythic" violence in the world of law.[77] As Derrida pointed out, however, Benjamin's text does not sustain that opposition either. The two forms of violence are reconnected, for example, in the notion of sacrifice which forms the vanishing point of Benjamin's text as well: "Die erste fordert Opfer, die zweite nimmt sie an" (200) ["The first demands sacrifice; the second accepts it" (250)].

A similar argument can be made for the aesthetic development of these themes in *Das Indische Grabmal*. In the film, too, we find that the aesthetics of narrative performance generate an affect against representation as the very play of difference and similarity. This affect may help to explain the film's indulgence in violence, specifically in the form of violent fantasies of separation. The argument returns to the question of the "violence in/of representation", further disentangling what is at stake here. Thus, the theme is arguably indicated already by the ways in which the yogi's magic interventions into European communication technologies are set up as violent acts that both manipulate and interrupt mediated long-distance communication. Beyond this emphasis on cinema technology with its self-reflexive potential, however, the film also pursues the theme of mediation and its fallacies by focusing on the unreliability of, in Benjamin's words, "discussion as a technique of civil agreement". Unlike the yogi plot, this aspect is already developed to a significant degree in von Harbou's novel, which suggests the theme's cross-media relevance in the cultural landscape.[78]

In the film itself, the plot unfolds not least through a series of performative speech acts, namely promises. In terms of apparent intention, these promises are very different, as they include the couple's above-mentioned protection promise to the servant, as well as the promise of "freedom" (behind the door of the tiger cage) made by a servant of the prince as he executes the British officer. In the encounters between the prince and our European couple, intention becomes murkier, for example when after confessing his desires for revenge in the mountains, the prince promises Herbert that he shall build a

---

[75] Benjamin: Zur Kritik der Gewalt. Pp. 191–192. Critique of Violence. P. 244.
[76] Benjamin: Zur Kritik der Gewalt. P. 191. Critique of Violence. P. 244.
[77] Benjamin: Zur Kritik der Gewalt. P. 199. Critique of Violence. P. 249.
[78] V. Harbou: *Das Indische Grabmal*. See Pp. 69, 124, 129, 184–185.

tomb "neither for the dead nor for the living", but rather "the tomb of a great love", and asks the architect for the return promise that he "will do nothing to thwart" his plans. Taking the hand extended by the prince, the architect attempts to resignify the deal by rewording the promise: "On the contrary, Prince, I give you my word that I will do anything to save you from actions that might lead you to eternal remorse".

Even while the facial features of the prince suggest that Herbert's compassion momentarily touches him emotionally as well as physically, Herbert's attempt at redirecting the promise fails to change the violent course of affairs. Well intentioned or not, the film's various promises share a general condition of infelicity: while they regularly *fail* as attempts to prevent violence, they succeed insofar as, or if, they function as media of violence. In accordance with Derrida, we can once more suggest that the film thus stages the violence in/of representation. Arguably attesting to the pitfalls of generalizing this argument all-too-quickly, however, *Das Indische Grabmal* makes the point in a "paranoid" way. As the realm of structural ambiguity qua play of signification, language functions *exclusively* violently. Sharing Benjamin's affect against representation as mediation, the film does not sustain a (Butlerian) concept of resignification and democratic negotiation within the "impure" realms of linguistic force.

Without such a possibility, however, the play of difference and similarity turns into a threat. Again, we can turn to Girard for the theoretical unfolding of the theme. Methodologically positioning himself against what he calls the "'anti-differential' prejudice" of modern anthropology and society, he asserts that it is the "loss" of (clear-cut) difference that "gives rise to violence and chaos".[79] As if following the same logic, the film answers the loss of clear-cut differentiations in its aesthetic play of difference and similarity with fantasies of violent distinction. While, in other words, the film's techniques of narrative performance indulge us with a play of contact between seemingly contrary forces, they also stage that contact as "contamination", embedding it in the racial rhetoric of early 20th-century hegemonic rhetoric. The theme is prefigured in the repeated, and variously highlighted gesture of the handshake which accompanies the mutual promises between the prince and the Europeans. In the openly sexualized encounter between the prince and the architect's fiancé, the "contaminating" nature of such a cont(r)act becomes particularly clear. Early on, the prince promises Irene that she will see her fiancé, asking for the counter-promise that she will not try to do so without his knowledge. As he extends his hand, she takes it hesitantly. A close-up highlights the handshake which is different from that between the two men, a gesture of courtship rather than just a deal.

---

[79] Girard: *Violence and the Sacred*. Pp. 50–51.

As the film unfolds, this "moral contamination" is dramatized through the tropes of illness. Herbert becomes afflicted with leprosy after accidentally stepping on a half-buried penitent who cursed him: "Leprosy shall eat away your white skin". While the yogi heals him, Irene is punished for her (virtual) transgressions by accidentally getting trapped in the yard of lepers herself. Aligned with her perspective, we experience the violent threat of contaminating hands stretched out at her. In the very last moment, the servant of the princess saves her by quickly opening a gate and shutting it again, just in time to keep the lepers enclosed. In close-up, the film highlights how her heroic act crushes the hands of a leper, voyeuristically indulging the spectator in this twofold violence of contact staged as threat and its cruel prevention.

In conclusion, my discussion of the film's aesthetic "Kritik der Gewalt" confirms its politically equivocal character. Even more than Benjamin's philosophical performatives, its filmic acts of narrative performance with their openly racist connotations can be read in the context of a society obsessed with discourses of purity as a means of negotiating its "particularly extreme and extremely dysfunctional relation between 'self' and 'other.'"[80] Beyond the narrow Weimar context, the return of Benjamin's critique of representation in Fischer-Lichte's turn-of-the-21st century performance concept might even invite speculations on the continued prominence of related epistemological themes in the German imagination. At the same time, the transnational flows constituting Fischer-Lichte's arguments – including Girard's anthropological theory of violence – as well as the aesthetic politics of our Weimar film show that the evoked specters of historical violence cannot be neatly enclosed in some German horror yard. Beyond a new diagnosis of the proto-fascist German soul, the film's overdetermined, ambivalent aesthetic scenario exemplifies the complex, intricate nature of our attempts to map intermedial, trans-national imaginations of violence in their multi-faceted contexts.

---

[80] Elsaesser: *Weimar Cinema*. P. 438.

IV. Modernism, Modernization, and Representation

Lutz Koepnick

The Violence of the Aesthetic

Modern German thought and aesthetic practice was driven by a curious dialectic of the focused and the fuzzy, one which has produced often highly contradictory positions on the relationship between the work of visual perception and the perceived violence of overabundant images. Whereas theorists and practitioners of pictorial photography around 1910 considered blurry images to be an aesthetic strategy protecting the viewer's eye from stressful forms of looking, another tradition considers a lack of focus as a viable code for representing experiences of violence and communicating these in visceral form to the viewer. It is the task of this paper to shed light on some paradigmatic episodes of this dialectic of the focused and the fuzzy in modern German culture. It is not least of all the work of Walter Benjamin that will be of central importance to elaborate on the extent to which this dialectic is implicated in larger controversies about the general location of the aesthetic in modern industrial culture, about the role of the aesthetic to either defend our sensory perception against, or open it up to, the assaults of visual overflow, and about the give and take between art and violence in face of modern culture's ubiquity of mediated images and virtualized forms of transport.

Swamped by today's barrage of mediated images, at times it is difficult not to envy people with myopic vision. What a blessing it must be not to be forced to react to each and every visual stimulus approaching our eyes. What a stroke of luck it must be to escape the multitude of screens and other windows of representation around us, not by shutting one's eyes altogether, but simply by making most signals flow by as if they weren't meant for us. What a bliss it must be to look calmly right through our age's compulsive connectivity and ceaseless information. But merely to squint our eyes with the intention to blur the work of vision isn't much of a help, for part of the promise of nearsightedness is of course to evade the vicissitudes of instrumental vision in the first place: to inhabit a visual field in which we, rather than actively warding off overstimulation, simply enjoy the pleasures of drift, of no longer playing the Pavlovian Dog, and intend non-intentionality.

In such moments of civilizational discontent, the fuzzy seems to hold the promise of a better life, an existence liberating perception from the assaults of visual culture and its ongoing demands to keep our eyes sharpened. It doesn't take a truly nearsighted person's protest, however, in order to evoke second thoughts about this utopian equation of the indistinct and the non-violent. What it takes, instead, is our recollection of the modern dialectic of the focused and the fuzzy, one in whose course we can observe fundamental sea changes in the meaning of blurred vision, and one which has produced often highly contradictory thoughts on the nexus between attention, visual perception, and the violent overabundance of mediated images. It is the task of this essay to shed light on a paradigmatic moment of this dialectic, and it is the work of Walter Benjamin that will be of central importance here in order to render visible what is myopic itself about any understanding of myopia as an aesthetic remedy against the violence of visual overflow.[1]

1. The Art of Being Out of Focus

In the first decades of the twentieth century, German theorists and practitioners of photography such as Willi Warstat and Heinrich Kühn were emphatically dedicated to defending the medium's artistic status, its legitimate membership in the pantheon of high art. In books such as *Allgemeine Ästhetik der photographischen Kunst auf psychologischer Grundlage* [*A General Aesthetic of Photographic Art from a Psychological Point of View*] (1909) and *Die künstlerische Photographie: Ihre Entwicklung, ihre Probleme, ihre Bedeutung* [*Artistic Photography: Its Development, Its Problems, Its Significance*] (1913), Königsberg professor Warstat provided intricate aesthetic, psychological, physiological, and technological observations in order to assure his readers that photography could do much more than merely indexing the real, i.e., offer ample opportunities for individual self-expression and aesthetic transfiguration.[2] Warstat's approach to the photographic process was anything but naive. He left no doubt about the fact that photographic representations, because they suspend the temporality of human perception and arrest the flux of the visual field, have little in common with the kind of images iris and retina transmit to our brains. Unlike the human eye, which has the ability to readjust its focus and can therefore single out certain zones of attention, photographic images have the tendency to map visible space without allowing the viewer to differentiate between fore- and background, the important and the marginal. Cameras, when left to themselves, essentially present too much at once and thus fail to structure the world of appearances in any meaningful fashion. They favor product over process and thus overwhelm the viewer with an excess of visual information. Hobby photographers might succeed in

---

[1] This essay was critically inspired by Wolfgang Ullrich: *Die Geschichte der Unschärfe*. Berlin: Wagenbach 2002; and Philippe Garnier: *Die Entdeckung der Unschärfe*. München: Liebeskind 2002.
[2] Willi Warstat: *Allgemeine Ästhetik der photographischen Kunst auf psychologischer Grundlage* and *Die künstlerische Photographie: Ihre Entwicklung, ihre Probleme, ihre Bedeutung*. In: *Willi Warstat on the Aesthetics of Art Photography*. Ed. by Peter C. Bunnell. New York: Arno Press 1979. (Reprinted with permission of Wilhelm Knapp Verlag.)

putting a frame around the real, but their images usually fail to distinguish between sights of greater and those of lesser importance.

Enter what Warstat considers the art photographer, manipulating the apparatus in such a way that it will overcome the amateur's hapless positivism. Photography, for Wartsat, becomes art whenever it understands how to beat the medium's perceptual violence at its own game. Photographers can do so in two ways: either during the process of capturing their images – by choosing evocative perspectives that screen out unnecessary detail and help define structural relationships within the image; or when developing and printing their image – with the help of certain reframing strategies, light filters, and other manual transformations of the negative. Art photography in Warstat's understanding assumes aesthetic qualities because it contains the medium's latent violence and excess. What defines photographers as true artists is their unique gift to reduce the image's aggressive spread of detail and focus; their talent to have the apparatus – somewhat ironically as it were – emulate the very procedures of human vision, to remake technology in the image of organic qualities.

In Warstat's view, the task of art and the aesthetic was to elevate the viewer above the aggressive intrusions of modern industrial culture, and photography deserved the name of art whenever it succeeded in protecting the viewer's eye from disquieting forms of perception. The work of Heinrich Kühn, one of the leading figures in the international pictorial photography movement around 1910, is helpful for illustrating and complicating this understanding. Similar to Warstat, Kühn conceived of the aesthetic as an antithesis to violence, and of art photography as a relaxant meant to calm the modern subject's over-agitated sensory systems. "By photography", Kühn wrote in his 1921 textbook *Technik der Lichtbildnerei,* "we understand a pictorial representation expressing a seamless intermingling of different tones, created and conveyed by the effect of light".[3] In his work as a photographer Kühn relied largely on gum-bichromate printing methods in order to achieve his goals, but he also used compositional principles showing landscapes as picturesque and framing techniques soliciting empathetic identification with the subject on display. Strongly influenced by his American colleague Alfred Stieglitz, Kühn developed a photographic style that emphasized planar simplicity and a rhythmical order of individual elements. No matter whether he experimented with color reproduction or explored the expressive potential of the grayscale, Kühn's photographs avoided strongly perspectival perceptions of space and instead, due to their stress on the decorative poetics of light, often collapsed any clear separation of pictorial foreground and background, of figure and ground. Kühn may have been dedicating much of his attention to picturing family members in

---

[3] Heinrich Kühn: *Technik der Lichtbildnerei*. Halle: Wilhelm Knapp 1921. P. 12.

rural settings, as if trying to play out the preindustrial against the modern, the familiar against the alienated. The deliberate blur of his photographic technique, however, often situated his figures in strangely unsettled relationships to their surroundings, a state of suspension whose uncanny aspects can barely be overlooked. Privileging atmospheric values over representational detail, the sfumato effects of light over the force of contour, Kühn's images set out to celebrate the intimate, the scenic, and the simple, but they also – surreptitiously – seemed to reveal the very modern dynamic of rupture and displacement Kühn's brand of pictorial photography so adamantly sought to reject.

Throughout his entire career, Kühn's primary interest was to use photography as a means to reproduce the feeling of the human eye. His photographic work mimicked the generic conventions and compositional methods of eighteenth and nineteenth-century genre painting, not in order to obscure the difference between the paintbrush and the camera, but in the hope of developing his medium to the fullest and, precisely in doing so, promoting the perceived task of all good art, namely to establish empathetic interaction between subject and object and to emancipate viewers from merely analytical or practical perceptions of the world. To favor the fuzzy over the focused, for Kühn, was to supersede a world submerged by strategic thought and utilitarian practice. Far more than a mere stylistic signature, sfumato effects defended the legacy of aesthetic autonomy against the visual overflow of modern mass culture; they modernized the way in which art had once sought to establish reciprocal and hence violence-free relationships between non-identical particulars. While Kühn's approach to the medium no doubt often appeared conservative and retrograde, we therefore would be wrong to exclude his work from the modernist canon altogether. Dedicated to shielding the eye against overstimulation, Kühn engaged his medium in an ongoing process of formal experimentation and self-questioning. His camera remediated the language of the older medium of painting, not in order to mask its own base in technology, but to drive photography's expressive potential to the fullest. Like any other modernist, Kühn self-reflexively explored aesthetic form as his work's most viable content. To blur our vision of things, for him, did not mean to depart from artistic rigor. On the contrary. What was undeniably modern about his work is the fact that his experiments with blur and his pursuit of aesthetic autonomy were propelled by a very focused politics and ethics, one whose central mission was to provide a remedy for the violence to which industrial culture subjected the modern observer's eye.

2. Aesthetics and Ballistics

Kühn's campaign against the surfeit of focus and visual stimulation in modern life were launched simultaneously with the invention of narrative cinema and its rise to modern culture's most successful means of reengineering the structures of attention. Only a few years after Kühn's greatest successes, this new hegemony of film caused Weimar photographers to develop a language of blur quite different from the aspirations of pictorial photography. Its principal task was now no longer to reveal the projective empathy of the human eye, but to capture the spirit of a world resolutely dedicated to experiences of speed, mobility, and motion pictures. Rather than wrestling with the unsettling effects of modern industrialization, the lack of focus in photographs such as Anton Stankowski's 1929 *Zeitprotokoll mit Auto* [*Time Protocol with Car*] came to pay tribute to the age's devotion to velocity, but also to contest the perceived role of film as the most effective tool of representing accelerated movements and transitory actions. Whereas Kühn and Warstat, in spite of their promotion of blur, had categorically favored the reproduction of still over that of moving subjects, the 1920s saw a rapidly evolving culture of photography in which newly developed light-weight cameras and faster film stock allowed photographers to engage ever more creatively with the tempo of high-speed objects, be they racing cars, airplanes, trains, or bullets.

It was this dual hegemony of film and speed in the first decades of the twentieth century that, in the course of the 1930s, would cause Walter Benjamin to rethink the violence of mechanical images, and to emphasize the extent to which the modern dialectic of the focused and the blurred is symptomatic of larger changes in the role of art and aesthetics in society. For Benjamin, photographers such as Kühn were guilty of trying to simulate what had been auratic about the very early products of nineteenth-century photography. They retouched their images in order to imitate how early photography, due to long exposure times, had "caused the subject to focus his life in the moment rather than hurrying on past it",[4] whereas the true challenge would have been to use the technology's advancements in order to pry objects from their auratic shells. Gum-print photographers such as Kühn, for Benjamin, fiddled with special effects so as to produce impressions of permanence, even though the apparatus had long developed into a versatile device for capturing the fleeting and impermanent in all its flux and motion. Kühn's lack of focus inscribed the past as present; it prevented the new from unsettling the meaning of tradition and revolutionizing the observer's sensory systems. For the advent of mechanical reproducibility, so of course Benjamin's perhaps most famous argument, not only added photography and film to the canon of existing art forms, it changed the entire concept of art and its location in society. Because technical images, in Benjamin's understanding, no longer owed any original,

---

[4] Walter Benjamin: Little History of Photography. In: *Selected Writings, 1927–1934*. Ed. by Michael W. Jennings, Howard Eiland, and Gary Smith. Cambridge, Massachusetts: Harvard University Press 1999. Vol. 2. Pp. 507–530. Here: P. 514.

they had the ability to brush away the institutions of bourgeois art and reconnect the aesthetic to the spheres of everyday life. Photographers such as Kühn, in Benjamin's perspective, betrayed this task and logic. They considered photographic images as heir to the bourgeois cult of art and its veneration of the self-contained art work, instead of realizing that the inherent temporality of photography and film, their power to disrupt the continuum of time and administer visual shocks to the observer, would drive aesthetic experience beyond the realm of art and reclaim much older definitions of the aesthetic, definitions which had emphasized the transformative experience (and pleasure) of sensory perception.

According to Benjamin's understanding, film's principle task as medium is to provide a training ground for the overflow of visual stimulation in modern culture: film becomes film not by turning away from, but by immersing, the viewer into the discontinuous perceptual assaults so typical for modernity. Rather than – like Kühn's camera – appeasing the modernite's strained eye, Benjamin's cinema requires the viewers constantly to readjust their focus and attention. To be on guard. Never to pause or lag behind. To sharpen their concentration and fend off any desire to be absorbed by the visual world. Benjamin's cinema fulfills its inherent potential whenever it succeeds in fundamentally remaking the nature of human perception; it administers ongoing shocks to the viewer to overcome the peculiarly modern separation of the senses and wed our sense of sight to that of touch. Though Benjamin discusses photographic effects such as slow motion and the disruptive power of extreme close-ups as well, he understands the art of cutting and editing as cinema's principle mechanism to shock the viewer. What allows film to fuse aesthetics and ballistics is less the individual take or camera position, but the very caesura in-between individual shots violently yanking the viewer's eyes from one perspective to another. It is in the abyss between two discontinuous shots that cinema actualizes its intrinsic program and redefines the task of post-autonomous art.

This is not the place to recount the thrust of Benjamin's theory of shock in further detail. What I would like to point out, however, is first that Benjamin understands the ballistic qualities of modern media not simply as a new way of artistic representation, but as a mechanism emancipating the viewer from the traditional strictures of time and place.

> By close-ups of the things around us, by focusing on hidden details of familiar objects, by exploring commonplace milieus under the ingenious guidance of the camera, the film, on the one hand, extends our comprehension of the necessities which rule our lives; on the other hand, it manages to assure us of an immense and unexpected field of action. Our taverns and our metropolitan streets, our offices and furnished rooms, our railroad stations and our factories appeared to have us locked up hopelessly. Then came the film and burst this prison-world asunder by

the dynamite of the tenth of a second, so that now, in the midst of its far-flung ruins and debris, we calmly and adventurously go traveling.[5]

Benjamin's camera throws into sharp focus what escapes the normal operations of organic vision. It reconstitutes the real as a clearly defined realm of action which bonds vision to the tactile and haptic and eliminates the ground for contemplative attitudes. Yet even though Benjamin's cinema invites the viewer on unprecedented journeys to virtual elsewheres and elsewhens, we should not mistake its products for a couch potato's dream fare. Cinematographers and editors cut into the visible world like psychoanalysts reveal the presence of unconscious impulses, and for this reason cinema has the ability to rattle sedentary viewers out of their fuzzy daydreams. Far from turning spectators into mindless voyeurs, film's task is to assault the viewers' eyes so as to sharpen their attention, to produce new forms of knowledge with the help of discontinuous montage sequences, and to clear the field for transformative projects by redefining what we perceive as the topographies of the real in the first place.

What strikes me as equally important to note in this context is – secondly – the fact that Benjamin, when stressing the ballistic qualities of the medium of the film, operates with a conceptual model according to which certain media have their own internal program or logic, and that the products of certain media practices are at their best whenever their practitioners make best use of this program or logic; whenever they succeed in purifying the medium from external influences and develop its inherent potentialities to the fullest. For Benjamin, montage editing isn't simply one of many different features of film, translating the urban dweller's everyday experience of perceptual disruption into a timely aesthetic form. It is at the very heart of what makes film into film in the first place: the medium's essence, the apparatus's inherent meaning to which both filmmakers and audiences need to live up. Benjamin's puzzling inability to recognize the possibilities of sound film after 1927 was a direct result of his purist conception of the medium's identity.[6] Sound, for him, like for many other modernist theorists of the time, messed up the medium's structural organization and charge; it transformed film into something hybrid and unwieldy, multiplied its channels of expression and communication, and in this way muffled its programmatic power to burst the prison-worlds of bourgeois society asunder.

---

[5] Walter Benjamin: The Work of Art in the Age of Mechanical Reproduction. In: *Illuminations: Essays and Reflections*. Ed. by Hanna Arendt. Trans. by Harry Zohn. New York: Schocken 1969. Pp. 217–251. Here: P. 236.
[6] See Lutz Koepnick: Benjamin's Silence. In: *Sound Matters: Essays on the Acoustics of Modern German Culture*. Ed. by Nora M. Alter and Lutz Koepnick. New York: Berghahn Books 2004. Pp. 117–129.

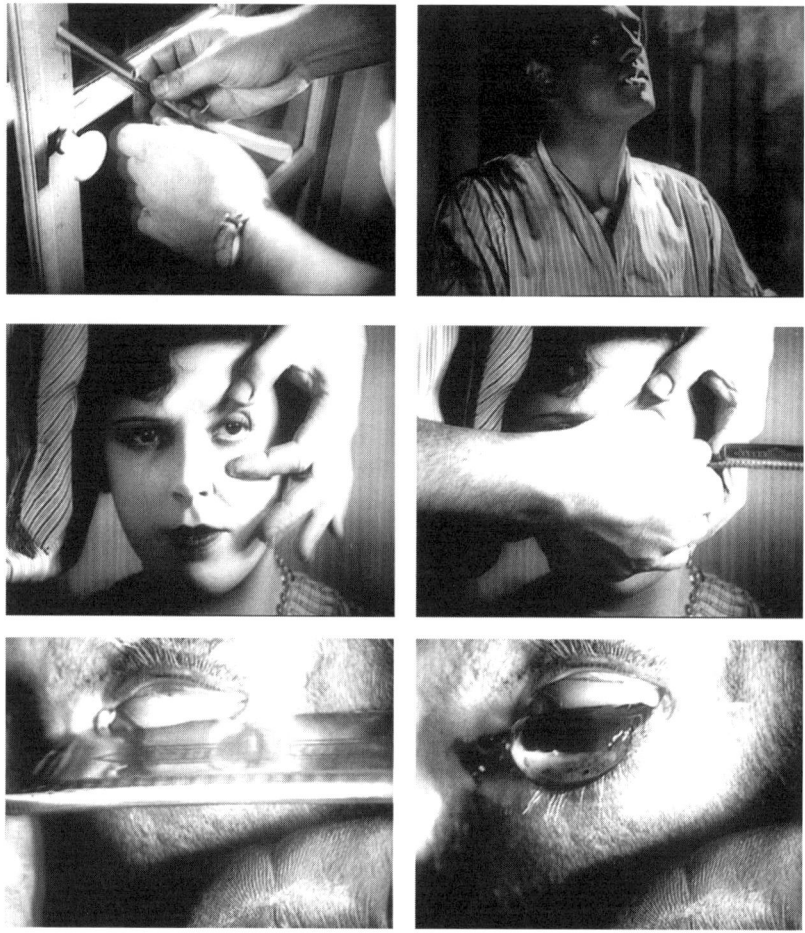

Figure 11.1 Louis Buñuel's *Un chien andalou* [*An Andalusian Dog*] (1929). Video stills / frame enlargements.

It should for this reason come as no surprise that we can locate the two single most important models of Benjamin's fusion of aesthetics and ballistics in the era of silent film. First, I am thinking of the famous close-up from Louis Buñuel's *Un chien andalou* [*An Andalusian Dog*] (1929) in which a hand slices a woman's eyeball with the help of a razor (Figure 11.1). As gruesome as it may be, this shot is highly allegorical of what Surrealists such as Buñuel and theorists such as Benjamin expected from the art of filmmaking and its effect on the viewer's perception in general: to hit the spectator like a bullet, to undercut contemplative distance and detachment, to force open new ways of seeing the world and to sharpen our eyes for the repressed imagery of the unconscious. Buñuel's *Andalusian Dog* allegorized in one single frame what Benjamin saw emerging from the chasm in-between individual filmic images. Buñuel's hand is that of Benjamin's film cutter; Buñuel's razor is the editing device of Benjamin's filmmaker, eager to slice disparate images together so as to shock spectators, focus their gaze, and heighten their presence of mind.

Secondly, I am thinking of the work of Sergei Eisenstein and how in films such as the 1925 *Battleship Potemkin* he marshaled his whole repertoire of montage editing and visual counterpoint in order to stage violent conflicts between masses and repressive political regimes. In 1924, Eisenstein saw the task of future filmmakers in liberating film from the dictates of plot-driven scripts and exploring new relationships between screen and the spectators' physiological infrastructure. The central idea of this new approach was that of creating effective structures linking the viewer's motoric dispositions to the events presented on screen. Its principle instrument was what Eisenstein called the montage of attractions, the concept of attraction being understood as

> any demonstrable fact (an action, an object, a phenomenon, a conscious combination, and so on) that is known and proven to exercise a definite effect on the attention and emotions of the audience and that, combined with others, possesses the characteristic of concentrating the audience's emotions in any direction dictated by the production's purpose.[7]

Based on the assemblage of discontinuous attractions, Eisenstein's early montage cinema wasn't simply a Brechtian apparatus interrupting the viewer's process of affective identification so as to elicit cognitive processes and spectatorial activity. Though Eisenstein understood the different techniques of montage as a dialectical practice, his juxtapositions of lines, volumes, planes, movements, and intensities sought to lodge dialectics straight in the viewer's motoric, sensual, and affective registers. To serve as an effective tool of political intervention, film was to violently crack the affective indifference of the viewer; its task was to dramatically reshape and focus the viewer's attention and thus allow for comprehensive physiological rather than exclusively optical modes of response. In this, Eisenstein's aim was no less than to emancipate Dziga Vertov's cine-eye from its perceived underlying aestheticism and intellectualism and turn it into a cine-fist.[8]

Consider one of the most pivotal segments of Eisenstein's *Battleship Potemkin*, the shooting of the elderly woman with the eye glasses, after we

---

[7] Sergei Eisenstein: The Montage of Film Attractions. In: *The Eisenstein Reader*. Ed. by Richard Taylor. Trans. by Richard Taylor and William Powell. London: BFI Publishing 1998. Pp. 35–52. Here: Pp. 35–36.
[8] See David Bordwell: *The Cinema of Eisenstein*. Cambridge, Massachusetts: Harvard University Press 1993. P. 116.

Figure 11.2 Sergei Eisenstein, *Battleship Potemkin* (1925). Video stills / frame enlargements.

had seen her in earlier moments first trying to motivate a number of middle-class citizens to talk the soldiers out of massacring the people of Odessa, and then empathizing with two other women and their loss of their respective children (Figure 11.2). The last moments of this woman's life are presented such: we cut from her close-up to the famous image of the baby carriage rolling down the stairs, seen from various angles and interrupted by a few more shots of the panicked crowd and of a younger man hiding behind a wall, his face strangely reflected in an unidentified glass pane. Suddenly, we cut to a medium-close up of a soldier whacking his sword diagonally in the direction of the camera and hence at us. After the first blow, Eisenstein reframes this shot, now offering an even closer view of the soldier's face during two additional whacks at both the camera and the viewer. Next, we finally cut again to the sight of the woman, her glasses shattered, blood protruding from her right eye, her face in final agony before what we must assume to be her certain death.

Similar to Buñuel, Eisenstein once again associates the cinematic means of cutting and editing with a gory assault on the human eye. Yet whereas in Buñuel's film, the slicing of the woman's eye served as an allegory for cinema's ability to displace repressive forms of rationalism and consciousness, in Eisenstein's sequence it makes us feel for and with the victims of political violence and repression. Yanked around by Eisenstein's editing strategies and thus unable to locate the depicted events in a meaningful spatial and temporal continuum, we are meant to become her: spectators physiologically hurt by the work of the cinematic apparatus. But in becoming her and concentrating our own attention on her death, we are also, in line with what Eisenstein in 1924 called "production's purpose", urged to realize that the women's earlier hope to talk is of no use in stopping state violence; that neither words nor empathetic gestures – these mainstays of bourgeois culture – are adequate to liberate the masses. Becoming blind and dying with her, we are asked to understand that it takes physical action and organized struggle to open the door toward a different future, that the rule of violence cannot be broken without counter violence.

Though Benjamin rarely discusses specific films explicitly, there are good reasons to believe that his thinking about the ballistics of art in the age of mechanical reproducibility borrowed heavily from both Buñuel's Surrealist and Eisenstein's militant slicing of the cinematic dream screen. Both filmmakers, in their skillful use of montage and special effects, understood expertly how to burst the prison-world of bourgeois culture asunder and thus to open unexpected fields of action, whether they included the repressed domain of the unconscious or the arena of political transformation. Both of them explored the technical structure of film as a mechanism, not simply in order to hit spectators like bullets, but in doing so to disrupt contemplative attitudes and reorganize the viewers' senso-motoric systems. In the work of both, Benjamin found what he expected the medium of film to do to count as film in the first place, namely to develop an aesthetic that would not shy away from addressing the perceptual violence inherent in modern industrial culture. In this new form of art, aesthetic structures did not simply come to represent violence, but actually administered violence to the spectator's senses in the name of social change.

Nothing, one might therefore conclude, could be more different than Benjamin's and Heinrich Kühn's view of mechanical images. Whereas Benjamin understood cinema as an ideal training ground for modern shock perception, Kühn did everything at his disposal to protect his viewers from disruptive experiences. Whereas Benjamin wanted audiences to heighten their presence of mind in front of the screen, Kühn asked his viewers to relax vis-à-vis the photographic image and free their perception from the visual overstimulation of modern everyday life. Whereas, in Benjamin's understanding, the razor-sharp editing maneuvers of film had the ability to endow sight with haptic and tactile qualities, Kühn's photographs endorsed the unfocused as the medium's most viable strategy of producing pure and autonomous forms of vision. Whereas Benjamin, in sum, embraced the violence inherent in the aesthetic of modern media for the sake of revolutionary interventions, Kühn hoped to preserve the aesthetic as a panacea for what he perceived as the violent ills of industrial culture.

And yet, we should be careful not to overlook what both Kühn and Benjamin, in spite of all their overt differences, have in common. For both Kühn and

Benjamin base their respective approaches to their medium upon ontological assumptions about the unity and structural identity of this medium; both not only think that aesthetic works are at their best whenever they fulfill the inherent technological program of their medium, but they assume that formal rigor – i.e., an artist's attempt to live up to the medium's built-in technological potential – is the very key to the social value of art and aesthetic experience. In a characteristically modernist fashion, both Kühn and Benjamin consider formal integrity itself to be ethical or political, and both resist any understanding of media as potentially hybrid, messy, and incoherent. Whether fuzzy or focused, whether suspending or rechanneling the violence of visual overflow in modern life, form, in the eyes of both Kühn and Benjamin, defines content and didactically encodes the very way in which audiences should learn how to look, not simply at works of art, but at social reality in general. What both share, then, is that no doubt violent gesture itself with which aesthetic modernists often sought to purify their respective medium from hostile influences and unwanted sensory data. What they share is a certain modernist militancy stressing the autonomous specificity of various art forms and understanding an artist's rigorous adherence to the logic of his medium as key to the social relevance – the power – of aesthetic experience.

3. The Rumbling of Violence

In a famous 1969 essay, Hannah Arendt defined power as the human ability to act in concert. Never the property of one person alone, power always belongs to a group and, in the final analysis, aims at building communicative infrastructures as an end in and of itself. Violence, on the other hand, is distinguished by its instrumental character. It is used by those trying to enforce something on someone else. Whereas power precedes and outlasts all aims and should therefore be understood as "the very condition enabling a group of people to think and act in terms of the means-end category",[9] violence will always remain tied to instrumental perspectives and lopsided forms of interaction; it remains caught within the logic of means and ends, unable to produce any sense of human reciprocity, intersubjectivity, and understanding. Whereas power, according to Arendt's conception, helps build legitimate networks of human interaction, violence requires tools and instruments that cannot but fracture human bonds and channels of communication and action. True power can never rest on the imperative structure of violence, whereas violence has the force to obliterate the binding glue of power:

> Those who oppose violence with mere power will soon find that they are confronted not by men but by men's artifacts, whose inhumanity and destruc-

[9] Hannah Arendt: *On Violence*. San Diego: Hartcourt Brace & Company 1970. P. 51.

tive effectiveness increase in proportion to the distance separating the opponents. Violence can always destroy power; out of the barrel of a gun grows the most effective command, resulting in the most instant and perfect obedience. What never can grow out of it is power. (53)

Arendt's notions of power and violence are helpful in order further to illuminate the subterranean link between Kühn's and Benjamin's understanding of modern vision and the mechanical image. Kühn's gum-print practice endorsed the fuzzy in the name of shutting out the violent overflow of visual stimulations in modern industrial culture. Rarefying detail, his photographs hoped to realize the medium's specificity with the intention of defining the aesthetic as an alternative to the overwhelming effects of modern perceptual conditions. The blurred contours of Kühn's images essentially operated as a formal equivalent to Rainer Maria Rilke's aesthetic injunction: "You must change your life!" ["Du mußt dein Leben ändern"].[10] Benjamin, by contrast, privileged the focused over the fuzzy because it promised to translate perceptual violence into political change. Not hesitant to overwhelm the viewer with oversaturated sequences of images, his aim was to play out the specificity of film against the strictures of bourgeois society, the distracted, albeit highly attentive, viewer being Benjamin's operative building block for the formation of new post-bourgeois communities. To be true to the perceived logic of one's medium, then, for both was end and means at once. It either contained or explored the violence of visual overstimulation with the intention of establishing improved conditions for human receptivity and reciprocity; it negotiated the surfeit of visual perception in modernity in an effort to undo present-day threats to operative forms of subjectivity and interaction. Yet whereas Kühn's pictorial photography insisted on the exclusivity of power and violence in Arendt's sense, Benjamin's montage cinema learned its message from Eisenstein's bourgeois lady and was designed to do the seemingly impossible: to climb the ladder of violence so as to reach out beyond it; to put violence in the service of building new communicative infrastructures powerful enough to do away with the stultifying logic of means and end.

Arendt might also be helpful for understanding what separates us today from Kühn's and Benjamin's competing views on violence, perception, focus, and the aesthetic. Consider the cinematic techniques dominantly in use since the 1990s to communicate narrative action and violence. Rather than emphasizing an actor's performance and physicality, Hollywood directors now on the one hand tend to create jerky editing rhythms that abruptly cut away after movement has begun and before it has come to completion, while on the other hand they systematically seek to unsettle the viewer with erratic and

---

[10] Rainer Maria Rilke: Archaischer Torso Apollos. In: *Ausgewählte Gedichte*. Frankfurt am Main: Insel Verlag 1932. P. 47.

Figure 11.3 Michael Bay, *The Rock* (1996). Video stills / frame enlargements.

often extremely rickety camera movements. As Michael Bay, the director of the 1996 *The Rock* (Figure 11.3), explicates his strategies for filming a spectacular car chase in San Francisco: "I film actors driving in these scenes from a dolly a few feet in front of a stationary car. I do whip pans and whip zooms and violently shake the camera, trying to make the whole screen rumble. Used in snippets, it looks as if the actors are driving ferociously".[11] Though such nervous editing creates visceral arousal indeed, the viewer's sense of excitement and danger remains diffuse and undifferentiated as we are often unable to connect individual shots to each other and to determine spatial and temporal relationships. Fierce action and violence are thus suggested, not by what happens in front of the camera, but mostly through camerawork and editing: the camera's spasmodic motions, the editor's seemingly arbitrary cut-aways, the frame's frantic rumbling. That we do not exactly see what is going on and

---

[11] Quoted in David Bordwell: Aesthetics in Action: *Kungfu*, Gunplay, and Cinematic Expressivity. In: *At Full Speed: Hong Kong Cinema in a Borderless World.* Ed. by Esther C. M. Yau. Minneapolis: University of Minnesota Press 2001. Pp. 73–94. Here: P. 76.

how one action might lead to another; that individual actions never really achieve concreteness and remain literally out of focus and illegible; that crucial steps within the action are often entirely omitted for the sake of creating a general sense that something dynamic is going on – all this has now come to serve as a primary tool for presenting violence on screen. As David Bordwell puts it, "The rapid cutting, constant camera movement, and dramatic music and sound effects must labor to generate an excitement that is not primed by the concrete event taking place before the lens".[12]

Unstable camera work and elliptical editing today often produce sensory impressions of violence without putting the bodies of our star commodities in harm's way. Such strategies are of course not entirely new. Robert Rossen, for instance, relied heavily on the labor of wobbly cameras and jerky editing in the intense boxing sequences of his 1947 *Body and Soul*, in part to evoke greater realism and draw the viewer into the action, in part to protect the fragile physicality of lead-actor John Garfield. A former flyweight boxer himself, cinematographer James Wong Howe described his work for Rossen as such:

> When I used the hand-held camera in *Body and Soul*, the unsteady effect was desirable. When a fighter would get a hard punch, I would even shake the camera a little, and the audience would get a jolt, too. The resulting effect was very exciting. I brought the audience right into the ring. In movie theaters, the audiences would stand up and yell and root for the fighters.[13]

Like Michael Bay, Howe and Rossen considered cinema a tool to deliver a series of physical shocks to the spectator, a mechanism whose realism was defined by the viewers' impulse to rear back before the screen and protect their own senses from the images' threats and blows. Like Bay, Howe pictured action and violence as *perception-images*, to refer to Gilles Deleuze's Bergsonian vocabulary.[14] Not what the camera pictured, but how it looked at certain events, and how it mimicked the operations of visual perception under duress, here became the primary technique of startling the audience and encoding ferocious action.

And yet, we should not overlook certain fundamental changes in the cinematic representation of violence today compared to Rossen's and, for that matter, Eisenstein's era. I am thinking here in particular of the extreme manipulation of cinematic time due to the use of temporal overlaps – one action been shown multiply from different points of view – as well as the stylizing

---

[12] Ibid. P. 76.
[13] Quoted from the special feature portion of the film's 2001 DVD release.
[14] Gilles Deleuze: *Cinema: The Movement-Image*. Trans. by Hugh Tomlinson and Barbara Habberjam. Minneapolis: University of Minnesota Press 1991. Vol. 1. Pp. 71–86.

use of slow motion photography. As if meant to offset the blur, illegibility, and spasmodic nature of camerawork and editing, contemporary directors – including Bay in the car chase sequence of *The Rock* – tend to repeatedly decelerate the pace of certain scenes within the filming of frantic action so as to stress exceptional moments of spectacle and emphasize the quasi-lyrical or even super-human qualities of pivotal conflict. Even if average shot lengths may no longer last for more than one second, the special effect of slow motion here encourages the viewers to sharpen their eyes for certain details and be astonished by the extraordinary events on screen. A quick and moralizing response to this use of slow motion would be to say that it underwrites a precarious aestheticization of violence, one in whose context Hollywood seeks to capitalize ruthlessly on the viewer's at once naive and perverse pleasures. More, however, is at stake here, I would like to emphasize, once we recall the peculiarly modern dialectic of the blurred and the focused, of aesthetic pleasure and the mechanical image, that I sought to trace in the preceding pages. For the pleasures produced by slow motion in contemporary action cinema have less to do with our identification with and immersion into the violence on screen, than with our curiosity and astonishment about the power of the apparatus to produce such images in the first place.[15] What we are both shocked and thrilled about is not the speed of cars violently assaulting our eyes and bodies and hence extending reality effects, but the magic of camera and filmmaker to produce brazen artifice while at the same time triggering visceral responses.

To put this differently: by combining the poetics of slow motion with the effects of jerky camerawork, by joining the seemingly opposing strategies of utter stylization and sheer illegibility, contemporary representations of violence move us beyond the dialectic of the fuzzy and the focused so prevalent in modernist discourse. Contrary to Warstat and Kühn, the blurred now no longer is charged with the task of maintaining contemplative modes of looking, shutting out unwanted violence, and securing bourgeois order and the autonomy of high art. And contrary to Benjamin, cinematic images here no longer heighten our attention in order to pave the way for post-bourgeois communities, but simply for the sake of astonishing us about the magic of cinema itself. Though many might mourn their suspension of realism and authenticity, the images of contemporary action cinema – at once blurred and decelerated – cast critical light on what we perhaps only now come to understand as

---

[15] Tom Gunning's pathbreaking work on early cinema and the factor of astonishment can be of great use in theorizing the attractions of contemporary action photography as well. See Tom Gunning: An Aesthetics of Astonishment: Early Film and the (In)Credulous Spectator. In: *Viewing Positions: Ways of Seeing Film*. Ed. by Linda Williams. New Brunswick: Rutgers University Press 1995. Pp. 114–133.

modernism's central naiveté, as modernism's own aesthetic myopia: namely, the assumption that the purity of form itself could manufacture specific ethical or political responses in the viewer, whether these effects were meant to counteract violent overstimulation or turn the shocks of modern experience into an engine of social reform. Today, neither the aesthetics of the blurred nor the aesthetics of heightened attentiveness can claim to support unequivocal projects. That formal integrity no longer warrants a predictable politics, that nothing can really shock us anymore, is the shocking truth of contemporary representations of action and violence. We might disparage the pluralism and hybridity of today's codes of cinematic violence as a vacuous attempt to bond our pleasures to nothing more and nothing less than the incredible work of cinema itself. But, in a somewhat more generous perspective, we may also see this representation as testimony to Hannah Arendt's perhaps most provocative thesis: that violent interventions can be justifiable, but will never be legitimate; that operative structures of human interaction, understanding, and reciprocity can never grow out of the instrumental nature of violence.

Patrizia McBride

Montage and Violence in Weimar Culture: Kurt Schwitters' Reassembled Individuals

This essay examines the emergence of an innovative discourse on montage in Weimar culture in the early 1920s. In this context montage denotes both an aesthetic principle that encompasses a wide range of artistic practices – visual and literary collage, photomontage, and sculptural assemblage – and a discursive medium for problematizing the role violence played in constituting subjectivity after the trauma of World War I. After briefly tracing the relationship between montage, subjectivity, and violence during the breakthrough phase of montage practices in the 1920s and 1930s, the essay examines two narratives composed in 1919–20 by Kurt Schwitters, one of the most innovative practitioners of collage and montage in the twentieth century. Schwitters' stories paradigmatically deploy a montage aesthetics in order to interrogate the role of violence in attaining agency. At the same time, they implicitly ask what kind of understanding of experience is enabled by montage, understood as a perspective that combines epistemological, aesthetic, and ethical considerations.

In his 1920 "dada manifesto on feeble love and bitter love" Tristan Tzara explained that to compose a Dadaist poem one simply needs to clip words from a newspaper article, place them in a bag and

Shake gently
Next take out each cutting one after the other
Copy conscientiously in the order in which they left the bag
The poem will resemble you
And there you are - an infinitely original author of charming sensibility, even though
    unappreciated by the vulgar herd.[1]

The provocation of Tzara's instructions lies not only in the idea of the collage poem assembled according to the principle of chance, but also and especially in the suggestion that this montage principle of composition provides a blueprint for understanding subjectivity. If the poem can resemble the self that fabricated it, Tzara intimates, it is because both are at bottom the result of random cutting and pasting. While Tzara's instructions rehearse the avant-garde attack on the myth of a singular subjectivity that exercises itself in original poetic acts, they also draw attention to an important problem that

---

[1] Quoted in Matthew Gale: *Dada and Surrealism.* London-New York: Phaidon Press 1997. Pp. 63–64. Tzara's manifesto was first published in 1920 in Picabia's journal *391*. The whole text of the manifesto can be found in Tristan Tzara: *Seven Dada Manifestos and Lampisteries.* Trans. by Barbara Wright. London: Calder 1977.

the perspective of montage makes visible.[2] This is the issue of how to rethink agency given the haphazard nature of subjectivity and artistic practice. Within this framework, active intervention appears to require the cutting and pasting of existing materials in acts that are bound to violate the integrity of the materials and are thus inherently violent.

In this essay, I will focus on the emergence of a discourse on montage in Weimar culture in the early 1920s. Montage denotes in this context an aesthetic principle whose ideological reach extends beyond the wide range of innovative practices it encompasses (visual and literary collage, photo-montage, and sculptural assemblage). My hypothesis is that at this time montage also functioned as a discursive medium for reconceptualizing subjectivity and agency after the trauma of the Great War – specifically, for problematizing the role of violence in the constitution of subjectivity within a framework that rejects the psychological and ethical postulates of late-nineteenth century humanism. Violence in this context connotes a number of entwined phenomena. At the aesthetic level, it encompasses the portrayal of the violated body, as well as depictions of larger processes of disruption and disfiguration that trespass on an explicit or intuitive normative threshold. Historically these accounts are framed by a perception of the novelty of the violence produced by World War I, both in terms of its quality and of its magnitude. Finally, violence refers here to specific defamiliarizing effects that textual montage procedures elicit in the reader and that have been customarily analyzed by drawing on the category of "shock".[3] After briefly tracing the relation between montage,

---

[2] Tzara's discourse is emblematic for a modernist understanding of randomly constituted subjectivity driven by a poetic principle that whimsically scrambles words and meanings. In this context, originality, the cherished chimera of the bourgeois artist supposedly endowed with unique genius as a source of inspiration, is recoded as the singularity of a random assemblage. Tristan Tzara (1896–1963) was one of the most radical and imaginative writers associated with Dadaism. Born in Romania, in 1916 he helped found the Cabaret Voltaire, the hub of Zurich Dada. Upon leaving Zurich at the end of World War I he settled in Paris, where he lived until his death. He authored a number of influential Dadaist manifestos and was a steady contributor to the main journals of Dadaism. In Paris he temporarily joined forces with André Breton in propagating the cause of Dadaism in the early 1920s, but he became marginalized as the Dada circle collapsed and Breton started building the following of intellectuals and artists that formed the core of Surrealism. See Gale: *Dada and Surrealism*. Pp. 35–80.

[3] As is well known, the modernist discourse of defamiliarization and shock finds one of its first conceptualizations in the theories of the Russian formalists, especially the momentous articulation of poetic language offered by Victor Shklovsky: Art as Technique (1917). In: *Russian Formalist Criticism: Four Essays*. Ed. and trans. by Lee T. Lemon and Marion J. Reis. Lincoln: University of Nebraska Press 1965. Pp. 3–24. Within the German-speaking context, Walter Benjamin was

subjectivity, and violence during the breakthrough phase of montage practices in the 1920s and 1930s, that is, before montage became a staple of advertisement and political propaganda in photography and film, I will examine two narratives composed in 1919–20 by Kurt Schwitters, one of the most innovative practitioners of collage and montage in the twentieth century. Schwitters' stories paradigmatically deploy a montage aesthetics in order to interrogate the role of violence in the attainment of agency. At the same time, they implicitly ask the question of what kind of understanding of experience is enabled by montage, understood as a perspective that combines epistemological, aesthetic, and ethical considerations.

In *Theorie der Avant-Garde,* Peter Bürger offered a momentous analysis of montage as the aesthetic principle that guided the reconceptualization of artistic practice spear-headed by Dada during and after the war.[4] Within this framework, montage connotes both an analytical category and a set of practices that involve combination, overlap, and juxtaposition. Its defamiliarizing potential operates at two levels. In the first place, the unsublimated incorporation of found objects, be they images, things, or linguistic material, destroys the bounded contours of the artwork, as the collaged fragments unremittingly point back to the extra-artistic contexts from which they were culled. Secondly, the anti-illusionistic reshuffling of elements from everyday experience produces unfamiliar and startling juxtapositions. This potential for unusual perceptual constellations was aggressively exploited by the Berlin Dadaists as a weapon for undermining an art establishment that in their eyes was bent

---

one of the first theorists to link montage to a mode of aesthetic reception predicated on shock. See Walter Benjamin: Das Kunstwerk im Zeitalter seiner technischen Reproduzierbarkeit. In: *Gesammelte Schriften.* Ed. by Rolf Tiedemann and Hermann Schweppenhäuser. Frankfurt am Main: Suhrkamp 1974 (Dritte Fassung). Vol. I.2. Pp. 471–508. Walter Benjamin: The Work of Art in the Age of Its Technological Reproducibility. In: Walter Benjamin: *Selected Writings, 1938–1940.* Trans. by Edmund Jephcott and others. Ed. by Howard Eiland and Michael W. Jennings. Cambridge, Massachusetts: Harvard University Press 2003 (Third Version). Vol. 4. Pp. 251–283. Benjamin's reflection was in part inspired by Bertolt Brecht's theory and practice of epic theater. For an influential discussion of the avant-garde aesthetics of shock in relation to montage practices see Peter Bürger: *Theorie der Avantgarde.* Frankfurt am Main: Suhrkamp 1974. Pp. 98–111. Peter Bürger: *Theory of the Avant-Garde.* Trans. by Michael Shaw. Minneapolis: University of Minnesota Press 1984. Pp. 73–82.
[4] See especially the section on montage in chapter 3, in which Bürger develops analytical categories for describing the new understanding of the artwork he ascribes to the historical avant-garde. Peter Bürger: *Theorie der Avantgarde.* Pp. 98–111. Peter Bürger: *Theory of the Avant-Garde.* Pp. 73–82.

on affirming the reactionary entrenchments of Weimar Germany with its unquestioning pursuit of verisimilitude.[5]

Violence appears quite prominently in Dada's discourse on montage in part because of its emphasis on the montage procedure itself, which is bound to foreground the invasive, potentially disruptive quality of the act of cutting and pasting. One is reminded here of the startling effects of the works exhibited at the First International Dada Fair, which ranged from Hannah Höch's jagged tapestry of Weimar Germany as a beer-belly culture, "cut with the kitchen knife", to various instances of machine-like bodies that combine anthropomorphic and mechanical forms. The effect of these works, one can surmise, resides primarily in the blatant sense of violation of boundaries they convey. In her study of Berlin Dada, Hanne Bergius has drawn attention to the Nietzschean framework that authorizes such transgressions.[6] Much like Nietzsche, the Dadaists sneered at the late-idealistic dualism that regarded unsanctioned violence as the aberrant expression of the instinctual, physical side of human nature, which the mind (or spirit) needs to hold in check. Nietzsche's belief that some measure of violence is unavoidable, indeed, even salutary for the healthy human animal, resonated with the vitalistic discourse that had purchase at the turn of the century. It also provided ammunition for Georges Sorel's notorious celebration of the purifying, regenerative power of violence, which he legitimized as a tool of political struggle.[7]

One can ask to what extent this Sorelian constellation inspired the parallel between the cameraman and the surgeon drawn by Walter Benjamin in his classic analysis of filmic montage in the *Kunstwerk* essay. Benjamin, who was a sympathetic reader of Sorel, describes the cameraman's relation to his material by comparing him to a surgeon who heals the diseased body by violating its integrity. Significantly, the common term of the comparison involves the idea

---

[5] See for instance Wieland Herzfelde's appropriation of montage for an anti-illusionistic aesthetics aimed at challenging the bourgeois art establishment in Wieland Herzfelde: Introduction to the First International Dada Fair. Trans. by Brigid Doherty. In: *October* 105 (2003). Pp. 100–104.

[6] See Hanne Bergius: *Montage und Metamechanik. Dada Berlin: Artistik von Polaritäten.* Berlin: Gebr. Mann 2000. Pp. 2–13.

[7] See Sorel's discussion of Nietzsche's *Genealogy of Morals*. Georges Sorel: *Reflections on Violence.* Ed. by Jeremy Jennings. Cambridge: Cambridge University Press 1999. Pp. 230–238. Georges Sorel (1847–1922), the prominent theorist of revolutionary syndicalism, published his *Reflections on Violence* in 1906. In this work he amended his initial endorsement of Marxism by promoting the legitimate, indeed, rejuvenating role of violence in the working-class's struggle to transform society. The primary means of revolutionary practice was for Sorel the general strike, which he conceived not as a means of bargaining or negotiation, but rather as a radical practice aimed at the revolutionary undoing of extant social structure.

of cutting, "schneiden", which in German denotes both the surgeon's activity and the cameraman's framing and editing.[8] The example of the surgeon who cuts into the patient's body serves to foreground the degree to which the cameraman reaches into the fabric of reality in order to alter it and functions as a foil to the presumably detached, neutral attitude traditionally claimed by the painter. To be sure, the surgeon analogy does not directly entail violence or coercion. However, Benjamin's characterization of the potential of montage in relation to the new filmic medium draws on examples that markedly emphasize its capacity for disruption and violation. A case in point is his discussion of the alienation experienced by the film actor who, unlike the stage actor, has no final control over his performance, which in the film is pieced together in the cutting room, and is thus metaphorically exiled from his own person.[9]

Sally Stein's analysis of the montage practices deployed by German and American artists in advertisement sheds further light on the perceived link between montage and violence. Stein contrasts American advertisers' distinctive reluctance to make adventurous use of photomontage – especially when it came to tampering with the human figure – with the practices of the German avant-garde, for whom representations that could be construed as a violation of the body's intactness did not seem to constitute a taboo. Stein accounts for these different approaches by pointing to the risk-adverse attitude of American advertising agencies and artists, especially as it related to their fear of alienating audiences who would likely interpret the non-naturalistic representation of the human body as an actual violation. While one can debate whether American advertisers rightly gauged or rather underestimated their audiences' ability to deal with patently distorted representations of the body and the natural world, their fear of offending audiences is noteworthy because it underlines the perceived violence entailed in the use of montage for non-naturalistic representations.

---

[8] See section XI in Walter Benjamin: Das Kunstwerk im Zeitalter seiner technischen Reproduzierbarkeit. Pp. 495–496. Walter Benjamin: The Work of Art in the Age of Its Technological Reproducibility. Pp. 263–264. The comparison with the surgeon is at first warranted by a semantic association revolving around the multiple meanings of the term "Operateur", which in German means both projectionist and surgeon. In other words, the analogy is immediately authorized by the term's linguistic multivalence rather than by the idea of cutting. As the comparison unfolds, however, "cutting" gains prominence as the crucial practice that distinguishes both the cameraman's and the surgeon's intervention. The juxtaposition between the surgeon and his pre-modern foil, the magician, centers around the issue of the distance that separates the healer from the patient. The surgeon/cameraman erases this distance by intervening in the body, while the magician/painter claims to be able to heal the body by keeping his distance and never violating the integrity of the person.
[9] For this discussion see section IX of Das Kunstwerk im Zeitalter seiner technischen Reproduzierbarkeit. Pp. 488–491.

That manipulating representations of the human figure could come across as a literal defilement underscores how the practice of disarticulating and reassembling elements of experience proper to montage was indeed understood as a disconcerting rupture of intact experience unless it could be defused by couching it within an overall naturalistic depiction.[10]

As Stein's discussion intimates, the advertising practices of German artists suggest that they could expect their audiences to have a comparatively high threshold of tolerance for the distortions inherent in their use of montage, even when it came to tampering with the human figure. One can wonder to what extent the sight of the prosthetic bodies of war invalids begging on the streets of Germany's cities contributed to making these representations appear more like an honest record of the lasting devastations wrought by the war than the morbid fantasies of sensation-seeking artists. It is helpful to juxtapose George Grosz's graphic depiction of mutilated war veterans, for instance in *Republican Automatons*[11] and *These War Invalids Are Getting to Be a Positive Pest*,[12] both from 1920, with the sculptural assemblage he produced together with John Heartfield, and which was exhibited at the First International Dada Fair under the caption "The Middle-Class Philistine Heartfield Gone Wild".[13] In each case, the human figure is portrayed as a piece-meal assemblage of removable parts, with the prosthetic limbs – all three images feature prosthetic legs – standing in for the artificial, inorganic quality of the whole body. In this context, it is also important to note the fundamental ambiguity attached to the bodies assembled of human and mechanical parts that were exhibited at the Dada Fair. While it is true that representations of montaged bodies were often meant to symbolize the alienation of individuals made pliable for the requirements of militarism and industrial capitalism, at times they also gave voice to a proto-constructivist and productivist imagination committed to exploring a new type of human whose range of action is enhanced by mechanic prostheses

---

[10] Sally Stein: "Good Fences Make Good Neighbors": American Resistance to Photomontage between the Wars. In: *Montage and Modern Life: 1919–1942*. Ed. by Matthew Teitelbaum. Boston: The Massachusetts Institute of Technology Press 1992. Pp.133–148.
[11] Reproduced in Uwe M. Schneede: *George Grosz: His Life and Work*. Trans. by Susanne Flatauer. London: Gordon Fraser 1979. P. 66.
[12] Ibid. P. 76.
[13] Reproduced and discussed in Brigid Doherty: The Work of Art and the Problem of Politics in Berlin Dada. *October* 105 (2003). Pp. 73–92. Doherty sees this sculpture as a mockery of Rilke's poem *Archaischer Torso Apollos* aimed at challenging the philistine cultural politics of the German Communist Party. Doherty also discusses the association of Dada montage, violence, and surgery as a practice that both mitigates and deepens the disfigurations of the war in Brigid Doherty: Figures of Pseudorevolution. In: *October* 84 (1998). Pp. 64–89, esp. Pp. 75–80.

in a vaguely utopian industrial-technical fantasy, as Wieland Herzfelde's introduction for the exhibition's catalog suggests.[14]

Helmut Lethen's analysis of Weimar culture offers an illuminating framework for reconstructing the link between montage, violence, and subjectivity suggested by these representations. According to Lethen, Weimar literary and anthropological discourses portray interwar German society as an agonistic arena that compels individuals to armor themselves by putting on a protective façade, or the mask of a cold persona, in Lethen's suggestive terminology. In drawing on Helmut Plessner's anthropological observations Lethen reconstructs the understanding of subjectivity that underwrites these discourses and that regards individual identity as being inherently artificial. That is, individuals are not endowed with some essential core of identity, but are rather substantially shaped through constant exchange with their environment, their sense of self harnessed in the reciprocal, potentially hostile gaze of others. In other words, Weimar culture is a culture of exteriority, in which the inner guide of conscience has given way to the exterior pressure of shame. The outward, performative character of identity requires clear models of conduct, which are provided by literature and other cultural objects. Success in this environment depends on the incessantly vigilant performance of the visible self. This calls for repressing unchecked emotional or physical impulses and for subjecting the body, which is the veritable stage of the cold persona's performance, to a cold-blooded, steely discipline, which is no longer tempered by the warm humanist postulates of compassion and the repudiation of suffering. Notably, the violence that flows from the ruthless castigation of instinctual impulses remains unacknowledged in the discursive model of the cold persona, but resurfaces in its foil, the type of the defenseless, wretched creature.[15]

---

[14] Compare, for instance, Herzfelde's commentary on George Grosz's *"Daum" Marries Her Pedantic Automaton "George"*, in which marriage is denounced as a normalizing institution that reduces individuals to productive cogs in the social machine as symbolized by Grosz's self-portrayal as a mechanic puppet, to his gloss on another picture by Grosz, *"The Convict" Monteur John Heartfield After Franz Jung's Attempt to Get Him Up on His Feet*, in which a pugnacious-looking Heartfield is depicted with a complex mechanical gear-work where his heart should be. Herzfelde invests this figure, part human and part machine, with positive valence, though his characterization also expresses a residual ambivalence: "We see a deformed body, whose forms bespeak uncommon reserves of energy, which swell up in every direction against those indifferent walls. Beyond this the sole and material reflections: the intimate knowledge of the machine (which indeed is an element of the art of the criminal) and the obsession with good food and freedom" Herzfelde. P. 103.
[15] See especially sections I-III of Helmut Lethen: *Verhaltenslehren der Kälte. Lebensversuche zwischen den Kriegen*. Frankfurt am Main: Suhrkamp 1994. Helmut Lethen: *Cool Conduct: The Culture of Distance in Weimar Germany*. 1994. Trans. by Don Reneau. Berkeley: University of California Press 2002.

Lethen foregrounds the affinity between the new models of agency, predicated on the combinatory, performative character of identity, and the sensibility of montage aesthetics, by pointing to Brecht's early play *Mann ist Mann* [*A Man's a Man*], which recounts an individual's symbolic disassembling and remaking.[16] In the play, conceptualized at the end of World War I, though not staged until 1926, the "Ummontierung" ["reassemblage"] of the protagonist Galy Gay offers a meditation on the malleability of individual identity, specifically, on the fundamental interchangeability of the attitudes and dispositions that make the difference between ruthlessly asserting oneself and being on the receiving end. As a parable detailing the transformation of a creature into a cool persona, Galy Gay is an attempt at coming to terms with the dread elicited by the montage process – at stake is especially the violence that lurks behind this process.[17] One can conclude with Lethen that the flipside of montage as a principle for shaping subjectivity and grounding agency is an unprecedented increase in what counts as acceptable violence, combined with a problematic disregard for its consequences.

In the wake of World War I Kurt Schwitters penned two narratives that deploy montage as a prism for reflecting on the constitution of subjectivity and agency.[18] Schwitters articulated his distinctive theory of *Merz*, or abstract montage, around this time in order to defend and promote his radical collage

---

[16] Bertolt Brecht: *Mann ist Mann*. In: *Werke: Große kommentierte Berliner und Frankfurter Ausgabe*. Ed. by Werner Hecht et. al. Frankfurt am Main: Suhrkamp 1988. Vol. 2. Pp. 93–168.

[17] According to Lethen, the play's copious revisions document the laborious process of providing the reassembled protagonist with the backdrop of the "right" collective in the face of the deterioration of Weimar's political situation. Lethen: *Verhaltenslehren*. P. 143; *Cool Conduct*. P. 109.

[18] Born in Hanover in 1887, Schwitters became associated with the influential Berlin Expressionist journal *Der Sturm* around 1918. Though he remained based in Hanover, in 1920 he sought admission to the Berlin Club Dada, but was unceremoniously rejected by its ring leaders George Grosz and Richard Huelsenbeck, who were suspicious of his ties to Expressionism and found him too unpolitical and too bourgeois in appearance and demeanor. Schwitters' creation of the label *Merz*, which denotes a radical montage practice that cuts across available artistic genres and media, was in part a response to his exclusion from "official" Dadaist circles. He nevertheless collaborated with some of the most innovative artists of Dada, De Stijl, and Constructivism throughout the 1920s. In 1937 he was forced to flee Nazi Germany and emigrate to Norway and later to Britain, where he died in 1948. For a discussion of Schwitters' impact on post-World-War-II art, see Gwendolen Webster: *Kurt Merz Schwitters: A Biographical Study*. Cardiff: University of Wales Press 1997. See also the essays in the volume *In the Beginning Was Merz. From Kurt Schwitters to the Present Day*. Ed. by Susanne Meyer-Büser and Karin Orchard. Ostfildern Ruit: Hatje Cantz 2000.

practice. He advocated an artistic practice that is free to appropriate any element of experience so as to imaginatively hybridize media and genres.[19] Schwitters' emphasis on the formal aspects of the montage procedure and his insistence on upholding art's autonomy from political activity earned him the contempt of the activist phalanx of Berlin Dada, which accused him of advancing an hermetic and at bottom escapist understanding of art rather than turning art into a weapon for piercing the ideological screen buttressing the status quo.[20] Yet the charge of formalism and lack of social commitment brought by declared Schwitters foes such as Richard Huelsenbeck is belied by the exploration of individual identity that unfolds in his literary work in the immediate postwar period. It is this reflection, particularly as it draws on the principle of montage that sustains his artistic practice, which interests me in this paper. I will focus in particular on two prose narratives from 1919 and 1922. These short stories juxtapose two competing models of agency that hinge on an understanding of subjectivity as assembled and inessential. At the same time, they explicitly thematize the montage procedure as a perspective for scrutinizing the relation between violence, political practice, and available moral frameworks. In so doing, Schwitters' stories deliver a caustic commentary on the self-deluded politics of Berlin Dada and a meditation on the shortcomings of available normative horizons for dealing with the phenomenon of violence as magnified by the experience of the Great War.

---

[19] *Merz* represents Schwitters' label for his theory of abstract, i.e. non-figural and non-narrative montage, which encompasses hybrid practices ranging from poetic and visual collage to sculptural assemblage. At bottom *Merz* underwrites a combinatory, semiotic understanding of artistic practice. It denotes the ability to seize on just about any element or object of experience, divest it of its semantic and contextual valences, and refunctionalize it by inserting it in a new context, where it will acquire new meaning by establishing new relations with other, surrounding elements. For an early characterization of *Merz*, see his essay from 1920. Kurt Schwitters: Merz. In: *Das literarische Werk. Manifeste und kritische Prosa*. Ed. by Friedhelm Lach. Köln: DuMont 1981. Vol. 5. Pp. 74–82, here especially Pp. 76–77. Kurt Schwitters: From Merz. In: *Kurt Schwitters Poems Performance Pieces Proses Plays Poetics*. Ed. and trans. by Jerome Rothenberg and Pierre Joris. Cambridge, Massachusetts: Exact Change 2002. Pp. 215–221. Henceforth, citations from Lach's five-volume edition of Schwitters' collected works are identified in parenthesis in the body of the text as *Werk*; citations from the English translation by Rothenberg and Joris are identified as *Trans*.
[20] See Huelsenbeck's attack on Schwitters in the introduction he drafted for the *Dada Almanach*. Richard Huelsenbeck: Introduction. (1920.) *Dada Almanach*. Ed. by Richard Huelsenbeck. Hamburg: Edition Nautilus 1987. Pp. 3–9. Here: P. 9. See also: Huelsenbeck: *The Dada Almanac*. English ed. and trans. by Malcolm Green. London: Atlas Press 1993. Pp. 9–14. Here: P. 14.

The first narrative, titled *Die Zwiebel* [*The Onion*] is a surreal fantasy of reassemblage cheerfully told in the first person by its protagonist, Alves Bäsenstiel, who describes in graphic detail the process of his disemboweling.[21] The event, which Bäsenstiel has himself helped to organize, recasts religious ritual and juridical execution within the gory context of butchering livestock. A surprising turn occurs when the king, the star guest at the event, which is also being witnessed by an unspecified *Volk*, greedily ingests the narrator's eyes. This fare proves noxious, burning two holes in the king's innards. At this point the king's daughter hastily orders that the narrator's scattered intestines be reassembled so that he can be resuscitated. The newly collaged narrator however refuses to give the king a life-saving antidote and marries the princess instead.

The narration in this short piece is patterned after the unruly logic of fairy tales. For instance, the protagonist is able to witness his disemboweling even after his skull has been cracked open and he is for all purposes dead. In a similar vein, the reassemblage of his body unfolds as a cinematic sequence played in surreal, reversed, slow motion. The various phases of the narrator's disemboweling are recounted with chilling detachment and occasional forays into black humor, as in the intimation that knowledge of an individual's introspective space is tantamount to figuring out how his innards fit together: "Ich zog und zerrte magnetisch an den Eingeweiden, bis alle wieder richtig an gewohnter Stelle lagen. Dabei kam mir meine Kenntnis des inneren Menschen sehr zugute" (*Werk* 2:25) ["I pushed and pulled magnetically on the intestines, until they lay in their accustomed places. My knowledge of man's inner nature came in handy" (*Trans.* 125).[22]]

The slaughterhouse setting explicitly evokes the carnage of the war. The theme of a sacrificial offering rehearses the blood-thirsty rhetoric of self-immolation that had purchase among intellectuals and artists in the latter years of the *Kaiserreich*. The protagonist is a man who will be disemboweled and quartered like livestock in a cannibalistic ritual that recalls the Christian tale of sacrificial death freely accepted by a savior who offers his own body as a redemptive meal. There is however a peculiar twist, because in Schwitters' tale the sacrificial victim ends up bringing death instead of life. Furthermore, Bäsenstiel's resurrection delivers a sardonic commentary on the Expressionist trope of the New Man,[23] for the individual reborn from the slaughter in

---

[21] Kurt Schwitters: Die Zwiebel. In: *Werk*. Vol. 2. Pp. 22–27. Kurt Schwitters: The Onion. In: *Trans*. Pp. 121–127. The story first appeared in Schwitters' own collection *Anna Blume Dichtungen* in 1919, and was reprinted that same year in the Berlin avant-garde journal *Der Sturm*.
[22] This translation has been slightly modified.
[23] The mocking reference to the New Man has been noted by commentators, especially John Elderfield: *Kurt Schwitters*. London: Thames and Hudson 1985. P. 100.

which he has acquiesced is identical to the old one, being nothing more than an assemblage of the same old parts:

> Man begann mich wieder zusammenzusetzen. Mit einem sanften Ruck wurden zuerst meine Augen in ihre Höhlen gedruckt. (Fürchte dich nicht, Glaube, Liebe, Hoffnung sind die Sterne.) Dann holte man meine inneren Teile. Es war zum Glück noch nichts gekocht, auch noch nichts zu Wurst zerhackt. (*Werk* 2:25)
> [They started to put me back together. With a little gentle pressure they pushed my eyes back in their sockets. (Have no fear: faith, hope, love, are thy stars.) Then they gathered up my innards. Happily nothing had been cooked yet, and nothing had been ground up for sausages.] (*Trans.* 125)[24]

By the same token, the narrative debunks the fantasy that the individual's heroic self-immolation will usher in a new society.[25] In fact, the destruction of greedy power as a result of the king's death is ambiguously followed by Bäsenstiel's marriage to the princess. It is unclear how the story's political and patriarchal order will be affected by this turn of events, which may just be an instance of a new tyrant replacing the old one.

The ambiguity of Bäsenstiel's character in *Die Zwiebel* is dispelled in another story Schwitters wrote around the same time, *Franz Müllers Drahtfrühling* [*Franz Müller's Wire Springtime*].[26] Here Bäsenstiel plays a key role as an opportunist politician with ties to the activist phalanx of Dadaism. His character recalls Schwitters' archrival, Richard Huelsenbeck, who in 1918 denied Schwitters membership in the Berlin Club Dada for being insufficiently political and too bourgeois in his appearance and demeanor. In three chapters, *Franz Müllers Drahtfrühling* tells of the revolutionary uprisings unleashed by the purportedly subversive behavior of an artist, Franz Müller, whose indifference to the questioning of well-situated citizens and a policeman first sparks street riots and then prompts the convening of the country's parliament. Here Bäsenstiel, who, in the narrator's words, holds no specific

---

[24] Translation modified.
[25] This central trope of Expressionist discourse is found for instance in Kandinsky's influential essay *Über das Geistige in der Kunst*, which calls artists to sacrifice themselves and form a vanguard. They will thereby show the way to spiritual purification to the unenlightened masses and the philistine bourgeois, who are both presumably drowning in the swamps of materialism and soullessness. Wassily Kandinsky: *Über das Geistige in der Kunst*. Bern: Benteli 1952. Wassily Kandinsky: *On the Spiritual in Art. Complete Writings on Art.* Ed. by Kenneth C. Lindsay and Peter Vergo. Trans. by Peter Vergo et. al. New York: Da Capo 1994.
[26] Kurt Schwitters: Franz Müllers Drahtfrühling. In: *Werk*. Vol. 2. Pp. 29–46. The story was published in *Der Sturm* in 1922. Hans Arp, who was a close friend of Schwitters in the 1920s, claims to have been involved in drafting parts of the narrative. *Werk*. Vol. 2. P. 391.

ideological creed except for a marked belief in authority, continues to instigate against Müller, whom he accuses of being a criminal and a seducer of the people (*Werk* 2:41). The story's various episodes are strung together, indeed, collaged, without much regard for continuity or motivation. They are topped by a happy ending of sorts, consisting of Müller's erotically charged encounter with a young woman, whose white clothes he symbolically soils.

If one considers the two narratives merely from the standpoint of their characterization of contemporary political institutions (monarchic rule in the *Kaiserreich* and parliamentary democracy in Weimar Germany), one may conclude that they share a vantage point of uncompromising and indiscriminate contempt. Their stock descriptions of political actors driven by the basest human instincts – greed, dishonesty, grandstanding, and power-mongering – deliver at best a cranky and trivializing record of events during and after the war. This could be interpreted as a defensive response on the part of an apolitical artist who felt goaded by the radical engagement of fellow avant-gardists like Huelsenbeck and Herzfelde. Alternatively, it could be seen as symptomatic for the cosmic nihilism boldly professed by Dada and that distinguishes the heroic phase of cynical reason in Peter Sloterdijk's account.[27] One can however also draw on the perspective mapped by the work of Jonathan Crary for reading these stories, and examine montage as a prism for exploring a realignment of discourses of perception, aesthetic practice, and power in the historical construction of subjectivity.[28] Specifically, the question is how the montage principle of taking apart and putting together anew, which the narratives both portray and formally enact, can be put to work to explore competing understandings of malleable individual identity and the social constructedness of the self in the wake of World War I.

Both narratives unfold in highly theatrical settings that underscore the centrality of acts of watching and witnessing – the slaughterhouse/gallows/sacrificial altar in *Die Zwiebel*; the street and parliament chamber in *Franz Müllers Drahtfrühling*. Indeed, *Die Zwiebel* markedly portrays the self of the first-person narrator as the constant object of an other's perception, including its own. Traditional psychological observation, which presupposes the existence

---

[27] See especially Peter Sloterdijk: Dadaistische Chaotologie. Semantische Zynismen. In: *Kritik der zynischen Vernunft*. Frankfurt am Main: Suhrkamp 1983. Vol. 2. Pp. 711–740. Peter Sloterdijk: Dadaistic Chaotology. Semantic Cynicisms. In: *Critique of Cynical Reason*. Trans. by Michael Eldred. Minneapolis: University of Minnesota Press 1987. Pp. 391–409.
[28] See especially Jonathan Crary: *Techniques of the Observer. On Vision and Modernity in the Nineteenth Century*. Cambridge, Massachusetts.: Maschusetts Institute of Technology Press 1990.

of an inward space qualitatively different from the bodily realm, is lampooned through remarks steeped in black humor:

> Es ist doch ein eigentümliches Gefühl, wenn man in zehn Minuten geschlachtet werden soll. (Die Opfer der Mutterschaft.) Ich war bislang in meinem ganzen Leben noch nicht geschlachtet worden. Dazu muß man reif sein. (*Werk* 2:22)
> [Knowing that you will be butchered in ten minutes gives you a funny kind of feeling. (The sacrifices of maternity.) Until then I had never in my life been butchered. One must be ripe for it. (*Trans.* 121)[29]]

The prominence of the theatrical makes the stories into early dramatizations of the culture of exteriority that for Helmut Lethen distinguishes Weimar Germany from the *Kaiserreich*. Against this cultural horizon, subjectivity is formed through individuals' interaction with their environment and in the reciprocal gaze they exchange with others. The emphasis here lies on shaping and controlling the ways in which an individual is perceived, because being perceived is all that counts in a culture that no longer believes in essential identity. Bäsenstiel, the character that connects the two stories, is a paradigmatic example of the cool persona described by Lethen, staging the performance of a self that asserts control over its environment by exerting the utmost control over its body, whose disemboweling it willingly presides over. His cool acquiescence to his dismembering empowers him to the most radical political act, namely, regicide, for the king is killed not by the poisonous eyes per se, but by Bäsenstiel's refusal to administer the antidote that could save him. In other words, Bäsenstiel's very passivity, his refusal to intervene, translates into a paradoxical assertion of agency, subverting the tale's political order. As the reader realizes in hindsight, the narrator's cheerful tone throughout the story is warranted by this unsettling happy ending. On the whole, *Die Zwiebel* provides a scathing commentary on the organicist discourse of sacrifice and rebirth that had authorized the war, which it literalizes via the slaughterhouse setting. The portrayal of butchering draws attention to the violence this discourse helped to legitimize, while the blatantly impossible procedure of instilling life into a body's reassembled limbs exposes the fraudulence of its premise.

In *Franz Müllers Drahtfrühling*, Franz Müller embodies a very different montage procedure. Unlike Bäsenstiel's gory spectacle, Müller's montage practice is markedly non-violent and grounds an unorthodox, anti-heroic mode of artistic agency. As it turns out, Müller's *sprechender Name* is not related to the word "Mühle", mill, as one would expect based on the etymology of this common German family name, but rather to "Müll", garbage.[30] In

---

[29] Translation modified.
[30] In other words, Schwitters' word play seizes on the quasi homophone "Müll" to semantically refunctionalize the term as "Müll-er", which in the context of his story acquires the meaning of "garbage man".

this way Müller's name hints at his distinctive attire, which is assembled from trash gathered from the gutter:

> Der Anzug war auch etwas eigenartig. Anna Blume dachte dabei etwa an die Merzplastiken des Autors. Er war nicht etwa gestopft oder geflickt, sondern mit Brettern vernagelt und mit Draht umspannt. Anna Blume dachte dabei etwa an die Merzplastiken des Autors; ekelhaft, so etwas in die Tat umzusetzen; eine wandelnde Merzplastik. (*Werk* 2:34-35)
> [His suit was also somewhat peculiar. It reminded Anna Blume of the author's Merz sculptures. It was not darned or patched up, but rather made of planks hammered together and bound up with wire. It reminded Anna Blume of the author's Merz sculptures; how revolting to execute something like that; a walking Merz sculpture.[31]]

Müller's clothes pointedly resemble the collages of refuse created by the self-identified narrator/author, and this makes of him a strolling *Merz* sculpture. But trash is also Müller's favorite food, a circumstance that provides for some humorously disgusting narrative digressions. The contrast to Bäsenstiel could not be more striking. Bäsenstiel's ostensive willingness to provide nourishment by immolating his own body proves toxic. Müller, on the other hand, is willing to eat refuse, i.e., to draw nourishment from the debased domains of everyday life. While this entails engaging experience in a nonviolent manner, the humorously repulsive description of his behavior prevents any idealization or heroization of his character. Indeed, Müller's propensity for eating rotting garbage makes him no more a point of identification than Bäsenstiel. He is neither a hero nor a savior, but simply a practitioner of *Merz*, the montage principle advocated by Schwitters. As the prototype of an artist who literally feeds on the trash that is also the stuff of his work, Müller symbolizes Schwitters' avant-garde agenda of erasing the divide between artistic and non-artistic realms. This polemical erasure is not framed by the traditional narrative of a quest for authenticity pursued through attempts at eliminating the dualism of outside and inside, appearance and essence, signifier and signified. Rather, Müller's unheroic and repulsive behavior challenges the late-idealistic narrative that elevates art to a transfiguration of everyday life and instead portrays

---

[31] For *Franz Müllers Drahtfrühling* I offer my own translation rather than drawing on the 1927 translation/adaptation by Eugène Jolas, which is reprinted in *Werk*. Vol. 2. Pp. 383–391. Anna Blume is the main character in Schwitters' homonymous nonsensical poem from 1919, *An Anna Blume* [*To Anna Blume*] whose unexpected success made of Schwitters a literary sensation of sorts. For several years Schwitters wove references to Anna Blume in his works. They are part self-ironic exercise and part shrewd attempt at exploiting the poem's scandalous success.

both the artist and the artwork as made of the same smelly and unflattering stuff of ordinary experience.[32]

In both stories, montage offers a key framework for contrasting alternative modes of constituting subjectivity and conceptualizing agency. Specifically, the montage procedures through which Bäsenstiel and Müller are constituted as agents appear as the literal implementation of two very different discourses. If Bäsenstiel embodies narratives that promise the birth of a new man through the violent sacrifice of the old one, Müller exemplifies the results of transposing onto the body an artistic practice that revolves around the incorporation of materials from everyday experience, including refuse. What makes the montage procedure at the heart of the two stories notable is not so much the fact that in both cases bodies are taken apart and pieced together anew, in other words, that one can no longer assume the fundamental intactness and integrity of the body. Rather, it is the specific type of assemblage that calls for closer scrutiny, as well as the circumstances under which it takes place. In both stories the contexts that frame the montaged body are marked by violent occurrences that contribute to overturning the established order, yet the violence relates in very different ways to the moment of assemblage, and it is this difference that the narratives emphasize.

While violence is integral to the unnatural disassembling and reassembling of Bäsenstiel's body and is instrumental to his empowerment following the king's poisoning, for Müller the incorporation of disparate elements, which symbolizes artistic montage, does not produce violent effects per se but rather occurs via the ordinary bodily function of eating. In other words, in this second narrative violence does not relate to the process of montage directly but rather to the revolutionary circumstances the story recounts. To be sure, Müller's unresponsiveness to the questioning of bystanders sets in motion the chain of events that lead to revolution. However the narrative leaves little doubt as to who is ultimately responsible for the upheaval. Indeed, it is the vain, vicious, and dim-witted conduct of several bystanders that causes the situation to get out of control. The simmering brutality that drives the actors' behavior is exemplarily illustrated by the chilling death of a child who is

---

[32] Numerous statements in Schwitters' theoretical texts make clear that the practice of incorporating refuse in his art is not meant as a polemical debasement of art and the artwork that would offer a critique of violated reality by foregrounding its defilement. Rather, Schwitters pleads for an expansion of artistic practice beyond the stifling constraints of academic art; the artist is thus free to include all possible materials from everyday experience, whether noble or humble, whether belonging to traditional artistic idioms and practices or rather deriving from non-artistic realms. Within this logic even refuse lends itself to artistic expression. See his 1919 essay *Die Merzmalerei* [*Merz Painting*]. In *Werk*. Vol. 5. P. 37.

squeezed between two oversized women and whose corpse is used as a stepstool of sorts by onlookers eager to secure a higher vantage point to observe the revolutionary events. Bystanders who trip over the body in an ensuing stampede are themselves trampled to death (*Werk* 2:37). The surreal detachment with which the callously utilitarian and idiotically vain behavior of the participants is described is punctuated by amusing details that make the narrative even more disturbing. The question becomes how to make sense of the odd mixture of humor and violence that distinguishes both stories. Answering this question requires taking a closer look at the montage procedure that underlies the making of the body and the specific grotesque effects it engenders.

It is at first significant that for both Bäsenstiel and Müller the process of assemblage involves more than the rearrangement of attitudes and behavioral patterns that is at the heart of Brecht's *Mann ist Mann*. In Schwitters' tales, montage affects the body materially in ways that directly recall Mikhail Bakhtin's discussion of the grotesque body in his study of Rabelais. Here Bakhtin rejects the conventional notion of the grotesque as aimed at the satirical portrayal of human flaws via a physiognomy of caricatured physical attributes. In Rabelais' grotesque bodies Bakhtin finds instead a concept of subjectivity that lies outside the modern understanding of a closed individuality harnessed by "an entirely finished, completed, strictly limited body". Rather than presenting an impenetrable façade, Bakhtin's grotesque body is "never finished" and "constantly in an act of becoming" as it messily comes into contact with other bodies and objects.[33] This concept of the grotesque is, I believe, key to understanding Schwitters' portrayal of Bäsenstiel's gory dismemberment and Müller's revolting eating habits. Specifically, Bäsenstiel's tale deploys a grotesque montage of the body to explore a discourse that demands the individual's self-immolation while steering clear of the late-idealistic concept of heroic subjectivity which bred this very discourse. In Müller's case, the grotesque body is used to present the artist's relation to everyday life outside the strictures of the dominant tropes of genius, beauty, and purity.[34]

---

[33] Mikhail M. Bakhtin: *Rabelais and His World*. 1940. Trans. by Helene Iswolsky. Cambridge, Massachusetts: Maschusetts Institute of Technology Press 1968. Pp. 336 and 317 respectively.

[34] Another instance of a grotesque body whose incontrollable expansion helps to unmask the stupidity of a political system in which inept rulers are obeyed by mindlessly subservient underlings is offered in a story Schwitters published in 1923, titled *Er* [*He*]. In this tale the inordinate growth of a soldier's body proves a threat to his superiors, who order the soldier incarcerated only to discover that the man's incontrollable growth makes imprisonment unfeasible, since building large enough prisons to keep up with his body's steadily increasing size proves impossible. Finally, the king orders the soldier to drown himself by jumping into the ocean, which the soldier readily does. *Werk*. Vol. 2. Pp. 97–105.

It is important to note that Schwitters' grotesque portrayal of collaged bodies has nothing inherently celebratory. This sets it off from the reading of Rabelais developed by Bakhtin, for whom the grotesque body joyfully affirms the cosmic cycle of death and rebirth in order to temper the dread caused by the experience of individual death and suffering. Schwitters' collaged bodies are also not inherently subversive, as in Bataille's vision of an excessive "formless" and unproductive expenditure.[35] Rather, the presentation of the unfinished body constitutes a cognitive medium for exploring the unstable and contourless nature of individuality and subjectivity.[36]

The grotesque also defines the narratives' epistemological horizon by eliciting a hybrid reaction from the reader that incongruously mixes humor and dread. This is achieved through the tales' distinctive montage form, which intersperses passages that develop the main story line with inserts of various kinds: clichés, puns, fragments from ads, and proverbs, as well as words strung together without an explicit syntactic nexus in the tradition of the Expressionist

---

[35] Bataille's concepts of the formless and of unproductive expenditure point to activities and practices that exceed the parameters of instrumental rationality and conceptual knowledge. In their marked aimlessness and uselessness, these practices constitute acts of insubordination that unconditionally affirm life while defying the straitjacket of extant economic and social structures. Georges Bataille: Formless. In: *Visions of Excess. Selected Writings, 1927–1939.* Ed. by Allan Stoekl. Trans. by Allan Stoekl and others. Minneapolis: University of Minnesota Press 1985. P. 31. Georges Bataille: The Notion of Expenditure. In: *Visions of Excess: Selected Writings, 1927–1939.* Pp. 116–129.

[36] Leah Dickerman has incisively drawn on Bakhtin's understanding of the grotesque body to describe the inordinate, boundless, and temporally fluid quality of Schwitters' *Merzbau*, the sculptural installation Schwitters worked on for over a decade in his Hanover apartment. See Leah Dickerman: *Merz* and Memory: On Kurt Schwitters. In: *The Dada Seminars.* Ed. by Leah Dickerman and Matthew. Witkovsky. Washington, D.C.: National Gallery of Art, Washington 2005. Pp. 103–125, esp. Pp. 112–13. It must be noted that Schwitters' treatment of the body in his visual work is far less radical than that of contemporaries and close associates such as Hannah Höch and Raoul Hausmann. In fact, the human body is rarely recognizably addressed in Schwitters' visual pieces with the exception of the *Merzbau* itself and of a few irreverent collages, which however never go so far as to distort the human figure in some patently incongruous, monstrous fashion. One can only speculate about the reasons that account for the paucity of iconic representations of the body in Schwitters' work. One possible explanation lies in his declared predilection for a radical type of abstraction in his visual work, which prompted him to abstain from representing the experiential world in any way that may seem even remotely naturalistic. For a discussion of Hannah Höch's deployment of the grotesque body as a critique of contemporary scientific discourses see Thomas Haakenson's dissertation: *Grotesque Visions: Art, Science, and Visual Culture in Early-Twentieth-Century Germany.* University of Minnesota 2006.

Wortkunst circle. While these inserts can at times be read as a humorous commentary on the narrated events, for the most part they appear unrelated to the main story. The incongruity produced by the clash of the collaged elements engenders a comic effect that helps deflate the gravity of the narration, but also bestows on it a chilling quality. This mix of tragic and comic elements works to block an immediate moral response that would be congruous with the outrage elicited by the gory violence in *Die Zwiebel* or the disgust provoked by the crass descriptions in *Franz Müllers Drahtfrühling*. And this is perhaps the most unsettling feature of these stories. On the one hand, they recount events that clearly violate established normative frameworks and are bound to provoke strong emotional reactions. On the other, they not only fail to thematize this violation in moral terms, but also befuddle the reader by defusing moral judgment through black humor.

This is not to say that the narratives espouse the standpoint of a complacent or celebratory amoralism. Rather, their lack of an explicit moral standpoint directs the reader's attention to montage and its effects. Specifically, Schwitters' tales present and enact an understanding of montage as an innovative principle of artistic intervention that also allows for rethinking subjectivity and agency – a connection emblematically drawn in the passage from Tzara's manifesto I quoted at the onset. Paraphrasing one of Jonathan Crary's central arguments in *Techniques of the Observer*, one can maintain that montage is not just a symptom of the transformed field of perception available to a subject whose historical status remains unchanged.[37] Rather, montage reflects a reconceptualization of subjectivity that proceeds from an awareness of the lack of ontological intactness of experience and the body that was produced by the war. This awareness engenders an exploration of embodied subjectivity that departs from the dualistic model of the bounded, intact body conceived as the receptacle for a loftier, spiritual side with which it finds itself in permanent tension. The grotesque helps to direct attention to the materiality of the body outside this dualism and turns it into a starting point for a wide-ranging inquiry into possible options for reshaping subjectivity.

Where this reshaping involves violence or suffering, this is provocatively investigated within an epistemic horizon that pointedly avoids invoking a specific normative framework. Schwitters' collaged body offers a medium for examining discourses that prescribe a violent refashioning of the individual – discourses that had currency both before and after the war. Alves Bäsenstiel, Schwitters' prototype of a cold persona, attains agency after willingly subjecting

---

[37] See the first chapter of Crary's *Techniques of the Observer* for the study's overarching argument regarding the ways in which the ascent of new technologies and instruments of vision in the course of the nineteenth century correlated with a realignment of the prevalent understanding of visuality and subjectivity. Pp. 1–24.

himself to a ritual that entails his physical disemboweling and reassembling. The final implications of his empowerment remain ambiguous, as the reader is left unable to decide whether Bäsenstiel is a messiah or rather just the new tyrant. In this respect, a comparison with Jünger's cold-blooded depiction of steely male subjectivity forged in existential combat is highly instructive. Jünger's portrayal of violence as purifying ritual and beautiful spectacle is bound to underplay its effects in order to foreground the positive moment of empowerment.[38] Schwitters' grotesque portrayal of the disassembled body instead relies on an ambivalent ending to prevent the montage procedure from being evaluated in terms of some heroic outcome. In so doing, it focuses attention on the violence the procedure engenders.[39]

This raises the question of what broader implications are to be drawn from Schwitters' deployment of the trope of montage in the two tales. Montage here serves as a hybrid ideological perspective, one that is primarily aesthetic, in the sense that it connotes a principle of artistic production. Yet it also suggests a distinctive cognitive vantage point, in this specific instance, a way of seeing that draws on and literalizes contemporary discourses concerned with refashioning identity. Its grotesque portrayal of the violated body acknowledges and problematizes the heightened threshold of acceptable violence that characterizes these discourses, but refuses to judge it in terms of the normative framework of late-nineteenth century humanism, which attributes violence to an inability to control the instinctual side of human nature. It also steers clear of the materialist pathos that subscribes to a biological or physiological understanding of violence as the ineluctable and perhaps even salutary release of repressed aggression, a standpoint that easily lends itself to an indiscriminate glorification of violence as a source of regenerative self-expression. Instead its ethical contribution lies, paradoxically, in blocking moral judgment via grotesque strategies that thematize the absence of an adequate ethical frame of reference, which it presents as a challenge rather than a condition to be mourned.

Schwitters' refusal to adjudicate the question of violence in terms of a late-idealistic or biological framework shows that this question can no longer be adequately explained by drawing on an essentialist understanding of immutable human nature, if it ever could have been. His discourse effectively resituates the question of violence within the arena of political behavior, thus anticipating Hannah Arendt's cautionary statement that

---

[38] For an analysis of depictions of violence in Jünger's work see Andreas Huyssen: Fortifying the Heart Totally: Ernst Jünger's Armored Texts. In: *New German Critique* 59 (1993). Special Issue on Ernst Jünger. Pp. 3–23.

[39] This cool emphasis on violence marks the distance that separates Schwitters' protagonist from Lethen's type of the cool persona. In Schwitters' account the violence perpetrated on the body is not swept under the rug but rather literalized and exhibited in a grotesque fashion.

neither violence nor power is a natural phenomenon, that is, a manifestation of the life process; they belong to the political realm of human affairs whose essentially human quality is guaranteed by man's faculty of action.[40]

The resonance with Arendt's account also helps to cast into sharp relief the limitations of Schwitters' portrayal of political life. In her apprehensive analysis of the deployment of violence as a legitimate political tool in the decolonization movement and the student protests of the 1960s, Arendt explains this higher tolerance for violence by pointing to the perceived frustration of political action in modern societies dominated by faceless and unaccountable bureaucracies. Whether one agrees or rather takes issue with Arendt's appraisal of violence as a subordinate and limited instrument that needs to be deployed sparingly lest it destroys the political power it is supposed to serve, one would be hard pressed to find an even remotely comparable analysis of the relation between power, violence, and politics in Schwitters' tales. In both narratives, political life appears as an unsavory domain of dishonesty and unabashed self-interest. The revolution unleashed by Müller's appearance is not caused by unsustainable social or material conditions; it is also utterly devoid of ideological content. By the same token, neither the regicide that ensues from Bäsenstiel's disembowelment nor the sleazy and nonsensical behavior of the participants in the parliamentary session recounted in chapter two of *Franz Müllers Drahtfrühling* offer the least glimpse of emancipatory politics.

The political harangue held by Bäsenstiel in *Franz Müllers Drahtfrühling*, which parodically echoes the discourse of Dadaist activists like Richard Huelsenbeck, gives a clear indication of what is ultimately at stake in Schwitters' bleak and oversimplifying portrayal of political life. Here Bäsenstiel recycles the acerbic, confrontational word games perfected by Zurich Dada to rehash tired Expressionist clichés protesting the war and celebrating the virtues of humanity and world-wide peace (*Werk* 2:39). This caricaturing portrayal of Dadaist politics shows that Schwitters' narratives are not so much concerned with providing a reading of the revolutionary events that shook Germany at the end of the war as in settling the score with militant Dadaists like Huelsenbeck and Grosz by exposing their disingenuous political aspirations. At the same time, what makes these narratives significant is not their limited portrayal of current political events, but rather their avant-garde amalgamation of cognitive, aesthetic, and ethical considerations made possible by the perspective of montage. This hybrid perspective engenders an exploration of new models of subjectivity and agency predicated on an acceptance of the constructed and inessential quality of individual identity. In addition, the montage technique that formally shapes the narratives engenders grotesque effects that call

---

[40] Hannah Arendt: *On Violence*. San Diego, CA: Harcourt Brace & Company 1969. P. 82.

attention to the lack of an adequate normative framework for evaluating the violence perpetrated in the name of discourses that call for a rebirth of the individual. The violent consequences of these discourses are also investigated via a montage procedure that affects the body directly. This troubling actualization of heroic subjectivity is contrasted to an alternative, nonviolent, and non-heroic model of agency, which is associated with artistic subjectivity as the instantiation of *Merz*, Schwitters' own conceptualization of artistic montage.

In closing I would like to underscore the distinctive cognitive import of the understanding of montage enacted in Schwitters' tales. Montage in the early phase of Weimar culture is commonly discussed as a set of devices whose timeliness lies in its ability to give expression to the transformed perception of modern life, as marked by dislocation, incongruity, fragmentation, and sensory overload.[41] The underlying premise of this account is a theory of mimesis, one that no longer endorses some form of illusionism, to be sure, but nonetheless postulates a motivated relation between the formal qualities of montage (jaggedness, disjointedness, lack of closure) and corresponding, perceived qualities of modern experience. The understanding I have illustrated in my discussion of Schwitters differs from this account. Its emphasis lies in the ability attributed to montage practices to present something not yet seen or experienced, based on visualizing the effects of discourses concerned with refashioning subjectivity.[42] This is not a utopian exercise; it does not entail projecting a desirable vision onto an imagined non-place. It is more an experiment that presents a state of affairs that does not exist in the given form, yet is offered to perception in the interest of expanding knowledge and judgment.

---

[41] This argument has been advanced under various guises. Following Adorno, Peter Bürger suggests that the moment of incongruity that characterizes montage practices dramatizes the unresolved contradictions of reality under the aegis of mature capitalism. Bürger: *Theorie*. Pp. 105–106; *Theory*. Pp. 77–78. In her study of Hannah Höch, Maud Lavin suggests that the disjointedness and incoherence of montage correlates with the fragmentation of everyday experience in Weimar culture. Maud Lavin: *Cut with the Kitchen Knife: The Weimar Photomontages of Hannah Höch*. New Haven: Yale University Press 1993. Pp. 47–48. This argument is echoed in Dorothea Dietrich's study of Schwitters, who asserts that Schwitters' collages and watercolors offer a medium for representing the chaos and fragmentation of experience in Weimar culture. At the same time, they seek to restore to it a sense of totality and a hierarchical order. Dorothea Dietrich: *The Collages of Kurt Schwitters: Tradition and Innovation*. Cambridge: Cambridge University Press 1993. Pp. 93–96, 106.

[42] For this suggestion I draw on Matthew Teitelbaum's assertion that "montage practice sought not merely to represent the real (as Cubism did through the integration of new material) but, also, to extend the idea of the real to something not yet seen". Matthew Teitelbaum: Preface. In: *Montage and Modern Life: 1919–1942*. Ed. by Matthew Teitelbaum. Boston: The Massachusetts Institute of Technology Press 1992. Pp. 6–19. Here: P. 8.

Peter M. McIsaac

Preserving the Bloody Remains: Legacies of Violence in Austria's Heeresgeschichtliches Museum

This essay examines attempts by the Heeresgeschichtliches Museum (HGM) to bring Austria's violent past into productive relationship with the present. The essay proceeds by considering the museum as an institution that seeks to shape key societal discourses by telling stories with objects. In analyzing the museum's strategies, it argues that problems of violence inherent in the museum's program and the history it treats, prevent the HGM from rescuing the unrealized potential of the Austrian past. The essay demonstrates this by generating a genealogy of the radically different purposes to which key objects in the museum's holdings have been put in varying historical periods. After presenting this genealogy in the first two parts of the paper, in the final section I explore whether alternative strategies might exist for dealing with the problems of violence inherent in the museum's program.

In Gerhard Roth's *Eine Reise in das Innere von Wien*, Vienna's Heeresgeschichtliches Museum (HGM) serves as an indispensable vehicle for exposing Austria's violent "other history". "Die österreichische Geschichte ist eine gewalttätige", Roth writes,

> auch wenn es nicht den Anschein hat und alles verklärt und im Dreivierteltakt dargeboten oder, so nicht anders möglich, in zwölftonreihige Kammermusik zersplittert und in atonalen Opernarien zu Gehör gebracht wird.[1]
> [Austrian history is a violent one, even if it does not appear to be and everything is transfigured and offered in three-quarter time or, if nothing else is possible, fragmented into twelve-tone chamber music and presented to the ear in atonal opera arias.]

In contrast to the presentation of Austrian history as a history of high aesthetic culture, the war museum's artifacts and narratives help dispel Roth's sense that Austria wishes to view itself as a society lacking a significantly violent past. For Roth, notions that the Habsburgs preferred to pursue happily by marriage what other rulers had to seek by warfare (thinking of the Habsburg motto, "Bella gerant alii, tu felix Austria nube!")[2] or that Austria was only ever serious about cultivating genius "im Dreivierteltakt" blunt awareness of

---

[1] Gerhard Roth: *Eine Reise in das Innere von Wien. Essays*. Frankfurt am Main: Fischer 1991. P. 185. Subsequent references will be made parenthetically. Translations are mine unless otherwise noted.
[2] This phrase roughly translates as, "Others may lead wars, you, happy Austria, marry".

the brutality and militaristic spirit that also shaped this land and its culture. Devoted as it is to capturing the military's role in Austrian history, the HGM represents a setting where Austria's belligerence against real and imagined enemies forms the backbone of the museum's explicit presentation.

Yet this presentation likewise operates according to specific, historically rooted aesthetic strategies that require the museum to be approached in terms of its own configuration of aesthetics and violence. On one level, the displays themselves are configured so as to appear beautiful wherever possible. In addition to appearing in an architectural program executed using sumptuous materials such as marble and artistically executed frescoes and mosaics, the displays contain artifacts such as paintings and certain types of weaponry selected wherever possible for both historical authenticity and beauty deriving from high levels of artistic performance or craftsmanship. On another level, the museum's presentations construct narratives that "beautify" the historical record, both by emphasizing views of war centered on leadership and heroism and by excluding any number of complicating perspectives. Though exclusions inhere to practically any narrative construct – and as will become clear, telling stories with objects leads to certain kinds of exclusions and invisibilities – this official state museum manipulates the past in a recognizably Austrian, bureaucratic fashion: by expunging the record of certain crimes and their victims.[3] Where blood is not shown to flow explicitly in this museum, its traces nonetheless remain detectable by particular modes of museological critique.

To develop such a critique, I will consider the museum as an institution that seeks to shape key societal discourses. In some approaches, museums are thought to accomplish this by naturalizing certain basic narratives that underwrite a culture's core beliefs. In museum settings, these core beliefs are grounded through the exposition and exposure of corroborating objects and texts that work to elaborate the basic narratives in terms of larger cultural stories.[4] Theoretically, the stories museums tell with objects thus potentially

---

[3] Roth writes: "Die österreichische Geschichte ist eine gewalttätige, auch wenn es nicht den Anschein hat [. . .]. Die Gewalttätigkeit, und sei es die einer Bürokratenarmee, die mit spitzen Schreibfedern und blaublütiger, schwarzer und später brauner Tinte den stillen Krieg gegen das freie Denken führte, ist in der Buchhaltung des Landes festgehalten, auch wenn noch so viele Konten gefälscht, durch Tintentod und Radierkunst unsichtbar gemacht". ["Austrian history is violent, even when it appears not to be [. . .]. The violence of Austrian history, and be it that of a bureaucrat army that waged war with sharp fountain pens and blue-blooded, black, and later brown ink, has been registered in the country's ledgers. This is so even if so many accounts have been forged, made invisible through a kind of killing accomplished on the level of writing, as a kind of erasure".] (Roth 185–186).
[4] Mieke Bal: *Double Exposures: The Subject of Cultural Analysis*. London: Routledge 1996. P. 5.

structure thought and behavior, insofar as they provide environments for grounding the veracity of the basic narratives societies wish to tell about themselves. But while the stories told by museum displays no doubt affect some visitors in this manner, the complexity of museum environments and visitors' individual interests in viewing them leaves a very real possibility that several alternative, and in fact conflicting, narratives can be generated by any one museum layout. This condition raises important questions about the likelihood that a given visitor will reach certain conclusions about a museum display, but it does not mean that museum displays can mean just anything. Museum environments are the product of agents who select, order, and frame contexts that make certain notions more likely to be thought relative to others. As such, they can be evaluated in terms of the strategies they employ to stabilize certain meanings over others. In the case of the HGM, questions can be raised about the extent to which the museum displays can in fact shape societal thinking in the ways curators expect.

Over the past decade, the discourses supported by the HGM have been increasingly framed in terms of Austria's Second Republic and its place in a united, peaceful Europe. That is to say, the current republican political order increasingly provides the points of orientation for regarding the Austrian past. Nowhere has this become clearer than in the debates about whether to build a so-called "Haus der Geschichte" ["House of History"].[5] Though this institution

---

[5] The earliest proposals for such a museum reach back to 1988, arising in the wake of the Waldheim affair and the fiftieth anniversary of the Anschluss in 1938. Though originally a project initiated by Leon Zelman, the head of the Jewish Welcome Committee and conceived of as a "House of Europe" dedicated to tolerance and antifascism, it was eventually transformed into a project that, while acknowledging the Holocaust, would focus primarily on providing an Austrian national narrative. A turning point in this development was the study conducted by Stefan Karner and Manfried Rauchensteiner, then the director of the HGM. The project received official state backing as a "Haus der Geschichte" in Wolfgang Schüssel's 2003 *Regierungsprogramm*, with proposals accelerating after the series of temporary exhibitions on Austria since 1955 made Austria's recent history seem urgently topical. The government favored making the Arsenal into a historical museum complex as late as March 2006 until stiff opposition from historians and politicians forced rethinking the project. On the merits of a Holocaust-focused conception, see Anton Pelinka, Sabine Juffinger, Ekkehard Kappler, Stephan Laske, and Claudia Meister-Scheytt: 'Die Geschichte verstehen, um die Gegenwart zu begreifen.' Machbarkeitsstudie für 'Haus der Toleranz' dem Parlament vorgelegt. In: Parlamentskorrespondenz Blatt 527 (26.11.1999). Wien: Austrian Parliament 2006. http://www.parlinkom.gv.at/portal/page?_pageid=908,469763&_dad=portal&_schema=PORTAL. For the government's position and funding proposal in 2003, see Regierungsprogramm der Österreichischen Bundesregierung für die XXII. Gesetzgebungsperiode. Wien: 2003. P. 34. http://www.austria.gv.at/site/3354/default.aspx.

would focus on events after the signing of the Austrian State Treaty in 1955, such a museum would likely need to reach back into the nineteenth century – probably to 1848, if not 1804 – in order to tell Austria's national story.[6] This has meant that the HGM and its version of the past have figured prominently in the debates, with some proposals going so far as to turn the entire Arsenal complex into an array of historical museums (a Viennese "Museum Island", in emulation of the one in Berlin) that would extend the historical narrative as begun in the HGM. What recommends the HGM for this task, beyond the fact that the museum finds its origins in the aftermath of 1848, is the claim that the HGM provides a narrative of events that productively situates past regimes relative to today's republican democracy.

In the minds of its directors, visitors to the museum are supposed to come away with the insight that the Austrian past offers united Europe the multinational state of the Habsburg Empire as a model for peaceful, multi-national coexistence. Already in 1960, the HGM's director Heinz Zatschek argued that the museum's configuration imparted this view of history when he wrote,

Das Heeresgeschichtliche Museum in Wien vereint in seinen Schausälen Leistungen der verschiedenen Völker auf den verschiedensten Gebieten: des Kriegshandwerks, der Gewerbe, der Künste, der Forschung, durch Jahrhunderte hindurch. In ihm wird deutlicher als anderswo sichtbar, dass die Völker Europas eine Schicksalsgemeinschaft bilden [. . .], [das Museum] wirbt für Europa.[7]
[The Military History Museum in Vienna unites in its galleries the achievements of various peoples in the most diverse areas: in the artisanry of war, the trades, the arts, research, throughout centuries. In this museum it is clearer than elsewhere that the peoples of Europe share a common destiny [. . .]; [the museum] campaigns for Europe.]

By enabling the salvage of a useful past from the ruins of Austrian empire, the museum retains, for Zatschek, pertinence for today's peaceful Europe. This is a view that a recent director, Manfried Rauchensteiner, has sought to amplify, albeit without seeking to instrumentalize the past.[8]

---

[6] Most proposals in circulation argue for the need for a larger historical sweep than 1955. See for instance the "roadmap" for developing the museum. Haus der Geschichte der Republik Österreich. Umsetzungsstrategie (roadmap). Wien: Dokumentationsarchiv des österreichischen Widerstandes 2006. http://www.doew.at/frames.php?/thema/haus_der_geschichte/roadmap.html.
[7] Heinz Zatschek: *Das Heeresgeschichtliche Museum in Wien*. Graz: Böhlau 1960. Pp. 28–30.
[8] See Rauchensteiner's comment on the potential that relating the past in terms of present-day priorities could become an exercise in manipulation. Manfried Rauchensteiner: Das Heeresgeschichtliche Museum in Wien. In: *Der Krieg und seine Museen*. Ed. by Hans-Martin Hinz. Frankfurt am Main: Campus 1997. Pp. 57–72. Here: Pp. 62–63.

This essay seeks to question the museum's ability to achieve this goal. In raising questions about the museum, I am not disputing, at least not in the abstract, that the Austro-Hungarian multi-ethnic state might well offer lessons for today's Europe. Rather, I will argue that for formal reasons, the HGM in its present configuration cannot adequately rescue the unrealized potential of that past. This occurs in large part because certain problems of violence inherent in the museum's program and the history it treats remain unaddressed. In thinking through this problem, I wish to focus on the objects that, by all accounts, have formed the notional center of the museum's holdings for much of the twentieth century: the car, bloodied uniform and other artifacts from Franz Ferdinand's June 28, 1914 assassination in Sarajevo. These objects constitute the imaginary and ritual core of the museum. Metonymically standing in for the historical-cultural-political context leading to the fall of the Austro-Hungarian Empire, the objects operate as a kind of historical and emotive pivot point where the disastrous violence of the Austrian past ostensibly becomes transformed into lessons for a non-violent Austrian and European present and future. Yet, as I wish to demonstrate through a genealogy of the museum, these objects have previously occupied such a pivot point earlier in the twentieth century, and in fact in order to serve very different, indeed violent, ends. In the National Socialist incarnations of the museum, the traces of bombs, bullets and blood visibly preserved in the Sarajevo artifacts was mobilized to oblige Austrians to accept and perpetuate further bloodshed against all its past and present, internal and external enemies. After presenting this genealogy in the first two parts of the paper, in the final section I explore whether alternative strategies might exist for dealing with the problems of violence inherent in the museum's program.

I

If Franz Ferdinand's bloody uniform, car and other effects were not always the HGM's most prized possessions, this is probably only because the Archduke was not yet born when the museum was first opened in 1857. In fact the first purpose-built museum on Austrian soil, the "Waffenmuseum" ["Weapons Museum"] as it was then known, arose as an integral part of the Arsenal, a massive complex designed to address the tactical and cultural aftermath of the 1848 revolution. Having had to fire on fellow Austrians after losing control of Vienna in October 1848, the military faced low morale and logistical challenges once it had defeated uprisings in Prague, Italy, Hungary and Vienna. Though debate continued for some years as how best to defend against subsequent uprisings, the revolution had, by all accounts, redefined the city and how its layout might aid "internal enemies" (peasants, the working classes, ethnic nationalists). Modernization of the military's facilities, coupled with a shift to an emphasis on troops' mobility, reshaped Vienna's urban fabric.

The initial cornerstone of this transformation of Vienna's layout and conception was the Arsenal. This massive complex, consisting of barracks, arms factories, a church and the "Waffenmuseum", took shape in lock step with the transformation of Vienna from a medieval fortress to a modern city ruled by the principle of mobility in both commerce and defense. On the military side, the principle led to the construction of new barracks, armories and the replacement of medieval fortifications with broad arteries such as the Ringstraße that would, in the words of Carl Schorske, "minimize barricading opportunities for potential rebels" and "facilitate the swift movement of men and materiel to any point of danger".[9] But while the Arsenal provided the new base from which troops would be able to sweep onto the Ringstraße in times of emergency and in and out of the city via either the nearby East or South rail stations, its buildings simultaneously provided a testing ground for some of the architects who would later build the historicist monumental buildings on the Ringstraße.[10] Ludwig Förster and Theophil Hansen, the latter the designer of Austria's neo-classicist parliament and five other buildings on the Ringstraße, pioneered a Byzantine historicist idiom as lead architects of the Army museum. Architects August von Siccardsburg and Eduard van der Null, designers of the Staatsoper, likewise tested historicist styles in the Arsenal.

The Arsenal and museum therefore emerged from the same modern cultural and political nexus as the Ringstraße. But while the Ringstraße was less visibly dictated solely by military needs following the Army's defeats in the 1850s and 1860s, in the museum it has managed to foreground a view of its contributions to Austria's cultural and dynastic achievements. The convergence of military and non-military exigencies in shaping Vienna's civil institutions makes the Arsenal and its museum an apt confirmation of Michel Foucault's point, elaborated in his lectures at the College de France in 1975–76, that modern civil society merely proves to be the continuation of war by other means.[11] On the face of it, the cultural function of the museum until the end of the Nazi era would seem to support at least some of Foucault's

---

[9] Carl E. Schorske: *Fin-de-siècle Vienna: Politics and Culture*. New York: Knopf 1979. Pp. 30–31.
[10] Peter Schubert: *Das Wiener Arsenal. Ein historischer Überblick*. Wien: Brüder Hollinek 1975. P. 16.
[11] Foucault sets this thesis out in reversal of Clausewitz's dictum. See Michel Foucault: *Society Must Be Defended: Lectures at the Collège de France 1975–1976*. Trans. by David Macey. New York: Picador 2003. Pp. 15–21. See also Beatrice Hanssen: *Critique of Violence: Between Poststructuralism and Critical Theory*. New York: Routledge 2000. Pp. 16–29.

major claims about war. Yet the steps necessary to achieve a reversal of that history's trend in the museum's postwar incarnation might well also reveal something about the place of violence in an Austrian civil society that is, as Roth would have it, ruled by aesthetics bordered by violence.

Knowledge and beautification of the military's contribution to the shaping of Austrian civil society – in today's terminology, an affirmative identity – was precisely what the museum was to instill in the military using then developing exhibition techniques. Indebted to the architectural program Schinkel used to sacralize sculpture and painting in his 1830 Berlin art museum (today known as the Altes Museum), the Viennese museum used two halls and a massive stairway where Schinkel had used a rotunda. As in Schinkel's rotunda, which was designed as a sacred space that would cleanse visitors' minds before they encountered art, the HGM's entry halls were meant to instill respect and fascination for Austrian military leaders and traditions.[12] Today, in the first hall, the Hall of Military Strategists ["Feldherrenhalle"], the visitor passes under fifty-six six-foot tall marble statues of Austria's greatest military leaders (the original plan called for fifty-two), before ascending the staircase into the large Hall of Fame ["Ruhmeshalle"]. This three-sectioned room is adorned with frescos representing significant moments in Austrian military history. These moments were subsequently rendered palpable by holdings from the Imperial weapons and art collections, objects whose authenticity, fine craftsmanship, and auratic uniqueness were meant to reinforce the veracity of museum's historical sweep. All told, the museum emerged as a sacred temple to the Army, an institution designed to reassure soldiers that they stood on the right side of history.

It is not productive to speak of the HGM today as a sacred temple to the military, though continuities can be detected in many other emphases. For one thing, the museum continues to be an official state institution, administered by the Austrian ministry of defense. For Manfried Rauchensteiner, one of the museum's recent directors, its mission is to function as Austria's "zentrales historisches Museum", making it a national museum with the ultimate goal of supplying a historical narrative for the Austrian Republic.[13] This mission, according to its directors, has required that the museum adhere to its tradition of presenting only authentic materials. As Rauchensteiner puts it,

> Dabei sollte allerdings die Linie des gesamten Hauses, nämlich herausragendes historisches Museum zu sein, unbedingt beibehalten werden, das heißt: Nur die ausgesuchtesten Objekte und die Originale bei der Ausstellungstätigkeit zu berücksichtigen. (67)

---

[12] Peter Schubert and Wolfgang Schubert: *Das Wiener Arsenal*. Klosterneuburg: Mayer 2001. Pp. 23–24.
[13] Rauchensteiner: Das Heeresgeschichtliche Museum in Wien. P. 58.

[In the process, the profile of the entire house – that it is to be an outstanding historical museum – certainly must be maintained unconditionally, which means: only the most exquisite and original objects can be taken into account for display purposes.]

The museum's past traditions require that its current displays not only be verifiably factual, but in fact unique and most exquisite. As I will show, this limiting criterion can become a self-fulfilling prophecy when it comes to defining which areas the museum can conceivably address and a source of suppression in its own right.

For now, I want to focus on those objects every director and catalog has held to be the museum's most exquisite: the car, bloody uniform (Figure 13.1) and other objects recovered from Franz Ferdinand's assassination in Sarajevo. These objects are still the objects of considerable state investment, with items from the assassination still hotly sought after by the museum. In 2004, it obtained Franz Ferdinand's bloodied undershirt and the ostensible murder weapon, which the museum insisted would need to undergo rigorous testing for authenticity. Requiring both verified provenance and forensic analysis that would, among other things, match the blood on Ferdinand's uniform to the blood on the undershirt, the museum's approach to authenticity underscored the correctness of the criteria it has used to collect and preserve its items.[14] The emphasis on utter caution in changing its holdings likewise serves to illustrate the commitment the state and the administration has to what it calls "quality". The museum accordingly saw fit only in 1995 to remove the black drapes set around the precious items before World War II.[15] Rauchensteiner noted, "Ich ordnete damit gewissermaßen ein Ende der Staatstrauer an" ["I decreed in a certain sense an end to state mourning"],[16] indicating that the state's presentation of these objects needed to become "more lively" in order to uphold the importance of the objects, both for the museum's larger narrative and its status as "authenticity machine".

But while the museum's ability to guarantee authenticity and quality works to imbue its presentation of the past with an aura of truth, the use of these criteria to attract visitors complicates its avowed mission of teaching about the Austrian past. In marketing campaigns, museum staff plays on the historical uniqueness of their prized objects, translating authenticity into spectacle. In summer 1999, for instance, posters proclaiming "Wir haben das Original!" ["We have the original!"] could be found all over Vienna. Outfitted with images of Franz Ferdinand's car, the posters sought to remind passers-by that

---

[14] Sammlung zum Attentat erweitert. In: Österreichischer Rundfunk. Wien 16 June 2004. http://wien.orf.at/oesterreich.orf?read=detail&channel=1&id=325761.
[15] See also Roth's description. P. 182.
[16] Rauchensteiner: Das Heeresgeschichtliche Museum in Wien. P. 67.

275

Figure 13.1 Uniform in which Franz Ferdinand was assassinated. Photo credit: Erich Lessing / Art Resource, NY.

the museum promised encounters with artifacts of assured significance.[17] In similar fashion, a more recent pamphlet promotes the museum as the place for a brush with "Weltgeschichte" ["world history"], in a building that is itself "eines der bedeutendsten historischen Museen der Welt" ["one of the most significant historical museums in the world"] as well as the "älteste[..]

---

[17] The phrasing plays on the Coca Cola slogan, "It's the real thing!".

Historismusgebäude[] der Stadt" ["the oldest example of historicist architecture in the city"]. In both forms of promotion, the museum's high standards of preservation promise singular forms of event culture, a place where the museum's version of authentic "Ereignisgeschichte" ["event-oriented history"] is thought capable of transforming events in one's own life and memory.

Though there might be nothing wrong per se in attempting to arouse visitor curiosity, visitors who might respond to such a campaign or otherwise find these objects fascinating might not, in the current display environment, necessarily interpret them in ways that conform to the stated intentions of museum directors. In Gerhard Roth's text, the museum's information officer, Oberst Krach, draws on his own desires and experiences when he gives tours, stating that "Ich persönlich brauche einen historischen Schauer" ["personally, I need an historical shiver"] as a motivation for encountering the objects. As Krach observes, Ferdinand's car and uniform clearly serve as exemplary objects that deliver an "historical shudder". He exclaims, "Der Aufenthalt in diesem Raum zählt zu den Höhepunkten jeder Führung. Wir stehen vor den stummen Zeugen des Mordes in Sarajewo" ["a visit to this room counts among the highpoints of every tour. We are standing in front of the silent witnesses to the murder in Sarajevo"]. What Sarajevo means remains unelaborated, however, with Krach stating only, "Damit der Stellenwert dieses Ereignisses klar ist, war die Ermordung des Thronfolgerpaares der unmittelbare Anlass zum Ersten Weltkrieg". ["so that the value of this event is clear, the assassination of the heir to the throne and his wife was the immediate cause of the First World War"]. Instead of historical detail, the real charge of these objects results from Krach's attempt to get visitors to reenact the bloody details of the assassination in the mind's eye:

> Der erste Schuss durchschlug die rechte Bordwand [des Wagens] und tötete die Gemahlin des Thronfolgers durch einen Bauchschuss. Gleich aber krachte der zweite, traf den Thronfolger in den Hals und zerfetzte ihm die rechte Schlagader. Was der erste Schuss angerichtet hat, können Sie sich mit eigener Phantasie vorstellen. [. . .] Wir suchen den zweiten Treffer auf der Uniform, der ihren Gemahl Franz Ferdinand von Österreich tötete. [. . .] In Verlängerung meines Zeigestabes blicken Sie bitte auf die Uniform. [. . .] Da sehen Sie unter der rechten Kragenstelle ein ganz kleines Einschussloch. Dort trat das tödliche Projektil in den Körper ein. Das Blut rann aus der Wunde in einem dünnen Strom, unter der Uniform von rechts nach links hinunter, sickerte auf der linken Brustseite, also ganz wo anders durch den Stoff und färbte die Uniform dunkelrot. [. . .] Der Generalshut ist stark beschädigt von Andenkenjägern – die Uniform noch deutlich behaftet mit Blutspuren.[18]
>
> [The first shot penetrated the right side wall [of the car] and killed the wife of the heir to the throne with a bullet to the stomach. Immediately, however, the crack of the second shot was heard that hit the heir in the throat and ripped his artery to

[18] Roth. Pp. 183, 184.

shreds. Using your own imagination you can imagine what the first shot brought about. [. . .] We will now look for the trace of the second shot on the uniform, the shot that killed her husband Franz Ferdinand of Austria. [. . .] Following the tip of my pointer please look at the uniform. [. . .] You will see there, under the right collar point, a quite small entry hole. The deadly projectile penetrated the body there. Blood ran out of the wound in a thin stream downwards from right to left under the uniform, it pooled under the left side of the chest, in a completely different place [from the actual wound] and where it colored the uniform a dark red. [. . .] The general's hat has been badly damaged by souvenir hunters – the uniform is still markedly stained with blood.]

The late twentieth-century mental reenactment of the bloodletting recalls the efforts of every catalog from 1941 to the present to draw attention to the blood stains, cuts and other traces of suffering not only on the uniform jacket (Figure 13.1), but also on Ferdinand's pants and hat. In this context, the flow of blood functions as the emotive signature of an event of tragic proportions: the bloody reenactment in the visitor's imagination is the image that metonymically stands in for the immense loss of life in World War I. Indeed, since Krach offers no further detail on the subject, the question arises as to whether the emotive charge of the mental reenactment is necessarily directed at any particular interpretation of history. Though the museum has delivered on its promise of satisfying curiosity with a relic from "world history", visitors might take away little more than a scene of bloody gore. Why something more is necessary to mobilize the violent past for peaceful ends is revealed by examining past attempts to make these objects bear on the present.

II

The investment of the bloodied uniform and car with pivotal meaning has a genealogy. The objects first entered the museum in 1914, though how they were precisely valorized is difficult to ascertain prior to 1938. By all accounts, the financial and planning difficulties prevented World War I material from being rapidly assimilated into the previous holdings, although a few rooms were eventually opened (a painting gallery in 1923, World War I ordinance in 1934, and a special exhibit on Franz Josef in 1937).[19] While catalogs from 1960, 2000 and 2005 mention that the car rested in the Feldherrnhalle from 1914 to 1944 (and little else), it is worth noting that the Franz Josef exhibition was held in the ceremonial rooms and that no extant catalog mentions either car or uniform, or attempts to link them to the pathos and nationalism they otherwise try to evoke.[20] Whatever feelings might have been stimulated for

---

[19] Isonzofront Saal 1 und 2. In: *Katalog des Heeresmuseums*. Wien: Verlag des Heeresmuseums 1934. Pp. 1–2.
[20] Zatschek: *Das Heeresgeschichtliche Museum in Wien*. P. 53.

visitors by the car and uniform, curators seem not to have elicited reactions to them prior to 1938. These objects begin to symbolize particular sentiments and worldviews only in their use in the Nazi era, when they formed the ritual core of the museum.

In order to grasp the centrality of these objects in the Nazi incarnation of the museum, I need to stress three things.[21] First, 1938 is a pivotal year in the history of this museum, insofar as the Nazis immediately halted work on a separate museum dedicated to World War I that was planned for the Hofburg. Without the Anschluss, the museum's present-day sweep from the sixteenth century to the present would have been lost. As Heinz Zatschek comments, "kein Zweifel, eine Ideallösung wäre auch ohne den Einmarsch der Deutschen nicht verwirklicht worden" ["There can be no doubt, an ideal solution would also not have been reached without the Germans marching in"].[22] Second, contrary to claims by postwar officials, the administrative structure of Nazi army museums did not leave the Viennese without decision-making powers.[23] Personnel in Vienna determined the directions taken by the Viennese museum according to their resources and local needs, particularly reaching the local population. By gauging visitor responses over time, staff learned that the most effective way to present their message was to couch it in terms of a historical mission Austrians seemed to identify with: the protection of European culture against peoples and cultures such as the Ottoman Empire. This message could be best presented by drawing on the museum's permanent collection, which became increasingly important over time. This contradicts the narratives offered by postwar museum directors who portray Nazi efforts as limited to the staging of temporary, propaganda exhibitions that somehow resided in the museum as some sort of alien implant that bore no relation to the standing

---

[21] In order to reach Austrian visitors, the exhibition style used in exhibitions such as "Entartete Kunst" was abandoned in favor of approaches that addressed visitors in terms of their local culture and history. Peter M. McIsaac: *Museums of the Mind: German Modernity and the Dynamics of Collecting*. University Park, Pennsylvania: Penn State University Press 2007.
[22] Zatschek: *Das Heeresgeschichtliche Museum in Wien*. P. 25.
[23] Historian Lars-H. Thümmler claims that the function of that office was primarily to advise and coordinate, especially to distribute material captured from the various fronts to the appropriate museums. That office did not, apparently, dictate that museums exchange objects or use their holdings in any particular way, only that they pursue similar overall goals with the means available to them. Lars-H. Thümmler: Das Zeughaus Berlin im Zweiten Weltkrieg. In: *Deutsches Historisches Museum*. Berlin: Deutsches Historisches Museum 2006. http://www.dhm.de/texte/zhwk2.html.

collections.[24] Yet in 1941 and again in 1943, the National Socialist leadership produced two separate catalogs covering the permanent collections as curators then viewed them. In addition to having significance on their own, the permanent collections formed a backdrop that framed the message of the temporary exhibitions, whose catalogs document that the temporary exhibitions used and referred to material from the permanent collections.

From catalogs, it becomes clear that the Nazis had made few but very telling changes to the overall collections in order to affect how exhibitions were framed by the ceremonial rooms. As such, temporary exhibitions and the permanent collection all fit into a larger narrative that attempted to cast the past struggles of the Austrian military as a kind of prehistory to the Nazi war effort. Under the Nazis, the Feldherrenhalle and the Ruhmeshalle were connected by a series of statues of World War I leaders, current generals, and, in the center, a bust of Hitler. With these extensions, the current Nazi military leadership was portrayed as seamlessly emanating out of the museum's celebration of homegrown military traditions. Discussing this fusion, the programmatic introduction to the 1941 catalog explains:

> In dieser Vereinigung [von Österreich und Deutschland] liegt [dem Museum] vor allem die Veranschaulichung des kaiserlichen Heeres des Ersten Reiches ob, das nach mannigfachen staatsrechtlichen Wandlungen und 300 Jahren ruhmvollen Bestandes im Herbste 1918 als gesamte bewaffnete Macht der österreichisch-ungarischen Monarchie mit dieser zerbrach.
> Verteidiger der Gemarkungen des Deutschen Reiches gegen Osten, Westen und Süden, Kolonisator Südosteuropäischen Bodens, Pionier deutscher Sprache und Kultur – diese dreifache Funktion steht auf dem Ehrenschild des alt-österreichischen Heeres – ihr diente es [. . .] bis zum letzten Pulsschlag jenes Herzens, das die kerndeutschen Stammlande der Babenberger und der Donaumonarchie mit ihrem sudetenländischen Zustrom bildeten. Das Heeresmuseum Wien ist seine Erinnerungs- und Weihestätte.
> Vom Führer, dem großen Sohn dieses Stammlandes, ins Reich, in *sein* Reich heimgeführt, haben Soldaten des einstigen Heeres unter neuen Fahnen alten Ruhm erneuert und mit ihren jungen Kameraden neuen Lorbeer in einem Maße geerntet, daß noch das Heldenlied fernster Zeiten das in seiner Größe kaum Faßliche künden wird.[25]

---

[24] See for instance Zatschek, Franz Kaindl, and Manfried Rauchensteiner et al. Zatschek: *Das Heeresgeschichtliches Museum in Wien*. Pp. 24–25. Franz Kaindl: Das Wiener Heeresgeschichtliche Museum. Ein historisches Nationalmuseum von internationaler Dimension. In: *Die Nation und ihre Museen*. Ed. by Marie-Louise Plessen. Frankfurt am Main: Campus 1992. Pp. 271–280. Here: P. 277. Manfried Rauchensteiner et al.: *Phönix aus der Asche. Zerstörung und Wiederaufbau des Heeresgeschichtlichen Museums 1844–1955*. Wien: Heeresgeschichtliches Museum/ Militärhistorisches Institut Wien 2005. Pp. 14–15.

[25] *Heeresmuseum Wien. Führer durch die Feldherren- und durch die Ruhmeshalle*. Wien: Heeresmuseum Wien 1941. Pp. 3–4.

[In this union [of Austria with Germany], it is incumbent on the museum above all else to exemplify the Imperial army of the first empire, which, in the fall of 1918 after several transformations in state form and after 300 years of glorious, continued existence as the collective armed forces of the Austrian-Hungarian monarchy, collapsed along with it.

Defender of the borders of the German Reich to the east, west and south, colonizer of the soil of south-eastern Europe, pioneer of German language and culture – this threefold function is represented on the shield of honor of the old-Austrian army – it carried out this function [. . .] until the last beat of that heart that forms the core German lands of the Babenbergs and the Danube monarchy with its Sudeten German influx. The Army Museum of Vienna is the site dedicated to its memory and consecration.

Brought home into the Reich, into *his* Reich by the Führer, the great son of this German land, soldiers of the erstwhile [Austro-Hungarian] army have renewed their old glory under new banners and have reaped new laurels with their young comrades to such an extent that the heroic song of the most distant future times will still tell of these deeds which are hardly comprehensible in their immensity.]

In keeping with fascist corporatist notions, the dual monarchy is envisioned as a vividly living body: blood pulsed through its veins until the last beat of its heart, blood that it shed in the name of protecting and upholding a particular notion of Europe.

This notion of blood was activated in a separate micronarrative that linked the display of Franz Ferdinand's car in the Feldherrenhalle to the bloody uniform in the Ruhmeshalle. Visitors encountered the car immediately in the Feldherrenhalle, which in the 1941 guide is framed with this narrative:

Kraftwagen, in dem das Thronfolgerpaar Erzherzog Franz Ferdinand und seine Gemahlin Sophie Herzogin von Honeberg am 28. Juni 1914 in Sarajewo ermordet wurde. (An der Rückseite des Wagens Spuren des ersten, erfolglosen Attentats, neben dem Wagenschlag rechts der Durchschuss des Geschosses, das die Herzogin tötete).[26]

[Automobile in which the heir Arch Duke Franz Ferdinand and his wife Sophie Duchess of Honeberg were murdered on the 28th of June in Sarajevo. (At the rear of the car traces of the first unsuccessful assassination attempt, near the car door on the right the hole from the shot that killed the Duchess).]

Much of the "work" done by the placement of the automobile was achieved without words. In depicting Ferdinand as an equal to the fifty-plus military leaders towering over visitors, the museum's spatial environment reduced the complexity of the events of June 28, making it more difficult to consider the assassination attempts to be anything other than attacks on a military figure. This framing sets the terms of all the events that follow in seemingly self-evident fashion. As an attack on its military leadership, the only appropriate response would be one of war.

[26] Ibid. P. 5.

Leaving this room, the visitor climbed the staircase and encountered Franz Ferdinand's uniform, the busts of WWI dead, and Adolf Hitler. In museological terms, the spatial sequentiality of the Sarajevo artifacts is converted into a causal relationship that articulates how one set of events follows from the other: the attack on the car resulted in the flow of blood and valiant but unsuccessful attempts to save the Crown Prince, which in turn caused the deaths of the WWI leaders placed around the room and finally the program in the present – waging war in the name of the past. By ascending through past Austrian leaders to Hitler, as I have mentioned, Austrian military history was thus figured as a precursor to the Nazi era.[27] This point was reinforced by the inflection of the blood on Franz Ferdinand's uniform:

> Die blutgetränkte Uniform des am 28. Juni 1914 in Sarajewo ermordeten Generals der Kavalerie, Admirals und Generalinspektors der gesamten bewaffneten Macht Erzherzogs Franz Ferdinand – Das Geschoß drang an der Goldborte zwischen den beiden unteren Kragen und blauem Stoff ein – wir stehen buchstäblich vor der Quelle zu den Strömen Blutes, die seither vergossen wurden.[28]
> [The blood-drenched uniform of the General of the Cavalry, of the Admiral and General Inspector of all the Armed Forces Archduke Franz Ferdinand who was murdered on June 28, 1914 – The shot penetrated between both lower collars and the blue material at the gold braid – we are literally standing before the source of the streams of blood that have been shed since then.]

By repeating date, place, and name of the archduke, this text links the uniform to information provided about the car and attacks. Within this narrative sustained by objects, the reconstruction of the bullets' path explains past and present Austrian suffering in terms of history's incursion on this body. Surrounded by the busts of fallen World War I leaders, the car and uniform become ritual objects at a crucial ideological pivot point, where the fall of Austria-Hungary is conjoined with Nazism using the metaphor of blood. By means of its past and present bloodshed, Austria is sutured into a vision of Europe maintained through an economy of violence.[29] That economy continues in the image of bloody relics from Sarajevo, with the Austrian past seeming to propagate further war and bloodshed in the present day. Constructed so as to uphold historical continuity, the Nazi era's use of the Sarajevo objects thus represents the precise inverse of what they are supposed to mean in the postwar era and provide a strikingly overt instance of war being extended to civil society through a public institution.

---

[27] Ibid. P. 6.
[28] Ibid. P. 8.
[29] A similar rhetoric is at work in the special exhibition *Kampfraum Südost: Sonderschau veranstaltet vom Chef der Heeresmuseen Wien: Juni-August 1944*. Wien: Verlag des Heeresmuseums 1944. P. 5.

III

What is remarkable about the Nazi interpretation of the Sarajevo objects is less that such a reading was attempted than that postwar officials seem to have made little effort to demonstrate its flaws. Such attempts might well have been expected given the rhetoric of radical change that accompanied the reconstructed museum, change that resulted voluntarily during the postwar political climate and involuntarily from the severe impact of the war on the museum. Official accounts make much of the constraints arising from allied looting and bombs on the remaking of the museum. As director Heinz Zatschek wrote, "es zeigte sich abermals, dass jedes Ding zwei Seiten hat. Die gute bei der Zerstörung und bei den Bergungen war die, daß man nicht irgendwo anknüpfen mußte, sondern ganz neu beginnen konnte" ["It again proved to be true that everything has two sides. The good one with respect to the destruction and the salvage was that one did not have connect up somewhere, but rather could start in a completely new manner"].[30] On an ideological level, too, the need for change was recognized. As director Franz Kaindl put it in 1991, the Nazi era represented "die entschiedenste Zäsur in der Geschichte unseres Museums" ["the most decisive caesura in the history of our museum"], implying that utter breaks with the past had been carried out.[31]

Yet it is literally difficult to see how the museological program enacts radical breaks. The car and uniform experienced relatively minor changes in their location and in phrasing on labels and in catalogs. Location-wise, car and uniform were taken from the ceremonial halls and presented in a single room that simultaneously marked the beginning of World War I and the end of the Habsburg Empire. Until 1995, this room framed the objects in the same black drape that was added to the objects before World War II. As had been the case in the Nazi era, the objects continued to be touted as the most significant of the whole museum, in some sense undercutting their relegation to a single spot in the historical sweep. Similarly, texts accompanying the objects maintained the focus on the militaristic narrative established after 1938. In 1960 the uniform's story read:

> Das tödliche Projektil aus einer 9mm Browning-Pistole des Attentäters Gavrilo Princip drang durch die Naht des Kragenansatzes unterhalb der rechtseitigen drei Generalsterne ein, zerriß die Halsvene und verletzte die Luftröhre. Die Einschnitte am linken Brustteil des Rockes, am linken Ärmel und von der Ruckseite des Kragens bis zur Taille stammen von den ärztlichen Hilfsmaßnahmen für den sterbenden Thronfolger. Der Rock ist an der Innen- und an der Vorderseite von Blut getränkt; Blutflecke sind auch an der Hose wahrzunehmen.[32]

---

[30] Zatschek: *Das Heeresgeschichtliche Museum in Wien*. P. 27.
[31] Kaindl: Das Wiener Heeresgeschichtliche Museum. P. 279.
[32] Zatschek: *Das Heeresgeschichtliche Museum in Wien*. P. 53.

[The deadly projectile from the assassin Gavrilo Princip's 9mm Browning pistol penetrated the seam of the collar below the row of general's stars on the right, it shattered the artery in the neck and damaged the windpipe. The cuts on the left portion of the chest of the jacket, on the left sleeve and from the back of the collar to the waist, stem from the medical attempts to save the dying heir to the throne. The jacket is drenched with blood on the interior and on the front; bloodstains can also be seen on the pants.]

In similar fashion to how the entry on Franz Ferdinand's car continues to highlight the traces of violence on it, this later catalog entry on the uniform employs many of the same words such as "drenched with blood". If anything, these depictions place even more emphasis on gore than did the Nazi-era installations, without, however, helping the viewer to understand how that gore necessitated a particular social order in the present. This set of emphases occurs because the gore itself has never much troubled museum directors in the way that revelations of the museum's use of gore in the name of National Socialism would seem to. It is that context of 1918–1945 that the museum renders invisible and thus harder to think about in the new arrangement, and it is because the displays are charged with obscuring the museum's history that its ability to put the past into productive relationship with the present is less effective than it might otherwise be.

An overriding concern with deflecting scrutiny from the museum's contributions to National Socialism makes sense in light of the priorities of those in charge of it from 1945–1965, Heinrich Drimmel and Heinz Zatschek. Drimmel, a prominent conservative ÖVP (Austrian People's Party) politician who served as Austria's Education Minister, had administrative control of the museum during Allied occupation (1945–55). He was unrepentant in his support of Austro-fascism, that phase of government from 1934 to 1938 in which reactionary forces outlawed the Socialist and Communist parties and by some accounts prepared the ground for the National Socialist takeover of Austria in 1938. Drimmel benefited from "Aryanization", living at Große Schiffsgasse 24 once two-thirds of its Jewish inhabitants lost their apartments there.[33] Drimmel's politics would have been a factor during the reconstruction of the museum, since, as a plaque in the Feldherrenhalle and a 2005 catalog on the museum from 1945–1955 make clear, Drimmel regarded the museum as "his"

---

[33] See Anton Pelinka and Walzer and Templ. Anton Pelinka: Austrian Identity and the "Ständestaat". In: *The Habsburg Legacy. National Identity in Historical Perspective*. Ed. by Ritchie Robertson and Edward Timms. Edinburgh: Edinburgh University Press 1994. Pp. 169–177. Here: Pp. 169–170. See also Tina Walzer and Stephan Templ: *Unser Wien. "Arisierung" auf Österreichisch*. Berlin: Aufbau 2001. P. 198.

special project.[34] Heinz Zatschek's credentials are also consistent with the notion that the museum harbored recidivist tendencies. A prolific historian and "long time supporter of Nazism" in the opinion of the Czech Academy of Sciences, Zatschek directed the Philosophical Faculty of the Prague University and its Research Libraries until 1945.[35] Though unusual for scholars, the denazification process stripped Zatschek of his Austrian citizenship and his academic credentials, which he regained in 1950 and 1955 respectively, the latter on the ground that he had continued to publish after the war. Lectures on the *Sudeten* Germans – one of Zatschek's specialties throughout his career – became a special focus by 1957, the time of his appointment as "Kustos 1. Klasse" ["Curator First Class"] of the HGM. But even if they had wished to, Drimmel and Zatschek probably would have had difficulty bringing the museum's past into the open, given the marked tendency of Austria's postwar political, military and bureaucratic entities to maintain a decorous silence with respect to the Nazi past irrespective of the personalities in particular positions.[36]

It is important to recognize the extent to which the avoidance of the period 1918–1945 has been tied to the maintenance of invisible gaps and discontinuities in the museum record. As Manfried Rauchensteiner notes, the museum decided not to collect World War II material so as not to invite undue attention.[37] Part of this motivation no doubt arose in order to avoid providing impetus for a resurgent neo-Nazism, as Rauchensteiner claims. Yet in combination with the dictate that the museum only display the most exquisite original objects, this decision also creates great difficulties when it comes to depicting events of the interwar and Nazi years, so much so that museological policy structures the decision to treat 1918–1945 as an ideological rupture with respect to the present. The question that arises is whether notional discontinuities – which might help to prevent a return to totalitarianism, racial

---

[34] The plaque is in the Feldherrenhalle. The catalog contains quotes from Drimmel, as well as photographs of his active participation in ceremonies. Rauchensteiner: *Phoenix aus der Asche*. Pp. 110–115.
[35] Vaclav Podany and Hana Barvikova: Heinz Zatschek. In: *History, Archaeology, Ethnography-Personal Papers*. Prague: Archive of the Academy of Sciences of the Czech Republic 1999. http://www.archiv.cas.cz/english/pages/histpers.htm.
[36] Wolfgang Kos: Entnazifizierung der Bürokratie. In: *Verdrängte Schuld, verfehlte Sühne. Entnazifizierung in Österreich, 1945–1955*. Ed. by Sebastian Meissl, Klaus-Dieter Mulley and Oliver Rathkolb. München: Oldenbourg 1986. Pp. 52–72. Here: P. 54. See also Oliver Rathkolb: NS-Problem und politische Restauration: Vorgeschichte und Etablierung des VdU. In: *Verdrängte Schuld, verfehlte Sühne: Entnazifizierung in Österreich, 1945–1955*. Ed. by Sebastian Meissl, Klaus-Dieter Mulley and Oliver Rathkolb. München: Oldenbourg 1986. Pp. 73–100.
[37] Rauchensteiner: Das Heeresgeschichtliche Museum. P. 67.

intolerance and genocide – are best achieved in museum space through gaps or through forms of display that might demonstrate the negative consequences of failing to understand history's full complexity. The upshot of the HGM's inability to reveal the full extent of its wartime activities has left their displays oddly ambiguous and made previous visitor knowledge the determining factor in reading the museum display in any particular way.

Changes to the installation of the Sarajevo artifacts illustrate the extent to which a visitor must be already keyed in to Austria-Hungary's multi-ethnic state form in order to recognize its contemporary relevance in the museum's displays. Since one of the ironies of Franz Ferdinand's assassination was that he supported reforms to enhance the Empire's multi-national character, the circumstances of his assassination could have helped to cue visitors to the topic. Yet only in the 1990 catalog was the issue of multi-ethnic coexistence relative to the fall of the Habsburg Empire raised at all:

> Die kulturelle und ethnische Vielfalt des großen Habsburgerreiches, das Kaiser Franz Joseph I. in eine konstitutionelle Monarchie verwandelt hat, kann *der aufmerksame Besucher* nicht nur an der in 11 Sprachen abgefaßten Formel für den Fahneneid und dem sogennanten "Farbenkastel" ablesen, den nuancenreichen Farbkennzeichen für jedes einzelne der 102 k.u.k. Infanterieregimenter und die übrigen Einheiten.
>
> Auch eine umfangreiche Bilderserie von Oskar Brüch anläßlich der ungarischen Milleniums-Ausstellung in Budapest 1896 zeigt alle Truppengattungen und "Branchen", vom Pferdehirten der Puszta-Remontierungsgestüte bis zu den Militärgeistlichen (my emphasis).[38]
>
> [*The observant visitor* can detect the cultural and ethnic diversity of the great Habsburg Empire that Emperor Franz Joseph I. transformed into a constitutional monarchy, not only in the oath of allegiance formulated in 11 languages and in the so-called "paint box", that nuance-rich color mark for each of the 102 Austro-Hungarian infantry regiments and other units.
>
> Also, a large series of pictures painted by Oskar Brüch on the occasion of the Hungarian Millennium Exhibition in Budapest in 1896 shows all the troop types and "trades", from the horse herders of Puszta studs to the military chaplains.]

According to the museum's own official text, an "observant visitor" is necessary even to notice that multi-ethic diversity factored in the military at that time, let alone understand how that issue impacted the society at large.[39] Perhaps having acknowledged this problem, the 2000 catalog goes into greater

---

[38] Liselotte Popelka: *Heeresgeschichtliches Museum Wien*. Graz: Verlag Styria 1980. Pp. 56–57.

[39] That such interpretations are possible is demonstrated by Gerhard Roth's explanation of why Sarajevo represents a tragedy from the standpoint of today's Europe, though, as Roth's text also shows, previous visitor knowledge and research culled from other sources, not to mention reading the museum *against* the grain, play a key role in reaching these conclusions (Roth. Pp. 176–177).

detail – eight sentences – on Austria's multi-nationalist heritage.[40] Yet even in this improved form, uninformed visitors will likely still lack sufficient knowledge for the museum's displays to make Austria's complicated legacies illuminate the present, particularly given latter-day marketing and tour-guide techniques that trade on the spectacle of gore preserved on the Sarajevo artifacts.

Significant changes in display and accompanying political conditions would be necessary for the museum to pursue strategies that would promote ideological rupture by demonstrating the ends to which the gore had been put in previous displays. By revealing the precise reasons why the museum and the Sarajevo artifacts proved attractive to the National Socialists, the museum could create the opportunity for visitors to differentiate between the respective visions laying claim to the Habsburg past. Accomplishing this goal in the museum setting would arguably require an approach that not only equips visitors with sufficient historical background to critique the National Socialist appropriation of the Habsburg past – something that would require a much more robust contextualization of military events than is currently the case – but one that also invites them to reflect on the museum's role in generating, and potentially manipulating, historical knowledge. It is only by abandoning the traditional, top-down presentation of the past that the contemporary HGM can show that it operates in a wholly different mode than the Nazi-era museum. For the HGM to become a better instrument of democratic engagement it would have to jettison the fiction that museum objects secure an incontrovertible narrative of the past independent of the context in which they are placed.

This kind of change might place curators in an uncomfortable position, insofar as it means relinquishing the authoritative position to which they have stubbornly clung since 1945. In some ways, however, such a shift would build on the principles under which the museum currently operates. For one thing, the past decade has seen the HGM incrementally acknowledge its activities under National Socialism. It now presents, for instance, the bust of Adolf Hitler that once adorned the Ruhmeshalle in its treatment of the World War II years. Gestures such as this would become more meaningful (and arguably less manipulative) if the museum were to explain exactly how the bust's original display laid claim to the Habsburg past and everything that the museum then represented. For another, the museum already has the "most exquisite and original" objects necessary to mount such a display, Franz Ferdinand's car and uniform. Their framing under the National Socialists could be treated using authentic but non-auratic items such as mass-produced catalogs and

---

[40] Manfried Rauchensteiner et al.: *Das Heeresgeschichtliche Museum in Wien*. Graz: Verlag Styria 2000. P. 65.

photographs. Their use would need to be balanced with the seriousness of concerns about enshrining such a problematic vision of the past, though what the museum would ultimately be prompting visitors to actively reject is not the past but a particular interpretation of it.

The likelihood of the HGM's undertaking such a new direction in its presentation of the Austrian past turns not only on curatorial willingness, but also the political implications of such a change. Such a full acknowledgement of this state museum's mobilization of the Habsburg past in the name of National Socialism would challenge core myths of the Second Republic's understanding of the Nazi era and German-speaking legacies of violence prior to 1938. To revise these myths would strike at the heart of the postwar political consensus that underwrote the Second Republic's first fifty years. As such, the museum might only be able to move once interventions such as Gerhard Roth's have prepared the discursive terrain, though the potential remains for the museum to shape itself into an instrument that brings the violent past into productive relationship with the present and future.

Index

Abitz-Schultze, Thaddäus 116
Adorno, Theodor W. 139–144, 149, 151–152, 156, 160, 188, 192–193, 265; works by Adorno: *Studien zum autoritären Charakter* / *The Authoritarian Personality* 149, 152, 156; *Dialektik der Aufklärung* / *Dialectic of the Enlightenment* 139–144, 151, 160
Agamben, Giorgio 193
Anderson, Benedict 176
Arendt, Hannah 70, 238–239, 243, 263–264; works by Arendt: *Macht und Gewalt* / *On Violence* 70, 238–239, 264
Aristotle 70, 94
Arp, Hans 255
Arquilla, John 14, 23–24
Auerbach, Erich 171
Austin, J.L. 210

Baasner, Rainer 127
Baer, Karl Ernst von 51
Bahr, Ehrhard 173, 182
Bakhtin, Mikhail 260–261
Bal, Mieke 268
Baldwin, Claire 94
Baldwin, James 183
Barker, Adam 203, 211, 215
Barner, Wilfried 174, 178–180
Bartels, Adolf 178, 180
Bartra, Roger 121
Bartsch, Kurt 157
Barvikova, Hana 284
Bataille, Georges 261
Baumann, Peter 159
Bay, Michael 240–242; works by Bay: *The Rock* 241–242
Becker, Nikolaus 57
Becker-Cantarino, Barbara 36–37
Beethoven, Ludwig van 17–19, 26; works by Beethoven: *Fidelio* 17–19, 26

Bell, Matthew 93–94
Benjamin, Walter 14, 18–20, 24, 154, 157–158, 167, 179–181, 185, 199, 202, 207–208, 210, 215–216, 218, 221–222, 224, 227–228, 231–235, 237–239, 242, 246–249; works by Benjamin: *Franz Kafka* 185; *Kleine Geschichte der Photographie* / *Little History of Photography* 231; *Das Kunstwerk im Zeitalter seiner technischen Reproduzierbarkeit* / *The Work of Art in the Age of Mechanical Reproduction* 232–233, 247–249; *Zur Kritik der Gewalt* / *On the Critique of Violence* 18–19, 154, 157–158, 167, 181, 199, 202, 207, 210, 218, 221–222, 224
Bergius, Hanne 248
Bernays, Michael 178
Bernheimer, Richard 123
Berry, Martin 51
Bhabha, Homi 176, 208–209
Bielschowsky, Albert 178–179
Binder, Hartmut 194
Bismarck, Otto von 168
Blanchot, Maurice 193
Bock, Hans-Michael 200, 204
Bohnert, Christiane 166
Bordwell, David 235, 240–242
Börne, Ludwig 174
Bornscheuer, Lothar 62–64
Bouilly, Jean Nicolas 17
Bourdieu, Pierre 29, 67, 71–72, 76–78; works by Bourdieu: *Language and Symbolic Power* 71–72, 77–78
Brecht, Bertolt 247, 252, 260; works by Brecht: *Mann ist Mann* / *A Man's a Man* 252, 260
Brennan, Timothy 169
Breuer, Josef 97
Brewster, Ben 215

Brod, Max 184–185
Bronfen, Elisabeth 97, 99, 102
Brooks, Peter 41
Brown, Theodore M. 93
Brüch, Oskar 285
Buñuel, Louis 234–237; works by Buñuel: *Un chien andalou / An Andalusian Dog* 234–235
Bürger, Peter 247, 265; works by Bürger: *Theorie der Avant-Garde / Theory of the Avant-Garde* 247, 265
Buruma, Ian 27
Bush, George W. 21
Butler, Judith 65, 202, 207–210, 214
Butzmann, Hans 116, 121, 129, 132

Campe, Julius 80
Carlson, Marvin 199
Castle, Terry 102
Chamberlain, Houston Stewart 180, 182
Cixous, Hélène 107
Clausewitz, Carl von 14, 22–23, 62
Coady, C. A. J. 70
Cook, James 36
Crary, Jonathan 256, 262; works by Crary: *Techniques of the Observer* 256, 262

Darwin, Charles 18
Das, Veena 14, 24
Deleuze, Gilles 45, 194, 241
Derrida, Jacques 141, 193, 202, 207–208, 210, 214–216, 221–222
Diamond, Elin 209–210
Dickerman, Leah 261
Dietrich, Dorothea 265
Doherty, Brigid 250
Dohm, Christian Wilhelm 169–172
Draper, Hal 75, 79
Drimmel, Heinrich 283–284
Dühring, Eugen 178
Dürer, Albrecht 123, 130–31, 134, 137

Eagleton, Terry 64–65
Ehrenfels, Elfriede von 26

Eisenstein, Sergei 235–237, 241; works by Eisenstein: *Battleship Potemkin* 235–236
Elderfield, John 254
Ellenberger, Henri F. 96
Elsaesser, Thomas 200, 202, 205, 209–214, 224
Engel, Eduard 178
Engels, Friedrich 20–21
Engelstein, Stefani 57
Evans, Richard J. 118

Fauth, Søren 116, 130, 132
Fischer, Bernd 64
Fischer, Jens Malte 180
Fischer-Lichte, Erika 201, 204, 206–209, 211, 224
Fontane, Theodor 116
Forster, Georg 35–36
Förster, Ludwig 272
Foucault, Michel 23, 49, 118, 141, 272
Frank, Manfred 141
Franz Ferdinand, Archduke 271, 274–277, 280–281, 283, 285–286
Franz Joseph I. 277, 285
Frenkel-Brunswick, Else 149, 152, 156
Freud, Sigmund 14, 18, 94–95, 97, 99, 101, 109, 141, 144, 156, 167; works by Freud: *Brief an Romain Rolland / Letter to Romain Rolland* 109; *Beobachtung einer hochgradigen Hemi-Anästhesie bei einem hysterischen Manne / Severe Case of Hemi-Anaesthesia in a Hysterical Male* 96; *Das Medusenhaupt / Medusa's Head* 110; *Über Fausse Reconnaissance (Déjà raconté) während der psychoanalytischen Arbeit / Fausse Reconnaissance (Déjà raconté) in Psycho-Analysis* 109; *Das Unheimliche / The Uncanny* 94–95
Freytag, Gustav 133
Friedrich Wilhelm III 51
Fuchs, Anne 189
Fuhrmann, Alexander 149

Gale, Matthew 245
Galen 92
Galtung, Johan 135
Garfield, John 241
Garncarz, Joseph 203
Garnier, Philippe 228
Geiger, Abraham 178
Geiger, Ludwig 178, 180
Gelus, Marjorie 63
George, Stefan 172
Geyer, Michael 67–68
Geyer-Ryan, Helga 140
Girard, René 207, 221, 223–224
Gneisenau, August Neidhardt von 62
Goebel, Rolf J. 189–190
Goethe, Johann Wolfgang von 30, 165, 168, 173–180, 182; works by Goethe: *Dichtung und Wahrheit / Poetry and Truth* 179; *Faust* 176–177; *Hermann und Dorothea* 174; *Wilhelm Meisters Lehrjahre / Wilhelm Meister's Apprentice Years* 175, 177
Goetschel, Willi 170
Goldhagen, Daniel 25, 143; works by Goldhagen: *Hitler's Willing Executioners* 25
Goldschmidt, Abraham Meyer 176
Greiner, Bernhard 60
Griffith, David Wark 211, 214
Grimm, Hermann 137
Gröning, Gert 149
Gross, Raphael 22
Grosse, Carl 105, 108; works by Grosse: *Der Genius* 105, 108
Grosz, George 250–252, 264; works by Grosz: *Republikanische Automaten / Republican Automatons* 250; *Diese Kriegsverletzten wachsen sich nachgerade zur Landplage aus / These War Invalids Are Getting to Be a Positive Pest* 250
Guattari, Félix 194
Gundolf, Friedrich 178–180
Gunning, Tom 203–204, 242

Haakenson, Thomas 261
Habermas, Jürgen 67, 70–71, 82, 141
Hague, Hope 178–179
Hake, Sabine 201, 205, 211
Hamblet, Wendy 115
Hansen, Theophil 272
Hanson, William 133
Hanssen, Beatrice 14, 158, 272; works by Hanssen: *Critique of Violence* 14, 272
Harbou, Thea von 200, 212, 222
Hartmann, Fritz 116
Harvey, William 94
Hausmann, Raoul 261
Hausschild, Jan-Christoph 73–74, 76
Haym, Rudolf 103
Heartfield, John 250
Hegel 81, 83
Hehn, Victor 178, 180–181
Heidegger, Martin 141, 143
Heine, Amalie 73–74, 76, 78
Heine, Heinrich 29, 67–87; works by Heine: *Aus der Harzreise / From the Harz Journey* 79; *Buch der Lieder / Book of Songs* 72–74, 78, 82; *Deutschland ein Wintermärchen / Germany: A Winter's Tale* 67–68; *Französische Zustände / Conditions in France* 67–68, 71, 80–86; *Gedichte / Poems* 73–74; *Die Heimkehr 62 / The Homecoming 62* 67, 74–75, 78, 80, 82–83; *Ideen: Das Buch Le Grand / Ideas: The Book Le Grand* 73–74; *Lyrisches Intermezzo 50 / Lyrical Intermezzo 50* 78–79; *Reise von München nach Genua / Journey from Munich to Genoa* 68; *Das Sklavenschiff / The Slave Ship* 68; *Tragödien, nebst einem lyrischen Intermezzo / Tragedies, Beside a Lyrical Intermezzo* 73–74; *Vitzliputzli* 68
Heine, Salomon 77
Heinemann, Karl 178
Helfer, Martha 112
Herder, Johann Gottfried 173

Hermand, Jost 69
Herminghouse, Patricia 52
Herrmann, Hans Peter 59
Herz, Henriette 174
Herzfelde, Wieland 248, 251, 256
Herzog, Dagmar 153
Hess, Jonathan 50
Hippocrates 94
Hitler, Adolf 140, 142, 145–146, 160, 200, 281, 286
Hobbes, Thomas 15–16, 19–21; works by Hobbes: *Leviathan* 15
Hobsbawm, Eric 67
Höch, Hannah 248, 261, 265
Hoffmann, Ernst Theodor Amadeus 113
Hoffmann, Volker 119
Hoffmann von Fallersleben, August Heinrich 57
Hofmann, Michael 196
Hohendahl, Peter U. 69–70
Höhn, Gerhard 68
Holitscher, Arthur 190–192, 195; works by Holitscher: *Amerika: Heute und Morgen / America: Today and Tomorrow* 190–192, 195
Holl, Adolf 159
Holub, Robert C. 69
Homer 139–140, 142–143; works by Homer: *Odyssey* 139–140, 142–143
Horkheimer, Max 139–144, 151, 160
Horváth, Ödön von 26, 30, 139–161; works by Horváth: *Italienische Nacht / Italian Night* 145; *Jugend ohne Gott / Youth without God* 26, 139–161; *Ein Kind unserer Zeit / A Child of Our Times* 144; *Sladek* 145
Howe, James Wong 242
Huber, Ludwig Ferdinand 36
Huber, Therese 29, 35–48; works by Huber: *Die Familie Seldorf* 29, 35–48
Huelsenbeck, Richard 252–253, 255–256, 264
Humboldt, Wilhelm von 170, 172
Hunt, Lynn 40–41

Huntington, Samuel P. 14, 25; works by Huntington: *The Clash of Civilizations* 14, 25
Huyssen, Andreas 141, 263

Israel, Manasseh ben 169

Jackson, Shannon 199
Jacobs, Lea 215
Jahn, Wolfgang 194
Janet, Pierre 99
Jarausch, Konrad 67–68
Jay, Martin 87
Jean Paul 91–93; works by Jean Paul: *Titan* 91–93
Jenisch, Daniel 106
Jensen, Wilhelm 116, 119, 133
Jesenská, Milena 188
Johns, Alessa 47
Jolas, Eugène 258
Jünger, Ernst 263

Kabatek, Wolfgang 209, 212–213, 218
Kadrnoska, Franz 157
Kafka, Franz 30, 183–198; works by Kafka: *Forschungen eines Hundes / Investigations of a Dog* 187; *Josefine, die Sängerin oder Das Volk der Mäuse / Josephine the Singer, or the Mouse Folk* 187; *Eine Kreuzung / A Crossbreed* 197; *Das Schloss / The Castle* 183; *Das Urteil / The Judgment* 188; *Der Verschollene / Amerika (The Man who disappeared)* 30, 183–198; *Die Verwandlung / The Metamorphosis* 185–186; *Wunsch Indianer zu werden / Wish to be a Red Indian* 185
Kaindl, Franz 279, 282
Kandinsky, Wassily 255
Kant, Immanuel 14–20, 23–24, 49–50, 98; works by Kant: *Anthropologie in pragmatischer Hinsicht / Anthropology from a Pragmatic Point of View* 16; *Kritik der Urteilskraft / Critique of Judgment* 15, 50; *Der Streit der*

Fakultäten / The Contest of Faculties 16–17; Versuch über die Krankheiten des Kopfes / Classifications of Mental Disorders 97–98; Zum ewigen Frieden / Toward Perpetual Peace 15–16, 18–19
Karner, Stefan 269
Kasten, Jürgen 201
Kennedy, Barbara 64
King, Geoff 203
King, Thomas A. 205
Kittler, Wolf 49, 61–62
Kleinman, Arthur 14, 24
Kleist, Heinrich von 29, 49; works by Kleist: Das Erdbeben in Chili / The Earthquake in Chile 53, 56; Die Familie Schroffenstein 53; Der Findling / The Foundling 53, 56, 63; Germania an ihre Kinder / Germania to her Children 51–52, 55, 61; Die Hermannsschlacht / Hermann's Battle 53, 59–65; Katechismus der Deutschen / Catechism of the Germans 52, 55–57, 61; Die Marquise von O... 52–54, 59–60, 63; Prinz Friedrich von Homburg / The Prince of Homburg 53; Über das Marionettentheater / On the Marionette Theater 65; Über die Rettung von Österreich / On the Rescue of Austria 61
Klemperer, Victor 181–182
Klibansky, Raymond 130–31
Klopstock, Friedrich 59
Koepnick, Lutz 19
Kohl, Stephan 16
Kohn, Hans 176–177
Koller, Ulrike 117
Kölliker, Rudolf Albert von 51
König, Christoph 180
Kontje, Todd 37
Kortländer, Bernd 72, 76
Kos, Wolfgang 284
Kouvelakis, Stathis 17
Kracauer, Siegfried 199–201, 203, 210, 213, 216–218

Kretschmer, Ernst 98
Krischke, Traugott 144–146
Krüger-Fürhoff, Irmela Marei 53
Kuhlemann, Ute 137
Kühn, Heinrich 228–232, 237–239, 242; works by Kühn: Technik der Lichtbildnerei / Technique of Pictorialism 229

Lämke, Ortwin 86
Landes, Joan 40
Lang, Fritz 140, 200, 204, 211–212, 214, 219
Lavin, Maud 265
Lehmann, Emil 175
Lenssen, Claudia 200
Lepenies, Wolf 94
Lerner, Paul 97–98
Lessing, Gotthold Ephraim 30, 38–39, 165–171, 174–178, 181; works by Lessing: Die Juden / The Jews 168; Miss Sara Sampson 38–39; Nathan der Weise / Nathan the Wise 165–171, 175–177, 181
Lethen, Helmut 140, 147, 155, 251–252, 257, 263
Levin, Rahel 174
Levinson, Daniel J. 149, 152, 156
Librett, Jeffrey 167–68, 171–172, 177
Lichtenberg, Georg Christoph 96
Liebbrand, Werner 92
Lillyman, William 113
Loose, Gerhard 195
Louis Philippe 80, 85–87
Ludwig, Emil 178
Ludwig, Otto 116
Lunzer, Heinz 145–146
Lunzer-Talos, Victoria 145–146

MacArthur, Elizabeth 46
Machosky, Brenda 178–179
Man, Paul de 194
Margalit, Avisha 27
Marighella, Carlos 62
Marr, Wilhelm 177–178, 181

Marshall, Jennifer Cizik 124
Marx, Karl 14, 20–21, 84, 156, 167
Matenko, Percy 103–04
May, Joe 30–31, 199–224; works by May: *Die Herrin der Welt / The Mistress of the World* 201; *Das indische Grabmal / The Indian Tomb* 30–31, 199–224
Mayr, Richard 178
Mazzoni, Cristina 98–99, 110
Meiner, Annemarie 116
Mendelssohn, Moses 166–170, 172–175
Menninghaus, Winfried 19
Mentzos, Stavros 96–97
Merrick, Jeffrey 41–42
Meyer, Richard Moritz 178
Meyer-Krentler, Eckhardt 117, 126
Moritz, Karl Philipp 93, 105–06, 109, 111; works by Moritz: *Erfahrungsseelenkunde / Journal of Empirical Psychology* 106, 109, 111; *Über die Schwärmerey und ihre Quellen in unseren Zeiten / On Enthusiasm and its Sources in Our Times* 106
Mosse, George L. 148, 173–174
Mueller, Magda 52
Muir, Edwin 196
Muir, Willa 196
Müller, Agnes 67
Müller-Funk, Wolfgang 159–160
Mulvey, Laura 205
Münz, Walter 100
Mussolini, Benito 27

Napoleon 51, 56, 61
Nelson, Victoria 101
Nicolai, Ralf R. 195
Niekerk, Carl 59, 96
Nietzsche, Friedrich 84, 141, 167, 248
Nüll, Eduard van der 272
Nussimbaum, Lev – see Said, Kurban

Oksiloff, Assenka 213
Oppermann, Hans 136
Outram, Dorinda 43

Panofsky, Erwin 130–131
Peitsch, Helmut 37
Pelinka, Anton 283
Pfeiffer, Joachim 63
Plessner, Helmuth 251
Podany, Vaclav 284
Politzer, Heinz 194
Popelka, Liselotte 285
Porter, Roy 42, 92, 94, 98
Prawer, S.S. 72–73, 113

Quaresima, Leonardo 200–201

Raabe, Margarethe 129
Raabe, Wilhelm 30, 115–137; works by Raabe: *Der Dräumling / The Dräumling Swamp* 126; *Im Siegeskranze / In the Victory Wreath* 126; *Krähenfelder Geschichten / Krähenfeld Stories* 115, 127–29, 136; *Des Reiches Krone / The Crown of the Empire* 126; *Stopfkuchen / Stuffcake* 135; *Zum wilden Mann / At the Sign of the Wildman* 30, 115–137
Rathkolb, Oliver 284
Rauchensteiner, Manfried 269–270, 273–274, 279, 284, 286
Reinhard, Carl von 58
Reiss, Tom 26–27
Richards, Anna 37
Richardson, Samuel 100, 105
Richter, Simon 43
Riesser, Gabriel 175–176, 178
Rilke, Rainer Maria 239, 250
Robespierre, Maximilien 86
Rogowski, Christian 201, 218
Ronfeldt, David 14, 23–24
Rossen, Robert 241; works by Rossen: *Body and Soul* 241
Roth, Gerhard 267–268, 273, 276–277, 285, 287; works by Roth: *Eine Reise in das Innere von Wien / A Journey inside Vienna* 267–268, 276–277
Rothfield, Lawrence 100
Rotter, Marcel 178–179

Rousseau, Jean-Jacques 40, 42
Ryan, Lawrence 64

Sade, Marquis de 139
Said, Edward 27
Said, Kurban 26–28; works by Said: *Ali und Nino* 26–28
Salzman, Leon 106, 108
Sammons, Jeffrey 64, 69–70, 87, 117, 119–21, 124, 133–34, 136
Sanford, R. Nevitt 149, 152, 156
Saxl, Fritz 130–31
Scharnhorst, Gerhard von 62
Schiller, Friedrich 99, 105, 113, 174; works by Schiller: *Der Geisterseher / The Ghost-Seer* 99, 105, 113
Schilson, Arno 170
Schings, Hans-Jürgen 94
Schinkel, Karl Friedrich 273
Schlegel, Dorothea (Veit) 167, 174
Schlegel, Friedrich 167
Schlegel, Johann Elias 58
Schlüppmann, Heide 205–206
Schlüssel, Wolfgang 269
Schmidt, Erich 180–181
Schmitt, Carl 14, 21–24, 49, 61–62, 64; works by Schmitt: *Der Begriff des Politischen / The Concept of the Political* 21–22; *Der Nomos der Erde / The Nomos of the Earth* 21–22; *Theorie des Partisanen / Theory of the Partisan* 21, 23, 61–62
Schneckenburger, Max 57
Schneider, Helmut 54
Scholem, Gershom 171–172, 174
Schorske, Carl 271
Schröder, Jürgen 150, 155–156
Schubert, Peter 272–273
Schubert, Wolfgang 273
Schwitters, Kurt 31, 245–265; works by Schwitters: *Franz Müllers Drahtfrühling / Franz Müller's Wire Springtime* 255–260, 262, 264; *Die Zwiebel / The Onion* 254–257, 259, 262–263

Sen, Amartya 14, 26; works by Sen: *Identity and Violence* 14, 26
Serner, Walter 206–207
Sethe, Christian 76–77
Shklovsky, Victor 246
Showalter, Elaine 96–97
Siccardsburg, August von 272
Simmel, Georg 178
Simson, Eduard 178
Slavney, Phillip R. 96–97
Sloterdijk, Peter 256
Solger, Karl Wilhelm Ferdinand 103–105
Solger, William 93
Sorel, Georges 248
Spary, Emma 49
Spies, Bernhard 159
Stalin, Joseph 26, 143
Stankowski, Anton 231; works by Stankowski: *Zeitprotokoll mit Auto / Time Protocol with Car* 231
Stein, Sally 249–250
Stekel, Wilhelm 110
Stephan, Inge 37
Stephens, Anthony 63
Stieglitz, Alfred 229
Stuart, Kathy 129
Sullivan, Heather 108, 113

Tabori, George 166, 181–182; works by Tabori: *Nathans Tod / Nathan's Death* 166
Tavris, Carol 135
Teitelbaum, Matthew 265
Templ, Stephan 283
Thalmann, Marianne 109
Thorbecke, Jan Rudolf 103–104
Thümmler, Lars H. 278
Thürmer, Wilfried 124
Tieck, Ludwig 29, 91–114; works by Tieck: *Franz Sternbalds Wanderungen / Franz Sternbald's Wanderings* 101; *Phantasus* 98; *William Lovell* 29, 91–114
Tworek(-Müller), Elisabeth 144–146
Tzara, Tristan 245–246, 262

Ullrich, Wolfgang 228

Varnhagen von Ense, Rahel – see Levin, Rahel
Veidt, Conrad 205
Vertov, Dziga 235
Virilio, Paul 24; works by Virilio: *Ground Zero* 24
Voß, Günter 123

Wackenroder, Wilhelm Heinrich 105, 108
Wagner, Richard 167, 180–182; works by Wagner: *Das Judentum in der Musik / Judaism in Music* 180–181
Walser, Martin 168
Walzer, Tina 283
Warstat, Willi 228–229, 231, 242; works by Warstat: *Allgemeine Ästhetik der photographischen Kunst auf psychologischer Grundlage / A General Aesthetic of Photographic Art from a Psychological Point of View* 228; *Die künstlerische Photographie: Ihre Entwicklung, ihre Probleme, ihre Bedeutung / Artistic Photography: Its Development, Its Problems, Its Significance* 228

Weber, Max 14, 20–21, 24; works by Weber: *Politik als Beruf / Politics as a Vocation* 20–21
Webster, Gwendolen 252
Weineck, Silke-Maria 54, 63
Wellbery, David 54, 112
Werner, Michael 73–74, 76
Wettley, Annemarie 92
Wiene, Robert 216
Wilhelm I. 122
Williams, John Alexander 147, 152
Williams, Raymond 176
Willis, Thomas 94
Witkowski, Georg 178
Wolff, Eugen 178
Wolschke-Bulmahn, Joachim 149
Wright, Richard 183; works by Wright: *Black Boy* 183

Zantop, Susanne 218
Zatschek, Heinz 270, 277–279, 282–284
Zelman, Leon 269
Zenge, Wilhelmine von 58
Zons, Raimar 61

Samuel Beckett: Debts and Legacies

Edited by
Erik Tonning, Matthew Feldman,
Matthijs Engelberts, Dirk Van Hulle

Amsterdam/New York, NY
2010. 483 pp.
(Samuel Beckett Today/
Aujourd'hui 22)
Bound €96,-/US$139,-
E-Book €96,-/US$139,-
ISBN: 978-90-420-3166-1
ISBN: 978-90-420-3167-8

Table of Contents
Introduction
Debts
Marjorie Perloff: Beckett in the Country of the Houyhnhms: The Transformation of Swiftian Satire
Chris Ackerley: "Delite in Swynes Draf": Husks and Lees, Sugarbeet Pulp and Roses in Samuel Beckett's "Draff"
Doireann Lalor: "The Italianate Irishman": The Role of Italian in Beckett's Intratextual Multilingualism
P. J. Murphy: Reincarnations of Joyce in Beckett's Fiction
Seán Kennedy: "First Love": Abortion and Infanticide in Beckett and Yeats
Ashley Taggart: Maeterlinck and Beckett: Paying Lip-Service to Silence
Peter Fifield: "Accursed Progenitor!" *Fin de partie* and Georges Bataille
Elsa Baroghel: From Narcissistic Isolation to Sadistic Pseudocouples: Tracing the Genesis of *Endgame*
Shane Weller: Staging Psychoanalysis: *Endgame* and the Freudian Theory of the Anal-Sadistic Phase
Paul Stewart: Sexual and Aesthetic Reproduction in *Malone Dies*
Matthew Feldman: Beckett and Philosophy, 1928–1938
Anthony Cordingley: Samuel Beckett's Debt to Aristotle: Cosmology, Syllogism, Space, Time
David Tucker: Towards an Analysis of Geulincx and the Ur-*Watt*
Julie Campbell: Bunyan and Beckett: The Legacy of *Pilgrim's Progress* in *Mercier and Camier*
Erik Tonning: "Nor by the Eye of Flesh nor by the Other": Fleshly, Creative and Mystical Vision in Late Beckett

Claire Lozier: *Breath* as *Vanitas*: Beckett's Debt to a Baroque Genre
Legacies
Steven Connor: Beckett and the Loutishness of Learning
Mary Bryden: "Stuck in a Stagger": Beckett and Cixous
Alastair Hird: "What does it Matter who is Speaking," Someone said, "What does it Matter who is Speaking": Beckett, Foucault, Barthes
David Addyman: Rest of Stage in Darkness: Beckett, his Directors and Place
Mark Nixon: Beckett – Frisch – Dürrenmatt
Daniel Katz: Where Now?: A Few Reflections on Beckett, Robert Smithson, and the Local
Katrin Wehling-Giorgi: "Splendid Little Pictures": Leibnizian Terminology in the Works of Samuel Beckett and Carlo Emilio Gadda
Laura Salisbury: Art of Noise: Beckett's Language in a Culture of Information
Bill Prosser: Beckett's Barbouillages
Interview
Rosemary Pountney and Matthew Feldman: An Interview with Dr Rosemary Pountney
Free Space
Rodney Sharkey: Beaufret, Beckett, and Heidegger: The Question(s) of Influence
Dror Harari: *Breath* and the Tradition of 1960's New Realism: Between Theatre and Art
Dan O'Hara: The Metronome of Consciousness
Natália Laranjinha: L'Écriture Aphasique de Samuel Beckett
Trish McTighe: Haptic Interfaces: The Live and the Recorded Body in Beckett's *Eh Joe* on Stage and Screen
Notes on Contributors

USA/Canada:
248 East 44th Street, 2nd floor,
New York, NY 10017, USA.
Call Toll-free (US only): T: 1-800-225-3998
F: 1-800-853-3881
All other countries:
Tijnmuiden 7, 1046 AK Amsterdam, The Netherlands
Tel. +31-20-611 48 21 Fax +31-20-447 29 79
Please note that the exchange rate is subject to fluctuations

New Insights into Audiovisual Translation and Media Accessibility

Media for All 2

Edited by
Jorge Díaz Cintas,
Anna Matamala and
Josélia Neves

This volume aims to take the pulse of the changes taking place in the thriving field of Audiovisual Translation and to offer new insights into both theoretical and practical issues. Academics and practitioners of proven international reputation are given voice in three distinctive sections pivoting around the main areas of subtitling and dubbing, media accessibility (subtitling for the deaf and hard-of-hearing and audio description), and didactic applications of AVT. Many countries, languages, transfer modes, audiences and genres are considered in order to provide the reader with a wide overview of the current state of the art in the field. This volume will be of interest not only for researchers, teachers and students in linguistics, translation and film studies, but also to translators and language professionals who want to expand their sphere of activity.

Amsterdam/New York, NY
2010. 310 pp.
(Approaches to Translation Studies 33)
Paper €62,-/US$90,-
E-Book €62,-/US$90,-
ISBN: 978-90-420-3180-7
ISBN: 978-90-420-3181-4

USA/Canada:
248 East 44th Street, 2nd floor,
New York, NY 10017, USA.
Call Toll-free (US only): T: 1-800-225-3998
F: 1-800-853-3881

All other countries:
Tijnmuiden 7, 1046 AK Amsterdam, The Netherlands
Tel. +31-20-611 48 21 Fax +31-20-447 29 79
Please note that the exchange rate is subject to fluctuations

Selbst und Bild

Zur Person beim letzten Fichte (1810–1814)

Franziskus von Heereman

Durch die jahrzehntelange Editionsarbeit der Fichte-Gesamtausgabe der *Bayerischen Akademie der Wissenschaften* ist nun das gesamte Oeuvre Fichtes der Forschung zugänglich. Von besonderem Interesse sind dabei die Jahre 1810–1814, die nicht zuletzt aufgrund der lückenhaften Quellenlage bisher kaum als eigenständige Periode untersucht worden sind. Dabei verdienen sie größte Beachtung, nicht bloß weil sie Fichtes letzte Untersuchungen zur Transzendentalphilosophie beinhalten, sondern weil Fichte hier erstmals wieder seit Jena dauerhaft akademisch tätig ist – als Professor an der neu gegründeten Berliner Universität. Dieser Umstand führt zu einer ungeheuren Fülle an ausgearbeiteten Texten, die das hochspekulative Anliegen neu auf eine akademische Hörerschaft ausrichten und uns heute ermöglichen, intensiv und umfassend den letzten Stand Fichtescher Transzendentalphilosophie aus erster Hand zu studieren.

Bewegt von der Lebensfrage Fichtes nach dem Wesen endlicher Freiheit, will die vorliegende Untersuchung erstmalig eine diesbezügliche Gesamtauswertung dieser Spättexte liefern. Dabei stößt sie auf die tragische Konkurrenz von Selbst und Bild; ein Entweder-Oder, an dessen Ende das Selbst das zu Vernichtende ist. Dies führt nun andererseits zu der systematischen Frage, ob man Selbst und Bild anders denken könne – als sich implizierend im Horizont absoluter Güte.

Amsterdam/New York, NY
2010. IX, 214 pp.
(Fichte-Studien-Supplementa 26)
Paper €45,-/US$65,-
E-Book €45,-/US$65,-
ISBN: 978-90-420-3195-1
ISBN: 978-90-420-3196-8

USA/Canada:
248 East 44th Street, 2nd floor,
New York, NY 10017, USA.
Call Toll-free (US only): T: 1-800-225-3998
F: 1-800-853-3881
All other countries:
Tijnmuiden 7, 1046 AK Amsterdam, The Netherlands
Tel. +31-20-611 48 21 Fax +31-20-447 29 79
Please note that the exchange rate is subject to fluctuations

Klabund. Sämtliche Werke

Band I, Lyrik. Dritter Teil

Herausgegeben von Ramazan Şen

Verzeichnis & Register der abgedruckten Gedichte
Verzeichnis der abgedruckten Gedichte, Band I, Erster Teil _ Zweiter Teil _ Dritter Teil
Band I Dritter Teil
Kleines Klabund-Buch
Lesebuch
Der Leierkastenmann
Der Neger
Wie Ich den Sommernachtstraum im Film Sehe
Einzelveröffentlichungen (1911–1928)
Postume Einzelveröffentlichungen
Unveröffentlichte Gedichte
Register

Amsterdam/New York, NY
2010. 366 pp. (Klabund – Sämtliche Werke I, Lyrik Teil 3)
Paper €73,-/US$106,-
E-Book €73,-/US$106,-
ISBN: 978-90-420-3145-6
ISBN: 978-90-420-3146-3
Band I-V:
ISBN: 978-90-420-0523-5

USA/Canada:
248 East 44th Street, 2nd floor,
New York, NY 10017, USA.
Call Toll-free (US only): T: 1-800-225-3998
F: 1-800-853-3881

All other countries:
Tijnmuiden 7, 1046 AK Amsterdam, The Netherlands
Tel. +31-20-611 48 21 Fax +31-20-447 29 79
Please note that the exchange rate is subject to fluctuations

rodopi
Orders@rodopi.nl—www.rodopi.nl

Self-Reference in Literature and Music

Edited by
Walter Bernhart and
Werner Wolf

This volume contains a selection of nine essays with an interdisciplinary perspective. They were originally presented at the Sixth International Conference on Word and Music Studies, which was held at Edinburgh University in June 2007 and was organized by the International Association for Word and Music Studies (WMA).

The contributions to this volume focus on self-reference in various systematic, historical and intermedial ways. Self-reference – including, as a special case, metareference (the self-conscious reflection on music, literature and other medial concerns) – is explored, among others, in instrumental music by Mozart, Mahler and Satie, in the structure and performance of (meta-)operas, in operatic adaptations of drama and filmic adaptations of opera, as well as in intermedial novelistic references to music. The essays cover a historical range from the 18th century to the present and are of interest to literary and opera scholars and students, musicologists as well as all readers generally interested in medial self-reference and intermediality studies.

Amsterdam/New York, NY
2010. X, 192 pp.
(Word and Music
Studies 11)
Paper €40,-/US$58,-
E-Book €40,-/US$58,-
ISBN: 978-90-420-3158-6
ISBN: 978-90-420-3159-3

USA/Canada:
248 East 44th Street, 2nd floor,
New York, NY 10017, USA.
Call Toll-free (US only): T: 1-800-225-3998
F: 1-800-853-3881
All other countries:
Tijnmuiden 7, 1046 AK Amsterdam, The Netherlands
Tel. +31-20-611 48 21 Fax +31-20-447 29 79
Please note that the exchange rate is subject to fluctuations

The Popular Avant-Garde

Edited by
Renée M. Silverman

Orders@rodopi.nl—www.rodopi.nl

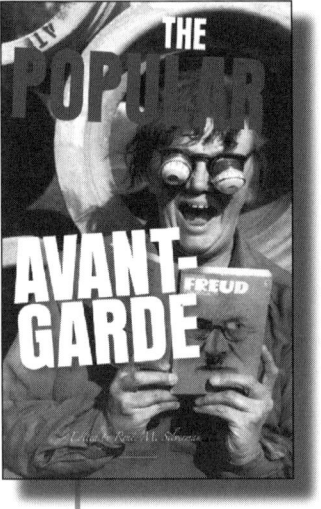

The avant-garde has been popular for some time, but its popularity has tended to fly under the radar. This "popular avant-garde," conceived as the meeting ground of the avant-garde and popular, avoids the divorce of art and praxis of which the avant-garde has been accused. *The Popular Avant-Garde* takes stock of the debates about both the "historical" ("modernist") and posterior avant-gardes, and sets them in relation to popular culture and art forms. With a critical introduction that examines the concepts of "the avant-garde," "the popular," and "the popular avant-garde," the series of essays analyzes the way in which the avant-garde employs popular genres for political purposes, as well as how the popular acquires a critical function with respect to the avant-garde. Each of the volume's three sections considers a different aspect of the productive exchange between the avant-garde and popular: the popular avant-garde as a culturally hybrid and cross-border phenomenon; the play between the popular avant-garde and developments in media and technology; and the popular avant-garde's upending of conventional ideas about "the people" and "the popular." *The Popular Avant-Garde* takes a fresh look at the now canonical Dadaist, Futurist, and Surrealist movements from the perspectives of gender and sexuality, and cultural and critical theory, while at the same time exploring less well-known avant-garde work in literature, film, television, music, photography, dance, sculpture, and the graphic arts. This volume's coverage of the American and Afro-American, Luso-Brazilian and Latin-American, East-European, and Scandinavian avant-gardes, in addition to the vanguards of Spain and other parts of Western Europe, will appeal to all those interested in avant-garde and popular art forms.

Amsterdam/New York, NY
2010. 324 pp.
(Avant-Garde Critical Studies 25)
Bound €65,-/US$94,-
E-Book €65,-/US$94,-
ISBN: 978-90-420-3160-9
ISBN: 978-90-420-3161-6

USA/Canada:
248 East 44th Street, 2nd floor,
New York, NY 10017, USA.
Call Toll-free (US only): T: 1-800-225-3998
F: 1-800-853-3881

All other countries:
Tijnmuiden 7, 1046 AK Amsterdam, The Netherlands
Tel. +31-20-611 48 21 Fax +31-20-447 29 79
Please note that the exchange rate is subject to fluctuations